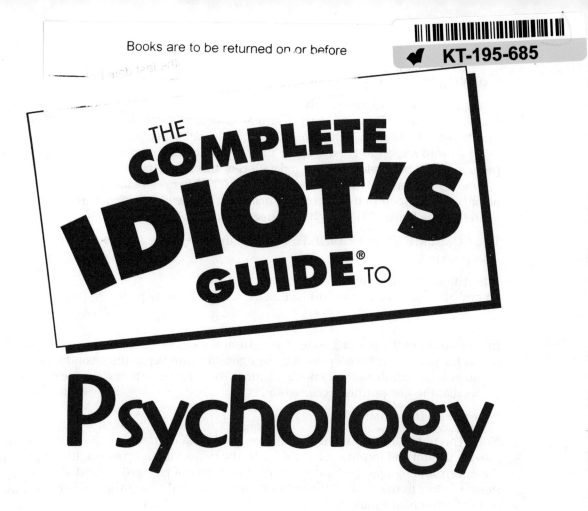

THE COMPLETE IDIOT'S GUIDE® TO

Psychology

by Joni E. Johnston, Psy.D.

alpha
books

Copyright © 2000 by Joni E. Johnston

International Standard Book Number: 0-02-863638-4
Library of Congress Catalog Card Number: Available upon request.

02   8   7   6   5

Interpretation of the printing code: The rightmost number of the first series of numbers is the year of the book's printing; the rightmost number of the second series of numbers is the number of the book's printing. For example, a printing code of 00-1 shows that the first printing occurred in 2000.

Printed in the United States of America

Publisher
Marie Butler-Knight

Editorial Director
Gary M. Krebs

Associate Managing Editor
Cari Shaw Fischer

Acquisitions Editor
Jessica Faust

Development Editor
Nancy Gratton

Production Editors
Jena Brandt
Michael Thomas

Copy Editor
Faren Bachelis

Cover Designer
Kevin Spear

Illustrator
Jody Schaeffer

Book Designers
Scott Cook and Amy Adams of DesignLab

Indexer
Chris Wilcox

Layout/Proofreading
Gloria Schurick, John Etchison

Contents at a Glance

Contents

Foreword

When introduced socially as a psychologist, I am often asked, "Are you going to psychoanalyze me?" Other times, an interested person will squint and ask, "What do you actually do?" In response, I often stammer and don't know exactly where to start or how to explain what psychologists do.

When I was in high school, I read every book I could find that was written by Sigmund Freud. By the time I took my first college course in Psychology, I knew I wanted to be a psychologist. As a psychologist, I feel privileged and honored that relative strangers share with me their deepest secrets, greatest fears, and most excruciating pain. However, not everyone is so enamored with psychologists.

In our society—through movies, theater, and TV—psychologists are often portrayed as whimsical characters who are well-intentioned but unethical do-gooders. Some people we meet say they "just don't believe in it." Others simply won't talk to psychologists. The joke about how many psychologists it takes to change a light bulb ("one") is revealing about perceptions. Not bad, but the light bulb really has to *want* to be changed.

This is not a signal of great faith in our abilities. Still, psychologists are human and we like to think of ourselves as empathic, caring people who do effective work that is delivered in the most skillful manner. It is humbling to recognize how others' opinions of us vary from our own perceptions. Maybe we haven't done a good job of describing ourselves to the public.

Despite the negative perceptions of some, psychology currently enjoys a great deal of popularity; it is even a favorite subject among college students. What new students find out is that there is much more to psychology than clinical work. Researchers and academicians study such things as brain-behavior relationships, sensations and perceptions, learning and motivation, and other aspects of human nature. They provide the scientific evidence to support the practice of those in applied settings. The results of their efforts are used in schools, courts, businesses, and organizations.

In this *Complete Idiot's Guide to Psychology* (by the way, psychologists don't use terms like "idiot" except to refer to themselves), Dr. Joni E. Johnston delineates what psychologists do and how they do it. In an easy-to-read format, and with many examples to illustrate her statements, she explains how psychology came into existence, how psychologists evaluate human nature, and what they actually do.

Psychology is a complex subject, but if you are interested, excited, or at all curious about it, start learning about it here. If you already know something about psychology, this will serve as a good reference. It pulls it all together. I am grateful for this guide—in the future, when people ask me what I do, I'll refer them directly here. This is a great book and I can't wait for it to become available to the general public. This is a book that I not only recommend buying but actually reading. Start now!

—Allen R. Miller, Ph.D.

Allen R. Miller, Ph.D. is a Licensed Psychologist. He is Associate Director of Behavioral Health Services and Chairman of Psychology at York Health System, York, PA.

Introduction

If you're into immediate gratification, psychology is for you. What other subject can you instantly apply to every aspect of your life? And it's practical. Learn about human nature and you can't help but understand and improve your own.

The purpose of this book is to give you a quick and comprehensive overview of psychology. While I've tried to stay off my soapbox, I'd be less than honest if I didn't tell you that my own "psychology" may at times color this book. Obviously, a book of this length can't cover everything, and you'll notice I spend more time talking about psychological disorders than psychological theory. And you'll certainly encounter my optimistic bias about human resilience (I never recovered from *The Grapes of Wrath*). However, you now hold in your hands a good place to start, a road map for your journey into the human psyche. Here's how it looks:

Part I "Putting It in Perspective," sets the stage for our human drama. In these chapters, you'll meet the major players in psychology and visit the various schools they started. We'll then shift to various theories of evolution—how psychology as a science evolved, how human behavior evolved, and how individual behavior evolves.

In **Part II, "Wake Up and Smell the Coffee,"** we'll explore how we make sense of the world, starting with our ability to touch, taste, hear, see, and smell. We'll investigate how information from the world around us becomes grist for our psychic mills, and how we raise our consciousness and all the ways we alter it. We then turn to the fascinating subjects of learning and memory—how we profit from experiences and the peculiar ways we remember them; how we organize things.

Part III, "The Forces Are with You," unleashes the forces that drive human behavior. We'll look at motives, drives, emotions, and all the other things that rouse us to action. We'll look at our hunger and sex drives in depth, and then switch gears to examine the power of language to shape our lives. And, we'll wind up with an exploration of stress—what people do when the forces in their lives get out of control.

While the first three parts look at qualities that we all share, **Part IV, "Self and Otherness,"** dares to be different. In this section, we'll cover all the characteristics that make each person unique, starting with the formation of our identity and ending with our individual brand of psychic self-defense. In between, we'll explore intelligence, personality development, and the difference between quirky personality traits and mental illness.

Part V, "Just What *Is* Normal, Anyway?" serves up the meat of clinical psychology—the ability to distinguish between what's normal and what's not. The first chapter in this section takes a close look at the pros and cons of psychological diagnoses, why we have them, and who decides what they are. The rest dissects the major psychological disorders, examines available treatments, and ends with the bottom line on self improvement—what you can change and what you can't.

Part VI, "Can't We All Just Get Along?" addressees all the good, bad, and ugly ways our interpersonal relationships influence us. Starting with peer pressure and conformity, we'll explore just how far most of us will follow the leader, why nonconformists are hard to find, and why some loves last forever.

Extras

In addition to the main narrative of *The Complete Idiot's Guide to Psychology*, you'll also find other useful types of information, including self-help tips, juicy nuggets that shed light on a confusing topic, quick definitions of psychology buzz-words, and strange and unusual (but true) facts. Look for these features:

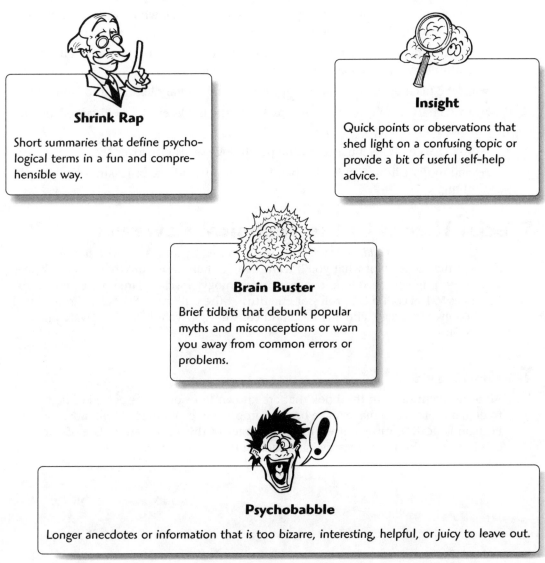

Shrink Rap

Short summaries that define psychological terms in a fun and comprehensible way.

Insight

Quick points or observations that shed light on a confusing topic or provide a bit of useful self-help advice.

Brain Buster

Brief tidbits that debunk popular myths and misconceptions or warn you away from common errors or problems.

Psychobabble

Longer anecdotes or information that is too bizarre, interesting, helpful, or juicy to leave out.

Dedication

In loving memory of Sara Elizabeth Johnston, and to all the wonderful people in Dothan, Alabama, who helped me say goodbye.

Acknowledgments

Hillary Clinton once said it takes a village to raise a child. Well, it also takes a village to write a book, or, I should say, for *me* to write a book. Here's where I get to say thanks to all the people who worked in my writing "village" and raised me (sometimes, it seemed, from the dead) while I was writing this book:

➤ to my literary agent, Evan Fogelman (a.k.a. Hercules), who has the patience of a saint and the heart of a lion;

➤ to my acquisitions editor, Jessica Faust, for giving me the chance to talk about psychology and then actually liking what I had to say;

➤ to the talented Nancy Gratton, for turning my literary lemons into lemonade;

➤ to Zachary, who gives mommy space to write books even if he'd rather she produce Power Rangers movies;

➤ to my sister, Julie, a master in the psychology of sisterly love;

➤ and to my editor-in-chief, husband, and best friend—Alex Tsakiris—for everything.

Special Thanks to the Technical Reviewer

The Complete Idiot's Guide to Psychology was reviewed by an expert who double-checked the accuracy of what you'll learn here, to help us ensure that this book gives you everything you need to know about psychology. Special thanks are extended to Dr. James V. DeLeo, Ph.D., professor emeritus at the California School of Professional Psychology, San Diego, and a clinical and consulting psychologist in private practice in San Diego.

Trademarks

Part 1
Putting It in Perspective

The study of psychology is as complex as its subject—the human psyche and human behavior. So it's no surprise that the development of the discipline took a lot of twists and turns to get to where it is today. In these first few chapters, you're going to have the opportunity to trace the development of the various schools of psychology and the singular contributions made by their founders. From there, it's on to a discussion of how human behavior, and the behavior of individuals, has evolved.

Chapter 1

A Little Psychological Insight

In This Chapter

➤ Understanding psychology

➤ A day in the life

➤ Psychology's major players

➤ How psychologists "do" psychology

➤ Psychology's many points of view

Psychology has come a long way, baby, from its early years. Way back when, in the nineteenth century, much of what passed for psychological practice was based on guesswork, informed by the social prejudices of the day. It took the contributions of a great many careful researchers and deep thinkers to give birth to the modern science of psychology—and every day, new insights are achieved.

This chapter will tell you what psychology is and what it's not. You'll meet the major players in the development of the science, and you'll understand the tools psychologists use to figure people out. By the time you've finished this chapter, you'll be well on your way to thinking like a shrink!

An Alienating Experience

The year was 1887. For many years, writer Charlotte Perkins Gilman had suffered from a severe and continuous nervous breakdown. Finally, out of desperation, she sought help from the most noted *alienist* in the United States.

This wise specialist in nervous disorders sent her home with the therapeutic advice to "live as domestic a life as possible," to "have but two hours of intellectual life a day," and to "never touch pen, brush, or pencil to paper again." Charlotte obeyed these instructions for three months—and came frighteningly close to the borderline of complete insanity. Fortunately, she survived the "help" of her doctor, and went on to write "The Yellow Wallpaper," a story of a creative woman who is trapped by the conventional lifestyle of her day and ultimately finds freedom through writing.

Shrink Rap

An **alienist** was a specialist who treated mental and nervous disorders before the science of psychology was developed.

What's Psychology?

Psychology is the science of human nature. It's all about studying the human mind and behavior so we can figure out why people think, feel, and do what they do. How do we fall in love, communicate with each other, solve problems, and learn new things? Psychologists are constantly asking questions, developing theories, and conducting experiments so they can better understand human nature and improve our lives. Whether they're therapists, professors, or researchers, psychologists are constantly trying to reach four goals:

➤ To describe what people do

➤ To explain why people think, feel, and act the way they do

➤ To predict what, when, and how they will do it

➤ To change the parts of human behavior that cause us pain

Let's take a look at each of them.

Telling It Like It Is

The first goal of psychology, describing human behavior, sounds easy; just watch what someone is doing and describe it. It's a lot tougher, though, than you might think. No matter how hard we try not to, we see each other through the filters of our prior experiences, our cultural values, and our beliefs.

For example, if you've just been dumped by the love of your life, it might be pretty hard to jump into a new relationship with complete optimism. You might try to protect yourself by watching closely for any sign of rejection. In fact, you might be so worried about getting hurt that you overlook evidence that your new love cares about you. Your mental filter has a worthy goal, to prevent more heartache, but it's still blinding you from seeing the world the way it really is.

Here's another example of how expectations and beliefs can cloud your vision: When asked to describe their newborns, parents of daughters will describe them as softer, smaller, and weaker than parents of sons, even when there is no actual difference in size, shape, or health. Even at birth, parents are "seeing" their children with eyes that reflect their expectations about gender.

Psychologists are people too—we have our share of biases, expectations, and prejudices. These can get in our way when we're observing human behavior. Whether we're doing therapy or research, we're constantly trying to keep our values, expectations, and opinions out of our work. That's why therapists consult with their *own* therapists: to make sure they're keeping their own "stuff" from interfering with their sessions with their patients. "Telling it like it is" is no easy task!

Insight

Want to start applying psychology to your life right now? Use what you learn in this book to solve just one real problem in your life—or at least, to understand it better.

Why, Oh Why, Oh Why?

Any mystery novel buff will tell you the motive in the whodunit is as important as who did it. Like mystery writers, psychologists often focus on the motives driving a person's behavior. They look for connections between things that happen and how people respond. Why do some—but not all—abused children become abusive adults? How does a brain tumor affect someone's personality? Does watching violent television lead to violent behavior? These are examples of the kinds of relationships psychologists try to explain.

Explanations are also useful in everyday life. People often seek therapy to make sense out of a painful situation such as a divorce or a loss. Even if we can't change what has happened to us, understanding the reason it happened gives us a sense of comfort and control, a sense that maybe we can prevent it from happening again.

What's Next?

Understanding why something happened is helpful, but being able to predict that something is going to happen gives us a lot more practical utility.

For example, here's a psychological fact of life: When it comes to human beings, the best predictor of future behavior is past behavior. How can that be useful in your day-to-day life?

Well, let's say you've been dating someone for six months and are starting to get serious. During a romantic dinner, your new love interest suddenly confesses he's been married nine times. This information might change your prediction about the odds that the two of you will turn gray together. You may be tempted to pull out your little black book of former loves and make a few calls. And you'd have good reason to do so—your dinner companion's past behavior suggests that, when it comes to long-term commitments, he's *not* a reliable candidate.

Psychobabble

Research shows that a psychologist is likely to overestimate the likelihood that prisoner Joe will become violent even after extensively interviewing and testing him. Asking a psychologist what a single person will do is like asking a physicist to predict what will happen to a particular drop of water in the ocean.

Or, at least, that's the obvious conclusion to draw. Unfortunately, the best predictor of human behavior isn't always accurate. As a profession, psychology has an abominable track record for predicting what any one person will do. Real life doesn't always cooperate with what theory says should happen—especially when you're dealing with what a single individual might do in a given set of circumstances. In that great deck of life, we're all wild cards!

When it comes to predicting behavior within a group, psychology does much better. For example, what if you wanted to predict the relationship between intelligence and success? Whether a smart individual will live up to his or her potential will be determined by lots of variables—maybe he or she is lazy, has a serious medical illness, or can't get along with others. A psychologist can't easily predict that intelligence in this *particular* person will result in success in life. But psychologists *can* accurately predict that intelligent people, taken as a group, are more likely to be successful than their unintelligent counterparts.

Similarly, an individual 19-year-old male may be the best driver in town—and wonder why he's stuck paying high premiums for car insurance. What he may not realize is that, because we can accurately predict that young men as a group are likely to be the worst drivers (we've got the accident statistics to bear this claim out), they are the most likely to get dinged on their car insurance rates.

Becoming the New, Improved Model

Human beings are always trying to improve, do better, or feel better, so it should come as no surprise that psychologists want to do more than understand human behavior. We want to shape it, mold it, and generally help people run their lives more effectively. The heart of all psychological treatment is teaching a client how to control his or her behavior in the desired direction—to stop drinking, to communicate more effectively, to cope with the memories of a painful childhood.

Try This at Home

Willing to do a little psychology on yourself? Apply the four goals of psychology to the most upsetting thing that's happened to you in the past six months.

> ➤ *Describe what happened:* Think like a journalist. Pretend that this event happened to someone else and objectively write down who, what, when, where, and how.

> ➤ *Explain what happened:* Why do you think this happened to you? What is the relationship between your own behavior and the situation?

> ➤ *Predict:* Has this event happened before? Knowing yourself and those around you, how likely is it to happen again? What would change your prediction?

> ➤ *Control:* What have you learned from this situation? What could you do to prevent it from happening again? How could you respond more effectively if it did?

There! You've just had a brief taste of thinking like a psychologist!

Brain Buster

We can spend years trying to understand ourselves, but if we don't use that information to make our lives better, what's the point?

A Day in the Life of a Shrink

Psychologists are a funny group. Take a psychologist to the movies and he or she will watch the audience. We shrinks are always trying to figure out who people are and why they think, feel, and behave as they do. But there are lots of different ways we go about our work.

The Couch Trip

Most people picture a psychologist sitting behind a couch or desk and listening to people's problems all day. They visualize Robin Williams in *Good Will Hunting* or Barbra Streisand in *The Prince of Tides*. These are images of clinical psychologists, the branch of psychology that trains us to deal with people's emotional and behavioral problems. However, while clinical psychology is the most popular area of specialization, most clinical psychologists aren't in private practice; most of us work in clinics, hospitals, or universities.

We're Everywhere, We're Everywhere!

And we do a lot more than therapy. We teach, we promote mental and physical health, we help businesses run more smoothly, and we conduct research. You can find us in just about any place you find human beings—courtrooms, campuses, locker rooms, hospitals, or board rooms.

Insight

Training in psychology can take us through some pretty unexpected twists and turns, professionally speaking. William Moulton Marston, a psychologist, spent years trying to develop a lie detector test measuring blood pressure. That failing, he applied his knowledge of human nature in a different direction, and created the comic book character "Wonder Woman."

And then there are the other branches of psychology. Not only do we study individual behavior, we study the relationship between individuals and anything they may do or influence. Social psychologists study how people influence one another. Environmental psychologists work with architects and city planners to improve the "relationship" between human beings and their work spaces and living quarters. Believe it or not, there's even a group, called human factors psychologists, who look at the relationship between workers and their machines!

"Doing" Psychology

There are lots of ways to study human beings. Astrologists use the moon and the stars, philosophers apply logic and reasoning, and psychics consult tea leaves and crystal balls. Psychology got *its* start when great philosophers began thinking about human nature.

How We Used to Do It

For hundreds of years, philosophers thought a lot about people, but most of them thought human nature was a spiritual matter that could not be studied scientifically. Luckily for us, in the seventeenth century, a philosopher by the name of René Descartes thought otherwise, and other people slowly began changing their minds.

It wasn't until the end of the nineteenth century, though, that people went beyond just *thinking* about human nature and started *studying* it. In 1879, Wilhelm Wundt founded the first psychological laboratory at the University of Leipzig, in Germany, and psychology as an academic discipline was born. This transformed psychology from philosophy to a science, and forever changed the study of human behavior.

Intuition, logic, common sense, and introspection were no longer acceptable ways to study human nature. Researchers now had to look at objective, outside evidence that either confirmed or disconfirmed their ideas about human beings. Psychologists developed a "show-me" attitude.

Psychology Today

In today's scientific climate, valid research questions about human behavior are those that are testable and replicable. They should be answerable through someone's first-hand experience, with no reliance on "experts," hearsay, or religious dogma. If I wonder whether studying before a test lowers test-taking anxiety, I'll research the question by finding students who hit the books before an exam and see if they're less nervous than their less studious counterparts.

Psychobabble

Common sense has led more than one person astray. Sir Francis Galton thought there was an obvious, common-sense link between a person's intelligence and his or her head size. We know today that there is absolutely no truth to this theory. It also makes you wonder about Sir Francis, whose head was reportedly so small he could have been nicknamed "pinhead."

Then, if you, too, are curious about the link between anxiety and studying, you can ask the same question, do the same research, and see if you get the same answer that I did. That's the *scientific method*.

Research psychologists are always checking up on each other's findings. After scientists publish results, their colleagues try to shoot holes through them, offering alternative explanations, and seeing if they can get the same result. This asking, theorizing, predicting, testing, and retesting forms the basis of what we know about human psychology today.

But not everything can be directly observed in a laboratory or field test. Many human activities, such as reasoning, creating, or dreaming, are private; we assume they happen, but we can't see them. Psychology as a science draws its conclusions about such activities by observing what a person does, when he or she does it, and how he or she does it.

Shrink Rap

The **scientific method** is a way of answering questions that helps remove bias from the study. First, you form your question into a statement that can be proven false, then you test it against observable facts. Other researchers who doubt your findings can duplicate your test and see if they get the same results.

Through their careful observations of human behavior, psychologists do make inferences about the mind. However, any judgments about thoughts or feelings must be checked out—after all, appearances *can* be deceiving. For example, if I greet my husband and he ignores me, I might immediately assume he's mad at me. If I ask him about it, however, I might learn that he wasn't giving me the silent treatment on purpose. Maybe he was preoccupied with work or, more likely, is temporarily hard of hearing after watching three football games at maximum volume!

Psychobabble

Not all questions about the mind and behavior can be answered by psychology. Questions like "Are some people born evil?" are important, but impossible to answer scientifically. How would we measure evilness? If evil is present at birth, we should find it in newborns; but how would we unlock the mind of a newborn? If we wait until the child is old enough to talk, his life experience may have contributed to his evil ways. What do psychologists do with questions like these? We pass the buck to philosophers.

Methods to Studying Madness

Science gave psychologists some pretty clear guidelines for studying human behavior:

➤ Be skeptical.

➤ Keep your values and opinions separate from your ideas and beliefs.

➤ Only ask questions that you can answer yourself.

➤ Show other people your results.

➤ Make sure other people can check your answers.

Psychology as a science dictates what kinds of questions we can ask—they must be objective and replicable. But how do we decide which questions to ask? *Theories,* my dear Watson. A theory is a set of related principles used to explain or predict something.

Because human beings are so complex, psychologists have theories for just about everything from learning to child development, from memory to mental illness. Personality theories try to explain why human beings are the way they are; development theory looks at how children become grownups. And the questions that can be asked are influenced by different theoretical perspectives about what parts of human nature are important.

If, for instance, we theorize that mental illness is a result of painful childhood experiences, we start to wonder what particular kinds of painful childhood experiences have the most impact. Or we may ask if the age at which the experience happens makes a difference.

Next, we start to generate *hypotheses*, predictions about what we would expect to happen if our theory is true. If we believe a person's childhood has a major impact on his or her adult life, for example, we might expect abused children to have some

problems when they grow up. To test our
hypothesis, we would conduct a study using
one or more scientifically appropriate research
methods, chosen to suit the kind of question
being asked. The most common research methods are *descriptive studies, correlational research,*
and *experiments.*

Delving into the Descriptive

If the question starts with "How often," "How
much," or "How many times," a *descriptive study*
is the way to go. In this method, the researcher
describes the behavior of a person or group of
persons. For example, we might ask how much
violence does the average child see on televi-

Shrink Rap

A **theory** is a set of assumptions
about a question. A **hypothesis** is an
answer to the question, based on
theoretical assumptions, that can be
tested to see if the answer can be
proven wrong.

sion? Or we might survey people to see what percentage of the population has been
treated for depression. Or, if we're assessing a person's assertiveness, we might count
the number of times he or she speaks up in a group.

Is There a Relationship?

Descriptive studies give us a good idea of what we're looking at, but they don't tell us
what it all means. For example, discovering the level of violence a child sees on television may be interesting, but we're more concerned about discovering if there's a
relationship between watching violent television and a child's aggressive behavior.
Correlational research tries to assess the relationship between two aspects of human
behavior.

Let's assume we were going to do a study on TV violence and aggressive behavior in
children, beginning with the theory that there is a positive relationship between
watching violent television and aggressive behavior in children. Our hypothesis is
that children who watch violent television are more aggressive than those who watch
little or no violent television.

Right away, we run into problems. How are we
going to measure aggression? This sounds simple
but it's not. We might count the number of
times a child is sent to the principal's office, but
that could be misleading: Some teachers run a
tight ship, while others may be real slackers.
Similarly, depending on siblings to tattletale
introduces all kinds of problems, such as loyalty,
sibling rivalry, and even the possibility of brib-
ery! All of these extra issues can make our measurements unreliable.

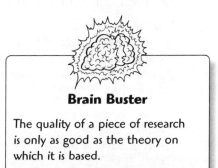

Brain Buster

The quality of a piece of research
is only as good as the theory on
which it is based.

One way to overcome such problems is to give the children's parents some kind of behavior rating scale that clearly defines aggressive behavior. We'll be equally clear in defining what we want to count as exposure to violent television: Do we measure the number of violent incidents in any show or just the number of violent shows? Does yelling count as violence? Do shoot-'em-up cartoons rate the same as live news coverage of Bosnia?

Once we have measured both behaviors, we compare the results. If children with high violent television viewing are also rated as more aggressive than children who watch tamer fare, we have some support for our theory. If, on the other hand, children who watch violent television are less aggressive, we'd have to look for another explanation. And we'd have a new hypothesis to test: Perhaps watching violent television serves as a safe outlet for children's anger and aggression and actually reduces the odds that they will act violently.

Psychobabble

A correlational study can tell us if a relationship exists between two things, but it can't give us the nature of that relationship. For example, it can't tell us if one thing causes the other. There might be all sorts of other factors that influence the relationship. So correlational studies are generally followed by another kind of research tool—the experiment.

The Experimental Experience

To tease out the cause and effect between two things, the researcher changes one and sees what effect this change has on the other. The thing the experimenter changes is called the *independent* variable; the thing that is influenced by the independent variable is called the *dependent* variable.

If we want to find out if exposure to violent television caused children to be more aggressive, we might show children violent television one hour this week, ten hours the next, and five hours the week after that. Each week, we'd see how changing the TV-watching time (the independent variable) affected aggression levels (the dependent variable).

But our experiment may still fail to give us clear-cut results. That's because of *confounding variables*—things that aren't supposed to be a part of the experiment but that creep in anyway and influence the results.

In our example, parental expectations might confound the results. If parents knew the amount of violent television their children were watching each week, they might unintentionally rate their children as being more aggressive during weeks of heavy viewing because they expected that behavior. We can try to safeguard against this by leaving the parents in the dark about the actual amount of their child's exposure to violent television during the period of our observations (but, of course, we'd get the parents' permission for this at the outset of the experiment).

Ethical Dilemmas

Psychological researchers face a dilemma when conducting experiments. On the one hand, they want to protect people's rights to be fully informed about the experiment and, on the other, they know that too much knowledge might skew the results. In our violence-and-aggression experiment, for instance, we would need to let the parents know that we were not going to inform them of the actual amount of violent programming the children watched each week—and we'd need to get their permission to keep them in the dark about it.

To help them walk that fine line, psychological researchers are ethically bound by the following guidelines:

➤ Tell the subject as much as possible.

➤ Make sure the subjects know they can quit the experiment at any time.

➤ Look for any possible way to conduct experiments without using deception.

➤ If deception is absolutely necessary in order to prevent bias, let subjects know that some details of the experiment are being withheld until all the data have been collected.

➤ Give the subject the full scoop after the experiment is complete.

Multiple Perspective Disorder

If you've ever seen the movies *Sybil* or *Three Faces of Eve*, you're aware of multiple personality disorder, a rare mental illness in which a person develops different personalities to cope with severe childhood trauma. Psychologists have their own version of this, and it has haunted the field of psychology since its early years: I call it multiple perspective disorder.

Imagine setting out to become the world's authority on elephants and only studying their legs. You can tell a lot about an elephant from his legs—the texture of its skin, the climate in

Insight

The human mind is amazingly complex. No single perspective—the biological, the behavioral, the emotional—can tell the whole story.

which it lives, maybe even its travel patterns. You might even make a few guesses about its size and weight. On the other hand, you would be clueless about its mating habits, eating rituals, or defense strategies. Even if you studied for years, the best you could do is become the leading expert on elephant legs. It'd be ludicrous to claim you truly understood elephants.

Yet for years, that's exactly what some psychologists did. Some groups studied the mind, while others focused on human behavior. Some believed childhood influences unlocked the key to our psyches and spent their time analyzing dreams and unlocking childhood memories. Others believed it was the here and now that mattered. Seven different perspectives emerged during the twentieth century, and most of them claimed to be *the* right way to study human nature. At times, battles became pretty heated over whose perspective was right.

Fortunately, psychologists today value the unique contribution of *each* psychological perspective. While some psychologists might still tell you that their beliefs about human nature fall in line with one particular perspective, in practice they are likely to apply whichever perspective best deals with the problem at hand. For, as you shall see, each perspective offers valuable insights into human nature. The seven perspectives most prevalent today include:

1. The biological perspective
2. The psychodynamic perspective
3. The behaviorist perspective
4. The humanist perspective
5. The cognitive perspective
6. The sociocultural perspective
7. The evolutionary perspective

Meet the Major Players in Psychology

René Descartes (1596–1650)	first philosopher to think human nature could be studied
Charles Darwin (1809–1882)	father of evolutionary psychology
Wilhelm Wundt (1832–1920)	father of clinical psychology, started first psychological lab
John Dewey (1887–1977)	published America's first psychology textbook
J. McKeen Cattell (1860–1944)	America's first professor of psychology
Sigmund Freud (1856–1939)	founder of psychoanalysis
John B. Watson (1878–1958)	first American behaviorist

continues

Meet the Major Players in Psychology   (continued)

Karl Lashley (1890–1958)	pioneer in biological psychology
Carl Rogers (1902–1987)	major humanist, argued for building self-esteem
Jean Piaget (1895–1980)	early cognitivist, studied how children learn to think and reason
Lev Vygotsky (1896–1934)	sociocultural pioneer, how children mind their culture

I Was Born This Way

Biological psychology has enjoyed its most recent vogue ever since Congress declared the 1990s the "decade of the brain." And what a decade it's been! Thanks to biological psychology, we have a much better understanding of the role our biological make-up plays in mental health and mental illness.

The biological perspective looks to the body to explain the mind. Biological psychologists look at the influence of hormones, genes, the brain, and the central nervous system on the way we think, feel, and act. How much of our personality is inherited? Is there a gene for suicide? Does mental stress cause physical illness? Do the brains of schizophrenics function differently than those of normal people? In the endless "nature versus nurture" debate of human behavior (see Chapter 3, "The Chicken or the Egg?"), biological psychology clearly sides with nature.

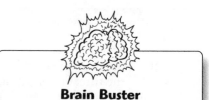

Brain Buster

Your genes may be causing your blues! We now know that depression runs in families, and that there are chemical changes in the brain that coincide with clinical depression. Medications can adjust these changes and chase depression away.

Biological psychology has been instrumental in the development of medications that effectively treat depression, anxiety, bipolar disorder, and schizophrenia. It has reawakened our awareness of the mind/body connection and given us specific ways to measure, and conquer, stress. Through its identification of the physiological components of many mental illnesses, it has helped tear down the false dichotomy between illnesses of the mind and illnesses of the body. This has helped to remove the stigma associated with mental illness—a development that has been as beneficial to people's mental health as any technique we've developed in the last 10 years!

It's Only the Tip of the Iceberg

The psychoanalytic perspective (psychoanalysis is the technique, not the theory) views behavior as driven by powerful mental conflicts locked deep within the

Shrink Rap

A **Freudian slip** is a mistake or substitution of either spoken or written
words. Freud believed that such
"slips" come from unconscious
wishes that pop up unexpectedly
through unintentional words. By
analyzing these "slips," a person
might get some clues into his inner
thoughts or "real" intent or wishes.

subconscious. Sigmund Freud, the father of psychoanalysis, thought most people were riddled with conflicts between their own needs and society's demands.

Freud thought that an adult's mind was like the tip of
an iceberg: he believed that conflicts arise, and are
pushed down, when we are children. Because of this,
we have little insight into the motives that drive our
behavior as adults. We do, however, get clues through
dreams, slips of the tongue, or sudden, unexplainable
behavior. Freud believed that unconscious conflicts
were the source of his patients' pain and frequently
led them to behave in an irrational manner.

Freud also believed that children are naturally sexual
and aggressive, but he believed that society was not
willing to accept these natural urges in youngsters.
He specifically pointed the finger at parents who, he
claimed, often became upset when faced with a child's
erection or natural interest in bodily functions, and
often punished the child for expressing natural urges.

Thus Freud explained the beginnings of psychological and behavioral problems. To
survive the threat of parental punishment, the child quickly learned to push these
natural urges out of sight and out of mind. Freud attributed much of human discomfort to the ongoing battle between our own individual needs and desires and society's
rules and norms, a battle that continues long after we pass through childhood.

Freud was perhaps the first to stress the influence of traumatic childhood events on
shaping our personalities and worldviews. He was the first to recognize that human
behavior is not always rational or easy to explain. He was also the first to use talking
in a therapeutic setting as a cure for mental illness, and to see the healing that can
occur when a client remembers, and works through, the trials and tribulations of
childhood. Last but not least, Freud certainly had a way with words; he gave us many
words that are now a common part of our lingo: Oedipal complex, penis envy, id,
ego, and superego.

We're Just Rats Caught in a Maze

The behavioral perspective all started with rats. After spending many years watching
rats race through mazes, a psychologist named John Watson realized he could accurately predict where a rat would run if he knew where it had found food on previous
trials. He was impressed with the amount of information he could learn about rats
just by watching their behavior and understanding the environment in which it
occurred. And he could change the rat's behavior pretty quickly by putting the food
in a different place.

Maybe, he thought, people aren't much different. Maybe we aren't as complicated as we think, and maybe all that mental mumbo jumbo like thoughts and feelings doesn't matter. Maybe, he proposed, human behavior is as simple as **ABC**:

Antecedent	Behavior	Consequence
the environmental trigger	the behavioral response to the environmental trigger	what happens next

Watson believed psychology should seek to understand people by studying what happens to them and how they respond. His focus was firmly on the bottom line: behavior. He theorized that behavior usually started as a response to an environmental event. From this he went on to reason that the consequences of that response would determine whether or not that behavior would increase over time or became less frequent.

Psychobabble

Watson responded a little too enthusiastically to one of the stimuli in his environment; an extramarital affair with his research assistant, Rosalie Raynor, became public knowledge and he was fired from his prestigious position at Johns Hopkins University. No other university would pick him up after that scandal.

Let's say that every time the phone rings, your new love interest is on the line. Chances are you'll start racing for the phone at the first ring. On the other hand, if bill collectors often give you a jingle, you might ignore the telephone no matter how many times it rings.

Behaviorism ruled the psychological roost for almost 50 years, and it contributed many practical tools and ideas. For one thing, it shifted the focus of psychological research from generating insights onto behavior change. It gave us behavior modification, a process of shaping someone's behavior by consistently rewarding the desired actions, thus earning the eternal gratitude of countless parents, teachers, and savvy spouses! And it gave us some pretty powerful weapons against irrational fears and phobias (see Chapter 18, "Swingers and Scaredy Cats").

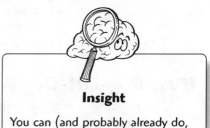

Insight

You can (and probably already do, sometimes) use behaviorism in your daily life. Anytime you use praise or rewards to get the kids to do their chores, you're acting like a behaviorist!

I Think, Therefore I Am

Cognitive psychology is the study of people's ability to acquire, organize, remember, and use knowledge to guide their behavior. Cognitive psychologists think we're much more than a bunch of rats. Yes, they say, we react to our environment, but we also act upon it: People solve problems, make decisions, and consider options and alternatives before we act.

The cognitive perspective assumes that there are connections between what people perceive, think, feel, and do. Unlike the behaviorists, cognitive psychologists think that what goes on inside someone's head is of critical importance. In fact, they believe that a lot of how we feel and what we do starts with what we're thinking, not with some impersonal stimulus from the environment. They would argue, for example, that someone who sees a cancer diagnosis as a meaningful personal challenge is likely to approach his or her treatment very differently than someone who views it as a death sentence.

Although the cognitive perspective focuses on the mind, it doesn't rely on introspection or intuition to study it. Cognitive psychologists study human behavior and then make inferences about the mind from their observations. For example, Swiss psychologist Jean Piaget gave children a series of problems to solve and then documented the mistakes they made and their reasons for their answers. After testing many children at varying ages, he developed his theory about how children develop their ability to reason.

Cognitive researchers develop theories about the mental processes that influence what we do. They test those theories by creating situations in which people would be expected to behave in one predictable way (if the theory were true) or in another way (if the theory were not true). Through the influence of cognitive psychology, we understand more about decision making, creativity, and problem solving than ever before. We've also learned how to do them better.

The influence of cognitive psychology is everywhere today. You see it in the numerous self-help books that proclaim the power of self-talk, and in the concept of attitude adjustment. If you've ever heard anyone say, "When life gives you lemons, make lemonade," he or she is speaking from a cognitive perspective.

It's a Dog-Eat-Dog World

You're probably familiar with Darwin's "survival of the fittest" idea. Darwin basically thought that the creatures whose inherited characteristics were best adapted to the environment were the ones that survived and reproduced. If a duck with a wide beak can get more food than narrow-beaked ducks, then wide-beaked ducks will survive. Over time, all ducks will have wider beaks.

Evolutionary psychology applies that same principle of *natural selection* to human behavior. It holds that human beings, as a species, have acquired innate problem-solving tendencies that promoted their survival and reproduction. Evolutionary psychologists study behaviors that are common among all humans and try to figure out how they helped us become top dog of the animal kingdom. They believe that a key to understanding human nature is in the behavior of our ancestors; if we can reconstruct the problems our ancestors dealt with, we can understand the problem-solving tendencies that helped them survive and thus became a genetic part of being human.

For example, all human beings hate, love, and get angry. Evolutionary psychologists would say we inherited the ability to express our feelings from our ancestors because the ability to communicate feelings and intentions helped them survive. Once we know how our emotions evolved, we can be more aware of, and therefore control, these natural tendencies.

Of course, who, what, or when any one human being will love is a lot more complicated; we must also look at his or her culture, life experiences, genes, and personality. And, we still have to contend with the here and now. A man might blame his having an affair on an ancestral legacy that called for men to ensure maximum reproduction by mating with multiple partners. He's still going to face his wife's wrath, and, possibly, the consequences of his behavior in court!

No Man Is an Island

Why do eating disorders only occur in countries like the United States, where the beauty ideal for women is to be thin? If aggression is a human instinct, why is the rate of violence so different from country to country? A sociocultural psychologist would tell you if you want to understand such human behaviors, you must start with the culture in which they live.

All human beings have minds, but each culture produces a different version. The sociocultural perspective focuses on the differences among people living in various cultures as well as the ways by which people's thoughts, feelings, and behavior are

Shrink Rap

Natural selection is the Darwinian principle that says the best-adapted traits are the ones that will be passed along from one generation to another in a species. Creatures with less well adapted traits will die out before they can reproduce, so their poorly adapted traits will eventually disappear from the population.

Insight

Evolutionary psychologists have identified 26 behavior traits that all humans on our planet share. Here are a just a few of the more interesting ones: deception, detecting emotions, gossip, humor, perception of status/rank, and romantic love.

influenced by their culture. From this perspective, our culture influences how we think, feel, and act. Culture teaches us about the roles we play and gives us informal rules about what is, and what is not, socially acceptable. If you've ever visited in another country, you've encountered the sociocultural perspective up close; it can be quite a shock realizing that what's "normal" is suddenly different!

Even psychology has cultural biases. In the United States, a country that values self-sufficiency and individualism, the focus of therapy is often on individual behavior change. In many Asian countries, where fitting into the group is a more highly valued trait, therapy would emphasize understanding and acceptance of ourselves and each other. And, in some Latin American cultures, where the family unit is numero uno, it would seem absurd to treat someone without including the whole family; behavior we would describe as healthy and independent might be viewed as selfish!

Look on the Bright Side

Undoubtedly, the stereotype of the "touchy-feely" psychologist started with a humanist. As a backlash against the doom and gloom of the psychoanalytic perspective and the behaviorist's robotic view of mankind, the humanists looked on the bright side of human nature. People are naturally good, the humanists said, and if left to their own devices, they will strive to become the best they can be. Problems only come up when other people get in their way.

According to this view, a parent or teacher might criticize a child's natural attempt to grow. If this happens often enough, such criticized children begin to doubt their own thoughts and feelings. They begin to see themselves as incapable and, as a result, start mistrusting their own judgment. As adults, they may not take charge of their own lives because they no longer believe they are capable of doing so.

With this theoretical viewpoint, it's not surprising that regaining a positive self-concept is a major therapeutic goal. The self-esteem movement started with humanists; in addition to their emphasis on promoting positive self-concepts, the humanists encourage therapists to look at their clients' *psychological reality*—the way they perceive their experiences, rather than focusing on the experiences themselves. From the humanist perspective, a person's view of his or her life is much more important than what actually happened—understand his perspective and you'll know why he thinks, feels, and acts the way he does.

Psychology in Action

Different psychological perspectives offer different explanations for the same behavior. Take a look at how each perspective might try to explain this fictional scenario:

Janine, a straight-A college student and track star, lined up to compete at the NCAA 5,000-meter regional finals—held later on the same day that she had to take her MCAT. Having spent the night studying for that all-important exam, Janine was operating on three hours of sleep. As the runners took off, Janine got off to a slow start and fell behind. Suddenly, she veered off the track, scaled an 8-foot fence, and jumped off a 45-foot bridge. Her injuries ended her running career and indefinitely postponed her dream of medical school.

A Potpourri of Psychological Perspectives

Perspective	Burning Questions	Possible Answers
Psychoanalytic	What forces drove Janine so hard that she "snapped"?	Maybe her parents pushed her too much, perhaps she overcompensated for feelings of inadequacy by "winning" and panicked at the thought of failure.
Behaviorist	What have been the previous consequences for Janine when she lost a race? In the past, did she usually lose when she fell behind?	Maybe past losses were followed by painful consequences (criticism or derision) and Janine was trying to avoid experiencing them again.
Humanist	Was Janine's self-image such that she only felt loved and respected when she won?	Maybe she was trying to change the basis of her self-worth or trying to test her friends' and family's love for her.
Cognitive	What was Janine thinking during the race? How did these thoughts lead her to act the way she did?	Maybe her fear of failure interfered with her ability to think rationally and thus impaired her judgment.
Sociocultural	What has American culture taught Janine about winning and the price of failure? How would she expect others to treat her if she lost the race?	Maybe Janine's behavior was so desperate because of the social consequences she anticipated if she failed, maybe she took "winning isn't everything, it's the only thing" to the extreme.
Biological	Did Janine have an undetected medical condition that was aggravated by the stress of running? Did she have a biological predisposition toward impulsive behavior?	Maybe Janine had an untreated chemical imbalance, maybe she had a brain tumor or some other physical problem that caused her to act out of character, maybe the physical effects of sleep deprivation were a factor.

A Potpourri of Psychological Perspectives   (continued)

Perspective	Burning Questions	Possible Answers
Evolutionary	Was Janine's behavior an example of adaptive behavior gone awry?	Maybe Janine perceived her fear of failure like our ancestors perceived threatening predators and was trying to flee from them.

Each perspective approaches the scenario from a different set of assumptions (theoretical position) and therefore comes up with a different question to answer. Each question has a certain amount of validity, but it's clear that no single perspective asks, and answers, every question that the scenario raises. In the chapters that follow, we'll look more closely at how insights from all of these psychological perspectives have contributed to the development of the science of psychology as we know it today.

The Least You Need to Know

➤ Psychology is the scientific study of human nature.

➤ Psychologists wear a lot of different hats: We help people solve their problems, and we use our knowledge about human behavior to help courts, companies, schools, and sports teams run more efficiently.

➤ Because psychology is a science, the questions it raises must be objective and testable, and research must be theory-based, systematic, and replicable.

➤ There are seven major psychological perspectives in psychology today: biological, psychodynamic, sociocultural, evolutionary, cognitive, humanist, and behaviorist.

➤ Each of the perspectives employed by psychologists have contributed important insights into the how and why of human nature.

Chapter 2

Bio Psycho What?

In This Chapter

➤ The biology of psychology

➤ The best communication system ever invented

➤ What "getting on your nerves" really means

➤ Left brain or right?

➤ Why the brain doesn't always mind

"Let's brainstorm." "Watch it, you pea brain." "She's the brains behind it." When we listen to the words we use, it's clear we know who rules the roost when it comes to human behavior. But we're still mystified by how it doesn't always listen to what we think we're telling it.

By the end of this chapter, you'll be up to speed on the biological hardware that programs human behavior. We'll explore the parts of the brain that cause us to think, feel, and do the things we do. We'll also explore how they do it; how different parts of the brain communicate with each other, how the brain gets along with the rest of the body, and how hormones and other chemicals influence human behavior. So, let's get started at the real beginning of psychology—why we have the brains we have.

You Are What You Think?

For hundreds of years, the Greeks thought the heart and blood were the head honchos of human beings. Who can blame them? Weighing in at around 3 pounds, the human brain looks like a wrinkled, gray cantaloupe. Even in the most vibrant human being it appears to be sitting around doing nothing. When you contrast this with our fiery red, pulsing, beating heart, no wonder the Greeks made the heart our chief executive organ.

But you can't tell a book by its cover, and you can't tell the marvels of the human brain by looking at it. If we want to understand human nature, we must first understand the nature of the brain because, in essence, psychology is the study of what the brain does. There's a biological counterpart to every thought or feeling we have. And, as you'll see, changes in the brain can dramatically change human behavior.

It's Evolutionary, My Dear Watson

We're all winners from an evolutionary perspective. The very fact that we're alive means our ancestors possessed favorable characteristics that allowed them to adapt and flourish in their natural environment. They passed these advantageous traits on to the next generation, who passed them onto their children, and so on until here we are. We're the "fittest" in the "survival of the fittest."

Adapting to Changes

Ever feel like you finally figured out the rules of life and then someone changes them? So did our ancestors. Here they were, trying to adapt to their environment as best they could and suddenly nature would decide to play a joke or two. Resources would become scarcer or maybe the average temperature would suddenly drop. These environmental shifts could dramatically change which organisms were favored.

A dramatic rise in temperature, for example, might select against the animals with the heaviest fur. In addition, scarcity of resources sharpens the competitive edge and speeds up the natural selection process. Think about the scores needed to get into medical school or a competitive corporate environment and you'll know what I mean!

In terms of human evolution, two environmental adaptations assured us the highest place on the totem pole, and, of course, these are things all humans share today. These adaptations were *bipedalism,* the ability to walk upright and *encephalization,* the development of a larger brain.

Shrink Rap

Bipedalism is the ability to walk upright on two legs. **Encephalization** is the development of a larger brain during the course of evolution.

On Your Feet, Big Head!

Bipedalism, which occurred between 5 and 10 million years ago, freed our hands for grasping and tool use. It made us better able to explore and relocate than other species. When the going got tough, human beings were the first who were able to get going.

Human evolution really took off a couple of million years ago, when our brains got bigger. Encephalization gave us more "head room" for thinking and ultimately led to our increased ability to reason, remember, and plan. Presto! The next thing you know, we were playing with fire and establishing home bases.

Bipedalism and encephalization were such handy tricks that, eventually, only intelligent bipedalists survived to reproduce. You've probably noticed that all human beings share these two characteristics, although some might to greater or lesser degrees!

From a psychological standpoint, though, we're more interested in what our evolutionary path means for brains living here and now. How do our brains help each one of us adapt to our environment today? How do they help us solve our problems, remember birthdays, and plan our future? To answer these questions, let's take a look at the human brain and what it does.

Psychobabble

If you doubt there's a link between our brain and our behavior, meet railroad manager Phineas Gage. In 1948, a construction explosion blasted an iron rod through his face and head. Astonishingly, he recovered from this injury and lived for another 12 years—but friends and family consistently said that he had changed from an efficient, capable manager to an irresponsible, moody, and at times vulgar human being. Phineas's altered brain created a changed man.

The Headquarters of Human Behavior

The brain contains more cells than there are stars in the universe. More than 100 billion of them, to be exact. And each part works together to produce, direct, and choreograph what we think, feel, and do.

A Living Record of Time Travel

One of the stories our brain tells us is the story of human evolution. From the neck up, it's structured in the order in which it evolved. The brain stem, the bulb where the brain meets the spine, is the oldest part of the brain; the midbrain and higher brain evolved on top of it in much the same way newer buildings are constructed on the old foundations of an ancient city.

As with your brain's structure, so developed the behavior each part of your brain controls. They too go from primitive to most sophisticated. The lower brain is responsible for aggression, territoriality, and rituals. The midbrain holds the limbic system, the seat of powerful emotions, sexual instincts, and the sense of smell. Over the top arches the cerebral cortex, that part of the brain that regulates higher levels of cognitive and emotional functioning. This is the site of reasoning, planning, creating, and problem solving, and it is the part that makes us human.

Hello Central!

The bottom-up approach is a useful way to organize the brain because it allows us to see the human brain's structural evolution inside each of us. We can also see how human behavior evolved from base instincts to thoughtful planning. From a psychological standpoint, you can see why it can be challenging to use your reasoning and self-control to keep from acting on powerful feelings or strong desires. After all, those desires have been around a lot longer than your logic!

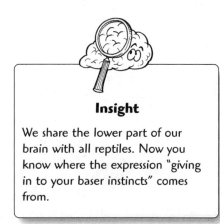

Insight

We share the lower part of our brain with all reptiles. Now you know where the expression "giving in to your baser instincts" comes from.

If the brain is the headquarters of human behavior, the cerebral cortex is unquestionably the commander-in-chief. Not only does it make up two-thirds of your brain, its job is to coordinate all the brain's units and strategically channel your resources in ways that will give you the best chance to survive and flourish in your environment. When we say "use your brain," the cerebrum is the part we're talking about.

Get Your Brain Organized

When psychologists talk about the brain, we're almost always talking about the cerebral cortex, primarily because it's the part of our brain that makes us uniquely human. The lower and middle portions of the brain often get overlooked. However, these more primitive parts of our brain are the foundation on which our mental houses are built. You couldn't survive long without them.

A quick rundown of the parts of the brain will give you a good sense of the way cognitive tasks are parceled out. Each part is a specialist:

Brainstem   regulates internal physiological state of the body

Medulla   regulates breathing and the beating of the heart

Pons   regulates brain activity during sleep

Reticular formation   arouses the brain to attend to new stimuli even during sleep

Thalamus   relay station between senses and the cerebral cortex

Cerebellum   organizes physical balance and movement

Limbic system   regulates motives, drives, feelings, and some aspects of memory

Hippocampus   key player in long-term memory

Amygdala   the tough guy, with roles in aggression, memory, emotion, and basic motives

Hypothalamus   regulates eating, drinking, sexual arousal, body temperature

Cerebrum   regulates higher levels of thinking and feeling

Cerebral hemispheres   each half mediates different cognition and emotions

Left Brain, Right Brain

Do you prefer geometry or English? Would you rather be a painter or a writer? Are you creative or logical? Depending on how you answered, popular psychology would classify you as "right-brained" or "left-brained."

Pychobabble

This "left brain/right brain" craze started with the discovery that the two sides of the cerebrum are not created equal. The two halves of the brain have different processing styles: The right half sees things holistically, while the left is more logical. In addition, they divide up the work. Some functions are more under the control of the right hemisphere and some are more under the control of the left.

Left-Leaning or a Rightward Slant?

For most people, the left brain is more involved in language and logic. The right half of the brain handles visual patterns and spatial relationships. Hence, painters are thought to be more "right-brained" and writers are thought to be more "left-brained." Sports psychologists have put the "right brain/left brain" concept to good use. By teaching athletes to use both sides of the brain, they help them improve their performance.

For example, tennis players naturally exercise their left brain every time they swing their tennis racket. The series of steps that form a backhanded swing is a left-brain activity. However, players can also use their right brain to play tennis: lying awake at night, they can mentally practice their game. Tennis players who visualize the perfect swing in their mind's eye and practice it are making creative use of the right hemisphere's holistic processing. And it works!

This division of labor holds true for our feelings as well. The left hemisphere is associated with anxiety and the positive emotions while the right hemisphere is responsible for the negative emotions. Given that painters and sculptors use their right hemisphere so much, maybe there's something to the idea of a tortured artist!

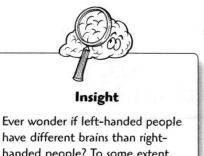

Insight

Ever wonder if left-handed people have different brains than right-handed people? To some extent, they do. For example, only 4 percent of right-handed people have speech centers located in their right hemisphere, but 15 percent of left-handers do.

Partners for Life

In reality, though, the popular left brain/right brain distinction is overly simplistic. These two halves of your brain are partners; they constantly talk to each other through a huge bundle of axons that connect the two hemispheres, the *corpus collusum*. They also work in sync. For example, when you run into an acquaintance, your left hemisphere remembers his name and your right hemisphere recalls his face.

Oddly enough, the left cerebral hemisphere controls the movement on the right side of the body and the right hemisphere controls the left. When you write your name with your right hand, your left hemisphere is actually doing the work. Specifically, your left parietal lobe is busy. Which brings me to the next topic of conversation: the four lobes that make up each hemisphere.

Meet the Mother Lobes

You have more lobes than the ones you hang your earrings on. Each half of your brain has four lobes—a parietal lobe, a temporal lobe, a frontal lobe, and an occipital lobe. You might not know them, but they know you. In fact, they make up a lot of who you are.

Front and Center

The frontal lobes, which sit just behind your forehead, are the newest additions to the human brain. These "babies" have some heavy-duty responsibilities. They are the seat of purposeful behavior; they plan, make decisions, and pursue goals. In addition, one of their most important functions may be to inhibit or override the more primitive behavior that might have once helped us survive but now gets us in social or legal hot water.

Temporally Speaking

Your temporal lobes sit directly behind your ears—a convenient place for them, given that a primary job is to make sense of what you hear. The left temporal lobe allows you to understand speech. Damage to certain parts of the left temporal lobe can leave you with perfectly good hearing but completely incapable of understanding a word that is said to you, a condition known as *Wernicke's aphasia*. To a person with Wernicke's aphasia, all languages are foreign.

Parietals Rule

Your right temporal lobe helps you understand music, the ringing of the telephone, and other nonverbal sounds. In neuropsychological terms, telling someone he has an ear for music translates into excellent right temporal lobe functioning.

Psychobabble

Oliver Sacks's *The Man Who Mistook His Wife for a Hat* gives you a close look at the impact of brain disorders on everyday life. The title of this book comes from one of Dr. Sacks's patients, who exhibited a condition known as facial agnosia (an inability to recognize faces). Mistaking his wife's head for a hat, he tried to pick it up off her shoulders and place it on a hat rack.

Your parietal lobes sit at the top of your head and integrate sensory information from the opposite sides of your body: Your left parietal lobe makes sense of information coming in from the right side of the body and your right parietal lobe takes care of the left side. These lobes help you understand what you're touching. When you reach into your purse, for example, your parietal lobes help you tell the difference between a quarter and a dime just by the way they feel.

An Occipital Complex?

Last but not least, if you cup your hand on the back of your head, you are hugging your occipital lobes. Your occipital lobes make sense of what you see; their primary job is to process visual information. The left occipital lobe controls the right visual field in both your eyes, while the right occipital lobe controls the left visual field. Contrary to popular belief, you do have eyes in the back of your head!

Here's how the occipital lobes divide our vision: Hold your hands out in front of your face so that your palms are facing you. Now, draw an imaginary vertical line down the middle of each hand. The right visual field is the right half of each hand; the left visual field is the left half of each hand.

Working with Half a Brain

Once psychologists realized that different hemispheres did different jobs, they started wondering what one would do without the other. What would happen if the two halves couldn't communicate back and forth? Would they fight with each other? Would they get along?

Two researchers by the name of Sperry and Gazzaniga found some amazing answers to these questions. They studied patients whose corpus collusum (which connects the two hemispheres of the brain) had been cut in order to reduce the severity and frequency of their epileptic seizures. On the surface, these patients seemed fine; they walked normally, had no drop in their IQ, and could carry on a good conversation. When information was presented to just one visual field, though, they behaved as if they had two separate minds.

Psychobabble

Use left-right differences to move yourself, or someone you love, in the right direction. To persuade a daredevil friend to be more cautious, get him or her to turn to the left when talking to you. This will increase activity in his or her right hemisphere, the side of the brain associated with more cautious behavior. And, if you're about to engage in risky business like asking for a raise, try to sit, stand, and walk so your attention is turned to your right!

In their experiments, Sperry and Gazzaniga flashed pictures of common objects on a screen and asked the subject to identify them. When the objects were flashed to the right, the person would look at the researchers as if they were complete idiots and say, "It's an apple." However, when the picture was flashed to the left, the subject would either deny that an object had appeared or would make a random guess.

When subjects were next asked to reach under a barrier and touch the object that had just been flashed, they could reliably identify the object with the left hand but not the right! The right hemisphere could remember the feel and shape of the apple but couldn't get the words for it. If you never forget a face and never remember a name, you can relate!

What was going on? Remember that the right hemisphere controls sensation and movement from the left half of the body and vice versa. Remember, also, that input from the right visual field goes first to the left hemisphere and vice versa. And, recall that, in most people, language is controlled by the left hemisphere and spatial perception (faces, pictures, geometry) is dominated by their right.

No matter how "smart" your brain is, if the different parts aren't communicating effectively, they don't work as well. And in the experimental subjects, the connection that let the hemispheres communicate had been cut. The information simply couldn't get where it had to go to be processed!

In a way, you might say the brain's parts are like relationships—they need communication in order to thrive. Unlike relationships, however, the brain can call upon some superpowered equipment that virtually guarantees good communication. Let me introduce you to the fastest communication system in the world—your nervous system.

You've Got a Lot of Nerve

The brain is a truly complex organ, containing more cells than there are stars in the universe. And each part works together with the rest to produce everything we think, feel, and do. Your nervous system is the choreographer; it constantly sends and receives messages that coordinate the stage show of human behavior.

The Internet has nothing on your nervous system—it's a huge network of more than 100 billion nerve cells that rapidly relays messages to and from the brain. These *nerve* cells, called *neurons,* are specialized cells that receive, process, and/or relay information to other cells within the body. The fastest of these messengers can send electrical impulses at a rate of up to 250 miles per hour; with 100 billion cells to coordinate, they have to.

The nervous system has two substations; the central nervous system (CNS) and the peripheral nervous system (PNS). The CNS is made up of all the neurons in the brain and the spinal cord, while the PNS is made up of all the neurons forming the nerve fibers that connect the CNS to the rest of the body.

Think of the body as an army—the CNS would be the general, synthesizing and coordinating all bodily functions, interpreting all the messages coming in from the body, and sending strategic commands appropriate to the environmental situation. The spinal cord, a trunk line of neurons that connects the brain to the PNS, would be the lieutenant.

Shrink Rap

A **nerve** is bundle of sensory or motor neurons that exist anywhere outside the central nervous system. When someone is getting on your nerves, you only have 43 pairs for them to get on—12 pairs from the brain and 31 pairs from the spinal cord. A **neuron** is a nerve that specializes in information processing.

All the messages directed to the CNS are sent and received through the spinal cord. Damage to the spinal cord disrupts the brain's ability to send and receive messages and, if the spinal cord is severed, the brain can no longer receive important messages from its limbs about what they are experiencing. So, for instance, you wouldn't feel pain even if a toe was roasting in the fireplace. Without the lieutenant, the general can't send commands for the body to protect itself. Your foot soldiers—your sense organs—are completely disabled.

No Pain, No Gain

I became painfully reacquainted with the efficiency of the body's communication system when my husband and I started swing dancing lessons. Mistakes are a natural part of acquiring any new skill and, when two beginners are dancing, this involves a lot of stepping on each other's toes. Over and over again, the nerves in my toes sent the painful message that 200 pounds of dancing male was standing on them. Time and time again, my brain prompted me to push him off and step aside. And, of course, my frontal lobes were busy reviewing the wisdom of my decision to take up swing.

Psychobabble

It's hard to believe wisdom comes with age when you realize that you lose almost 200,000 neurons each day. Fortunately, you start out with so many that even after 70 years you've still got more than 98 percent of your original supply. Besides, it's not the quantity that matters—it's the connections between the neurons that count. Albert Einstein had no more brain cells than you or I, but allegedly had incredibly dense connections between the various parts of his brain.

Speedy Delivery

Neurons are the basic unit of the nervous system. There are three types: sensory neurons, motor neurons, and interneurons. Sensory neurons carry information in from the senses toward the central nervous system. When my spouse stepped on my toes, it was the sensory neurons that got excited and sent the scoop to the brain.

Motor neurons carry messages from the central nervous system back to the muscles and glands. When they got the toe-stepping news, they probably said something like, "Get out of the way, you dummy. Move those feet and tell your partner to watch it."

Since sensory neurons rarely communicate directly with motor neurons, the interneurons act as brokers. They relay messages back and forth between the two and, occasionally, communicate with other interneurons. I'm sure they were quite busy during my dance lessons!

Doing the Neuron Dance

So, how do neurons do their thing? All neurons have a soma, dendrites, and an axon. The soma contains the nucleus of the cell and the cytoplasm that supports it. At one end of the soma are the dendrites, a bunch of branched fibers that receive messages from other neurons or sense receptors. The soma integrates the information from the dendrites and passes it on to a single, extended fiber called an axon. Still with me?

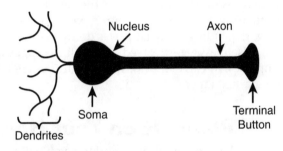

The parts of a neuron.

The axon's job is to carry electrical impulses, called action potentials, away from the cell body to other cells. A neuron's message lies in the number of action potentials that move down the axon. In Morse code, the message lies in the number and sequence of taps; with neurons, it lies in the speed with which electrical impulses are produced. The axon conducts these electrical impulses along its length until they literally reach the end of their rope—swollen, bulblike structures called terminal buttons that lie at the end of the axons. Action potentials trigger the release of chemical substances called *neurotransmitters* from each terminal button.

When a neuron is stimulated by another neuron's impulses or by sensory stimulation and begins to produce its own electrical impulses, it

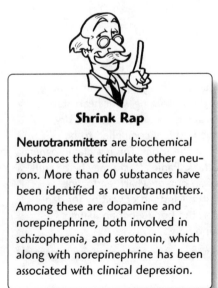

Shrink Rap

Neurotransmitters are biochemical substances that stimulate other neurons. More than 60 substances have been identified as neurotransmitters. Among these are dopamine and norepinephrine, both involved in schizophrenia, and serotonin, which along with norepinephrine has been associated with clinical depression.

fires off one of these impulses. The neural impulse travels the length of the neuron along the axon, finally arriving at the terminal buttons.

Synaptically Speaking

Here's where it gets a little tricky. There is no direct physical contact between a terminal button and the impulse's next destination. Instead, there's a gap at the near junction of two nerve cells—we call this gap a *synapse*. When an impulse is ready to leap the gap from a terminal button to the next stage in its journey, a small packet holding neurotransmitters (it's called a *synaptic vesicle*), moves to the inner membrane of the terminal buttons.

The vesicle ruptures, spilling its neurotransmitters into the synaptic gap, and they attach themselves to the neurons on the other side of the gap. If the neurotransmitter inputs are sufficiently stimulating, the receiving neuron will change—it'll either fire or be prevented from firing, depending on what it was doing before the inputs arrived. That's how the impulse message is relayed from cell to cell, as far as the strength of the relayed impulse can carry it. And, when your toes are hurting as bad as mine were, that's pretty darned far.

Insight

Imagine sitting in a restaurant and, without warning, your heart starts pounding, your mouth goes dry, and you feel compelled to bolt from the room. This is a classic *panic attack*. Panic attacks may be a result of an out-of-whack endocrine system—instead of waiting for danger, the body sends an alarm randomly.

Blame It on Your Hormones

Remember all the weirdness you went through in your teens? Hair sprouting in different places and body parts growing at different speeds? How about those mood swings? Blame it all on your hormones.

Your nervous system gets most of the press, but there's another communication system that can pack a powerful punch in terms of what you think, feel, and do. It is your endocrine system, and its messengers are your hormones.

Midbrain Magic

The endocrine system, controlled by the hypothalamus in the midsection of the brain, produces and secretes hormones into the bloodstream. These chemicals are involved in a lot of different bodily functions, from your sexual development to your arousal, mood, and metabolism.

Not only does your endocrine communication system help you regulate everyday alertness and mood, it helps you respond to emergencies. The most famous hormone is *adrenaline,* an energizer that responds to emergencies by preparing you for "fight or flight."

Adrenaline Alert!

Do you remember a time when you were driving and had a near miss with another car? Or any other close call? Then you probably remember your pounding heart, tensed muscles, maybe even a cold sweat.

Each of these "symptoms" is an example of your endocrine system preparing you to respond to a life-threatening situation. In fact, long after the danger had passed, you could probably still feel your endocrine system doing its job. As uncomfortable as it might feel, your ancestors wouldn't have survived without it.

The Brain Doesn't Mind

So, you've got the basics of how the brain works, but as a budding psychologist, you want to know about the *mind*. Learning about lobes, hemispheres, and neurons may be interesting, but you're probably itching to learn more about thoughts, feelings, and deeds.

Unfortunately, from a scientific standpoint, the mind is a much slipperier concept than the brain. You can't just go to the doctor and get him or her to take a picture of your mind, and since you can't see it, it's hard to define it.

The Make-Up of a Mind

Let's start by defining the mind as the sum total of all the thoughts, feelings, and sensations of which we are aware. It's the brain's consciousness. But the meaning of consciousness is subject to debate. Common sense says your mind rules as your brain, but science says there is strong reason to believe that your mind doesn't even understand a lot of what's happening in there.

Some research suggests that the mind's real job has been highly overrated—that, instead of controlling what we do, the mind may just interpret what the brain has already done. Experimenter Benjamin Libet wired subjects with electrodes that measure brain activity, then seated them in full view of a rapidly rotating clock and repeatedly asked them to flex one finger. Each time they flexed, he instructed them to tell him the exact time they "ordered" their finger to flex. He kept track of three events:

1. The onset of increased brain activity recorded by electrodes
2. The actual flexing of the finger
3. The point at which each subject said he or she had "told" the finger to flex

What You Think Ain't What You Get

Libet found that a flurry of brain activity took place *before* the order to flex the finger was dispatched by his subjects' conscious minds. Their neurons were firing a third of a second before they were even conscious of the desire to act. The brain had started moving before the mind had "decided" to do anything.

Psychobabble

John Searle (U.C. Berkeley) gave patients posthypnotic suggestions, then blocked their memory of them. When they later followed through with his suggestions, they offered seemingly rational explanations for their behavior, even though they had no idea why they were really doing it. Searle suggested that one patient crawl around on the floor. When the patient acted on the suggestion, he'd say something like, "I'm thinking of investing in floor coverings and I'd like to investigate this floor." More astonishingly, he truly *believed* his explanation.

Maybe, thought Libet, the mind only gives us the illusion of control. In his experiment, another brain mechanism seemed to delay the sensation of the finger moving long enough for the conscious mind to think it had commanded the action and then felt the muscles act. Time and again, the conscious order and the actual flexing of the finger took place at virtually the same time. But the brain activity showed that, by the time the mind ordered the finger to flex, the impulse had already been dispatched. All the mind got was a last-second opportunity to veto the decision!

Now you can see why we've spent so much time on biopsychology. Our mind may act as if it's running the show. We may think it is. But, from research like Libet's, we can see that much of what goes on in our brain is outside of our conscious awareness. Our mind may be more of an interpreter than a leader; while it gives us rational explanations for our behavior, it's not in the driver's seat. In the next chapter, we'll explore two areas that influence how well we drive: nature and nurture.

The Least You Need to Know

➤ The human brain evolved into its present form because it contained features that allowed our ancestors to thrive.

➤ The brain's structure reflects our evolutionary history: The old brain governs the most primitive human behavior, the midbrain is the seat of human drives and emotions, and the newer cerebral cortex guides the most complex thinking and feeling.

➤ The cerebral cortex—divided into two hemispheres and eight lobes—is the headquarters of human behavior.

➤ The human nervous system, which sends messages to and from the brain through electrical impulses—is the best communication system in the world.

➤ The mind is the part of our brain that we are conscious of—its main job may be to make sense of decisions our brain has already made.

Chapter 3

The Chicken or the Egg?

In This Chapter

➤ Refereeing the nature-nurture debate

➤ Let's get typical

➤ Getting into your genes

➤ Just what *are* you born with?

➤ You're *so* mature

The nature-nurture debate has been raging for 200 years. Whether they're studying personality, intelligence, or our susceptibility to mental disorders, psychologists are still trying to tease out how much our genes contribute to who we are and how much we're molded by our environment.

Some early researchers considered infants to be like blank pages, to be written on by their parents and teachers. Nurture was everything. Others believed that nature ruled the psychological roost. Today we know it's not so cut-and-dried an issue. In this chapter, we'll take a look at this "chicken or the egg" debate, at why we have the genes we have, and at the role our environment plays in nurturing our nature.

Dancing with Wolves

In 1801, a 12-year-old boy was discovered in the woods outside of Aveyron, France. He had apparently been raised by wolves; no one knew where he came from and he acted more like a wolf than a human being. A French doctor named Jean-Marie Itard renamed the boy "Victor" and took on the challenge of teaching him to be human.

Taming the Wild Child

Jean-Marie began an intensive training program with Victor. Initial results seemed promising. Fairly quickly, Victor became affectionate and well mannered and could utter a few words. After five years, however, Victor could learn no more. Although he lived with a caretaker until he died at age 40, Victor never became a fully functioning human being. From Jean-Marie's perspective, his experiment had failed.

Looking Beneath the Surface

But was it nature or nurture that failed? The good doctor had no information about Victor's genetic makeup; perhaps the boy had been abandoned because he was developmentally disabled to begin with. If that were true, Victor's nature was defective and no training program would have worked. Alternatively, maybe Jean-Marie's training program was off the mark and Victor could have whizzed through a different one. Or, maybe Victor could have learned the lessons of human nature at one time, but had outgrown his receptivity to language by age 12.

Brain Buster

There's danger in oversimplistic explanations for something as complex as human behavior. Overreliance on "nature" explanations has led to justifications of racism. Overreliance on the "nurture" side can lead to neglect of real, physical causes of arrested mental development, such as insufficient diet, lead poisoning (from paint chips), and other environmental hazards.

Nature or Nurture

Where did "you" come from? Are you the product of genetic Russian roulette, or have your life's experiences made you the person you are? For the past 200 years, scholars have debated these questions. It all started with an argument between two philosophers: John Locke and Jean-Jacques Rousseau.

The Great Debate, Philosophically Speaking

British philosopher John Locke formed the nurture camp. Babies, he argued, are born without knowledge or skills. We enter the world as blank slates upon which experience writes. Human development is directed by the stimulation received through experience and education.

"Hogwash," said French philosopher Jean-Jacques Rousseau. Human beings, he argued, are hardwired from birth with all our predispositions and abilities. Sure, we're unsophisticated when we enter the world, but we're also innocent and good. We're born noble savages.

When it comes to nature versus nurture, the issue is often more complex than it seems. Take Victor the wolf boy, for example. If his training program had produced a fully functioning, "normal" human being, this would have offered strong evidence that nurture is powerful. The fact that it didn't, however, doesn't prove the opposite. Since we have no information about Victor's genes, we can't say that Victor's stunted growth potential was due to nature *or* nurture.

Taking the Middle Road

In reality, complex skills are shaped by both our biological inheritance and our life experiences. Your heredity gives you your potential, but it is your experience that determines how, and how much of, that potential is realized.

Take language, for example. We appear to inherit a predisposition for language; it's programmed in our genes. However, there is evidence that environmental stimulation must occur during early childhood for maximum language development. If, like Victor, that optimal period is missed, our ability to learn language will be impaired. We can learn a little, but we'll never be the chatterbox we might have been if we'd had our environmental boost!

Asking the Right Questions

A common mistake made in the nature-nurture debate is in asking the wrong questions. For example, asking how much of your intelligence was a gift from your parents and how much was acquired by the sweat of your brow is, if taken literally, silly. In some respects, both nature and nurture contribute 100 percent. After all, if you didn't have any genes at all, you wouldn't be alive. And your mother's womb was your first environment—you wouldn't be alive without that either. No environment, no person—no person, no intelligence.

Psychobabble

Politics and genetics make dangerous bedfellows. Adolph Hitler distorted the science of genetics to justify genocide. As one of his well-respected geneticists wrote: " ... this alien Jewish population is somewhat inferior physically and mentally to the native population. We know and admit that some of their children from the academic standpoint have done brilliantly ... no breeder of cattle, however, would purchase an entire herd because he anticipated finding one or two fine specimens in it."

The real nature-nurture question is whether differences in a trait among a *group* of individuals are due more to differences in their genes or to their environment. In other words, why are some people smarter than others? Why do some people graduate from high school and others drop out? The nature-nurture question helps us look at groups of people and explain or predict their differences; it's not very good at helping us predict why individuals do the things they do.

Here's a useful analogy: It would be absurd to ask whether the area of a rectangle is due more to the length or width, because both must be present in order for it to be a rectangle. But it's not absurd to ask whether the differences among a given *set* of rectangles are due more to differences in length or in width.

Similarly, differences in intelligence may be due to genes for one set of people and environment for another. If you were raised in a loving family and I in solitary confinement, IQ differences are more likely to be due to environment. If we were raised in similar homes, though, differences in our genes might have more influence.

What Twins Tell Us

When scientists try to tease out the relative influence of nature and nurture, they are essentially trying to figure out how much of human nature is inherited. *Heritability* is the degree to which variation in a particular trait, within a certain group, stems from genetic differences among those members as opposed to environmental differences.

Insight

Ever wondered how much you were related to other relatives? You're 100 percent related to your parents as a team (50 percent to each). You're 50 percent related to your brother, 25 percent related to your grandparents, 12.5 percent related to half-siblings and first cousins, and 6.25 percent related to second cousins.

If a trait can be passed down from parent to child, we would expect relatives to be more similar in that trait than people who are not related. So, if we have smart parents, we should see smart kids, and assuming our kids don't marry any dummies, smart grandkids.

The catch, of course, is that relatives often live together. The fact that brothers and sisters have more similar IQs than unrelated people does not, by itself, tell us whether it's the egg (the genes) or the chicken (the home) that's responsible. Here's where the twins come in.

Identical twins have identical genes; they are the only human beings who truly have the same genetic nature. Fraternal twins and other siblings share only about 50 percent of their genes. In their journey through the nature-nurture tunnel, scientists have found that studying the natural differences between twins helps them see the light at the end.

For example, comparing the IQ scores between identical twins reared in the same home and identical twins adopted by different families at birth allows us to look at the influence of environment on intelligence. Since identical twins have exactly the same genes, we can feel pretty confident attributing any IQ difference to the different environments in which they were reared. On the other hand, if identical twins reared miles away have more similar IQ scores than fraternal twins who shared a bedroom since birth, nature pretty much wins the debate.

And, with regard to intelligence, nature has come out the winner. Identical twins consistently have more similar IQ scores than fraternal twins *regardless of the environment in which they are raised.* Anatomy, however, is not destiny. There's a surprisingly small relationship between intelligence and success, suggesting smart genes may give us a jump start in life, but they won't carry us over the long haul. Like our muscles, our intelligence can't help us that much if we don't use it.

Family Genes and Other Heirlooms

Research with twins does seem to tell us that smart parents make bright children and dumb parents don't have many children in graduate school. But, how does all this genetic passing down work?

When our dad's sperm and our mom's egg unite, the new cell it creates is a *zygote.* This zygote contains the full human complement of 23 paired chromosomes, with one member of each pair coming from each parent. The zygote grows up and becomes you. Because each sperm cell is different from each egg cell, each zygote is different from each other.

The fact that genes come in pairs helps geneticist calculate *percent relatedness,* the amount of genes you share with another human being. You may be the spitting image of your dad, but you have 50 percent of your genes from your mom and 50 percent from your dad. Genetically, you are 50 percent related to each of them.

The difference between the actual amount of genetic material you share and the way you physically look illustrates the difference between your *genotype* and your *phenotype. Genotype* refers to the entire set of genes you inherit, your biological potential. *Phenotype* refers to the observable properties of your body and your behavioral traits. Your phenotype might look just like your dad, but your genotype comes from both your parents in a 50-50 split.

Dominating Genes

Your genotype is predetermined—50 percent of your genetic makeup comes from Dad, 50 percent from Mom. Your phenotype, on the other hand, is a battle for control between your genes. And, just like the most aggressive warriors often win their battles, the most dominant genes dictate your phenotype.

Gregor Mendel was the first person to realize that some genes are dominant over others. A *dominant gene* is one that will produce its observable effects if it is present in either parent; a *recessive gene* will only show up if both parents possess it.

Jeepers, Creepers, Where'd You Get Those Peepers?

The reason there are more brown-eyed people than blue-eyed ones is because the gene for brown eyes is dominant: If one parent contributes blue-eyed genes and the other contributes brown-eyed ones, the child will have brown eyes. But we all know a few blue-eyed children whose parents are both brown-eyed. How can that be? Simple—sometimes brown-eyed parents have a recessive gene for blue eyes lurking in the background, and those are the ones that got passed along to form the blue-eyed child's zygote. (Since blue eyes are recessive, both parents must have contributed blue-eyed genes in order for them to show up in their offspring.)

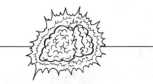

Brain Buster

A single recessive gene can dramatically alter a child's life. Take *phenylketonuria* (*PKU*), a genetic disorder carried by a recessive gene. Babies with PKU are unable to process a specific amino acid found in most protein-containing foods. This disorder can cause severe mental retardation and an inability to speak or understand language.

Genes and Mental Illness

Genes can also make us vulnerable to mental illness. Scientists can now predict our chances of inheriting schizophrenia, clinical depression, or bipolar disorder by looking at our family history of mental illness.

But once again, anatomy is not destiny: Even the grimmest genetic obstacle can be altered with the right environment. Infants with PKU, a genetic disorder that can cause mental retardation, can be immediately placed on a diet low in phenylalanine and grow up normally. And with the wonders of antidepressants, 70 to 90 percent of those who suffer from major depression lead happy, satisfying lives. Nature may deal us the cards, but we can play the game a lot of different ways.

Don't Blame Your Genes

If you were a smart kid, thank your parents for your good genes. If you dropped out of school to open a tattoo parlor, and now regret that you never lived up to your potential, blame yourself. Your genes aren't responsible for your behavior. It's pretty common to hear scientists at press conferences say things like, "We think we've found the gene for suicide." This is a bunch of baloney. Our genes may give us a predisposition for depression, but they don't make us overdose on pills.

The influence of our genes on our behavior is indirect. Their main task is building and organizing the physical structures of the body, including the brain. These structures interact with the environment to produce behavior. Good genes give us resources for coping with our environment, but a bad environment can challenge even the most resilient genes.

Psychobabble

The myth that behavior is controlled by genes has a long history. E.B. Ford, professor of eco-logical genetics at Oxford University, wrote: " ... the XYY genetic type is aggressive in a way which often leads to crimes of violence ... an instance of the widely established fact that intelligence and psychology are under genetic control." But studies have shown that only a maximum of 1 percent of XYY males might spend part of their lives behind bars.

Take, for example, a child growing up in an extremely violent neighborhood. Evidence suggests that the stress of living under these conditions may stimulate the development of the part of the brain that responds to threatening stimuli and organizes aggression. The child may, as a result, be more aggressive, because the environment in which he or she lives encourages the aggression centers of the brain to become more developed.

Over time, a high-crime environment might naturally select more aggressive individuals and, as a result, genes that promote the development of the brain's aggression center could be passed down to future generations. But be careful about the conclusions you draw from this: There's a big leap between inheriting a predisposition for aggression and actually committing a crime. We might be predisposed toward violence to help us survive a bad neighborhood, but our genes don't pick up a gun and shoot it.

The same is true for all human behavior. Natural selection has bred us to be better at doing whatever we needed to do to survive and thrive in our environment. As a result, certain behavioral mechanisms have evolved, including our capacity for language, our ability to learn and remember, and our problem-solving skills. The fact that you, a human, can read this page while a monkey or a lion cannot is the result of natural selection. However, not withstanding my writing skills, the fact that you as an individual can *understand* these words reflects what you have learned in your lifetime.

Insight

Functionalist psychology tries to explain behaviors in terms of the purposes, or functions, they serve for the individual. Evolutionary psychologists look at how human behavior functioned to promote the survival and propagation of the species.

Typical Human Behavior

Understanding our genes can help us understand our own behavior. Evolutionary psychologists look at the bigger picture and try to understand why human beings, as a species, act the way they do. In essence, they study universal human behaviors and try to figure out what caused them to evolve. Their questions are generally *functionalist* in nature, such as:

> ➤ Is it possible that some human behaviors evolved because ancestors who did those things had an environmental edge?

> ➤ What might that edge have been?

> ➤ How, for example, did talking help human beings get along better in the world?

Similarity Can Breed Content

Evolutionary psychologists are particularly interested in *species-typical behavior*— behaviors that are so common among the members of a species that they can be used as identifying characteristics. Barking, four-legged walking, and pooping on front lawns pretty much sums it up for dogs. Two-legged walking and talking are species-typical for humans.

So are human emotions. From an evolutionary perspective, human emotions may have motivated our ancestors to do the things they needed to do to survive. Perhaps ancestors who felt angry were more likely to protect themselves or defend their turf!

Psychobabble

A group of researchers, headed by Paul Eckman and Wallace Friesman, identified six basic emotions as universal among human beings: surprise, fear, disgust, anger, happiness, and sadness. When you're feeling sad, it can be comforting to know that every other human being has felt this way, too.

Not only do we all feel the same feelings, human beings are pretty darned good at knowing what others are feeling, too. Researchers showed photographs of American people expressing the six basic emotions to people in many different cultures, including a preliterate, geographically isolated tribe in New Guinea. In every culture, people were remarkably accurate at detecting the emotion expressed. You don't have to be Charles Darwin to see the survival benefits of recognizing the face of an enemy!

But Vive la Différence!

Species-typical behavior does not mean human beings are all alike. Not all human beings feel happy eating chocolate ice cream, nor does everybody cry when they're afraid. In humans, species-typical behavior means that we are biologically prepared for that behavior. But exactly when, how, and why each human experiences and expresses his or her unique feelings is a complicated jumble of biology, life experience, and cultural legacy. Species-typical behaviors identified by psychologists include

➤ living in communities

➤ male violence

➤ nepotism (favoring kin)

➤ marriage contracts

Evolutionary Theory Gone Awry

The application of evolutionary theory to psychology has stirred up a jumble of emotions, not to mention some pretty dark ulterior motives. Instead of explaining behavior through evolution, evolutionary psychology has, at times, been used to justify it.

Mother Nature's Morality

One misuse of evolutionary psychology is the *naturalistic fallacy*. According to this error in logic, nature is guided by a moral force that favors what is good or right. If male mammals in the wild dominate females through force, well, that's the way it "should be." British philosopher Herbert Spencer, a contemporary of Darwin, used this argument many times to justify the most extreme abuses of nineteenth-century capitalism. Of course, his biggest fans were those in power at the top of the industrialist ladder.

I Just Couldn't Help Myself!

A second misuse of evolutionary psychology is known as the *deterministic fallacy*. It's the genetic version of "the devil made me do it." According to this viewpoint, our genes control our behavior and there's nothing we can do about it. If natural selection teaches me to fight for my territory, can I help it if I slugged the man who took my parking space? It's genetic!

Insight

Self-control is a human characteristic that we often overlook. Yet nature has obviously favored it, since it appears to have selected those of our ancestors who exhibited it. After all, humans live in communities for greater chances of survival, so evolution must have favored cooperation and self-restraint.

The error in this logic is assuming that our genes directly influence our behavior, in a way that's beyond our control. But we human beings can control our environment, and we can control ourselves. I can choose to waste my energy fighting over parking spaces, or I can find more effective ways to deal with a crowded mall. I can go when it's less crowded or I can get there early. I can ask the person to move or I can change my attitude so I don't feel angry in the first place.

Home, Sweet Home

We've talked a lot about nature in this chapter—from genetics and species-typical behavior to evolution. As we've seen, though, even the clearest examples of nature's influence can be changed by nurture.

For example, common sense would lead you to expect that siblings growing up in the same family would have a lot in common. They have the same parents. They play in the same neighborhoods. They go to the same schools. In fact, they pretty much share the same learning opportunities. Even if siblings have no genetic relationship, as is the case with adopted siblings, you'd think all those shared childhood experiences would have an impact.

It should come as no surprise, then, to discover that family environment has a strong early influence on children's IQ scores. Adopted siblings living in the same home have more similar IQ scores than children who live apart. However, this similarity fades as the siblings grow up and begin to create their own environment. The intellectual advantage or disadvantage of being raised in a particular home fades by early adulthood.

How does this happen? It seems that intelligence is like a muscle; you either use it or lose it. Early environmental influences disappear in adulthood because, when they're grown, siblings choose different environments to live in. We can choose an environment that encourages us to either use our brain or lose our marbles!

Baby Builds on Blueprints

But even after taking into account the genes your parents gave you and the environment you're born into, there's still something more to be reckoned. And that "something more" is the unique, the individual, the personal *you*. You came into the world prepared to take your inheritance and grow with it and, from birth, you've been hard at work.

Babies come into this world with some pretty sophisticated equipment and some pretty strong preferences. Even while they're still in the womb they're moving around, listening to their mother talk, and preparing for their grand entrance into the world. When they're born, they are already biologically prepared to seek food, protection, and care.

For example, from birth, babies establish a relationship with people who can take care of them. They start out preferring female voices and, after just a few weeks on the outside, they can recognize their caregiver's voice. By seven weeks, they've learned to scan their caregiver's face and start to make eye contact when he or she talks. If Locke and Rousseau had spent any time around babies, they would have quickly given up the "blank slate" or "noble savage" descriptions. Pre-programmed "friendly" computers is a better description of newborns.

As early as 12 hours after birth, babies show distinct signs of pleasure at the taste of sugar water or vanilla and show aversion to the taste of lemon or the smell of rotten eggs. Days-old infants quickly learned to anticipate dessert when researchers stroked their foreheads and then fed them sugar water. Not only did babies turn their heads in the direction of sugar, they cried when the goods weren't delivered. From birth, it seems, we feel pain when a reliable relationship breaks down.

Insight

Our early years are very important. Our brains grow 50 percent larger in the first 12 months after birth, and by our second birthday, they are 80 percent larger than the brains we were born with. This growth eventually tapers off and, by age 11, we're pretty much stuck with the brains we have.

Let's Try Getting "Normal" for a Change

Genetic inheritance gives a baby a jump start on life, but he or she still has a lot of growing to do. After birth, a child's physical growth and abilities follow a genetically based timetable. This genetic blueprint is responsible for the appearance of certain behaviors at roughly the same time for all human beings, taking into allowance cultural variations. And, as you're about to see, it is the following of this timetable that, from a maturation standpoint, makes us "normal."

Oh, Grow Up!

If anyone has ever said that to you, they were giving you a clear message that you weren't living up to their expectations of how a person your age should behave. But how do we know how we're supposed to behave at what age? By looking at the human process of *maturation*.

Timely Development

That's a pretty fancy way of saying that, unless you are being raised by coneheads, you are expected to do certain things by a certain age. For example, by four months, most babies sit

Shrink Rap

Maturation refers to the process of growth typical of all members of a species who are reared in the usual environment of that species.

with support. Between five and six months, they stand holding on to something, and at about a year they start walking. If a baby can't do these things, parents start worrying.

Walking follows a fixed, time-ordered sequence that is typical of all physically capable members of our species. In cultures where there is more physical stimulation, children begin to walk sooner. However, contrary to many parents' beliefs, babies do not require any special training to learn to walk.

The Parental Part of the Equation

While baby's doing his or her developmental thing, part of a parent's emotional growth is learning to relax and trust his or her baby to develop at his or her own pace. That's because the parent's role in the process is to provide the emotional security that is necessary for his or her child's physical growth. For, as you're about to see, physical and emotional development go hand in hand.

What's Your Attachment Style?

The way we attach to our earliest caregivers can set the pattern for our relationships for the rest of our lives. To see how you tend to relate to others, put a check beside the self-descriptions that you most agree with:

1. ____ I am somewhat uncomfortable being close to others; I find it difficult to trust them completely, difficult to allow myself to depend on them. I am nervous when anyone gets too close, and often love partners who want me to be more intimate than I feel comfortable being.

2. ____ I find it relatively easy to get close to others and am comfortable depending on them. I don't often worry about being abandoned or about someone getting too close to me.

3. ____ I find that other people are reluctant to get as close as I would like them to. I often worry that my partner doesn't really love me or won't want to stay with me. I want to get very close to my partner, and this sometimes scares people away.

If you selected (1), you're expressing an avoidant, insecure attachment style. About 25 percent of us have this attachment pattern. Twenty percent of us will choose answer (2), which represents an anxious-ambivalent, insecure style. Fifty-five percent of us are lucky enough to answer (3), which suggests that we attached securely to our parents and are secure in our attachment to others.

Growing Up Emotionally

Watch a baby learn to walk and you aren't just witnessing physical development. You're witnessing emotional growth, too. From birth, our minds and bodies are intertwined.

Psychobabble

Monkeys deprived of social contact for six months were paired with normally reared, slightly younger monkeys. The socially deprived monkeys repeatedly attempted to withdraw from their younger playmates, but the younger "therapist" monkeys persisted. Used to the joys of social contact, these younger monkeys followed around and clung to the socially impaired monkeys. Within a few weeks, the "patient" and "therapist" were playing together and within six months, the "patients" were cured.

As babies begin to physically explore their worlds, they depend on their parents to make them feel safe. Time and time again, toddlers go back and forth between venturing out into the world and returning to check in and make sure Mom or Dad is still around should things move a little too fast. What does this pattern mean for a child's development? Children who don't trust their parents to be there often don't explore their environment.

Studies of infants reared in institutions have clearly demonstrated the criticalness of the parent-child attachment to social and physical development. Infants who were isolated for the first eight months of life rarely tried to approach adults later on, either to hug or caress them or to get reassurance when in distress. And, not surprisingly, this social impairment led to other developmental delays—such children failed to utter a single word by the first year of life.

Fortunately, few babies ever face the trauma of living in isolation for the first few months of life. However, none of us had perfect parents. Relationships between parents and children are complicated, and all of us have experienced at least one occasion where a parent couldn't be there for us. What impact does this have?

Psychologist Mary Ainsworth studied young children and their relationship with their primary caregivers. By placing them in novel situations where they were briefly separated from their parent, she identified three different attachment styles, one secure style and two insecure styles. And each of these attachment styles influenced the child's physical development.

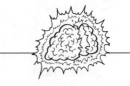

Brain Buster

Attachment disorders can be seriously disabling for the individual. The Academy Award–winning movie *Good Will Hunting* is a great example of the adult consequences of attachment disorder. Unlike the movie, though, in real life the hero or heroine rarely drives off into the sunset to have a happy-ever-after life.

Ainsworth discovered that securely attached children felt closer to and safer with their caregivers. As a result, they were more willing to explore or tolerate novel experiences. They were confident they could cry out for help or reunite with a caregiver if needed.

Insecurely attached children, on the other hand, reacted to separation and new situations with avoidance, anxiety, or ambivalence. Anxious or ambivalent children sought contact with their caregivers but were fearful and angry when separated from them. These children were also difficult to console when reunited with their parents.

Children with an avoidant attachment style, on the other hand, didn't seem to care if their primary caregivers left and they showed little emotion when they returned. Dr. Ainsworth hypothesized that these children were victims of long-term rejection and had given up on their efforts to have a consistent, caring caregiver. In reaction to an abusive or neglectful environment, these children developed an unhealthy protective shell around their hearts. In extreme cases, they became adults with little concern for anyone but themselves.

Nature? Nurture? It's Both!

In some respects, we're back where we started at the beginning of this chapter—in between nature and nurture. Children who aren't loved don't grow. Medication can control the influence of bad genes. Intelligence is in our nature, but success depends on nurture. When it comes to human beings, nature and nurture are inseparable. Given the amazing ways children develop, which we'll discuss in Chapter 4, "It's Only a Stage," perhaps that's the way it should be.

The Least You Need to Know

➤ We're the product of both nature and nurture: Our genes give us our biological potential and our environment determines how we express it.

➤ Every human being inherits certain behavioral tendencies that helped our human ancestors survive and thrive, but what triggers these tendencies and how often they are expressed varies across cultures and individuals.

➤ Genes never directly control behavior. None of us are born killers or saints.

➤ Emotional and physical development are inseparable. Children need emotional security to grow physically, and one source of that security is a healthy attachment to their parents.

Chapter 4

It's Only a Stage

In This Chapter

➤ The boon of boredom in baby research

➤ Learning the lingo

➤ Natural born psychologists

➤ Exploring the mind of a child

➤ Lurching from crisis to crisis

Human beings have historically had some pretty strange ideas about children. Maybe that's why the field of developmental psychology is still a baby; it wasn't born until the first half of the twentieth century. Since then, what we've learned is that children are pretty impressive. In this chapter, you'll learn how children's thoughts and language develop. You'll learn about a lot of different stages children go through, and how each stage prepares a child to deal more effectively with the world around him.

You'll also learn a lot about yourself. Understanding how children develop speech will not only teach you some healthy respect for children's built-in desires to communicate, it will give you valuable insight into how your present self-talk developed. And, as you learn how children learn, take time to reassess your life. As you'll see, children seem to intuitively seek out experiences and create adventures that help them make the most of their biological potential. Are you?

It's a Dog's Life

Once upon a time, an English animal shelter worker, responding to a neighbor's complaint about a mistreated dog, stumbled upon a badly neglected and abused child lying in a crib. Not knowing what to do, he turned the matter over to the police, who quickly contacted a judge. To the judge's horror, he soon realized it was safer to be a dog than a child. While there were laws protecting animals from abuse and neglect, there was no law that provided similar protection for children.

In England at that time, you see, children were the legal property of their parents. Luckily for all of us, this judge refused to go strictly by the book. He creatively declared the child to be "inhuman," thereby placing her under the protection of animal laws and allowing her to be removed from the home. A short time later, the first child abuse law was passed.

The Development of Child Development

The field of child development was born in the first half of the twentieth century. Sigmund Freud had begun talking about the influence of childhood on adult mental health, and scientists suddenly became curious about the life and experiences of children. Before that, people had some pretty strange ideas about child development.

Period	Prevailing Attitude About Children
1500	Children over 6 are small adults and should behave accordingly
1500–1700	Children are family property and contribute to household income
1800s	Decreased need for cheap labor; childhood extended to adolescence; beginning to be seen as valuable and vulnerable, children are "potential persons"; rise of child-oriented families, juvenile courts, and field of developmental psychology
1950–present	Children have legal rights, including the rights to due process in legal courts and to self-determination

Studying Bored Babes

Studying child development means studying babies. After all, the most rapid part of child development is in the first 18 to 24 months of life. But how do we do it? Babies aren't exactly giving speeches during these first few years. How do we know what babies know and how they know it? Through human nature's built-in tendency to become easily bored. Researchers call this *habituation,* and babies do it as much as grownups do.

Hundreds of experiments have shown that babies look longer at new things than at familiar ones. When shown a pattern, for example, babies show a lot of interest at first and then, over the course of a few minutes, look at it less and less. They become habituated to it. This aspect of baby nature is so reliable that developmental psychologists use it to assess infants' abilities to perceive and remember. Obviously, if a baby looks longer at a new stimulus than one that is old hat, he or she must perceive the difference between the two and, on some level, remember the old one.

Shrink Rap

Habituation is the process whereby a person becomes so accustomed to a stimulus that he or she ignores it and attends instead to less familiar stimuli.

And one of the things we've discovered while studying babies is that babies are constantly studying, and they're naturally drawn to studying things that provide them the most efficient opportunity to learn. For example, not only do babies waste little energy restudying objects they've already seen, they show a strong preference for objects in their environment that they can control.

Two-month-old infants show much more interest in a mobile that moves when they do as compared to a motor-driven one. And they get pretty mad when the device is disconnected. So much for Rousseau's noble savage idea that children are born all innocent and good!

Fast Learners and Good Teachers

Babies are fast learners, and by five or six months they've established some pretty good study habits. For example, infants across cultures engage in a sophisticated exploration called *examining*. When they encounter an interesting object, they hold it up in front of their eyes, turn it from side to side, pass it from one hand to the other, squeeze it, mouth it, and generally do whatever they can to figure it out. And they pay attention to detail: they look more at colorful objects; they feel objects with different textures; and they shake, rattle, and roll objects that make sounds.

Teenagers may not respect their elders, but babies do. They recognize the value of experience as a teacher and they start cashing in on the wisdom of their parents. Six-month-olds, for example, will look at their parents' eyes, follow their gaze, and then look at what the adult is viewing. The baby will then check back and forth periodically to see if the parent is still looking.

Six-month-olds are also much more likely to throw a ball if they've seen a parent throw it. Last but not least, they learn from their parent's mistakes. If a mommy looks fearful as a baby heads toward the stairs, babies are much less likely to keep going; it's as if they assume Mommy's been down that path and, as judged by her facial expression, lived to regret it.

Babies, it seems, are born students and their biggest teachers are mom and dad. And that's nowhere as clearly demonstrated as in the way that babies learn language.

Learning Baby Talk

Walking upright and growing bigger brains may be our two biggest evolutionary accomplishments, but language runs a close third. Not only is vocal communication useful for a group, it is also immediately useful and necessary for individual survival. As any parent can tell you, young children use sounds and gestures to show that they are hungry, tired, or unhappy.

Insight

Every baby is born fully capable of learning any language in the world. It's only after fairly long exposure to the language of his or her community that a child begins to lose some of that incredible linguistic ability.

I've spent seven years trying to learn Spanish and failed, so it depresses me to think I could have spoken any one (or more) of 3,000 languages, if only I'd started early enough. No matter what their native language, children have pretty much mastered it by the time they are 3 or 4 years old. In fact, between 18 months and 6 years of age, the average child learns about one word per waking hour!

Babies begin practicing cooing sounds at about 2 months, and progress to babbling at about 4 to 6 months. These early sounds appear to be wired in; deaf infants coo and babble at the same age and manner as hearing infants, and early babblers are as likely to contain foreign language sounds as native-language sounds. By 10 months, though, children start babbling in sounds that imitate their parents. If a deaf infant is exposed to sign language, he will start babbling with his or her hands.

Children learn language in three initial stages—one word, two words, and telegraphic speech. They start out by naming things that are present and then begin asking for things. At around 18 months, a naming explosion occurs and children begin to learn words at an astonishing rate. In the early two-word stage, children can use combinations of words to make meanings, although they stick to the bare necessities.

In their early two- and three-word sentences, children's speech is *telegraphic,* mainly consisting of nouns and verbs that get the message across. "Zachary eat" wouldn't have made my third-grade grammar teacher very happy, but it's pretty effective at getting Mommy to head for the refrigerator.

When it comes to getting their message across, children are downright geniuses. Parents certainly help by talking to them and providing them with plenty of opportunities. And, as you're about to see, lads and lasses may be born with some of their language talent built in.

Psychobabble

Apes pass vocabulary but fail grammar. Kanzi, the most fluent ape alive, has been pretty adept at acquiring a vocabulary. He will often announce his intention to go to the tree house before doing so and has been known, through his language symbols, to request a game of chase with his caretakers. No ape, however, has been able to grasp the basics of grammar, such as understanding the difference between plural and singular or understanding past or present tense.

LADS and LASSes

Language researchers have been so impressed with children's knack for languages that they began wondering if human beings were born linguists. Many theorists believe we have an innate, biologically based mental program for language acquisition. These theorists believe that we don't just repeat what we hear, but that we follow a pre-programmed set of instructions to acquire language and vocabulary. Noam Chomsky, a pioneer in this area of linguistics, called these speech-enabling structures *language acquisition devices,* or *LADs.*

Other researchers agree that human beings have a genetic predisposition for language, but that this built-in capacity for language is not a rigid device but rather a set of lessons and "listening rules" that helps us perceive and learn language. For example, babies pay attention to the sounds and rhythm of the sounds they hear others speak, especially the beginnings, endings, and stressed syllables.

In addition, children seem to be born using certain grammar rules. They come into the world with some natural biases in how to use and apply new words. For example, children have natural tendencies:

➤ to link new words to objects for which children do not already have a name (if a child has three objects and already knows the names of two, he'll assign any new name he learns the as-yet-unnamed object rather than wonder if it is a synonym for either of the named ones).

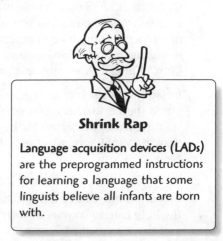

Shrink Rap

Language acquisition devices (LADs) are the preprogrammed instructions for learning a language that some linguists believe all infants are born with.

➤ to assume that all nouns are common nouns (calling all men "Daddy").

➤ to overextend common nouns to things that are similar (calling all round objects "balls").

Sure, these assumptions lead to some pretty funny talk, but think how efficient they are. If you're learning a new language, it's a lot better to group similar objects together and give them similar names than to assume every new item is a world unto itself. And think how confusing it would be if we wondered if every new word was merely a synonym of something we already knew? These built-in language teachers help speed up our early language development.

Shrink Rap

Language acquisition support systems (LASSes) are the circumstances that facilitate the efficient acquisition of language.

The jury is still out for LADs but not for *LASSes, language acquisition support systems.* In order for our language potential to blossom, we must grow up with a responsive environment with plenty of opportunity to practice. Without it, we miss the opportunity to fully express ourselves.

Remember Victor, the wolf boy from Aveyron (Chapter 3, "The Chicken or the Egg?")? Undoubtedly, one of the reasons his language skills never caught up is the fact that he was deprived of a language acquisition support system in childhood; he missed the critical period for language development. In every known case in which children are deprived of early language opportunities, their language skills are permanently impaired. When it comes to LASSes, we either use them or lose them.

Listen and Learn

Of course, there's another big influence that helps children talk faster: parents. If you're a parent, you're bilingual. You speak your native tongue and *parentese,* a lingo that involves speaking in an exaggerated, high-pitched tone of voice, emphasizing and repeating important words, and using short, staccato bursts ("uh-oh") to signal taboos. Most of us call this "baby talk" and it just happens to be the language babies learn best.

In fact, just as babies are amazingly skilled language learners, caregivers are incredibly gifted speech teachers. Not only do we speak in parentese, we engage our infants in training dialogues. From birth, we talk to our newborns and then wait for a reply. Early on, we'll accept just about anything as a valid reply before continuing—a burp, a sneeze, a yawn. Like any good teacher, though, we make more demands as our children grow, matching our expectations to their abilities.

Evolution must have thought talking was a pretty nifty ability to have, considering all the help it has given us in learning how to do it. Babies come programmed for speech and they're given parents who are natural language teachers. No wonder children have such a hard time being quiet; it's against their nature!

The Child Psychologist

Language is one area children are fascinated with. Psychology is another. They may start out exploring the outer world, but they pretty quickly show a fascination with their inner world as well. Most two-year-olds, for example, will label themselves as sad, mad, or glad depending upon the circumstances they are reporting. They also begin to use words like *dream, forget, pretend, believe,* and *hope* as they talk about internal states.

Psychobabble

Fifteen percent of the U.S. population has a learning disability. A common disability is dyslexia, characterized by problems in expressing or understanding language. The person with dyslexia has problems either translating language to thought (as in listening or reading) or thought to language (as in writing or speaking). It has nothing to do with intelligence.

And not just their own. By the time children have learned the words to say it, usually between 2$\frac{1}{2}$ and 3$\frac{1}{2}$, they begin to attribute thoughts, feelings, and motives to the things people do. A four-year-old soap opera fan will assure you the heroine of *As the World Turns* is crying because she's sad, or that Daddy is getting a beer because he's thirsty. Luckily for parents, an understanding of some of the ulterior motives that drive human behavior come later!

Toddlers two and three years old engage in an enormous amount of fantasy play, and even two-year-olds know the difference between make-believe and reality. This early distinction between make-believe and reality may be a necessary survival tool—a child who understands the difference has the foundation for understanding that beliefs can differ from reality and that people can fool others by manipulating their beliefs. Few of us would argue that the ability to detect deception is a key for psychological survival. By age four, children become pretty skilled at detecting deception in others—and using it for their own advantage as well.

All this worrying about the motives and intentions of other people can take its toll. Wouldn't it be wonderful if we were oblivious to the minds of other people? No more self-consciousness or worrying about making a good impression? Believe me, there have been plenty of times in my life when I would happily have subscribed to the "ignorance is bliss" school of thought.

As wonderful as it might be to imagine, our lives would be much more difficult if we were so blissfully oblivious. It would be like living among aliens. We might be able to

Shrink Rap

Emotional intelligence is the ability to understand, and use, our emotions successfully. It involves a group of skills, including the ability to motive ourselves, regulate our moods, control our impulses, and to empathize with others.

study them and fit in by copying their behavior, but we would never truly feel at home. Autistic children may know exactly what this feels like. Autism, a disorder characterized by severe deficits in social interaction and language acquisition, a tendency toward repetitive actions, and a narrow focus of interest, can result in a complete inability to relate to, or understand, people.

In the arena of child development, researchers have traditionally been more interested in the cognitive arena than in the touchy-feely world of emotional growth. However, as Dr. Daniel Goleman eloquently points out in his groundbreaking book *Emotional Intelligence,* a child's ability to develop his emotional skills may have more impact on his success in life than his grades and IQ scores put together.

Putting Our Thinking Caps On

The mind of my four-year-old, Zachary, fascinates me. He's still convinced the tallest glass holds the most juice even if he watches me pour the same amount back and forth. "Is Quasimodo real?" he wonders again after watching *The Hunchback of Notre Dame* for the 97th time. When he gets scared, he feels safe when I tell him about nice monsters. On the other hand, he isn't convinced if I tell him monsters don't exist. And, as sweet as he is, every time he ties up our cat I'm reminded that empathy is an acquired skill. No matter how grown-up our children try to be, their minds work differently from ours.

The Curious Child

Jean Piaget, the child-mind pioneer, was also fascinated by the minds of children. Watching his own three children develop sparked an interest in children's minds that lasted more than 50 years. What he concluded was that children are scientists who begin to experiment and explore their world from the moment they're born. Mental development, he believed, naturally arises out of this exploration.

Of course, infants start with what they can see, feel, taste, touch, hear, and smell. Before long, children start putting two and two together and realizing certain actions go best with certain objects. Sucking goes best with nipples. Banging goes best with rattles. Smiling goes best with Mommy's face. Piaget called this ability to develop mental blueprints linking actions and objects the development of *schemes*.

As soon as the baby develops a sucking scheme for nipples, no more effort is wasted in trying to squeeze milk out of a rattle or a teddy bear. Not only do these schemes save time, they are the foundation upon which babies learn more sophisticated lessons, through what Piaget calls *assimilations* and *accommodations*.

Coping with Curve Balls

One of the things we learn early on is that life is constantly throwing us curve balls and we have to find ways to hit them. Sometimes, we can fit that curve ball into our current environment with just a minor tweak (assimilation) and sometimes we have to adjust our way of thinking (accommodation). A baby who's a champion nipple sucker might easily be able to incorporate cups or bottles into his sucking scheme. Eating from a spoon, however, is a whole new challenge.

Piaget considered the assimilation of new experiences similar to the digestion of food. Two people might eat the same food, but the food will be assimilated into the body differently depending upon that person's digestive system, metabolism, and so forth. Moreover, just as

Insight

In Piagetian terms, life is a series of assimilations and accommodations. Children either fit new info into their current schemes or make room for entirely new ones. And they're usually a lot more willing to consider new schemes than their older, supposedly wiser, elders—that's what people mean when they refer to "childlike wonder."

wolfing down crayons or dirt will not help our bodies grow, new experiences that are too different from existing schemes can't be mentally digested, and will not result in growth. Give a toddler your hand calculator and you might get a stellar display of his banging scheme, but you won't teach him arithmetic.

Performing on Stage

Piaget was interested in more than *how* children think. He was also interested in *what* and *why* they think. Over and over, he watched children solve problems and asked them to explain their reasoning behind their solutions.

Not surprisingly, he found that four-year-olds thought differently than fourteen-year-olds. He also found that four-year-olds often came up with similar solutions to the same problems. Putting two and two together, he proposed that most children develop their thinking in stages, going from a concrete, here-and-now focus to a more abstract, future-oriented approach. He came up with four stages of cognitive development, each of which roughly correlated to a child's chronological age:

➤ sensorimotor stage (birth to 2 years old)

➤ preoperational stage (2 to 7 years old)

➤ concrete operations (7 to 11 years old)

➤ formal operations (12 years old and up)

Sensorimotor Stage

In the sensorimotor stage, thoughts and behaviors are pretty much one and the same. Infants spend their time examining their environment and placing objects into schemes for sucking, shaking, banging, twisting, dropping, and other categories that cause general mayhem for their parents.

At the end of the first year, babies take a giant leap forward when they begin to understand the concept of *object permanence*—that objects still exist even though they're out of baby's sight. This, of course, does not prevent them from wanting this concept confirmed over and over through endless games of peekaboo.

General Theme: Monkey see, monkey do.

Preoperational Stage

To you and me, a skillet is a cooking utensil. The only creative energy we spend on a skillet is in deciding what to cook in it. Give a preschooler a skillet and, alakazaam, you have the Spice Girls' lead guitar or the only Star Wars gun that will kill Darth Vadar. Children in this stage have a well-developed ability to magically transform everyday items into symbols and to recreate events that they have seen. However, while their thinking is no longer bound by the here and now, it is very much bound by appearances—witness my Zachary's insistence that the taller cup has more water, no matter how often I showed him otherwise.

This is also an age of profound self-centeredness. If a child falls off a chair, then it's a "bad" chair and needs to be punished—after all, *something* made him fall, and it certainly wasn't *his* fault. Ask a four-year-old to tell you another person's point of view, and she'll tell you her own thoughts and feelings because she hasn't developed the cognitive ability to do otherwise.

General Theme: You can do magic—and fall for it, too.

Shrink Rap

Conservation is the awareness that appearances can be deceiving and that, unless something is added or taken away, an object is the same no matter how it looks on the outside. Mommy in a mask and costume is still, recognizably, Mommy (unless that costume is *very* good).

Concrete Operations

By the time they reach the age of seven, children are starting to realize that appearances can be deceiving. They have, for instance, developed the concept of *conservation:* They realize that, no matter how much outward appearances change, physical properties don't change unless something is added or taken away.

Much of the problem solving done by children in this age group consists of what Piaget called *operations*, mentally reversing the consequences of an action to figure out cause and effect. Ask a 10-year-old bicyclist whether the chain or the fender is crucial to his cycling and he won't have to take apart his bicycle to tell you. By mentally removing each part, he'll know that the chain is connected to the pedals and the pedals move the wheels and, therefore, the chain is critical but the fender is not.

General Theme: Take things literally.

Formal Operations

Remember the game "20 Questions," where the winner is the person who guesses the right answer by answering the fewest yes/no questions? You have to enter formal operations to be really good at it, which is why children have trouble playing the game until they reach this stage, around the age of 12.

Children still in the concrete operations stage tend to limit their questions to specifics. If the correct answer is some kind of animal, a child might ask questions like, "Is it a dog?" or "Is it a monkey?" A formal thinker, on the other hand, might ask questions like, "Does it fly?" or "Does it have hair?" before moving to more specific questions. Formal operations allows us to see the "big picture"; in this stage, we develop general principles that we can apply to hypothetical situations.

General Theme: Think ahead.

The Human Computer

In the cognitive development arena, a quality versus quantity debate is being waged. Piaget believed that the quality of a child's thinking was different as it moved through each developmental stage. The five-year-old who assumes a taller glass holds more water thinks differently than a 10-year-old who understands that appearances can be deceiving.

Or does she? One perspective of cognitive development would argue that the difference in thinking isn't a matter of quality. Both the 5-year-old and the 10-year-old are doing the same kind of thinking, but the 10-year-old is doing it at greater capacity. This is the information processing perspective, which views a child's mind as something like a computer. It is wired like an adult's but, during childhood, is handicapped by limited memory capacity.

Insight

Even very young children who have been called to testify at trials can remember relevant details. The problem is that they are highly suggestible. A child's memory is most reliable when he or she was a participant in the event (such as a child abuse victim) and hasn't been exposed to people making suggestions about what might have happened.

The information processing model holds that the mind's basic machinery consists of attention devices for bringing information in, working memory for actively thinking about information, and long-term memory for holding that information so it can be used again in the future. In this view, cognitive development is a gradual increase in the capacity of working memory.

From this perspective, the five-year-old's inability to understand that the same amount of liquid can look different depending upon the shape of the glass is not due to poor quality. It's because their minds can't yet hold the information long enough for them to mentally reproduce the experiment and solve the riddle. As a result, their attention gets stuck on first impressions, the different sizes of the glasses.

Speak Before You Think—or Vice Versa

You still might not want to sit next to one on an airplane, but you've got to have a healthy respect for children by now. After all, what adult do you know who can learn any one of 3,000 languages, turn any household device into a lethal weapon, and train grownups to be at his or her beck and call? Kind of makes you wonder what happens when we grow up, doesn't it?

Children are linguists. They're psychologists. They're scientists. And according to a psychologist by the name of Lev Vygotsky, they're apprentices as well. In fact, Vygotsky thought children learn much more through their relationships than through their solo adventures in the world. According to this view, we speak first and think second.

Psychobabble

Ever notice how often children talk to themselves? Developmental psychologists call this noncommunicative speech, and its goal is to direct a child's thoughts rather than communicate intent to another person. Vygotsky thought noncommunicative speech was a transition in the development of verbal thought. It declines around age seven because by then we begin to have inner dialogues, the beginning of self-talk.

Piaget considered language to be a side effect of children's development of thought. Vygotsky argued that language is the foundation for the development of higher thought. He believed that words not only provide the building blocks for advanced thinking, they actually direct our thinking in ways that reflect the activities and values of our culture. Thus, children who grow up in cultures where counting is important develop an efficient set of number words. Some Eskimo cultures have hundreds of words for *snow* because differentiating between different types of snow is critical to their survival.

Human beings might be programmed to acquire language, but the specific language we learn is a product of our culture. According to Vygotsky, children first learn words to communicate with others, but then they begin to use those same words as symbols for thinking. In fact, he thought that much of our cognitive development is a matter of internalizing the symbols, ideas, and modes of reasoning that have evolved over the course of history and make up the culture into which we are born. A Vygotskyan would say that all human beings share the same brain, but our individual minds are a reflection of our culture!

The Moral of the Story

"Those are bad thoughts." "I think it's the right thing to do." "She made the wrong decision." From an early age, we do a lot more than think our thoughts. We evaluate them. In fact, by the time we're adults, rarely a thought goes by without us attaching some moral weight to it. But how do we learn to make these value judgments?

Shrink Rap

Morality is a system of beliefs, values, and underlying judgments about the rightness of human acts.

Lawrence Kohlberg was intrigued with how people develop their sense of morality: concepts of what is right and what is wrong. His curiosity eventually led him to develop the best known psychological explanation for moral development. Similar to Piaget's thoughts on cognitive growth, Kohlberg believed people acquired their morals in stages and that individuals in all cultures went through them in the same order. Kohlberg thought our moral development went from a self-centered focus to a higher level that focused on the good of society. Here's how he thought human moral development played out for most of us:

The Morality Play

The Stage	The Plot	The Motive
Stage 1	seek pleasure, avoid pain	avoid pain or getting caught
Stage 2	weigh the costs and benefits	achieve the most rewards
Stage 3	be a good kid	be popular and avoid disapproval
Stage 4	be a law-abiding citizen	stay out of jail, avoid penalties
Stage 5	make win-win deals	do what's good for society

continues

The Morality Play   (continued)

The Stage	The Plot	The Motive
Stage 6	live by your ethics	be just, don't disappoint yourself
Stage 7	be in tune with the cosmos	think about what's best for the universe

As you look at Kohlberg's stages, it may have occurred to you that, when it comes to developing morals, a lot of people you know seem to be developmentally delayed. Well, it's true. In reality, many adults never reach stage five and few go beyond it. I, personally, still wonder what the heck stage 7 really means!

Empathetically Yours

In addition, there is a big difference between moral beliefs and moral acts. If you want to predict whether someone will behave morally, skip right over these stages and measure his ability to empathize with others. *Empathy,* the ability to feel another person's feelings, is what motivates a child to behave morally. A child who gives up her favorite blanket to her crying baby sister may not be high up on Kolhberg's moral ladder, but she's well on her way to making good moral decisions.

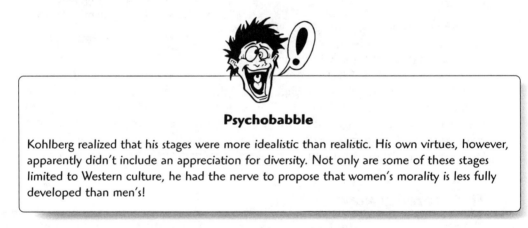

Psychobabble

Kohlberg realized that his stages were more idealistic than realistic. His own virtues, however, apparently didn't include an appreciation for diversity. Not only are some of these stages limited to Western culture, he had the nerve to propose that women's morality is less fully developed than men's!

Midlife Isn't the First Crisis

If your life is one crisis after the next, welcome to the club. Psychologist Erik Erikson's life was like that, too. As a middle-aged immigrant to America, he faced a lot of conflicts as he adjusted to his new life. He must have noticed that a lot of other people had crises in their lives, because he developed the theory that we all have conflicts and challenges at different stages in our lives. In his view, our emotional and social development depended upon how we deal with these crises.

Erickson coined the term *psychosocial crises* to describe successive turning points or choices that influence personality growth across the life span. Each crisis requires a new level of social interaction; if we turn in the right direction, we build up a sense of trust, security, and confidence in ourselves. If we don't, life keeps getting harder and harder; we may have ongoing feelings of insecurity, low self-worth, and a lack of self-confidence. Personal crises aside, here are the eight developmental crises we all have to go through:

Eight Human Crises and How They Turn Out

Age	Crisis	Good Ending	Bad Ending
0–1½	trust vs. mistrust	I can rely on others	insecurity, anxiety
1½–3	autonomy versus self-doubt, lack of control, feeling inadequate	I am my own person	helpless to change things
3–6 years	initiative versus guilt	I can make things happen	lack of self-worth
6 years–puberty	competence versus inferiority	I can lead	lack of self-confidence
adolescence	identity versus role confusion	I know who I am	unclear sense of self
early adulthood	intimacy versus isolation	I can be close to others	feeling alone, denial of need for closeness
middle adulthood	generativity versus stagnation	I can see beyond myself	self-indulgent concerns
late adulthood	ego-integrity versus despair	I have contributed	disappointment

A Self-Help Psych-Up

Want to boost your self-confidence? Try the same four strategies preschool teachers use to boost their students' sense of initiatives:

1. Encourage yourself to make choices and follow through with them.
2. Make sure at least some of your goals are small enough that you are bound to reach them.
3. Expand your horizons by trying lots of new and different things.
4. Be tolerant of your accidents and mistakes, especially when you are trying something new.

The theme of this chapter has been child development. As you've seen, however, the way children grow teaches us a lot about human nature in general. First of all, we come into the world with a lot of neat equipment and our environment is prepared to help us learn how to use it. Second, there is a time and place for everything; our language, our thought, our sense of morality, and our emotional development all take places in stages that can be influenced by our environment, but not necessarily altered by it. And, finally, there are few shortcuts in life; not resolving one of Erickson's stages is likely to come back to haunt us.

The Least You Need to Know

➤ Babies come into this world programmed to explore and conquer. Their natural interest in novel experiences and low tolerance for boredom helps us understand infants' inborn ability to learn.

➤ Children have a knack for languages. With the help of a responsive environment and plenty of opportunities to practice, they have a pretty good understanding of grammar by the time they are six years old.

➤ By the time they're two, children understand that people have reasons for what they do; by the time they are four, they know people's motives aren't always honorable.

➤ Psychologist Jean Piaget discovered that children mentally grow in stages, moving from a clumsy exploration of the immediate environment to the ability to hypothesize and think ahead.

➤ Morally speaking, children's understanding of what is right and wrong evolves as they get older, but their moral actions are more likely to be guided by their ability to feel empathy for others.

➤ Life is a series of turning points, and how we handle them will either move us forward or hold us back.

Part 2

Wake Up and Smell the Coffee

Is what you see the same as what's out there to be seen? Humans have some pretty miraculous sensory mechanisms—and an even more impressive data processing center, better known as the brain. In this part, you'll learn all about how you take information in from the world around you, and how your mind makes sense of all that data. From learning to memory, from remembering to organizing, your mind is a marvelous tool—here's where you'll learn all about its inner workings.

Knock
Knock

Chapter 5

Come to Your Senses

In This Chapter

➤ Making sense out of things

➤ When the pain is "all in your head"

➤ Coming to attention

➤ Discover why you're more organized than you think

➤ Life is but a dream

Conventional wisdom tries to have it both ways: "Seeing is believing," and "Life is but an illusion" are equally considered commonsense descriptions of how the world works. And in a very real sense, conventional wisdom is right. Our senses *do* provide us with reasonably reliable information—but the representations they give us of the world aren't as literally accurate as we tend to believe.

Without much conscious effort, we are constantly taking in information about the world and sending it on to our brains to make sense of it. In this chapter, we'll explore sensation and perception: how our senses process information, and how our first perceptions set the stage for how we think, feel, and interact with our world. In short, perception is the foreplay to the rest of psychology.

Insight

Penn and Teller, of course, are master illusionists, skilled in tricking our perceptions into seeing what they want us to see. But, while we might occasionally lose our senses to the professional manipulations of a great stage magician, most of the time our senses are right on target.

Smoke and Mirrors

My husband has been fascinated with magic since he was a child, so last December I took him to see the famous illusionists Penn and Teller. I was particularly amazed by their grand finale, a duel during which they appeared to fire guns at each other and catch the bullets in their teeth.

With my own eyes, I saw members of the audience inspecting the guns and loading them with real bullets. I heard gunfire. I smelled smoke. I saw glass behind Penn and Teller shatter as the guns were fired and I watched Penn and Teller's heads jerk back. And, I saw Penn and Teller reach inside their mouths and pull out fired bullets. Even while my intellect was assuring me that no human being could really catch a bullet between his teeth, my senses were arguing that Penn and Teller had done just that.

Creating a Sensation

We use our senses to guide us through life. Sometimes, they signal danger: A friend of mine recently commented that a blind date "made the hairs on the back of her neck stand up." She "sensed" that he wasn't trustworthy, and if she's smart, she'll trust herself and steer clear of him.

Our senses also give us pleasure—the feel of our boyfriend's lips, the sight of Van Gogh's paintings, or the taste of a double helping of tiramisu.

But for all the good they do us, our senses never get the credit. Human nature seems to hold fast to the belief that the joys of life are "out there"; we rarely recognize that, without our senses, we wouldn't have much joy at all. Instead of applauding the chef for a good meal, perhaps we should be thanking our taste buds!

In reality, it is your physiological response to these things that makes you feel good, not the things themselves. When you have a bad cold and can't smell for a few days, the sweetest perfume loses its allure. Your perception of things is even more complicated; you'll smell the same perfume, but perceive it differently depending on the circumstances: The same scent that had you drooling with lust can become nauseating after you've fallen out of love.

The discovery that our perception of the world differs from its physical reality led scientists to ponder the relationship between our mental world and the physical world in which we live. And this journey led them to another discovery.

On the Threshold of Discovery

The earliest psychologists were fascinated by the relationship between physical stimuli and the behavior or mental experiences they evoked. In fact, *psychophysics,* the study of psychological reactions to physical stimuli, is the oldest field of psychology.

The goal of psychophysicists was to map physical reality onto psychological reality. At what point, they wondered, does physical reality

Shrink Rap

Psychophysics is the study of psychological reactions to physical stimuli.

become human reality? To answer this question, pioneers began tracking the point at which physical differences in sound or light became mental distinctions. How bright does a light have to be in order for us to see it glowing? What's the softest sound we can still hear? It depends, they discovered, on the individual. People have different sensitivities to environmental stimuli.

Star Light, Star Bright

Let's say you and a friend are stargazing and you point out a faint star. Your friend says he can't see it. Thinking it's because he's not looking in the right place, you spend several frustrating minutes giving him the exact location of the star and pointing out brighter stars nearby. If he still can't see it, it may be because his *absolute threshold* for light is different from yours. An absolute threshold is the smallest, weakest amount of a stimulus that a person can detect. If you can see the star and he cannot, the star's light is above your absolute threshold and below your friend's.

Psychophysicists are also interested in our *difference threshold,* the smallest physical difference between two stimuli that can be recognized. Let's say you do your best studying with Nirvana blasting in the background. Your roommate, on the other hand, prefers a study atmosphere similar to a funeral parlor. Your earphones are broken and it's the night before a major exam. Your roommate asks you to turn down the radio; you want to be considerate but you also don't really want to turn the radio down. The least amount you can lower the volume to prove your good intentions while still keeping the volume audible would be the *just noticeable difference.*

Crossing the Threshold

Absolute and difference thresholds are constantly in use to guide safety regulations. For example, when warning lights are built into cars, safety engineers must make sure that they're bright enough to take your attention away from other dashboard lights. Without psychology, there'd be a lot more car accidents!

We may not be faster than the speed of sound or able to stop a speeding bullet, but our senses are pretty good at tuning in to our environment. The average person can:

see a candle flame at 30 miles on a dark, clear night;

hear the tick of a watch under quiet conditions at 20 feet;

taste 1 teaspoon of sugar in 2 gallons of water;

smell one drop of perfume diffused into a three-bedroom apartment; and

feel the wing of a bee falling on his cheek at a distance of 1 centimeter.

Get Your Signals Straight

The work of psychophysicists would be easier if perceptual differences between people were always due to physical reasons—if they were due to better hearing, sight, touch, smell, or taste. However, early psychophysicists failed to realize that differences in thresholds could be due to psychological reasons. And one of the biggest psychological reasons they overlooked was human bias. They did not recognize that our responses to environmental stimuli are biased by our past experiences as well as our expectations of the current situation.

Shrink Rap

Signal detection theory assumes that the ability to perceive environmental stimuli is influenced by both physical and psychological factors.

That's where *signal detection theory* comes in. This theory recognizes that our ability to perceive stimuli in the environment is influenced by psychological as well as physical factors. Perceiving sensory stimulation requires more than just responding to it, but making a judgment about its presence or absence as well. Just as jurors can be predisposed to vote innocent or guilty, our experience and expectations might lead us to be too ready to say we heard something or we didn't.

Here's an example of how this works. Suppose your boss is going to call at exactly 6 P.M. to tell you whether you are getting a promotion or not. You get home from the gym at 5:45 and would like to jump in the shower and rinse off the grit and grime of the day before he calls. However, you promised him you'd be available at 6 P.M. and you really want to answer that phone when it rings.

After thinking it through, you decide you have time for a quick rinse off before he calls. You jump in and start scrubbing away. However, you constantly find yourself tuning in to every little sound. You worry that you'll miss hearing the phone ring. You hear something—is it the phone or just shower noise?

Would you be more likely to jump out of the shower just in case it *was* your boss on the phone, or would you take your chances that you'll hear it over the shower? Either way, you're biased. If you would be a shower-jumper-outer in this scenario, you would be operating with a liberal bias. In your mind, the penalties (water splashed all over the floor) of a false alarm pale in comparison to the payoffs of hearing about that promotion. If, on the other hand, you would continue your shower unless you were certain it was the phone, you're a conservative.

Common Senses

Signal detection theory helps us understand all the things that influence our ability to make sense of our environment. But what are the "signals" that we detect? How do things "out there" (light waves) become things "in here" (the perception of a beautiful painting)? Through energy.

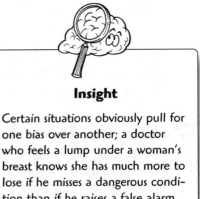

Insight

Certain situations obviously pull for one bias over another; a doctor who feels a lump under a woman's breast knows she has much more to lose if he misses a dangerous condition than if he raises a false alarm. When it comes to medical problems, give me a doctor with a liberal bias!

The study of sensation is a study of energy. Whether it's sound waves or light waves, physical energy from a stimulus in the environment stimulates our sensory neurons which, in turn, convert this energy into electrochemical signals that the nervous system carries to the brain. This process is known as *transduction*. These neural messages are the language through which our sense organs talk to our brain.

Your senses have a lot more in common than you might think. They all use transduction to communicate sensory input to the brain. They also tune out stimulation that does not change in intensity or some other quality, a process known as sensory adaptation. When you first put on your shoes, you are aware of how they feel on your feet. Wear them a short time and, unless they're pinching your toes or rubbing your heels, you forget about them.

Psychobabble

If asked to name our senses, most of us would list five—taste, touch, smell, sight, and hearing. In fact, all of us have a sixth sense—and a seventh and maybe an eighth. Our skin, for example, is sensitive to pain and temperature as well as touch. Aren't these senses, too? The common misperception that we have five senses started with Aristotle and we've been stuck with it ever since.

Sensory adaptation allows us to make the most of our senses by encouraging them to focus on novelty. From a survival standpoint, it was critical for us to be able to focus on sudden changes in our environment; abrupt changes most often signaled danger to our ancestors. If, for example, they had been too busy focusing on the constant sense of discomfort that comes from sitting on rocks, they might have missed real danger, like a large predatory animal emerging from the bushes.

What Stimulates You

Life is a stimulating experience. What stimulates us at any given moment depends upon the part of the body we're talking about. Take a look at what really stimulates you—and what really gets stimulated.

Sense	What Stimulates Us	What Gets Stimulated
Hearing	sound waves	pressure-sensitive hair cells in cochlea of inner ear
Vision	light waves	light-sensitive rods and cones in retina of eye
Touch	pressure on skin	sensitive ends of touch neurons in skin
Pain	potentially harmful stimuli	sensitive ends of pain neurons in skin and other tissue
Taste	molecules dissolved in fluid	taste cells in taste buds on the tongue
Smell	molecules dissolved in fluid	sensitive ends of olfactory neurons in the mucous membranes

The Big Five

We've already talked about some of the things our senses have in common. On a daily basis, though, we're much more aware of their differences. Seeing is different from hearing. We use our sense of sight to feast our eyes upon our loved one and our sense of touch to enjoy the pleasure of human contact. Let's look at the unique contribution each of our senses makes to our understanding of our world—starting with the "big five:"

➤ vision

➤ hearing

➤ smell

➤ taste

➤ touch

Vision

Most people say they would rather lose their hearing than their sight. Our ancestors would agree—from an evolutionary perspective, vision has been our most important sense.

Photoreceptors in our eyes gather light, convert its physical energy into neural messages, and send it on to the occipital lobe in the brain for decoding and analyzing. Transduction happens in the retina, which is composed of light-sensitive layers of cells at the back of the eyes.

Those cells in the retina are called *rods* and *cones*. Rods are receptor cells that permit vision in dim light; they are highly sensitive to the perception of light but can't distinguish colors or details. Cones, on the other hand, operate best in bright light, where they permit sharply focused color vision. With their help, we can visually discriminate among five million different colors—but we only have the language to identify 150 to 200 of them.

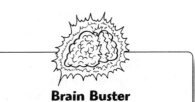

Brain Buster

All of us have a *blind spot,* a small part of the retina that is not coated with photoreceptors which creates a small gap in our visual field. We aren't aware of our blind spot because our eyes compensate for each other and our brain "fills in" the spot with information that matches the background.

Hearing

"If a tree falls in the forest and no one's there, does it make a sound?" This Zen riddle plays upon the fact that "sound" refers both to the physical stimulus we hear and to the sensation the stimulus produces. If we were using the term *sound* to refer to the physical stimulus, our answer would be yes. If we were referring to the sensation and no one was around to experience it, the right answer would be no.

Sounds are created when actions, like banging, cause objects, like drums, to vibrate. These vibrating objects push air molecules back and forth and, as a result, change the air pressure. These changes in air pressure travel in *sine waves* (see the following figure). Picture ocean waves breaking on the shoreline. How *fast* the waves crash determines the frequency we hear. High frequencies produce high sounds and low frequencies produce low sounds. How *high* the waves are at the crest dictates their amplitude. Sound waves with large amplitudes are loud and those with small amplitudes are soft.

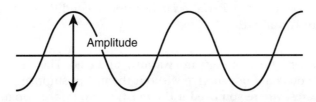

Amplitude

A simple example of a sine wave.

Hearing is made possible when the ear and the brain convert sine waves into the experience of sound. Sound waves travel into the ear, transfer from tissue to bones in the middle ear, and are transformed into fluid waves in the inner ear. The vibrations of these fluid waves stimulate tiny hair cells to generate nerve impulses to the auditory part of the brain. And, of course, our brain analyzes these sounds and responds appropriately, such as telling us to cover our ears when we hear fingernails scratching on a chalkboard!

Smell

Smell is our most primitive sense, which may be why we take it for granted. It's a real bummer, though, when we lose it; not only does the world seem bland, it tastes bland, too. Our sense of smell probably developed as a system for finding food, and anyone with a cold can tell you that our taste buds get a lot of the credit that our nose really deserves.

Odors are chemical molecules. When they hit the membranes of tiny hairs in our noses, the receptors there translate them into nerve impulses, which are relayed to the olfactory bulb, the part of the brain that decodes and interprets smells. Transduction strikes again.

Taste

A taste bud is no galloping gourmet. It can tell whether foods are sweet, sour, bitter, or salty and that's just about it. Food critics rely on their sense of smell to distinguish between subtle food flavors more than on their ability to taste them.

Your taste receptors, located on the upper side of your tongue, transduct chemical molecules dissolved in saliva to the taste center of your brain. If you've ever burned your tongue on hot soup, you may have noticed that your sense of taste was temporarily disrupted. But never fear! Those buds are amazingly resilient; they are replaced every few days. In fact, your sense of taste is the most resistant to damage of all your senses.

Touch

Food lovers aside, touch is the most pleasurable of all the senses. Not only is it the main avenue to sexual arousal, it is critical for healthy development. Children who are deprived of touch can develop *psychosocial dwarfism,* a condition whereby their physical development is stunted.

Your skin contains nerve endings that, when stimulated by physical contact with outside objects, produce sensations of pressure, warmth, and cold. These sensations are the skin senses, and you could not survive without them. Not surprisingly, your sensitivity to touch is greatest where you need it the most: on your face, tongue, and hands.

Pain in the What?

Although not included in the favored five, pain is a body sense that warns us of potential harm and helps us cope with sickness and injury. In the fight to survive, it's one of our best defenses. It is also one of our most puzzling senses, because our experience of pain is influenced by a number of psychological and social factors.

Insight

We need pain to survive, but there's a rare condition that prevents some people from feeling physical pain. Children with this disorder won't realize they should remove a hand from a hot stove. They often die young—from wound infections or tissue damage. Pain won't kill us, but the absence of pain will.

Nobody likes to be told a pain is "all in your head," but in truth, it often is. The way we experience our pain, the way we communicate about it to others, and even the way we respond to pain-relieving treatment may reveal more about our psychological state than the actual intensity of the pain stimulus. Stomachaches hurt; however, someone who's unhappy at work may find the discomfort unbearable, while someone energized at work may feel it's merely annoying.

Think of pain as your emotional experience of a physically distressing sensation. Things that intensify your emotions, like upsetting thoughts or catastrophic events, can magnify your experience of pain. Let's say you got a stomachache a few days ago. At first, you weren't concerned but you've had it for a few days now, so you're a little worried. Today also happens to be the day that your mom calls to tell you that your favorite uncle was just diagnosed with stomach cancer.

It would be pretty normal to find your thoughts suddenly shifting from, "Hmm, I've never had a stomachache this long before, I wonder if I should get it checked out," to, "Oh, my God, I wonder if I've got stomach cancer, too." Not only will your anxiety go up, chances are your belly will ache more, too.

Cultural attitudes and gender roles play a role in our relationship with pain. Early studies reported a consistent gender difference in pain perception—in the laboratory, women had a 20 percent lower pain tolerance than men. While these findings were initially attributed to biologically different pain thresholds, recent research suggests that the gender difference in pain tolerance may be in the expression of pain, not the perception of it.

In the lab, men tended to endure temporary discomfort rather than risk losing face by showing vulnerability to the researcher. Women, on the other hand, may be more accurate reporters because they feel less social pressure to endure unnecessary pain and are likely to speak up when something hurts. When it comes to your expression of pain, it's not all a function of biology; it's also your willingness to say "Ow!"

Psychobabble

We all have a built-in mechanism that temporarily prevents us from feeling pain when, for survival purposes, it is best to ignore our injuries. This phenomenon, *stress-induced analgesia*, helped U.S. Olympic Gymnastic member Kerri Strug momentarily overcome the pain of a just-sustained injury and execute a stellar performance on the vault.

Starting from the Top Down and the Bottom Up

If you think your senses are complicated, you ain't seen nothing yet. After your senses take in all that stimulation, your brain still has to make sense out of it. What is that round thing? Have we ever seen it—or anything like it—before? Is it a ball, an orange, or the moon? And, once we figure out what it is, we've got to figure out what to do with it.

If you've never been particularly proud of your organizing skills, your self-esteem is about to get a boost. Your brain has an amazing ability to automatically sort objects by size, distance, proportion, color, and many other categories. It solves mysteries hundreds of times a day by taking clues (sensory information from the environment) and using them to solve the puzzle by identifying the object. The "detective skills" you use are of two types—top-down processing and bottom-up processing.

Bottoms Up

Bottom-up processing is *data driven*—it starts with independent information from the outside and works its way inward to an interpretation of that information. When we process this way, we are starting with the environment; our eyes, for example, pick up colors or other visual cues as they look around. Using this data, our brain instantly tries to put together a visual image.

Interestingly, you are more likely to notice the "big picture" before you see details because your brain is so attuned to figuring out the whole landscape. For instance, you'll know that the shape coming toward you is a human being before you'll detect the color of his hair or eyes, or even his gender.

Of course, your brain doesn't just rely on information from your immediate environment to make sense of the world. It also makes use of your past experiences, knowledge, cultural background, motivations, expectations, and memories. This part of perceptual processing is known as *top-down processing* because your brain is comparing what you're currently seeing, hearing, or touching with your ideas, expectations, and memories of similar objects.

Watch Out! Reality Under Construction

The interaction of top-down and bottom-up processing means that your perception of reality is never truly objective. You are constantly constructing reality to fit in with your assumptions about how you think reality is, or ought to be. Because of our unique backgrounds, it really is true that no two people ever "see" the same thing.

Not only are we "topping down" and "bottoming up" at the same time, ideally, these processes are constantly balancing out. Consider what would happen if you relied exclusively on the current sensory stimuli of bottom-up processing to make sense of our world. You'd register experiences, but you wouldn't be able to learn from them.

Insight

Shake up someone's top-down processing about you and see what happens. Violate a friend's assumption about what you would "normally" do—wear different clothes, try a new hobby, or just express some different views about a hot topic. Not only will you surprise your friend, you might gain a new perspective on the "real you."

Similarly, if you're relying too much on top-down processing, you might be caught up in a fantasy world of hopes and expectations and overlook the reality that was staring you in the face. If you've ever stayed in a bad relationship because you kept pretending it was better than it was, maybe your perceptual processing was top heavy!

Life Is an Illusion

Do you ever wear dark clothes or vertical stripes to make yourself look thinner? If so, you're making use of illusion through your choice of clothing. By taking advantage of perceptual distortions, like dark colors appearing smaller than bright ones, we can artfully steer others into seeing us in a certain light.

Deceptive Appearances

We experience a perceptual illusion when our senses deceive us into perceiving an event or an object in a manner that is demonstrably incorrect. You might *look* thinner in vertical stripes than horizontal ones, but the tape measure or scale will clearly show that you aren't. If illusionists Penn and Teller would let my husband and me in on the tricks in their grand finale, we would see that they aren't really catching bullets with their teeth.

Illusions take advantage of our natural tendency to perceive objects in certain ways; in effect, they trick our senses. For example, from an early age, we learn cues that tell us about the relationship between size and distance. We learn that most objects that we see near the earth's horizon are farther away than objects we see near the zenith (straight up)—so birds or clouds seen near the horizon are usually farther away than those that are directly overhead.

Up, Down, Near, and Far

There are, however, exceptions to this rule. You may have noticed that the moon looks much larger when it is near the earth's horizon than when it's above us. When asked whether the horizon moon is farther or closer than usual, most people say closer. In this case, our perceptual systems apparently ignore the relative appearance of size, considering the fact that the moon does not change sizes, and imposes the interpretation that, because it appears larger at the horizon, it must be nearer to us. In reality, the moon is the same distance away from us at either position.

Typically, illusions are more common when the sensory stimulus is ambiguous. When information is missing, elements are combined in unusual ways, or familiar patterns are not apparent, our senses are much more vulnerable to deception.

Meet Ponzo the Western Illusion

In the following figure, which line is longer, the one on top or the one on bottom? People from the United States often say that the top line is longer, but not everybody sees it that way. The Ponzo illusion is an example of our cultural background influencing our perception of ambiguous information and, alas, leading us astray.

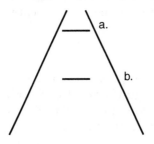

If you grew up in the United States, you are used to seeing long, flat highways or train tracks winding off in the distance. You've probably noticed that, if you look at them, the lines seem to come closer together off in the distance. People who grow up with these experiences learn to interpret converging lines as a cue for distance.

In the drawing above, the top line appears to be longer because its higher position implies it is further along the converging tracks. On the other hand, people who have spent their entire lives on Guam have had fewer opportunities to learn the perceptual cue that converging lines imply distance. They are much less likely to fall for this illusion and will report that the lines are the same length.

Pay Attention When I'm Talking to You

Great illusionists have the gift of commanding our *attention*. Through their smoke and mirrors, they focus our attention on one thing while they're doing something else in the background. Great illusionists know that attention is the first step in sensation and perception.

As we go about our daily activities, hundreds of things compete for our attention. Most of the time, we have a lot of conscious control over what we attend to. In fact, when our elementary school teacher told us to quit goofing off and "pay attention," she was relying on us to exert voluntary control over ourselves and tune in to our schoolwork.

If we are to fully understand anything, we have to focus on one source of information at a time. When we "pay attention," we are selectively attending to one source of information and blocking out others. Attention basically does three jobs:

➤ It helps us screen out irrelevant stimuli and focus on relevant information.

➤ It helps us consider the most appropriate response.

➤ It chooses the information that will enter in, and stay in, our awareness.

Shrink Rap

Attention is a state of focused awareness coupled with a readiness to respond.

Here's an example of how attention works. Have you ever been at a party and suddenly heard your name? You might have been standing in the same place for half an hour, aware that conversation was going on around you but clueless as to what was actually being said. The minute the person says your name, though, you find your head whipping around and tuning in to his or her words. It's almost as if the person said your name in a louder voice, although you know this isn't true.

It seems louder to you because your name rings an internal bell. Imagine your brain is a radio scanner and your attention is the station you're listening to. Personally interesting or perceptually meaningful information can grab your attention and cause you to suddenly tune in to a channel, just like a scanner picks up a strong signal.

But, you're probably wondering, how can you tell another station is broadcasting if it's not the one you're listening to? Because even ignored information gets processed at some level. Subjects who had separate messages playing in each ear were told to ignore one message and tune in to another. While they failed to recognize words in the unattended message even after it had been played 35 times, these same subjects instantly recognized their own name when it turned up in that message about one-third of the time.

Brain Buster

Attention deficit hyperactive disorder (ADHD) is characterized by inattention and a combination of hyperactive and impulsive behaviors. This disorder usually surfaces between three and five years of age, occurs worldwide, and affects boys nine times more often than girls.

The sounds that babies make have the same attention-grabbing impact on parents that hearing our name does on partygoers. Any new parent can tell you that the minute his or her baby cries, it is useless to try to pay attention to anything else. You could be immersed in your last chance to cram for the GREs or catch the climax in the final episode of *Seinfeld,* but the faintest cry will grab your attention as strongly as if the baby had walked up and slapped you upside the head. Whatever skills babies lack, commanding attention isn't one of them.

Working Smarter, Not Harder

Your closet might not be organized, but your brain is. But our brains are not only organized, they're efficient— they look for organizational strategies that require the least amount of effort. This brain trait is often referred to as the *law of Pragnanz.* Simply put, this law states that the simplest organization requiring the least amount of effort will always emerge.

For example, your brain automatically assumes objects having something in common go together. If, for example, you see three ducks sitting beside each other, your brain will assume that, since they're close to each other, they must go together. Similarly, objects that look alike are lumped together. And objects that are moving in the same direction and at the same rate are assumed to share a common fate.

So, at a minimum, your brain saves time and conserves energy by processing things in groups. Another natural organizational strategy is your brain's tendency to create maps. Using changes in color and texture as cues, your brain divides the world into meaningful regions. The fact that my shirt is blue and my pants are yellow helps you know that I'm not wearing a one-piece jumpsuit. Hair has a different texture than skin does and our brain instantly recognizes it as a different feature.

Two other perceptual strategies for organizing information have interesting parallels in human behavior. First, we have a tendency to fill in the gaps—our need for perceptual closure is so strong that our brain will often fill in the missing edges, making us see incomplete figures as complete. The fact that we aren't aware of our visual blind spot is one example of our brain's automatic ability to fill in the gaps. As a psychological parallel, our psyches tend to fill in the gaps, too. How many hours have you spent trying to fill in the gaps left by someone's inexplicable or hurtful behavior?

Psychobabble

In the late 1950s, advertisers attempted to sway movie viewers by flashing rapid visual images on the screen with the hope that these subliminal messages, although beyond our conscious awareness, would brainwash us into buying their products. The public outcry over this "mind control" was huge. Research has since found that, for the most part, our fears were unfounded. Subliminal visual messages can have a subtle influence, but they can't command us to do anything.

The second organizational strategy, our tendency to see a figure against a background, has similarly profound effects. Our brains naturally look for ways to categorize information into foreground (the primary object of interest) and background (the backdrop against which the figure stands out). Colors and textures create regions, and our brains naturally place some in front of others. And, of course, we do this psychologically as well; when you go to a party, a striking member of the opposite sex may quickly become the foreground and everyone else become background information.

Try This at Home!

What letters would you replace the asterisk with in the following two word series?

Sheep, goat, horse, cow, b*ll

Nickel, dime, quarter, dollar b*ll

The four words before the one with the fill-in-the-blank letter creates a certain perceptual *set;* they encourage you to see stimuli in a certain way. In this case, you were perceptually set to read "bull" for the first group of words and "bill" for the second.

Don't Take It Out of Context

The last stage of perception is identification and recognition—how your brain adds meaning to the facts it perceives. It takes all that sensory data and finds the appropriate context in which it belongs. We rely on context in our environment to help us make sense of things; so much so that if we encounter people or things that are out of their usual context, it can throw us for a perceptual loop.

Rodeo Time in Gay Paree

Fifteen years ago I was living in Dallas, where I saw hundreds of "Mesquite Texas Rodeo" bumper stickers on cars zooming down the 635 freeway. While on vacation in Paris that year, as I was strolling down the street one day, I suddenly saw a "Mesquite Texas Rodeo" bumper sticker on the back of a car. I must have looked at the back of that Parisian car for a good 10 seconds before I truly recognized what I was looking at.

Why? Because the bumper sticker was out of context. When we encounter things out of their normal context, it can be confusing. Identification and recognition relies on our memory, expectations, motivation, personality, and social experience to help us understand what is being perceived. If you always see a business associate in business meetings, you expect to see him in that context. When you see him at the beach, you may not recognize him right away—he's out of his usual context so it takes you longer to adjust.

Context? Which Context?

But your idea of a proper context is likely to be different from mine. Each of us works from what are known as *perceptual sets,* conditions that determine your readiness to detect a particular stimulus in a given context—and the specific conditions that make up one person's perceptual sets can be very different from the conditions that make up somebody else's.

One of the most fascinating things about psychology is how complicated human beings are. A famous saying in psychology is "don't confuse the map with the territory," meaning that our view of the world—our map—is just one of many possible interpretations of our environment. In the next chapter, we'll take a look at how you become aware of your map—through consciousness.

Psychobabble

Mothers and fathers are perceptually set to hear the cries of their child, which is why they seem to hear them long before you do. Some perceptual sets are useful, but some can be downright harmful; for example, someone who expects people of a certain race to behave in a certain way is likely to "see" things that confirm his or her beliefs and ignore behaviors that do not fit into these expectations.

The Least You Need to Know

➤ Sensation makes us aware of conditions inside or outside our body. Perception makes sense of them.

➤ Aristotle spread the rumor that we have just five senses—taste, touch, smell, sight, and hearing—but we have a lot more, including the ability to experience pain and temperature.

➤ Our senses convert physical energy from our environment into neurochemical signals, which they send up to the brain to be analyzed and interpreted.

➤ Our experience of pain is as much a product of our mind as it is of our body.

➤ While our ability to pay attention is often under voluntary control, we're programmed to tune into information that is personally meaningful or relevant.

➤ Our ability to make sense of our world requires the matching of information from our current environment with our prior experiences, memories, and expectations.

Chapter 6

It's Consciousness-Raising Time!

In This Chapter

➤ Getting the scoop on sleep

➤ We're all dreamers at heart

➤ Four paths to an altered consciousness

➤ The pharmaceutical problem

Imagine how you would feel if, in the middle of a breast exam, your doctor blurted out, "Oh, my God, I feel a lump in your breast! It could be cancerous." The fear this unprofessional remark would cause could be traumatic even if he turned out to be wrong. For good reason, doctors are trained to keep unfounded suspicions to themselves.

Doctors who'd never do this in an exam room have unintentionally terrorized patients with similar remarks in the operating room. Because the patient is under anesthesia, doctors assume the patient is unaware of what's being said. Not necessarily. Surgery patients under anesthesia may still hear what is going on around them. Even casual remarks in the operating room can be hazardous to our health!

How can we remember things that happened when we're unconscious? In this chapter, you'll learn that the line between consciousness and unconsciousness is blurrier than you might think. We'll take a look at how our brain produces consciousness, how our behavior interacts with our various states of mind, and why there appears to be a human need to alter our consciousness.

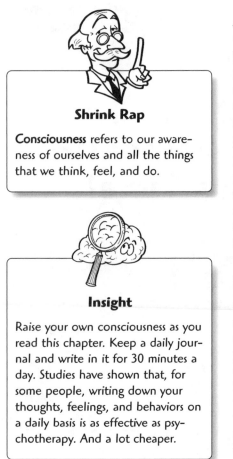

Are You Self-Conscious?

The word *consciousness* gets a bad rap these days, probably because it was overused in the sixties. Unless you're in California, you're likely to view anyone who talks of a "higher consciousness" with some degree of suspicion. However, to the extent that a "higher consciousness" is greater self-awareness, it is the ultimate goal of most psychologists.

As you learned in Chapter 5, "Come to Your Senses," we sense much more than we pay attention to. If you think of your consciousness as the front page of your mental newspaper, attention is the lead story that you can't resist reading. And, your senses tell you that the story is in the newspaper to begin with.

On the Wings of Fantasy

On a basic level, you're conscious that you are constantly perceiving and reacting to information in your environment. For example, while you're gazing out your office window at the beautiful grass below, you can imagine yourself lying on the grass and taking a nap instead of plugging away at your desk. You can wonder why the grass is so green outside and wonder what kind of fertilizer the groundskeeper uses. And, on a higher level, you are aware that you're sitting at your office desk daydreaming about being outside and you can feel guilty that you aren't getting your work done.

Consciousness is pretty complicated and, as a result, you aren't always aware of what's going on in your head. By the time you're grown up, you're so used to certain thoughts that entire conversations can be going on in your head without your even noticing them. But even though you don't notice them, they're still having an impact.

You Are What You Think

Ever felt sad or angry but didn't know why? If you traced the origin of these feelings, chances are you'd discover they were caused by self-defeating or negative thoughts. "I must be a loser going to another get-together by myself" is a surefire bummer of a thought, even if you're headed to the shindig of the year. If you let those thoughts stir around in the background of your consciousness long enough, you might decide to skip the party and go home and drown yourself in chocolate ice cream.

Being aware of your consciousness, on the other hand, gives you the power to understand your thoughts and feelings, evaluate their usefulness, and decide how much you'll let them influence your behavior. And the first step in raising your consciousness is understanding how your consciousness works.

Unconscious, Higher Conscious, and Everything in Between

For Freud, consciousness is just the tip of the iceberg. The stuff that crosses your mind lies on the surface, but underneath lurks a whole lot of dangerous activity that is completely outside of your awareness. In reality, consciousness is more like an elevator building. It has different levels, and information travels back and forth between them. Let's take a brief look at the four other levels of consciousness:

➤ nonconscious

➤ preconscious

➤ subconscious

➤ unconscious

Automatic Pilot

Your nonconscious handles information that is never represented in consciousness or memory but is critical to bodily and mental activity, such as information needed in controlling your heartbeat or regulating your blood pressure.

The File Cabinet

Your preconscious stores all the information that you don't need right now but that you can readily access if something calls your attention to it. If I ask you what you had for dinner last night, your preconscious opens that file and transfers it to your conscious. You aren't aware of that information until it is asked for.

The Secret Service

Subconscious awareness involves information that is not currently in your conscious but can be retrieved by special recall or attention-getting devices. Information stored in your preconscious, such as what you had for dinner last night, was once conscious; however, you may be completely unaware of information stored in

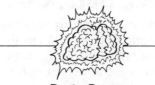

Brain Buster

If you find yourself thinking about something you don't want to think about, trying to push the thoughts away may make you obsess on it even more. The best way to win is to give up. Allow your mind to roam freely and the unwanted thoughts will become less intrusive and finally go away.

your subconscious. For example, under hypnosis, former surgery patients have re-called detailed operating room conversations that they were completely unaware of overhearing.

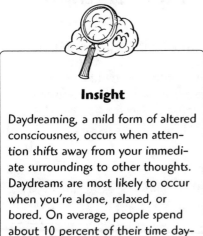

Insight

Daydreaming, a mild form of altered consciousness, occurs when attention shifts away from your immediate surroundings to other thoughts. Daydreams are most likely to occur when you're alone, relaxed, or bored. On average, people spend about 10 percent of their time day-dreaming.

The Clearinghouse

According to Freud, your unconscious handles memories, ideas, and emotions that are just too darned scary to face. Outside his school of thought, however, there has been little support for the existence of an unconscious. If it does exist, it is much more likely to store phone numbers and the lyrics of old songs than fearsome, repressed memories of childhood trauma. New research that studies unconscious thought processes suggests that your unconscious may act as a clearinghouse for sorting through and storing all the data you encounter but don't attend to.

The various levels of consciousness work together to run a pretty organized outfit. While your conscious mind is busy focusing on day-to-day operations, other parts are in the background making sure the office is running smoothly. Of course, even the hardest workers need a break to recharge their batteries. Let's take a look at a "vacation" your consciousness gets every day: sleep.

Alpha, Beta, Delta—The Sleep Fraternity

When it comes to consciousness, sleep is a paradox. On the one hand, we talk about "walking around in our sleep" when we're so tired we can barely hold our head up. We talk about being "knocked out" when our head hits the pillow after a hard day. At the same time, we can feel more "conscious" and alert in the middle of a dream than we do after a big meal in the middle of the day.

Until the *electroencephalograph* (*EEG*) came along, scientists pretty much thought sleep was a mindless activity. The EEG allowed us to record the electrical activity of the brain at any stage of alertness and quickly put this assumption to rest. The EEG soon made it clear that when you fall asleep, your brain goes through four predictable stages, indicating four distinct cycles of sleep.

Stage one is the brief transition stage that occurs when you're first falling asleep. On an EEG, your brain waves slow down and become large and regular *alpha waves*. Stages two through four are successively deeper stages of true sleep. They show up on the EEG as an increasingly large number of slow, irregular, high-amplitude waves called *delta waves*.

It takes about 90 minutes to move through the first four stages of sleep. After that, you move through the entire sleep cycle four to five more times during the night. After the first full cycle, however, you start going backward through stages three and two. You don't repeat stage one, however; in its place you enter the most exciting period of the night: REM sleep.

REM is the acronym for *rapid eye movement,* the condition that characterizes this stage of sleep. A lot goes on during REM sleep; in fact, if you couldn't see the person laid out in front you, the EEG would convince you he or she is wide awake. The EEG would show *beta waves,* the same irregular waves your brain makes when you're solving problems in the middle of the day. During your first sleep cycle, you spend about 10 minutes in REM sleep; in your last, you may spend up to an hour.

Shrink Rap

REM sleep is characterized by rapid eye movement, brain activity close to that of wakefulness, and a complete absence of muscle tone. Most dreaming takes place during REM sleep.

No one knows exactly why, but we need our REM sleep. If we are deprived of REM sleep one night, our brain waves play catch-up the next. It may be that REM sleep plays a role in stabilizing our emotions and cataloging and storing memories. One product of REM has captured the imaginations of amateur and professional psychologists all over the world—dreams.

I Must Be Dreaming

What do your dreams mean? The answer to that question depends on whom you're talking to. According to Native American tradition, dreams are messengers from the spirit world. Dreamcatchers, wooden hoops filled with a web made from nettle-stalk cord, were hung over the baby's cradle to bestow pleasant dreams and harmony. The good spirit dreams found their way through the tiny center hole and floated down the sacred feathers to the baby. The bad spirit dreams got caught in the web and disappeared in the morning light.

Freudian psychologists think dreams serve two purposes. One, they guard sleep by disguising disruptive thoughts with symbols. Two, they provide harmless ways for people to fulfill their darkest desires without suffering the social consequences.

Insight

Evolutionary psychologists think sleep evolved to restore your body from the wear and tear of the day and to help keep you out of trouble. Animals that eat low-calorie foods and thus need to spend a lot of time eating don't snooze much; animals that eat high-calorie foods sleep longer. Sleep is nature's way to keep idle animals from going astray!

Hard-core scientists suggest that sleep's major job is to provide regular group exercise for the brain's neurons. According to this somewhat skeptical view, dreams are simply an accidental by-product of random electrical discharges, and the only reason they have any meaning is because the brain tries to add meaning after these discharges happen.

The fact is, we don't know who has the right answer. But it's kind of depressing to think that dreams are random and meaningless, especially since some of our dreams seem to have fairly obvious relevance to what's going on in our lives. Almost everyone has had a dream that helped solve a problem or tough situation.

Actually, there is some scientific evidence that your psyche and your dreams are connected. Mental problems tend to extend REM sleep; it's as if our psyches need more time to work things out. And people who are going through similar crises often have dreams with similar themes. In one study, people who were depressed over a divorce described their dreams as being "stuck in the past."

The Ticking of Your Biological Clock

All of us have biological clocks that affect our arousal and energy levels throughout the day. If your clock is set to be a night person, and you have to get up at 6 A.M. every morning, you're in a difficult situation.

Your biological clock—or, more properly, your *circadian rhythm*—is pretty sophisticated; it is a coordinated set of physiological activities that coordinate your hormones, metabolism, body temperature, heart rate, and, of course, level of arousal. While biological clocks vary from person to person, they are amazingly consistent within the individual.

Shrink Rap

Circadian rhythm means "about a day"—it's the clock that regulates your sleep-wake cycle. When it's disrupted by flying across several time zones, you get **jet lag,** which can involve fatigue, sleepiness, and subsequent unusual sleep and wake schedules.

If you could rise at any time you choose and retire any time you like at night, how would your day differ from your present routine? Would you be up at dawn or snoozing till noon? Biological clocks are pretty resistant to change, so it can help to find a schedule that matches your natural biorhythms as closely as possible. And you can certainly cut down on relationship quarrels if your partner's clock ticks like yours; it can be pretty frustrating if the time you most feel like snuggling is the time your partner feels like snoozing.

Ticking clocks aside, human snoozers have more in common than you might think. Whether we're night owls or early birds, we're all tuned in to circadian rhythms, bodily patterns that repeat approximately every 24 hours. We all spend about one-third of our lives sleeping. And, as you're about to see, few things throw your consciousness for a loop like a lack of sleep!

Doc, I Just Can't Sleep

There's an epidemic in the United States and it's caused by lack of sleep. As many as 100 million Americans don't get enough sleep every night, and it costs the United States billions of dollars in lost productivity each year. More than half of all night shift workers nod off at least once a week on the job. It may be no accident that disasters such as the Exxon oil spill and the Chernobyl nuclear power plant accident happened during the late evening hours, when key personnel are likely to be less alert due to insufficient sleep. The average person needs six to eight hours of sleep a night; if we don't get it, the only thing that will wake us up is enough sleep.

Psychobabble

The world record holder for sleepless nights is Randy Gardner, a college student who stayed awake for 264 hours as part of a publicity stunt for a radio program. At the end of 11 days, he was alert enough to give an amazingly coherent radio interview. Some people experience extreme irritability and perceptual distortions after three or four sleepless nights, so don't try this at home!

If there's one thing worse than not getting enough sleep, it's not getting any sleep. *Insomnia* is a condition in which you have a normal desire for sleep, put in your seven or eight hours in bed, but, for some reason, can't go to sleep. Even if you lay perfectly still for seven or eight hours, you're likely to feel tired all day as a result of not sleeping.

Insomnia can be caused by a variety of psychological, environmental, and biological factors, including:

➤ anxiety or depression

➤ noisy next-door neighbors

➤ exercise too close to bedtime

➤ the use of stimulants (such as caffeine) prior to bedtime

➤ changes in work shifts

➤ physical illness or discomfort

Insomnia can take different forms. You can have trouble falling asleep, wake up off and on during the night, or crash immediately and wake up at 3 A.M. and be unable

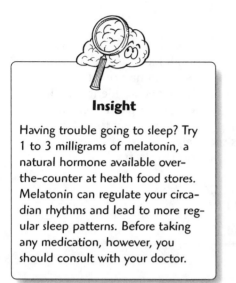

Insight

Having trouble going to sleep? Try 1 to 3 milligrams of melatonin, a natural hormone available over-the-counter at health food stores. Melatonin can regulate your circadian rhythms and lead to more regular sleep patterns. Before taking any medication, however, you should consult with your doctor.

to get back to sleep. The "cure" for insomnia can be as simple as earplugs or as complex as psychiatric medication or surgery.

Another form of insomnia is *excessive daytime sleepiness*. This disorder, which afflicts about four percent to five percent of the population, might sound hokey; after all, most of us would say we're sleepy during the day. However, sufferers of this disorder would argue otherwise. True daytime sleepiness is a persistent problem that can actually prevent you from functioning normally. Before doctors make this diagnosis, they have to rule out a number of medical problems, because chronic fatigue is a symptom of a number of serious medical conditions.

Last and most serious of the sleep disorders is *sleep apnea,* a potentially life-threatening condition most commonly found in overweight, older men. Sleep apnea is an upper respiratory sleep disorder that causes a person to quit breathing while asleep. When the blood's oxygen level drops low enough, emergency hormones are secreted and wake the person up. He starts breathing again and falls back asleep. This cycle can literally happen hundreds of times each night. Not only is this exhausting; without treatment, the sufferer runs the risk of literally dying in his sleep.

To make the most of your need to sleep, try a little self-help for the sleep-deprived:

➤ Take a 20-minute power nap in the middle of the day.

➤ Go to bed and get up at the same time every day (yes, even on the weekends).

➤ Get regular physical exercise, but not within three hours of bedtime.

Altered Consciousness

Sleep (and dreaming) is one form of altered consciousness. Human beings have invented thousands of others. There are roller coasters, ferris wheels, and merry-go-rounds. Young children spin around and around until they get dizzy. There's meditation and yoga, and there are drugs and alcohol. These are all ways of expanding or altering your state of mind, and they seem to be a universal part of human nature.

Albert Einstein once said that a problem can't be solved at the same level in which it occurs. The fact that we have to use our mind to solve our mind's problems is one of psychology's biggest challenges. One benefit of altering our consciousness is that it shifts us out of our normal way of looking at things. By changing our focus, we can get a different perspective on ourselves and our problems.

People also alter their consciousness to avoid their problems or escape from reality. When it comes to mind-altering drugs, there can be a fine line between using them for relaxation, for fun, or as an escape. Let's take a look at four ways we can alter our consciousness and the pros and cons of each:

➤ hypnosis

➤ meditation

➤ hallucinations

➤ drugs

Look Deeply into My Eyes

It is truly amusing to see old movies that include hypnosis as part of the plot. Inevitably, there is a Svengali look-alike waving a gold watch in front of an innocent and naive young woman, chanting, "Keep your eyes on the watch as it moves back and forth ... back and forth ..." His voice gets deeper and we see her eyelids droop lower and lower. She falls completely under his spell and the audience spends the rest of the movie watching her try to get out.

That's not the way hypnosis really works. If you've ever been hypnotized, you deserve much more credit than your hypnotist. The single most important factor in hypnosis is the degree to which a participant has a "talent" for becoming hypnotized. Clinical hypnotists call this talent *hypnotizability*.

Shrink Rap

Your **hypnotizability** is a measure of how susceptible you are to entering a hypnotic state.

You're Getting Very, Very Sleepy

Your hypnotizability is the degree to which you respond to hypnotic suggestions. Hypnosis is *not* the result of gullibility or a deep-seated need to conform to social pressure. It has much to do with a unique expression of human imagination. Are you the kind of person who gets so involved in a book or a movie that it feels like you're a part of it? If so, you're probably a good candidate for hypnosis. A hypnotizable person is one who is able to truly immerse himself in the imagination and feeling of life experiences.

Since the inception of hypnosis more than 200 years ago, it has been impossible to find agreement among professionals about what it is. But even though "hypnosis" is still clouded in mystery and confusion, there are some key elements that can be used when talking about hypnosis and hypnotic states. In a general sense, *hypnosis* is an induced state of awareness characterized by deep relaxation and increased suggestibility.

And When I Snap My Fingers, You'll Remember Nothing

A subject under hypnosis is highly responsive to the hypnotist's suggestion; however, it is not a form of mind control. No one under hypnosis can be made to do something against his or her will. The person under hypnosis is fully in control of him or herself at all times. And you can't get "stuck" under hypnosis.

Researchers may disagree about the psychological mechanisms involved in hypnosis, but they agree about the powerful therapeutic influence hypnosis can have in reducing the psychological component of pain. Children undergoing cancer treatment, for example, have successfully been taught to use their imagination to distract themselves from painful procedures. Watching a parent and child take a hypnosis-induced trip to Disneyland in the middle of an oncology ward is not only a powerful testament to the science of psychology. It's a testament to the human spirit.

Psychobabble

In 1897, a California murder defendant was hypnotized on the stand and swore he was innocent. Witnesses to the murder swore otherwise. Apparently, the jury was not in a trance; they recognized that a person could lie under hypnosis, believed the eyewitnesses, and convicted the defendant.

In Vivo Hypnosis

Want to know what it's like to be hypnotized? Close your eyes and pretend you're walking up to the front door of your home. In your mind's eye, open the door and walk in. Now walk through your home and count the doors. You may count only the doorways that have actual doors connected or you may count all the doorways. You may count all the doorways on all the floors or only the doorways on one floor. You can know that whatever you decide to do is perfectly right for you. Close your eyes and try it now.

How did that feel? Well, believe it or not, you were just hypnotized! You may have vividly pictured each door or you may have just had an inner sense about each door. Whatever you experienced was just right for you. There is no right or wrong way to be hypnotized. It's not even necessary to be in "trance," just a willingness to suspend your critical thinking. While many powerful things can happen during hypnosis, the process of being hypnotized itself is not mystical.

Don't Bother Me, I'm Meditating

Meditation is another way of altering consciousness. It took a while before it caught on in the Western part of the world, perhaps because its "sit still and listen" focus can be a little hard for those of us who grew up in a "get up and get ahead" culture. But although meditation got off to a slow start, it is now one of the fastest growing practices in the United States, and with good reason. If you're looking for a way to alter your consciousness, meditation may be the way to go.

First of all, anyone can learn it. *Transcendental Meditation,* the form of meditation that has received the most scientific investigation, basically involves sitting comfortably with your eyes closed and focusing on a mantra. A mantra is a word or phrase you repeat silently to yourself. Practiced 15 to 20 minutes twice daily, it apparently allows our mental activity to settle down naturally while alertness is maintained and enhanced.

Insight

Not only is meditation easy to learn, it has tremendous health benefits. Over a five-year study, practitioners of Transcendental Meditation had more than 50 percent fewer doctor's visits, drank less alcohol, felt less anxious, and felt more resilient and emotionally mature.

I Must Be Hallucinating

If you like having friends, hallucinations might not be the best way to alter your conscious. Western culture has little tolerance for unusual perceptual experiences. We're afraid of people who have them. This attitude is not universal; in some cultures, people who hallucinate are viewed as spiritual leaders with a direct connection to the spirit world.

We're Not Talking Beads and Lava Lamps Here

It's easy to confuse hallucinations with illusions—we *all* see illusions. When you look at the flashing lights on a movie marquee, you see the illusion of a single light zooming around the edge of the sign. The appearance of movement in stationary lights is common; they look that way to most of us. Most of us don't, however, "see" lights around the heads of the people selling tickets in the box office. If you do, you're having a *hallucination*. An illusion is a distortion of something that's there, a *hallucination* is seeing something that isn't there.

In general, hallucinations occur when your brain metabolism is altered from its normal level. They can be a symptom of many different diseases or conditions: high fever, an adverse reaction or side effect from a drug, ingestion of a hallucinogen, renal failure, migraines, or epilepsy.

Is This a Dagger I See Before Me?

Most of us, though, associate hallucinations with mental illness and, in particular, with schizophrenia. People with schizophrenia often hear voices inside their head but truly believe the voices are coming from outside themselves. Imagine how frightening it would be to hear a voice saying mean things about you but not knowing who was talking or where the voice was coming from.

Fortunately, even Western culture is becoming more tolerant of different perceptions of reality as overwhelming evidence points to schizophrenia being as much a physical disorder as diabetes or cancer. In addition, under certain conditions, we might all see reality differently. Trauma can cause just about anyone to hallucinate; some Vietnam vets, for example, were bombarded with "flashbacks," visual and auditory replays of traumatic combat scenes. And a significant number of ordinary people actually "see" or "hear" a deceased loved one within six weeks of his or her death.

Psychobabble

Is religious ecstasy a form of altered consciousness? In many religions, followers speak in imaginary languages that others cannot interpret. This "speaking in tongues," nicknamed glossolalia by scientists, is valued as a sign that the speaker has received important spiritual gifts. One explanation for its occurrence is that it reflects an altered state of consciousness; the goal for the speaker is to enter a trance and have his or her actions "taken over" by another power.

Operating Under the Influence

And now, ladies and gentleman, for the winner in the Most Popular Way to Alter Your Consciousness Contest—drugs and alcohol. Given the risks involved in this particular form of consciousness altering, it makes you wonder about the judges. Regular use of drugs and alcohol is so darned bad for you that it's hard for me to talk about it without sounding like the poster child for a "Just say no" campaign.

However, drug use does not always lead to drug addiction. Most teenagers try drugs and alcohol and the vast majority of them never become serious users. And yes, there are studies that suggest that one to two drinks a week can be good for your physical health, although, if you have a strong family history of substance abuse, it's probably not worth the risk.

Some Pills Make You Larger

Psychoactive drugs—the ones that work on your brain and change your mood—are the ones most likely to become addictive. They attach themselves to synaptic receptors in the brain and block or stimulate certain chemical reactions. It is these chemical reactions that we experience as increased relaxation, lowered inhibition, or greater self-confidence. Psychoactive drugs affect your mental processes and behavior by changing your conscious awareness. Let's take a look at the five classes of major mood changers:

➤ hallucinogens

➤ marijuana

➤ opiates

➤ depressants

➤ stimulants

Hallucinogens, also known as psychedelics, distort your senses and alter your perceptions. They can also temporarily blur the boundaries between yourself and the things around you. Someone on an acid trip, for example, may feel as if he is a physical part of the guitar he or she is playing, or he can "see" the music notes floating around him.

Marijuana is often classified as a hallucinogen, although it has some distinct properties of its own. The experience depends on the dose; small doses create mild, pleasurable highs, and larger doses result in long, hallucinogenic reactions. The positive effects include a sense of euphoria and well-being, and distortions of time and space. The effects, however, can also be negative, such as fear, anxiety, and confusion. Marijuana impairs motor coordination, making it risky to smoke and drive.

Dead to the World

Opiates are highly addictive drugs that suppress your ability to feel and respond to sensations. Prescription versions are routinely used as painkillers. The most popular street version is heroin—users typically report a "rush" of euphoria when they first use, followed by a trancelike state of relaxation (known as a "nod").

Depressants and stimulants are the most widely abused substances, although they tend to have opposite effects. Depressants, including alcohol, slow down the mental and physical activity of the body. They can temporarily relieve anxiety and stress but also quickly impair physical coordination and judgment. Someone who drinks too much is likely to slow down to the point of passing out.

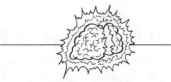

Brain Buster

Self-medicating for stress with alcohol or drugs is generally not a good idea. You risk trading off one problem for another. Don't believe me? Try volunteering a few hours at the local detox center. You may never chug another Samuel Adams after that.

On the other hand, stimulants like cocaine are "uppers." They speed up mental and physical activity. Cocaine and amphetamine users report increased confidence and higher energy when they first start out. An overdose of amphetamines can cause frightening hallucinations, dramatic mood swings, and paranoid delusions.

Risking Addiction

Your risk for addiction depends on lots of things—your personality, your genetic makeup, your coping skills, and your family history of drug and alcohol abuse. It also depends on your drug of choice.

Mood Alterer	Most Popular Drug	Risk of Dependence
Hallucinogens	LSD	no psychological, unknown physical
Cannabis	marijuana	unknown psychological, moderate physical
Opiates	heroin	high psychological and physical
Depressants	alcohol, Valium	moderate to high psychological and physical
Stimulants	cocaine, speed	high psychological and physical

The Monkey on Your Back

Being addicted to drugs has been called "having a monkey on your back." And for good reason! The harder you try to shake it off, the harder it clings to you. It demands to be fed at all hours of the day and night. It screams louder when you try to ignore it. No matter where you go, it's always there.

It All Sneaks Up on You

Continued use of certain psychoactive drugs lessens their effect over time, so that more of the drug is needed to achieve the same effect. The body develops a tolerance to the substance. To make matters worse, physiological dependence often goes hand in hand with tolerance. So, at the same time a user needs more of the drug to get the desired mental effects, he or she needs more of the drug for physical reasons, too.

After a while, addicts only feel "normal" when using. When they try to cut back or quit, they go through a process called withdrawal. Unpleasant physical and mental symptoms occur when a physically addicted substance abuser discontinues the drug.

The Addictive Mind

Psychological dependence can take place with or without physical dependence. When cocaine use became popular in the early 1980s, common wisdom held that it was not physically addictive, but highly addictive psychologically. It was easy for people to become emotionally dependent on the "pseudoconfidence" that cocaine generated. A little closer to home is the panic you may feel when you run out of coffee. While the physical dependency potential of caffeine is unknown, many of us experience the psychological addiction to coffee on a daily basis!

The "psychology" of drug use is amazingly complex. Even the immediate effects of drugs on your consciousness may be influenced more by your psychological factors than by the physical properties of the drug. The mood that you're in before taking the drug, your expectations of what will happen, and your history of prior drug use all play a crucial role. If you've ever had a few drinks when you were down in the dumps, and then wound up feeling more depressed, you know what I mean.

Insight

We often think *suicide* when we hear of an accidental overdose, but the body of a habitual drug user may develop a defense against the drug that increases the risk that he or she might accidentally take too much. Using environmental cues, the body secretes substances that counteract the drug. When users are in a familiar environment, they need more of the drug to overcome those cues. When users shoot up in a new place, the "normal" amount of drug can be lethal.

The Least You Need to Know

➤ Our consciousness is our awareness of who we are and all the things we think, feel, and do.

➤ Sleep is a form of altered consciousness that probably evolved to restore our bodies after all the wear and tear of the day and to keep our ancestors from having too much idle time on their hands.

➤ REM sleep is the most important of the four sleep stages. It's the time we dream and it seems to help stabilize our mood and store our memories.

➤ Sleep disorders (including insomnia, excessive daytime sleepiness, and sleep apnea) are caused by a complex combination of psychological and physical factors.

➤ Four ways people have purposefully altered their consciousness are meditation, hypnosis, hallucinations, and psychoactive drugs.

Chapter 7

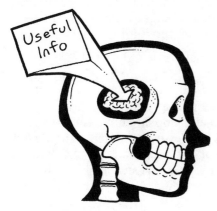

Get *That* Through Your Thick Skull!

In This Chapter

➤ Learn which associations we're all members of

➤ Learning and your love life

➤ Thorndike's cats and Pavlov's dogs

➤ Facing irrational fears

➤ Banishing bad habits

This chapter is all about learning: *how* we learn, *what* we learn, and *when* we learn. As you read, you'll meet some interesting psychologists who, through their work with animals, pioneered our understanding of learning. You'll learn about the power of association and how our interpretation of the consequences of our actions influences our learning curve. And you'll learn how to apply the magical principles of learning to get rid of irrational fears, alter bad habits, and maybe even improve your love life!

Helpless

"I can't do it," four-year-old Sabrina whines as she hands you the magazine and scissors. "You do it for me." "But Sabrina," you argue. "You haven't even tried. I know you can cut out that picture yourself." Inwardly, you sigh, frustrated and confused by Sabrina's constant clinging and refusal to attempt new things.

Shrink Rap

The term **learning** refers to any process through which experience at one time can change our behavior at another.

What's going on with Sabrina? Why is she constantly demanding assistance from you while other children her age are eager to do things for themselves? Doesn't she want to learn to do things for herself?

We all need a little help now and then, but if we need it all the time, we may have learned helplessness. Children as young as four can develop the belief that they lack the ability to impact their environment and, as a result, give up and stop attempting new tasks. Not only does learned helplessness interfere with our ability to take charge of our lives, many psychologists believe it causes depression. Learning obviously isn't just about developing new skills; it's also about believing that you can.

Learning About Learning

We've all heard the saying "Experience is the best teacher." Learning theorists would say it's the *only* teacher. By definition, learning involves changing our behavior in response to experience. And, since much of psychology deals with the effects of experiences on our behavior, learning about learning is important.

Learning is one of those psychological concepts that's easy to understand but hard to see. Since learning is something that happens inside us, it can never be observed directly. Teachers give us tests because they are looking for evidence, or lack thereof, that we are learning the material in their class. Similarly, learning researchers have to depend on measurable improvements in performance when they're studying learning. Whether it's a grade on a calculus test or the number of trials it takes a rat to find food in a maze, behavior is the ultimate evidence of learning.

But the benefit you get from learning is not confined to behavioral change. Learning also expands your options. For example, even if you decide not to quit smoking right now, by learning effective smoking cessation strategies you can increase your ability to quit in the future. Similarly, an inspiring book, perhaps like the one you are reading, can increase your appreciation for its subject, motivate you to learn more, and affect your attitudes and choices for years to come. Now, wasn't that money well spent?

Drooling Like a Dog

Association is the key to learning. I come from a long line of teachers and, believe me, the joys of learning were preached and the benefits of education drilled into my head. On the reverence ladder, school was right up there with church, and studying was considered as important as praying. I probably hid out in graduate school for so many years because my associations with hard work weren't nearly so pleasant!

A man by the name of Ivan Pavlov first discovered the power of positive associations and he used it to teach old dogs new tricks. As a scientist, he had spent many years studying the digestive processes in dogs. To speed along his studies, he frequently asked his assistants to put powdered meat in their mouths so they would salivate. One day, he noticed a strange thing; his dogs were drooling before the meat powder even touched their tongues. The sight of the food, or the sound of food being poured into the dish, sent these dogs into a frenzy of anticipation.

Shrink Rap

In **classical conditioning**, two stimuli become so closely associated that one of them can elicit the same reactive behavior as the other.

At first, Pavlov was annoyed. These "psychic secretions," as he called them, were messing up his work. He unsuccessfully tried numerous ways to get rid of them, but eventually gave in to the old maxim "If you can't beat 'em, join 'em."

Pavlov began deliberately controlling the signals that preceded the food. In one famous experiment, he sounded a bell just before placing the food in the dog's mouth. After several pairings of a bell with food, the dogs would drool in response to the bell sound alone. Pavlov was so fascinated with these events that he abandoned his original work on digestion, discovered *classical conditioning*, and changed the course of psychology forever.

If you're a pet owner, you're probably wondering what all the fuss was about. After all, within a week after getting your pet, you probably observed your little darling drooling to the sound of an electric can opener or the sound of food being poured into a dish. At the time, however, Pavlov's discovery was revolutionary.

For the first time, scientists could systematically study human learning by varying the associations between two stimuli and charting out what effect this had on a subject's response. Not only did Pavlov's research help us understand and use the power of positive association, it ultimately paved the way for understanding the role negative associations can play in the development of irrational fears and phobias.

On a gloomier note, classical conditioning has also given advertisers a lot of effective ammo. Every time they pair sex with their products, they're betting the association between the two will have you drooling just like Pavlov's dog!

Learning the Classics

You, my friend, have been conditioned—and I'm not talking about your hair. Maybe you've formed an association between a certain piece of music and a relationship breakup and now you feel sad every time you hear that song. Maybe you came down with a stomach virus after eating poached salmon and now every time you even smell fish, you feel nauseous. Maybe you've been in a recent car accident; now, even though you know it wasn't your fault, you're a little nervous about getting behind the wheel. Whether you know it or not, you have thousands of associations living in your head and many of them got there through classical conditioning.

Psychobabble

Remember the old *Gong Show?* John B. Watson and his assistant, Rosalie Raynor, invented a different version. They quickly taught an infant named Little Albert to fear a white rat by banging a loud gong just behind the tot whenever the rat appeared. After just seven gongs, Little Albert was scared to death of the same rat he had played with before the training began. His fear was so great that it generalized to other furry objects, including a Santa Claus mask.

Let's take the common association of a song on the radio and breaking up with your lover. For years after the breakup, just hearing that song may bring up the same feelings of pain and hurt that the breakup did, years ago. Similarly, if you associate salmon with the stomach flu, just the smell of salmon can recall the nauseated feelings you once had. This happened to a friend of mine and she swears to this day that the word *salmon* still makes her feel queasy.

Coming In on Cue

Here's how these associations happen: Human beings are biologically programmed to respond certain ways to certain things in the environment. We salivate when we eat food. We jump if we hear a sudden, loud noise. We jerk our hands away if we touch something hot. These natural reactions are unconditioned responses; we don't have to learn them.

Over time, though, we start noticing that certain cues might help us predict when an environmental stimulus (food, noises, burning) is about to appear. From an evolutionary standpoint, such cues signaling danger or benefits would be highly adaptive. Learning that a grizzly bear makes a certain noise in the bushes would be pretty useful information, especially if it keeps you from having to wait for physical confirmation of his presence! Similarly, the smell of something burning is a pretty good clue that fire is near, and it gives you the chance to respond to the smell in the same way you would to a fire—take it seriously and investigate immediately, before you get burned.

Where There's Smoke

In the fire example, the smell of smoke is the conditioned stimulus and fire is the unconditioned stimulus. You'll naturally avoid fire—it's your unconditioned response to the unconditioned stimulus signaling danger. But over time, you'll associate that smoke smell with danger and respond to it as if the smell were the same as an actual fire. What separates unconditioned responses from conditioned ones is learning—you have to *learn* conditioned responses. The urge to avoid or escape is an unconditioned response to fire, but it's a conditioned response to the burning smell, because you had to learn it.

Here's another example:

Unconditioned Stimulus   Intimate body contact (heavy petting)

Unconditioned Response   physiological arousal (getting "turned on")

Environmental Cue   Chanel No. 5

At first you get this sequence of behaviors:

Unconditioned Stimulus (petting)

+ Environmental Cue (the scent of Chanel)

Unconditioned Response (getting turned on)

After several repetitions, you can cut directly to the chase, so to speak:

the scent of Chanel = getting turned on

In this example, intimate bodily contact is a natural stimulus for physiological arousal. On the other hand, contrary to what advertisers may say, you have not been biologically programmed to respond to the perfume Chanel No. 5. But if you've had enough pairings of this perfume and sexual arousal in, say, the backseat of your car on Friday nights, you can bet even a whiff of Chanel will send those hormones flying!

Learning Isn't Always Fun

It would be great if all our classical conditioning was built on positive associations. Unfortunately, life doesn't work that way; we also get negatively conditioned by stimuli. Sometimes, in fact, learning can be downright aversive.

If the door to your office has a lot of static electricity and you get a jolt every time you touch it, the shock is an example of painful unconditioned stimuli. Your unconditioned response is avoidance. Over time, you may start approaching this innocent door with dread. You may begin to devise all kinds of quirky strategies for avoiding the shock—using a handkerchief to open to the door, always going in after someone else, or rubbing your feet on the floor to ground yourself. This kind of learning is called *aversive conditioning:* You learn an aversion to something that was previously perceived as harmless.

Brain Buster

Agoraphobia is an example of classically conditioned fear. People who have panic attacks often associate their physical symptoms with the environment in which they occur. In an attempt to ward off future attacks, they'll restrict their activities until they're literally unable to venture out of the house.

Aversive conditioning can be very powerful because of the fear associated with it. Not only do you want to avoid the object of your aversion, you become afraid of it. Fear is a hard emotion to unlearn—in fact, when strong fear is involved, conditioning can take place after only a single pairing between a neutral stimulus and an unconditioned stimulus. And it can last a lifetime.

During World War II, the signal used to call sailors to battle stations aboard U.S. Navy ships was a gong. To personnel on board, this sound was quickly associated with danger. Researchers found that, even 15 years later, the sound of the old "call to battle stations" struck fear in the hearts of the navy veterans who had been aboard these ships.

If you find yourself having an "irrational" reaction to something, chances are you're the victim of negative classical conditioning. For this to happen though, certain conditions have got to be met.

Learning About Meaningful Relationships

Timing is as critical in classical conditioning as it is in good joke telling. During your lifetime, you'll form thousands of associations among the situations and events in your life. Not all of these become classically conditioned. For example, that song might give you the blues because it was playing on your car radio during a relationship breakup, but you probably aren't heartbroken every time you drive your car.

Shrink Rap

Stimulus generalization is when an individual who has become conditioned to respond to one stimulus in a certain way will also respond in that same way to any similar stimuli.

That's because all associations are not created equal. In a child's early years, just about anything resembling the conditioned stimuli will prompt a similar response. A child who has been bitten by a large dog will initially regard all dogs with suspicion. This is called *stimulus generalization*. It seems that evolution first teaches us it's better to be safe than sorry.

Developing Discrimination

Over time, though, we become more discriminating. We learn to distinguish between the conditioned stimuli and its relatives. The child begins to realize that one bad dog does not spoil the whole bunch, and that he doesn't have to spend the rest of his life fearful of *all* dogs. When Little Albert realizes that the rat causes the gong to ring, while Santa Claus brings toys, he is engaging in *stimulus discrimination*.

Classical conditioning is a lot like dating; it's a balancing act between discriminating too much and responding the same way to too many stimuli! To find the proper balance, we rely on certain clues to help us figure out which associations are worth learning and which ones are not. There are three stimulating qualities that are most likely to result in classical conditioning:

➤ contrast

➤ contingency

➤ information

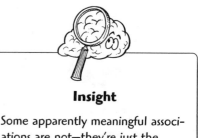

Insight

Some apparently meaningful associations are not—they're just the result of an accidental pairing between two stimuli. These accidents result in superstitious behavior, like the athletes who believe their "lucky" socks will help them win the championship—so they'd rather sit on the bench than change their socks during the playoffs!

Contrast

The smell of your mother's favorite perfume is more likely to stir up fond memories of her if you smell it in the middle of a business meeting than if you get your whiff of it at a perfume counter. Stimuli that stand out from others around them are more likely to be noticed. At the perfume counter, her perfume may get swamped by competing fragrances and lose its power over your associations.

Contingency

The most powerful associations occur when the conditioned stimulus *reliably* predicts the unconditioned stimuli. If you wear a certain perfume every time you and your boyfriend get together, he will be more likely to associate that fragrance with you.

Information

Conditioned stimuli are most likely to be conditioned if they provide *unique* information about the unconditioned stimulus. Where there's smoke there isn't always fire, but the smell of something burning generally means there is. That's why you're likely to immediately investigate the smell of something burning; the smell provides important, generally reliable information about danger.

Think of the Consequences

Classical conditioning is a powerful form of learning. From an early age, we learn to associate good feelings with certain things in our environment and bad things with others. These feelings affect what we do. But there's a much more direct way the environment shapes our behavior, and it's one parents rely on every day when they interact with a child. It's the fact that every act has consequences, and the method of teaching that uses this principle is called *operant conditioning*.

Parents know the power of rewarding a child for good behavior and punishing him or her for bad. Children do too. They quickly learn that, no matter how good it might feel to punch a brother's lights out, the consequences can be pretty painful. They also learn to do things that have negative associations, like homework, if there's a big enough reward at the end.

Kitty in a Box

Psychologist Edward Thorndike was the first to get us thinking along these lines. While Pavlov was preoccupied with drooling dogs, Edward Thorndike was into cats. He spent a lot of time watching them try to escape from puzzle boxes. At first the cats tried a number of things that didn't work. Sooner or later, though, they would accidentally do something that allowed them to escape.

Escape was the reward for their efforts—and when Thorndike put them back in the box, they usually found the escape route a little sooner than the last time. After several trips to the box, the cats would immediately trip the lever or push the button that let them out.

Thorndike coined the term *law of effect* to explain his observation that consistently rewarded responses are strengthened and those that aren't are gradually weakened, or "stamped out." Just like natural selection favored the evolution of characteristics that allowed the human species to survive, the law of effect says that behavior that gives rise to good consequences will be selected again in the future. From an operant perspective, you might say that learning is your own personal evolution!

Teaching Seamore to Dance

What about behaviors that would never occur if animals were left to their own devices? In Thorndike's box, even the dumbest cat could eventually figure out the right answer. On the other hand, if the animal trainers at Sea World waited for Seamore the sea lion to dance a jig on its own, we'd all be in for a long wait. To get Seamore to do tricks he would never do naturally, they use a form of learning called *shaping*.

Here's how it works: Let's say the trainers want Seamore to dance on two flippers. They first look for a natural behavior that resembles the desired one. Maybe Seamore temporarily balances on two flippers when he climbs up on a rock. The trainers then start rewarding Seamore with a fish every time they catch him balancing. Pretty soon Seamore realizes that he gets fed if he stands up. Naturally, he stands up more often.

Next, the trainers start rewarding another behavior step in the right direction. Maybe they hold a fish out and get Seamore to walk on two flippers. This process continues until Seamore is the dancing star of a Sea World show. If shaping can get sea lions to dance, imagine what effect patience and praise can have on the people you love.

Psychobabble

Shaping has been successfully used to help mentally impaired adults learn complex behaviors like getting dressed by themselves. Every small step in the right direction, such as pulling a shirt over the top of the head, is rewarded by a token he or she can exchange for food or another treat. The criticism of this approach has been that it teaches pretty materialistic values; the person starts expecting to be rewarded every time he or she does something right.

There's More Than One Way to Skinner a Cat

Thorndike may have gotten the operant conditioning ball rolling, but it was B.F. Skinner who really invented the game. Not only did he invent much of the lingo we use to talk about the process, his views came to dominate much of psychology for almost 50 years. According to Skinner, understanding another person was simply a matter of understanding the consequences he or she experienced during a lifetime. To Skinner, operant conditioning and psychology were one and the same.

If you're trying to understand why your boss does the things he or she does, Skinner would tell you to evaluate the consequences of his or her actions. For example, what do other employees do when the boss yells at them? Do they snap to attention or get their work done more quickly? And don't forget to take a look at the boss's reinforcement history; maybe that habit of yelling was begun because yelling was the only way your boss could get attention at home. One thing is certain—somewhere along the line, your boss was rewarded for yelling and, as a result, you suffer the consequences.

Calling in Reinforcements

Skinner called this phenomenon *reinforcement,* any consequence that increases a particular behavior over time. A smile, a pat on the back, and a gold star are all examples of positive reinforcers (as we get older, we might prefer a raise or a vacation). Reinforcers can also be negative: If you take out the garbage because you don't want your mom to nag you, then her nagging is a negative reinforcer for your garbage duty. As moms know all too well, if those potential consequences weren't there, kids might be tempted to slack off.

Oddly enough, constantly rewarding someone is less effective than rewarding them only occasionally. If you got a raise every week at work, you would darned sure notice the week you didn't get it. It wouldn't take too many weeks before your motivation took a nosedive. On the other hand, if you get a raise once a year, you're likely to keep on keeping on for the other 51 weeks. (I sure wouldn't mind it if someone tried this experiment on me!)

Shrink Rap

Reinforcements are any consequences that increase the occurrence of a particular behavior over time. They can be both positive (a hug, a raise in pay) or negative (a punishment, for example).

Consequentially

In fact, understanding consequences can be risky business. It's not always easy to tease out all the reinforcers for the things we do, and what is reinforcing to one person can be punishing to another. And negative consequences don't always work. Bad habits, like drinking too much or overeating, have negative consequences yet we keep doing them!

Insight

If you speak softly, you don't have to carry a big stick: Soft reprimands spoken only to the misbehaver are more effective than loud scoldings in front of others. And physical punishment must be immediate and consistent to be effective. Even when it works, it sends the message that physical aggression is okay if you're big enough to get away with it.

The Terminators

Reinforcers explain how we learn new behaviors and why we keep doing them. But if you want to unlearn a behavior, you have only two choices: extinguish it or punish it.

"Just ignore it." "Don't pay any attention to him." Children throughout time have been given this advice from parents and teachers alike. Withhold the reinforcers for a certain behavior and, over time, the behavior is likely to stop. If you're a child, though, the time it takes to extinguish your classmate's torture can feel like a lifetime, which is why kids routinely reject this advice.

Nipping Bad Behaviors in the Bud

And kids aren't fools—trying to extinguish behaviors rarely works outside of a laboratory because it's difficult to remove all the reinforcers for a particular behavior. You may give your classmate the silent treatment for a year, but if other classmates are giggling every time your teaser calls you "four-eyes," he or she is still getting *plenty* of reinforcement. In the real world, extinction is much more likely to work if it is paired with *positive* reinforcement of the desired behavior.

"Spare the rod and spoil the child" refers to the other way to correct behavior—by punishing it. Like extinction, punishing a behavior reduces its frequency over time. Spanking, time out, grounding, taking away privileges, and yelling are all examples of punishment. The purpose of punishment is to reduce pleasure, either by taking away something we like (dessert, attention, TV privileges) or by giving us something we don't like (a swat on the behind, a parking ticket).

Of Carrots and Sticks

But punishment works best in conjunction with positive reinforcement. All companies have disciplinary procedures for unacceptable behavior, but in recent years, one of the most popular recommendations to managers seeking to build employee morale has been for the manager to "catch them doing something *right.*" Managers are encouraged to pay attention to examples of effective employee behavior, like getting to work on time, meeting project deadlines, or building teams. When they see it, they are encouraged to call attention to that employee, point out the stellar behavior, and praise, praise, praise.

The theory is this: A manager can move employees in the right direction with praise, while the disciplinary policies are the "big stick" for behavior that gets out of line.

The Behavior Police

It's easy to confuse negative reinforcement with punishment because they both involve negative or unpleasant experiences. However, they have opposite effects on our behavior; punishment always decreases behavior while reinforcers increase them.

Terminators and Reinforcers

Kind of Stimulus That Follows Response	Do More of the Same (Reinforcer)	Cease and Desist (Punisher)
Positive	reward, food, prize, praise, thanks	criticism, disapproval, pain
Negative	easing pain or discomfort	privileges, ignoring, grounding

115

If you treat your significant other well to avoid getting jilted, then the possibility of getting dumped is a negative reinforcer. However, if, in spite of your good behavior, your significant other is dumb enough to dump you, you might feel punished for all of your good deeds. And, as all of us know if we've been the rebound in a rebound relationship, you might not be so inclined to make such an effort in the next one!

Learning on the Liberal Side

Some of Skinner's followers thought his strict emphasis on behavior was too conservative. They took a second look at all that mental stuff Skinner had discarded and concluded that the thoughts and feelings we have about the consequences of our behavior play a key role in the way we learn. They realized, for example, that we don't all feel the same way about what happens to us—a reward for one person might feel like a punishment to another.

This is the view held by cognitive psychologists, who say that the way you interpret the world has a big impact on how you feel and what you do. In other words, the meaning you give to the things that happen to you might be more important than the actual events themselves.

Psychobabble

Recent research indicates that thoughts and feelings don't influence only human behavior. Chimps can also be motivated by their feelings. In one dispute among chimpanzees, one chimp backed up another, which then failed to return the favor. In response, she chased and hit him. Apparently, even in the animal kingdom, one good turn deserves another, and a bad turn can lead to revenge.

Attitudes and Expectations

Cognitive psychologists believe classical conditioning occurs because the conditioned stimulus creates an expectation that the unconditioned stimulus is about to appear. When your cat hears the clanging of its food dish, it has come to expect that it's dinnertime, and it'll run to its dining spot.

Cognitive psychologists also think operant conditioning is much more complicated than the simple history of our rewards and punishments. The cognitivists believe that learning involves understanding the means to the end in addition to any thoughts and feelings we have about those means and ends. Whether you eat or not depends

116

much more on how hungry you are than it does on your knowledge that opening the refrigerator will give you access to food. That knowledge gives you options; it doesn't force you to use them.

Experience and Interpretation

It doesn't take a rocket scientist to know that your interpretation of things has a lot of influence over what you do. One factor that influences your present "take" on things is your past experience—you're likely to compare current consequences with past ones and be either happy or sad about the results.

My mom's savvy dating advice clearly took this into account. From the time I was a teenager, she would say things like, "Don't ever start out doing things for a man that you don't plan on continuing." My mom was warning me of the *negative contrast effect,* the well-documented tendency for people to compare rewards and to be highly dissatisfied with any drop in reinforcement. In fact, we're much better off capitalizing on the *positive contrast effect* in our love lives, starting out slowly and then being kinder and more generous as time goes by. Sometimes, Mom really does know best!

Modeling Behavior

Thanks goodness you don't always have to learn from your own mistakes. You learn a lot about getting along in the world by observing those around you. You can climb the corporate ladder by imitating your boss, you can learn from your parents' mistakes, and you can set a good example for your children. All of these are examples of *observational learning.*

The positive version of this is known as *modeling.* Children really do model what their parents do much more than what their parents say. Not only do they imitate their parents' behavior, they also learn general rules about what is acceptable and what is not by watching others. Grownups also use modeling—if you're going to a party and aren't sure of the protocol, you may spend a few minutes watching the people around you to get the lay of the land.

Unfortunately, modeling doesn't always influence us in a positive direction. Albert Bandura found that children who first watched adults beat up a large inflated Bobo doll were much more aggressive in their play with the doll than children who had watched a gentle adult or no adult at all. Not only did the children imitate the adults' behaviors, they were also amazingly creative at devising torture strategies of their own. Obviously, they were learning more than

Brain Buster

A side effect of television violence is *psychic numbing,* a reduction in emotional arousal while witnessing violence. In situations where people are getting hurt, reducing the emotional distress of witnesses is a risky social outcome.

certain punches and kicks: They were getting the bigger message that aggressive behavior was okay.

Don't Be So Scared

Fear is easy to learn and hard to unlearn. Classical conditioning helps us understand irrational fears as links between our emotions and certain stimuli in the environment. You might fear heights, for example, because you have associated them with falling, or you might fear public speaking because you associate all that attention with rejection or humiliation. The process of unlearning them is called *systematic desensitization*.

Systematic desensitization is a therapeutic process that involves three steps:

➤ Listing the stressful situation in order of scariness.

➤ Developing an emotion that is incompatible with fear.

➤ Gradually confronting the situation, starting with a very mildly stressful one.

You don't have to have a full-blown phobia to benefit from systematic desensitization. Learning the three steps will help in any situation, like asking someone on a date. Let's say you've been wanting to ask your next door neighbor out for a date but just haven't got up the nerve to do it. Take the following steps:

1. Write down several situations related to your fear, ranging from least scary to most scary. Before you declare your undying love to your neighbor, or die from the fear the thought of this evokes, think of several baby steps that would get you where you want to go—on a date. You might ask a friend's advice about approaching this person, then ask a friend to role-play your date request, and then start making small talk with your neighbor. The key is to break down your fear into 10 to 15 small, progressive steps. No matter what your fear is, or how strong, there is always a first step that is acceptable to you.

2. Relax. There are numerous relaxation resources that will teach you the relaxation response (check Appendix B for a few). Relaxation is a powerful weapon against fear, and there are others. Assertiveness can also help. As a last resort, you might try running a couple of miles before you knock on your neighbor's door: It's hard to get all worked up about anything when you're tired!

3. Just do it—gradually. Sooner or later, you've got to enter the lion's den. Here's where systematic desensitization really earns brownie points. If you've listed your 15 scenarios, and role-played with your friends through the first 14, then the toughest one isn't going to be all that tough.

Psychobabble

Famous author and sexually active playboy Johann Wolfgang Von Goethe became obsessed with the fear of "diseased organs" after five years of hardy partying and a year-long illness. Throughout his life, he described his decision to study medicine and his greatest work, *Faust,* as his method of overcoming his morbid fears. Now *there's* an example of turning lemons into lemonade.

Getting Rid of Bad Habits

Bad habits are often a combination of classical and operant conditioning. Take smoking, for example. There's the classical conditioning component—over time, you associate smoking with a lot of other things that you do. You reach for a cigarette after a good meal, you smoke in the morning when you're drinking coffee, and you light up when you're angry or stressed. These activities and conditions become deeply ingrained triggers for smoking.

Then there are the reinforcements. Inhaling smoke causes a temporary relaxation response, so smoking "feels good." If you're physically addicted, your body is rewarded by the nicotine entering your bloodstream. If you use smoking to handle strong feelings or stress, then smoking gives you a "time out" to regroup and think through the situation. You're caught in a conundrum—you have all these cues and triggers that remind you to smoke, and the reinforcements that encourage you to keep smoking.

That's why bad habits can be so persistent—in the short term, they're so gratifying. I might know that eating a chocolate cake might add a few pounds, but man, does that chocolate taste good.

Getting rid of bad habits is more than a matter of willpower; you must systematically disarm your triggers, get rid of your reinforcers, and gradually replace your behavior with healthier alternatives. Here are a few tips for starters:

➤ *Avoid the triggering situation:* If you smoke with your coffee, switch to tea. If you can't go to the mall without buying a new outfit, don't go window shopping. If you scarf down potato chips whenever they're around, don't keep them in the house.

➤ *Change the situation:* Sit in the nonsmoking section of the restaurant. Put your clothes purchases on hold for a few hours and then decide if you will go back and buy them. Don't eat with the television on or standing at the kitchen counter.

➤ *Substitute:* Keep a journal of your thoughts and feelings that lead up to your habit and find other ways to fill these needs. If you shop in response to stress, take a bubble bath instead. If you eat when you're emotionally hungry, get a massage or talk on the phone to a friend. The next time you get angry and feel the urge to light up, try a short power walk first.

Chances are you came into this chapter with some bad habits; whether it's overeating, smoking, or overspending, most of us have at least a few. And, in spite of the negative consequences, we keep doing them over and over. I hope, however, this chapter has given you some insight into breaking them. In the next chapter, we'll shed some more light on why we keep doing things that aren't in our best interest.

The Least You Need to Know

➤ Learning is the ability to profit from experience.

➤ Much of what we learn is the result of either classical or operant conditioning.

➤ Classical conditioning occurs when we realize a previously neutral stimulus predicts an unconditioned stimulus. If this happens often enough, we start responding to the neutral stimulus alone.

➤ If you're rewarded for a temper tantrum, chances are you'll do it again; if you don't get what you want, you'll eventually stop—this is called operant conditioning.

➤ It's not just the consequences that influence your behavior, it's how you interpret the consequences—a reward for one person can be perceived as a punishment for another.

➤ Understanding how you learn can help you unlearn fear or get rid of bad habits.

Chapter 8

Coming to Terms with Your Memory

In This Chapter

➤ The court jester of the brain

➤ Understand how your memories are made

➤ How to remember what you learn about memory

➤ The truth about false memories

➤ Explore the mystery of repressed memory

For awhile it seemed as if stories about recovering repressed memories were all over the news. Then there were all those stories about how those recovered memories were false. How is it possible to remember something that never happened? And how does a repressed memory happen, anyway? Memory distortion research has clearly shown that information that happens after the event, such as stories other people tell us about what happened, can actually be incorporated into our memory. And studies have given us lots of insights into the process by which the mind buries memories you find difficult or painful.

In this chapter, we'll take a look at the myths and realities of memory, how your memory normally works, and when and why it doesn't. We'll look at some ways to improve your memory, and how research into false memory and repressed memory has improved our understanding of both these phenomena. As you read through this chapter, keep in mind one thing about memory: It's a lot trickier than you might think!

Kidnapped!

Until he was 15, child psychologist Jean Piaget believed his earliest memory was of nearly being kidnapped at the age of two. He remembered vivid details of the event, such as sitting in his baby carriage and watching his nurse defend herself against the kidnapper. He remembered the scratches on his nurse's face, and the short cloak and white baton the police officer was wearing as he chased the kidnapper away.

However, the kidnapping never happened. When Piaget was in his midteens, his parents received a remorseful letter from his former nurse, confessing that she had made the whole story up and returning the watch she had been given as a reward. Piaget's memories were false.

But the nurse's confession raised a whole new mystery: How did Piaget remember something that never happened? Obviously, Piaget heard many accounts of this story as a child, imagined what he thought had actually happened, and projected this information into the past in the form of a visual memory.

The Court Jester

Your brain can store 100 trillion bits of information, so why can't you remember the name of the person you sat next to in homeroom during high school? If your brain is a kingdom, surely your memory is the court jester. It's always playing tricks. You can, for example, instantly recall things you never tried to learn (like popular song lyrics), and you can easily forget things you spent hours memorizing (like material you've studied for an exam).

Shrink Rap

Implicit memory is your ability to remember information you haven't deliberately tried to learn. **Explicit memory** is your ability to retain information you've put real effort into learning.

And has anyone ever told you to "just forget" something that happened? Tell *him* to forget it; your memory doesn't work on command.

Whether you want it to or not, your brain stores all kinds of information. *Implicit memory* holds all those trivial facts, song lyrics, and general nonsense that your brain files away while you're concentrating on something else. Most of the time, however, researchers are more interested in studying *explicit memory,* which contains the information that people consciously spend energy processing.

Learning About Remembering from Forgetting

When it comes to memory, the proverbial elephant is way ahead of human beings—members of our species constantly forget, misremember, and make mistakes. These mistakes offer valuable clues about how memory normally works. For example, researchers have found that people forget for one of three reasons:

1. They don't get it to begin with.

2. They had it but they lost it.

3. They have it but they can't find it.

These mistakes reflect a failure in one of the three mental operations necessary for memory: encoding, storage, and retrieval.

For instance, I simply can't seem to remember my high school classmate's name, even though I sat next to her for years. Chances are my memory failure is due to a retrieval problem—I have her name filed someplace but can't seem to open the right filing cabinet. If someone gave me a hint, I could probably come up with it. This "hint" would be a retrieval cue—information that will help me find and open the right cabinet.

On the other hand, if I was so self-absorbed in high school that I never learned my classmate's name in the first place, my inability to come up with it now would be an encoding problem. One clue that a memory failure is due to encoding is the ineffectiveness of hints or clues to prompt memory. If I never knew my classmate's name was Denise Johnson, she could tell me her nickname, her initials, and her astrological sign—and I still wouldn't have a clue.

Try This!

If you're the kind of person who never heard a name you could remember, here's a trick to try the next time you meet someone new.

1. Discretely look for an unusual facial feature—ears, hairline, eyes, nose, complexion, or anything else that stands out.

2. Create a mental association between that characteristic, the person's whole face, and the name. You can build this association in a couple of ways:

   a. Associate the person with someone else you know (Jack Sjinski has Uncle Jack's nose).

   b. You might make up a rhyme or image (visualize Jack Sjinski skiing down the tip of his nose).

Alternatively, maybe during my high school years I was a conniving social climber and Denise didn't fit my idea of the popular crowd. Maybe I learned Denise's name long enough to ask her for a favor a few times, but then didn't think it was important to remember on a regular basis. In this case, my failure to remember her name today would be due to a *storage* problem. That's what happens when you look up a phone number, hold it in your head long enough to dial the number, and then forget it a few seconds later.

Memory Tests

When teachers give us tests, they aren't just measuring our capacity for learning. They're also measuring our ability to remember what we've learned. Common sense might tell us that we either know something or we don't, so that any method of testing will give us the same results. Not so. The way we're tested can have a lot of influence over the results, because different types of tests engage our retrieval system differently.

Shrink Rap

Amnesia is the partial or complete loss of memory, and can be caused by physical or psychological factors. Psychologically based amnesia can be triggered by a traumatic event; memory almost always returns after a few days. Soap operas aside, very rarely does a person lose his memory for large portions of his life.

For instance, keeping your eyes on this line, tell me the three mental operations that are required for memory. No peeking! Did you remember them? If not, see if you can recognize them from this multiple choice:

retrieval

categorization

storage

encoding

filing

Encoding, storage, and retrieval are the three mental operations required for memory. If you couldn't recall all three, but you recognized them in the multiple-choice question, your recognition is better than your recall. Recall questions give fewer cues than recognition questions and thus seem "harder" to those taking the test. It is possible to learn information but have trouble retrieving it without those cues, although try telling that to your teacher after you've bombed an essay test!

The Long and Short of It

Think of memory in terms of threes. We've already gone over the three mental processes necessary for memory—encoding, storage, and retrieval. Each of these mental processes happens at least three times as the information makes its way through the three memory systems: sensory memory, working memory, and long-term memory.

Photographer at Work

Ever notice how you can still hear the sound of the television right after you turn it off? That's your sensory memory. Sensory memory holds an impression a split second longer than it's actually present, to make sure that you have time to register it. Its goal is to hold information long enough to give you a sense of continuity but short enough that it doesn't interfere with new information coming in.

Sensory memories capture impressions from all our senses. If the impression is a sound, the memory is called an *echoe,* while a visual sensory memory is called an *icon.* At the most, your sensory memory works for only a second or two, but what it lacks in stamina, it makes up for in volume. For example, if I showed you a picture with a bunch of words on it for only a fraction of a second, you could only say about four of the words before you started forgetting the rest. However, you'd be able to pick out as many as nine. It seems we can remember words faster than we can say them!

The Organic Data Processor

Working memory has more stamina than sensory memory, but it's no marathon runner; it only lasts for about 20 seconds. It works pretty hard for those 20 seconds, working through and sorting out information that has been transferred from either long-term or sensory memory. When information enters your working memory, it has already been reorganized into meaningful and familiar patterns. For example, when subjects are asked to recall lists of letters they have just seen, they are much more likely to confuse letters that sound similar—like B and T—than letters that look familiar. Yet another example of how misremembering teaches us about remembering!

Insight

Only about 5 percent of people truly have photographic memories, known technically as *eidetic imagery.* Such individuals can envision a previously viewed scene in their minds, as if they were experiencing the scene directly rather than scanning memory for traces or details. Apparently, such people are able to directly transfer their sensory impressions into long-term memory.

Insight

Advertisers know how to manipulate their prospective customers. One trick they use is "chunking": When they want customers to remember their business line, they'll get a phone number that clusters the numbers into meaningful patterns. How does it work? Well, if I wanted you to buy my hot new psychology product, which number would you remember—1-800-568-3362 or 1-800-LOVE-DOC?

Working memory deals exclusively with the here-and-now, preserving recent experiences or events. Because it is short term, its capacity is limited. When the items are unrelated, like the digits of a telephone number, you can hold between five and nine bits of information in your working memory. There are, however, strategies that expand your working memory and you use at least one of them all the time. When you look up a phone number and repeat it before you dial, you're using a rehearsal strategy to enhance your working memory.

The Curious Curator

Just as a museum curator takes care of historical artifacts, your long-term memory collects and stores all the experiences, events, facts, emotions, skills, and so forth that have been transferred from your sensory and short-term memory. The information ranges from your mom's birthday to calculus equations. Essentially, the information in long-term memory is your library of knowledge of the world; without it, you'd be lost.

Long-term memory stores words and concepts according to their meaning, and files them next to similar words and concepts already in your memory. The smallest unit of meaning that you can store is a *proposition:* an idea that expresses the relationship between ideas, objects, or events. "Men are from Mars, women are from Venus" is a proposition about men and women. "Trees have green leaves" is another proposition. Some psychologists believe these propositions are the building blocks of long-term memory, while others believe we store verbal information in propositions and visual information in images.

Psychobabble

One of the strangest neurological disorders is Korsakoff's syndrome. Korsakoff's sufferers are fully alert and conscious, but are often unable to store information longer than a few seconds before they forget it. Perhaps in an attempt to compensate for their memory deficits, these patients frequently make up elaborate and convincing memories of events that never happened, and more than one medical professional has believed them.

Visiting the Museum

We all have different "artifacts" in our mental museum, but the structure of the "building" looks remarkably similar for each of us. It can be helpful to think of your memory museum as having two wings, with each holding different kinds of information. These wings are actually two types of long-term memory—*procedural* and *declarative*.

I Was Only Following Procedure

The procedural "wing" of your memory museum stores information about how things are done. Remembering how to ride a bicycle, tie your shoelaces, and put on your makeup are all stored in your procedural memory. All of the skills you learn consist of small action sequences, and it is these skill memories that get implanted in your long-term memory.

Shrink Rap

Procedural memory is the long-term memory for how things are done. **Declarative memory** stores the "who, what, when, where, and why"; it is the part of long-term memory that holds information and facts.

Skill memories are amazingly hardy. Even if you haven't ridden a bike in 30 years, the memory comes back amazingly fast once you have your behind on the seat and your feet on the pedals. The frustrating thing about skill memories, though, is that they are difficult to communicate to others. Ask a gold medal gymnast to tell you exactly how she does her stuff on the balance beam, and she can't. And if she tries to consciously think it through while she's doing it, chances are her performance won't be as good.

Well, I Declare!

Declarative memory, on the other hand, deals with the facts. It is the part of our memory that allows us to survive school, win at *Trivial Pursuit,* and win friends and influence people. Unlike procedural memory, declarative memory requires conscious effort, as evidenced by all the eye rolling and facial grimaces that you see on the faces of people taking their SATs. Remembering the directions to the dance studio is an example of declarative memory; remembering how to dance is procedural.

Insight

Research indicates that all of us have some degree of amnesia. Most of us can accurately recall what has happened in the last half of our lives. If you're 20 years old, you can remember the past 10 years. If you're 60, your memory's good for the last 30. Your 10-year-old child can recall the last five. For most of us, the rest is a blur.

The declarative wing of your memory museum has two rooms, one for *episodic memory,* the other for *semantic memory.* Episodic memory stores autobiographical information, such as thoughts, feelings, and things that happen to us. Semantic memory is more like an encyclopedia; it stores the basic meaning of words and concepts.

One way we know that episodic memory is different from procedural memory is the way it is organized. For example, when autobiographical information enters long-term memory, it is tagged with the time it happened and the context in which it took place—a kind of marking that doesn't appear to happen with information stored in procedural memory.

On the other hand, you probably can't remember exactly when or where you learned your multiplication tables. When you do remember when or where you learned factual information, it is often because an emotional experience was attached to it. My brother remembers when and where he learned his multiplication tables because he was rapped on the knuckles several times for not practicing them as part of his third grade homework. As in my brother's case, sometimes episodic memory can greatly assist semantic recall!

Now, *Where* Did I Put That Thought?

It happens to most of us about once a week. You see someone you've known for years, yet his or her name suddenly eludes you. You remember other things about this person, like where you met or past conversations you've had. But, temporarily, his or her name escapes you. Frustrated, you exclaim, "But it's right on the tip of my tongue!"

The tip-of-the-tongue experience has intrigued psychologists since the 1800s. Long-term memory preserves information for retrieval at any later time; a tip-of-the-tongue experience appears to be a breakdown in this retrieval process. Putting information into memory is half the battle, but you still have to find it when you need it.

Retrieval failure demonstrates an important concept in long-term memory—the difference between accessibility and availability. Your relationship with long-term memory is kind of like a crush; just because the object of your affection is single (available) doesn't mean he or she is interested in you (accessible). Sometimes, long-term memories are available somewhere in your mental filing cabinet, but you can't access them.

Generally, when you're trying to retrieve a memory, you'll simply use *retrieval cues*. These are prompts to help you recover information from memory. An example of such prompts would be the options presented on a multiple-choice test—they help you recognize the material you learned the night before.

Another retrieval aid is something most of us do frequently: When you're trying to remember where you put your car keys, you'll probably try to retrace your steps from the time you last saw them. Or you might think about where you've found those darned keys all the other times you've misplaced them. In either case, your internal retrieval cues help you remember.

Retrieval cues are helpful because they capitalize on your memory's natural tendency to organize and store related concepts and experiences together. Of course, if you'd just put the keys in the same place every time, you wouldn't be having this trouble to begin with! And, as you're about to see, you wouldn't have so many retrieval failures if you encoded it right in the first place.

Shrink Rap

Retrieval cues are mental or environmental aids that help us retrieve information from long-term memory.

Will You Gain Wisdom or Grow Senile?

If I had a dime for every joke I've heard about "old" people and memory problems, I'd be sipping Piña Coladas in Tahiti right now! For years, physicians believed forgetfulness is an inevitable part of growing old. Many elderly people still do; they consistently list memory problems among the most critical ones they face. But are these beliefs accurate?

It depends on what kind of memory you're talking about. For example, aging has relatively little effect on short-term memory. Young adults and seniors differ, on the average, by less than one digit in the number of numbers they can hold in short-term memory.

Insight

Alzheimer's disease causes brain deterioration in middle or later life, usually after age 65. Family history plays a role in about 40 percent of people with early-onset Alzheimer's. There's no way to prevent it, but some studies have offered tentative leads at reducing the risk.

Coming to (Memory) Terms

Some information in short-term memory is transferred and stored in long-term memory. It is this kind of memory that elderly adults have in mind when they complain about forgetfulness. Their most prominent complaint is remembering the names of people they met recently. Laboratory tests (using lists of words to be remembered) reveal that a moderate decline in memory for recent events accompanies normal aging. Some elderly adults remember as well as many young adults, indicating that this decline is a general pattern and not the inevitable fate for every person over 60.

Long-term memory for remote events (things that happened years ago) is pretty consistent over time. All of us forget personal information at some point during the first five to six years after it's been acquired. What's left after that usually sticks around. In general, elderly adults do have more trouble remembering some things—like when pain medication was last taken (temporal memory) and where they left their umbrella (spatial memory), but if they use cues as reminders of things that need to be done (for example, leaving out the empty cereal box as a reminder to go to the grocery store), they are no more absent-minded than the rest of us.

You Can Always Make a List

What does all this mean? While I can't promise you that you'll gain wisdom in your golden years, you can rest assured that your memory doesn't have to trip you up as you age. When memory problems do exist, the use of written reminders and visual cues is highly effective at minimizing their impact. So, quit worrying about losing your marbles and concentrate on putting more marbles in there!

Get It Right in the First Place

The way we put information in has a lot to do with how easily we can get it out. Have you ever studied for a multiple-choice test and then been ambushed by an essay exam? It's not a good feeling. No matter how prepared you were for multiple choice, chances are you didn't do so well with the essays. If we're smart, the way we prepare for an essay test is by memorizing the "big picture"—general information about the topic, broad concepts, and an overall analysis of the material. On the other hand, concrete facts and specific distinctions are most easily translated into multiple-choice tests.

Since long-term memory stores information logically and meaningfully, it makes sense to organize information when you first encode it in memory. Let's say you are really interested in the psychology of memory and want to maximize the chances you'll remember the information in this chapter. One of the best encoding strategies was developed by Francis Robinson in 1970. It's the SQ3R method:

S = Survey

Q = Question

3R = Read, Recite, Review

Here's how to use the SQ3R method to remember this chapter:

Survey the chapter subheadings and get an idea of how the material is organized.

Develop specific **questions** concerning each subheading. (What is memory? What is the difference between short- and long-term memory? Why do we forget? What is repressed memory, and is it real?)

Read the chapter and write down the answers to the questions you have raised.

When you have finished reading and answering, **recite** the answers to the questions back to yourself without looking up the answer.

Now, **review** the material again and continue to recite the answers to each of the questions.

The SQ3R method makes the most of your long-term memory's natural organizer. By getting the lay of the land before you dive into the material, you're helping your brain decide how to organize the material. Breaking down the material into smaller parts helps your memory file the information in a way that will be most useful to you. By asking and answering your own questions, you're making the information personally meaningful. Rehearsing the information several different ways helps you store the information. And, of course, taking the time to use these encoding strategies helps you overcome one of the biggest personality traits that leads to forgetfulness—plain, old-fashioned laziness!

Hooked on Mnemonics

"Use *i* before *e* except after *c*." "Thirty days hath September, April, June, and November." "In 1492, Columbus sailed the ocean blue." No, I haven't regressed back to the third grade. I'm giving you examples of *mnemonics:* short, verbal devices that encode a long series of facts by associating them with familiar and previously encoded information.

In the world of grownups, acronyms and jingles are commonly used mnemonics. AT&T is a lot easier to remember than American Telephone and Telegraph. Marketers weren't born yesterday; they regularly use jingles and rhymes to build product recognition and keep that annoying commercial playing in your head long after you've changed the channel.

Shrink Rap

Mnemonics are short, verbal strategies that improve and expand our ability to remember new information by storing it with familiar and previously encoded information.

Mnemonics are very effective memory aids. They not only help us encode the information in a creative and distinctive way, they make it much easier for us to recall it when we need it. Psychological research has studied three types of mnemonic strategies:

1. natural language mediators
2. the method of loci
3. visual imagery

Using *natural language mediators* involves associating new information with already stored meanings or spellings of words. Creating a story to link items together is an example of using natural language mediators. For instance, to remember the three stages of memory, you might say to yourself, "It doesn't make sense (sensory memory) that she's working (working memory) so long (long-term memory)."

The *method of loci* could help you remember a grocery list. Imagine a familiar place, like your office or bedroom, and mentally place the items on various objects around the room. When you need to recall them, you take a trip around the room and retrieve them.

Visual imagery is a third mnemonic device. In this method, you just create vivid mental pictures of your grocery items. Mentally picturing

Insight

Getting ready for a high school reunion? Get out that yearbook and you're sure to be "Most Popular." Forty-eight years after graduation, students were only able to recall 20 percent of their schoolmates' names. After looking at old photos, though, they could name them 90 percent of the time.

a cat mixing *shampoo* and *eggs* to make *cat food* would certainly create a lasting impression on your memory.

Mnemonics Boosters

When it comes to mnemonics, all images are not created equal. Here are five tips for boosting the power of your mnemonics:

1. Use positive, pleasant images. The brain often blocks out unpleasant ones.
2. Use humor. Funny or peculiar things are easier to remember than normal ones. (Yes, rude or sexual rhymes or images work, too.)
3. Vivid, colorful images are easier to remember than dull ones.
4. Use all the senses. Give your visual images voices, smells, touch, taste, and feelings.
5. Give your images movement.

Warning: Under Construction

Your memories are often under construction. They can change with time and are influenced by your past history, current values, and future expectations. In addition, they can be strengthened, or even built, by social influence. Piaget believed that his false memory (discussed earlier in this chapter) developed as a result of the numerous accounts he heard of the kidnapping; over time, he thought, he must have unconsciously turned the kidnapping story into a vivid visual memory. His memory was "real" to him, but "false" in reality.

How accurate and reliable is memory? It's a hard worker, but it gets easily confused. Memory studies show that we often construct our memories after the fact, and that we are susceptible to suggestions from others that help us fill in any gaps. One way a police officer can screw up a victim's identification of an assailant is by showing a photograph of the suspect in advance of the lineup. When this happens, the lineup is contaminated by the photograph—it is impossible to know whether the victim recognizes the suspect from the crime scene or the photograph.

And don't rely on your gut instincts to improve your memory. Studies have clearly shown that a feeling of certainty about a memory means nothing about whether your memory is accurate. If you really want to be sure your memory is accurate, your best bet is to do some detective work and look for corroborating evidence!

The Truth About False Memories

In 1990, teenager Donna Smith began therapy with Cathy M., a private social worker who specialized in child abuse. Although Donna had entered treatment reporting that she had been sexually abused by a neighbor at age three, Cathy M. repeatedly interrogated Donna about her father. After several months of pressured questioning by her therapist, Donna lied and said her father had "touched" her. When her therapist reported her father to the authorities, Donna tried to set the record straight, only to be told by her therapist that all abuse victims tried to recant their stories.

Donna was confused and continued to work with Cathy M., who continued to make suggestions and reinforce any suggestion of incest. Over the course of several months, Donna actually came to believe her father had been a chronic sexual abuser. She began "remembering" him practicing ritual satanic abuse on her younger brothers. Only after she was placed in foster care away from her therapist did Donna regain her perspective and the courage to tell the truth. By this time, her family was emotionally and financially devastated.

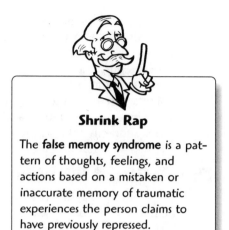

Shrink Rap

The **false memory syndrome** is a pattern of thoughts, feelings, and actions based on a mistaken or inaccurate memory of traumatic experiences the person claims to have previously repressed.

Sorting the True from the False

Unfortunately, Donna's experience is not an isolated incident. There are similar stories of adults who enter therapy to resolve some conflict or gain happiness and, with the therapist's "support," suddenly start remembering traumatic abuse or incest. As these "repressed" memories are unleashed, the person may take long-delayed action such as criminal prosecution or public denouncement.

Psychobabble

Are memories of past lives false? In 1952, therapist Morey Bernstein hypnotized Virginia Tighe. Virginia immediately began speaking in an Irish brogue and claimed she was redheaded Bridey Murphy, a nineteenth-century woman from Cork, Ireland. The news spread, and reporters went to Ireland to investigate. They found her, all right, except she wasn't in a grave across the sea. They found her in Chicago; Bridey Murphy Corkell was a neighbor who lived right across the street from where Virginia grew up!

But while false memories do occur, by no means are most memories of child sexual abuse false. Given that studies estimate that one out of every four girls will be sexually exploited before the age of 18, odds are that anyone who remembers child sexual abuse is telling the truth. The rare occurrence of false memory is likely to happen when a vulnerable person hooks up with a therapist who, intentionally or not, implants false memories through hypnotic suggestion, by asking leading questions, and/or by defining "abuse" and "incest" so broadly that, in retrospect, innocent actions suddenly take on menacing meaning.

The Political Problems

As you might imagine, the false memory syndrome is a political hot potato. On the one hand, survivors of sexual abuse have fought a long and hard battle to gain credibility, protection, and help. On the other hand, the concern remains that there is no scientific evidence for repression of multiple traumatic events that happen over an extended period of time. Still, there is the very real fear that a few misguided therapists and their clients could undermine the true stories of thousands of others. Whatever is the outcome of this heated controversy, we can all agree that our society will not benefit from having more victims—neither victims of sexual abuse nor victims of false memory.

Exploring Repressed Memories

I vividly remember the exact moment the space shuttle *Challenger* exploded in 1986. I was in my tiny office at work and my colleague Jan came running in to tell me about it. My mom has a vivid recollection of where she was and what she was doing when she heard that John F. Kennedy had been assassinated. Nineteenth-century researchers discovered the same phenomenon when they asked people what they were doing when they heard that Abraham Lincoln had been shot.

These memories are called *flashbulb memories,* long-lasting and deep memories in response to traumatic events. Not everyone has flashbulb memories and not every tragic situation causes them. Recent research, in fact, has questioned the validity of the flashbulb effect, but what it does support is our tendency to remember upsetting or traumatic events.

Real-life traumas in children and adults—such as school ground shootings or natural disasters—are generally well remembered. Complete amnesia for these terrifying episodes is virtually nonexistent. People who have repeated war traumas, even children, generally remember their experiences. In fact, many of them report having great difficulty getting the events out of their dreams or minds; they can't repress them even though they want to.

We know that people forget things. We know that people later remember things that they had forgotten earlier. And psychologists generally agree that it is quite common to consciously repress unpleasant experiences, even sexual abuse, and to spontaneously remember such events long afterward.

Intuitively, the ability to block out repeated childhood trauma seems like a pretty good survival strategy; if you can't get away from it physically, at least you can in your mind. However, until we have more evidence, Sigmund Freud's idea that we might store the memory of traumatic events in a place outside of our unconscious will stay up in the air.

I can tell you that I've had therapy clients who were victims of documented incest (the perpetrator had confessed and been sent to prison), and yet siblings who were also victims claimed to have no memory at all that abuse had occurred.

Shrink Rap

A **repressed memory** is the memory of a traumatic event retained in the unconscious mind, where it is said to affect conscious thoughts, feelings, and behaviors even though there is no conscious memory of the alleged trauma.

The Least You Need to Know

➤ Your memory doesn't mind very well—it often misremembers, forgets, and makes mistakes.

➤ The three mental operations required for memory are encoding (putting information in), storage (filing it away), and retrieval (finding it). Forgetting is a failure in one of these areas.

➤ While elderly adults seem to have more problems remembering recent events, using written reminders and other memory strategies can minimize their impact.

➤ Mnemonics are very effective memory aids that help us store information in a way that we can easily recall it later on.

➤ False memories can fool us. Although not likely, it is possible to remember serious childhood trauma that never happened.

➤ The truth about repression is still up in the air. Most people remember ongoing traumatic events.

Part 3

The Forces Are with You

What's the most important thing a detective looks for when solving a crime? Elementary, my dear Watson: It's motivation, of course. Almost all of human behavior is driven by motives—whether or not we're conscious of them at the time. Here's where you'll get the scoop on the major motives that drive us to do the things we do, and how we can harness our motivations to make our lives better.

Chapter 9

What's Your Motive?

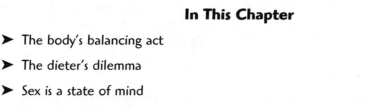

In This Chapter

➤ The body's balancing act

➤ The dieter's dilemma

➤ Sex is a state of mind

➤ The roots of sexual orientation

➤ The thirst for power and the drive to achievement

Motivation is what makes us do what we do. But where does motivation come from? And how do we get more of it? How do we stick to our diet, study when we feel like sleeping, and keep going when life tries to knock us down?

In this chapter, we'll explore the drives that power human behavior. We'll explore juicy motives like hunger and sex, and you'll see why you need them and what you'll do to get them. We'll explore the mind-motive connection, and the pluses and minuses of having a brain that can influence our base instincts. And we'll visit some of the "higher" motives, such as the need for achievement, and give you a chance to find out what motives drive you to work every day.

Running on Willpower

Wilma Rudolph was the seventeenth of 19 children. At the age of four, she had polio, scarlet fever, and double pneumonia. She didn't walk again until she was 11. And yet,

Insight

Understanding and applying the principles of motivation can accelerate learning, improve performance, increase perseverance, and overcome obstacles. How much more motivation do you need?

in spite of all these obstacles, at the age of 20, she won three gold medals in the Olympics and set a women's record for the 200 meter run.

Wilma Rudolph is a testament to the power of motivation. Nothing could stop her. She was so driven that, in one race, she twisted her ankle and yet still managed to come in first. Odds that would have prevented many people from leading a normal life never stopped her from leading an exceptional one.

It's a Jungle in Here

How are you feeling right now? Hungry? Sleepy? Angry? How you feel will affect your ability to focus on this chapter. If you're hungry, fantasies of home cooking may get sandwiched in between these appetizing paragraphs. If you're sleepy, you might respond to my wittiest comments with, "Oh hmmm … zzzzzz."

Your mental state will also cause you to pay attention to some things over others. If you're feeling down, you might have started out reading the chapter on mood disorders. If you're trying to diet but having a little problem keeping the refrigerator closed, this chapter might have caught your eye. Clearly, your mental state affects your thoughts and your actions.

But what makes you hungry, or sleepy, or angry? What causes you to behave in a certain way at a particular time? When we look at the complexity of human motivation, one thing becomes clear: It isn't just a jungle out *there*. It's a jungle in *here*, too.

Shrink Rap

Motivation is the physical and psychological process that drives us toward a certain goal. If the "push" comes from within, we call it a **drive**; if it comes from an external source, we call it an **incentive**.

Let's Get Motivatin'

When psychologists use the term *motivation,* they're talking about all of the factors, inside us and in the world around us, that cause us to behave in a particular way at a particular time. Lots of things, like our genes, our learning histories, our personalities, and our social experiences, all contribute to motivation. Internal conditions that push us toward a goal are called *drives.* External motivations are called *incentives.*

Motivated behavior is always directed toward an incentive—the sought-after object or result that will satisfy a drive. My hunger drive sends me heading toward the refrigerator and the mint chocolate-chip ice cream in the freezer is an incentive for me to walk a little faster.

Hungry Like a Wolf

Drives and incentives always complement each other. If one is weak, the other must be strong enough to motivate the goal-directed behavior. If the only thing in the fridge is cottage cheese, I've got to be pretty darned hungry to traipse to the refrigerator. Of course, if I'm hungry enough, even cottage cheese can look pretty tasty. So, not only can drives and incentives influence one another, they can also influence each other's strength; hypothetically, at least, I could be full enough so that even mint chocolate-chip ice cream wouldn't be very appealing.

Professors wonder whether students who fail exams "aren't motivated enough." Coaches speculate that winning teams were "hungrier" and "more motivated" than their opponents. Detectives seek to establish the motive for crimes. Clients come to therapy looking for the motivation to quit bingeing. Not only is motivation one of the most commonly used psychological terms, it's something we never seem to have enough of!

What Drives Your Body?

If you were attracted to psychology because of all the big words, you'll like this one: *homeostasis.* Homeostasis is the equilibrium our bodies must maintain to keep us alive. For example, body temperature, oxygen, minerals, and water must be kept within a certain range, going neither too high nor too low. When our equilibrium is off, our bodies encourage us to take action to regain our balance. When you chug a quart of water after running a few miles, your motivation to drink is an upset in homeostatic balance, and your behavior is designed to correct it. You can even blame your high air-conditioning bills on homeostasis; when you're too hot, your body signals you to find cooler temperatures!

Psychobabble

Your body is wiser than you think. D.W. was a year old when he developed a craving for salt. His favorite foods were loaded with salt, *salt* was one of the first words he used, and, when salt was denied to him, he would pitch a fit until his parents gave in. When D.W. was hospitalized at age $3\frac{1}{2}$ for other symptoms, medical staff would not yield to his demand for salt. He died within a few days. An autopsy subsequently revealed that his adrenal glands didn't work; his strong drive for salt, and his ability to manipulate his parents into providing it, had kept him alive for $2\frac{1}{2}$ years.

Homeostasis is helpful in understanding thirst, hunger, and our need for oxygen, salt, and temperature control. But many things that motivate us aren't necessarily for our immediate survival. Take sex. Most of us are pretty motivated by it, but despite what an overly amorous paramour may have told you, nobody can die from lack of sex.

Psychologists have puzzled over this glitch in the homeostasis theory until their puzzlers were sore. To solve this dilemma, they distinguish between *regulatory* drives that are necessary for physiological equilibrium, and *nonregulatory drives,* like sex, that serve some other purpose. Although, as you're about to see, even regulatory drives like hunger can have hidden motives.

Investigating Motives

Psychologists must always infer motives from behaviors—after all, you can't *observe* motives directly. If you're eating, it's fair to assume that you're hungry. If you're drinking (water, at least), you must be thirsty. Psychologists are constantly looking for links between the stimuli (including conditions and situations) that lead to motivation, and the responses (behaviors) that are produced by motivational states. For example, do food commercials trigger hunger motives which lead to eating?

They also look for the "whodunit" in your behavior, which, in this case, refers to the brain. In the early 1950s, scientists began poking around in the brains of animals to see which parts controlled what drives. They'd either create lesions to remove any stimulation from reaching that part of the brain, or they'd plant electrodes that would provide more stimulation. Then they'd watch to see what happened. What they observed formed the basis of a lot of what we know today about human drives, particularly hunger.

Insight

I always remember that the hypothalamus has to do with hunger, maybe because the word *hypothalamus* reminds me of hippopotamus and that reminds me of fat. If that association works for you, please feel free to use it. In reality, the hypothalamus can make us fat or skinny, depending on what part of the hypothalamus you're talking about.

The Mystery of Hunger

In the 1950s, scientists discovered the hunger-hypothalamus connection. They found that animals with lesions to the lateral area of the hypothalamus were completely disinterested in food. These animals would literally starve to death if they weren't force-fed through a tube. On the other hand, if the lateral part of the hypothalamus was stimulated, the animals would gorge themselves. Excited, these researchers quickly proclaimed the lateral hypothalamus as the "hunger center" of the brain.

Inside the Pleasure Dome

If you're looking for a scapegoat to blame those few extra pounds on, don't jump the gun. Later experiments showed that the hypothalamus was interested in a lot more than food. When researchers presented these same overly stimulated animals with other incentives, like sexual partners, access to water, or nest-building materials, these animals engaged in a frenzy of behavior that matched whatever incentive was provided. If sexual partners were available, they had an orgy. If water was handy, they drank it until they were about to explode!

While stimulation to the lateral part of the hypothalamus causes bingeing, manipulating another part of the hypothalamus, the ventromedial part, has the opposite effect. Animals that have lesions in this area are hungry and overeat; stimulation here causes the animal to stop eating. Occasionally, a tumor at the base of the brain damages this area in humans, and, in such cases, the person becomes extremely obese.

Is Your Hunger in Your Head?

We've come a long way in understanding the roots of the hunger drive. It's now believed that a tract of neurons running through the hypothalamus was actually responsible for the initial research findings. This bunch of neurons isn't actually part of the hypothalamus; they just travel through it on their journey from the brainstem to the basal ganglia. Also, as previously noted by the frenzy of activity, this tract seems to be part of a general activation system—stimulation seems to give the message "you've got to do something." What that "something" is depends upon the available incentives.

We're All Picky Eaters

When it comes to hunger, the hypothalamus isn't completely innocent. It has neurons that, at the very least, can modify your appetite. When researchers destroy parts of the lateral hypothalamus, lab animals cut back on their eating but don't completely quit. They eat enough to survive, but at a lower-than-normal weight, and most of their other drives are normal. No, this procedure isn't available in humans!

To see if the lateral hypothalamus did indeed play a role in hunger, and wasn't just a thoroughfare for that tract of hungry neurons, researchers implanted very tiny electrodes in this part of a monkey's brain. What they found is that the hypothalamus is a picky eater.

First of all, the monkey would only become excited by food if it was hungry and food was available. The cells would become active when the hungry monkey saw or smelled food, but not when the monkey was exposed to stimuli that had never been associated with food. In

Insight

Apparently, the beginning of a new year is not enough motivation for most of us to shed extra pounds. At the stroke of midnight every New Year's Eve, more than 130 million Americans make weight loss a New Year's resolution. Only 14 percent will keep it.

addition, the hypothalamus would get "tired" of certain foods; if it had eaten several bananas, the cells would stop responding to that food but would continue to respond to peanuts and oranges!

What all this means to us, then, is that the hunger motive involves a part of the brain that is programmed to respond to food cues when we're hungry. When we're not hungry, those same food cues would leave us cold, at least from a physiological perspective. If you've ever been on a diet and found yourself drooling over every food commercial, your response is literally "all in your head"! It's in your brain.

The Dieter's Dilemma

Let's get a few things straight. Your weight has little to do with willpower. Studies show that thin people have no more willpower than fat people do. Skinny people are not more conscientious, or less anxious. They are not morally superior. In fact, fat people and thin people do not differ on any personality characteristics.

But don't obese people eat more than people of normal weight? Maybe. It does appear that people who are overweight eat more in response to stress. However, all dieters, regardless of their weight, are more likely to eat in response to stress; the weight difference between stress eaters and nonstress eaters may be that overweight people are more likely to be on a diet. Stress can make all of us vulnerable to the munchies, but if we've been fighting hunger cues already, we're more likely to give into temptation.

Mmmmmm, It's So Appetizing!

Another challenge for dieters is our culture's *appetizer effect,* which tricks our bodies' normal methods of food-regulation. Here's how this works: All of us have built-in bodily signals for hunger and fullness. When we're hungry, our stomachs growl; when we're full, our stomachs send signals to the brain telling us to stop eating. The amount of sugar (glucose) in the blood also cues our bodies to start, or stop, eating; high blood sugar says stop, low blood sugar says go. And our fat cells secrete a hormone, *leptin,* at a rate that is proportional to the amount of fat being stored in our cells. The greater the amount of leptin, the less our hunger drive is stimulated.

The problem is that our hunger isn't just dictated by the amount of food in the stomach, blood, or fat cells. Our environment can have a powerful influence. Any stimulus in our environment that reminds us of good food can increase our hunger drive—and that's where the *appetizer effect* kicks in.

Anyone who's ever had a second slice of pecan pie can attest to the fact that the appetizer effect, plus the

Shrink Rap

The **appetizer effect** occurs when hunger is stimulated by external stimuli, such as the smell or sight of food or food advertisements.

availability of yummy foods, can easily over-whelm his body's fullness signals. In addition, the appetizer effect can actually stimulate physical hunger. Just the smell of McDonald's french fries can cause our insulin to drop and cause us to head to the drive-through.

My Genes Made Me Do It!

Just in case you aren't completely bummed out by now, there's yet another reason why dieting is so hard. We each inherit a certain weight range, and it is difficult, without a major life change, to get below it. If your genetic weight range is between 120 and 140, you can comfortably maintain a weight of 120 through a healthy diet and regular exercise. If, however, you wouldn't be caught dead in a bathing suit until you're below 110 and are constantly dieting to reach this goal, you're setting yourself up for failure.

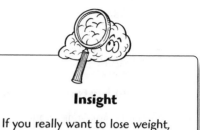

Insight

If you really want to lose weight, strike the word *diet* from your vocabulary forever. Instead, exercise five times a week (for at least 30 minutes), don't dip below 1,200 calories, quit depriving yourself of favorite foods, and get reacquainted with your body's hunger and fullness cues.

Even if you starve yourself down to this weight, you'll have a lot of trouble maintaining it. And, losing and regaining weight, known as *yo-yo dieting*, tends to make you fatter over time. In fact, while dieting is often promoted as a solution for weight gain, it is often what causes average-sized people to gain weight in the first place!

Come On, Baby, Light My Fire

Enough about food. Let's talk about sex. First of all, how interested are you in it? How much do you know about it? Interest and knowledge are not the same thing, and interest without knowledge can cause serious problems. Here's a little quiz to assess your knowledge about male and female sexuality.

Answer true or false to the following questions:

1. Men and women go through the same sequences and phases of sexual response. _____True _____False

2. Many women can have multiple orgasms, while men rarely do in a comparable time frame. _____True _____False

3. Penis size is generally unrelated to any aspect of sexual performance. _____True _____False

4. Women tend to get aroused more slowly, but often remain aroused much longer. _____True _____False

Brain Buster

If you've been complaining about "not getting enough" from your partner, take a deeper look. Masters and Johnson found that the frequency of sex was almost never the real problem—more likely, it was the quality of the sex, a lack of communication about sexual needs and interests, or unresolved feelings or conflict in the relationship.

Insight

If you're getting ready for a hot date, don't skimp on the cologne. A recent study found that a few whiffs of men's cologne actually increased physiological arousal in women. Maybe those advertisers aren't exaggerating as much as we thought!

If you answered true for all of them, go to the head of the class. Masters and Johnson shocked the nation when, in the 1960s, they began studying human sexuality by observing and recording what people actually did when they had sex. Surveys about American sexual behavior had been done before, but Masters and Johnson were well aware that people aren't always honest about what does or doesn't happen in the bedroom. Perhaps they had overheard one too many locker room bragging sessions and decided to see the truth with their own eyes.

What they saw were men and women exhibiting remarkably similar patterns of sexual arousal and response. Differences that did exist had to do with timing and stamina. Women were slower on the uptake, but once they got going, they could last longer than the Energizer Bunny. Men, on the other hand, got off to a faster start, but fizzled out sooner.

Penis size had nothing to do with any aspect of sexual performance, with one exception. Men who thought it mattered were less secure about their sexual prowess, leading the researchers to conclude that a man's attitude about his penis size could have a big impact on his sexuality even when his actual penis size doesn't. On the other hand, a big attitude can quickly make up for a small penis.

As it turns out, the same is true for a woman's feelings about her body. You don't have to be built like Cindy Crawford to enjoy a roll in the hay. And, if you believe it, your sexual confidence alone will turn a few heads!

Ready, Set, Blast Off

Both men and women go through four stages of sexual response. Hopefully you've experienced them for yourself. Just in case you haven't, or you want to see if your experience matches everybody else's, they are:

1. **Excitement.** This is the beginning of arousal. Everything heats up; blood rushes to your pelvis and your sex organs enlarge.

2. **Plateau.** This is the peak of arousal. You breathe faster, your heartbeat speeds up, and you get ready for the climax.

3. **Orgasm.** This is the release of sexual tension. Men ejaculate and women experience genital contractions.

4. **Resolution.** This is the letdown. The body gradually returns to normal.

Driving the Sex Machine

I hate to burst your bubble, but calling someone "an animal" in bed is not a compliment. When it comes to sex, we humans are much wilder and have a lot more fun. A lot of female animals, for example, only have intercourse at certain times of the month, while women are liberated from the control of their menstrual cycle. We can, and do, get turned on any time during the month. Among nonhuman animals, intercourse occurs in a stereotyped way. Among humans, sexual positions are limited only by our imagination. It'd be much more flattering for a rat to playfully paw her sexual partner and call him "a sexual human."

Those Sexy Hormones!

We do have some things in common with our less sexually evolved friends, however, and one of those things is hormones. In all mammals, including humans, the production of sex hormones speeds up at the onset of puberty. Men get jolted with testosterone and women get an estrogen charge. However, these famous hormones have a silent partner that gives us a head start in the sex department. This less-known helper, produced by our adrenal glands, is called *droepiandrosterone,* or *DHEA.*

Before we enter that tumultuous time called puberty, DHEA is already behind the scenes stirring things up. Boys and girls begin to secrete DHEA at about age six, and the amount rises until the midteens, where it stabilizes at adult levels. Most men and women recall their earliest clear feelings of sexual attraction as occurring about 10 years of age, well before the physical changes brought on by estrogen or testosterone. Research suggests that these feelings are brought on by DHEA.

Tanking Up on Testosterone

Once things get stirred up, though, testosterone keeps us stirred up. Testosterone maintains a man's sexual drive during adulthood by stimulating his desire; this hormone has little to do with sexual performance. Men castrated in accidents almost always experience a decline in their sex drive and behavior, and testosterone injections bring it back. Similarly, men with unusually low levels of testosterone show a dramatic increase in sex after a few booster shots. However, a couple of extra testosterone doses won't turn you into a sex maniac; if your testosterone is within normal limits, any additional amount doesn't seem to have any effect.

Psychobabble

Looking for a great sex partner? Look for a jazz-loving, politically active college graduate. A 1995 study of sex demographics found these three factors to be related to above-average sexual activity. Steer clear of those Ph.D.s, though; people who had completed graduate school may have bucks and brains, but they have sex less often than any other group!

In women, ovarian hormones like estrogen play a rather small role, if any, in our sex drive. Our adrenal glands play a larger one; they produce DHEA and, believe it or not, testosterone. Women who've had a hysterectomy rarely report a lower libido, while women whose adrenal glands have been removed generally do. Like men, women who complain of sexual disinterest also change their tune with a few testosterone treatments. When it comes to curing a lack of interest in sex, a little testosterone never hurt anybody!

Sex in Low Gear

Fabulous orgasms aside, sex is mainly in your head. Unlike other animals, what turns humans on has less to do with physiological need than with cognitive desires. We fantasize, we interpret sexual experiences, and we have sexual beliefs and values. Even the subjective experience of an orgasm can depend on interpersonal factors (feeling safe or liking a person) as well as physical stimulation. For humans, the real sex organ is the brain.

I Love You for Your Mind

The complexity of human sexuality is wonderful, but the rewards have their risks. Because human sexuality is as influenced by the mind as it is by the body, a number of physical and psychological factors can throw your sex drive out of gear. Traumatic sexual experiences, fears of pregnancy or disease, relationship conflict, performance pressure, and shameful messages about sexuality can reduce sexual desire and can even prevent your body from functioning normally. Physical causes include various drugs, medications, and chronic medical conditions. The causes of sexual difficulties are as varied and unique as the problems they cause.

When a person has ongoing difficulties, he or she may have a *sexual dysfunction*—a frequently occurring impairment during any stage of the sexual response cycle that prevents satisfaction from sexual activity. These disorders generally fall into four categories: sexual desire disorders, sexual arousal disorders, orgasm disorders, and sexual pain disorders. Interestingly, sexual dysfunctions are more common in the early adult years, with the majority of people seeking treatment during their late twenties and early thirties. The two most widely publicized disorders have been sexual arousal disorder in women and impotence in men.

Dealing with Dysfunction

The most effective treatment, of course, depends upon the nature of the sexual dysfunction. Some sexual dysfunctions, like arousal problems, tend to be psychological in nature, while others, like sexual pain disorder and impotence, can have numerous causes. In many situations, a combination of physical and psychological treatments is most effective.

Insight

Half of all men experience occasional impotence, and, for one out of every eight men, it's a chronic problem. With these stats, it's no wonder that Viagra, a drug that increases the body's ability to achieve and maintain an erection during sexual stimulation, has been heralded as a wonder drug.

Oriented Toward Sex

Clearly, human sexuality is pretty complicated. Even your most primitive sexual urges are often at the whim of your thoughts and feelings. And, while these thoughts and feelings can certainly add spark to your sex life, they can also dampen your ardor. Your sex drive can go up or down depending on a lot of physical and psychological factors.

Sexual orientation, however, is not a matter of "getting up" or "laying down." It's a different ballpark altogether, and its causes have been a matter of political debate and scientific inquiry. In fact, so many theories have been thrown around, so many political agendas mixed in with science, and so much misinformation distributed that it's hard to tease out truth from fiction.

Psychologists haven't exactly been at the forefront of the tolerance movement; in the 1980s, homosexuality was still classified as a mental disorder.

Birds Do It, Bees Do It

In the past, most psychologists argued that sexual orientation was learned. Some still do. However, as anyone with more than three brain cells can see, there are a few problems with this explanation. First of all, there is no evidence that the style of parenting, absence of a male or

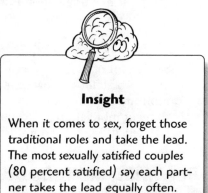

Insight

When it comes to sex, forget those traditional roles and take the lead. The most sexually satisfied couples (80 percent satisfied) say each partner takes the lead equally often.

female parent, or degree of opportunity for any type of sexual experience in adolescence contributes to the development of sexual orientation. Early seduction or rape by someone of the opposite or same sex does not cause it.

Second, between 1 percent and 5 percent of men and women are homosexual in every culture, with a larger percentage practicing bisexuality. This is true in cultures that accept homosexuality and in cultures that punish and outlaw it. If sexual orientation is learned, it's pretty darned hard to see the payoffs in doing something that might land you in jail.

Insight

The feeling of attraction to one sex or the other often exists for years before it is expressed. Considering how hard it can be to rid yourself of sexual feelings for a partner who's clearly bad for you, imagine trying to change your attraction toward an entire gender. It's almost impossible.

It's Just the Way It Is

We know genetic differences play some role in determining sexual orientation. Roughly 50 percent of identical twins share the same sexual orientation. In contrast, if you have a gay sibling, your chances of also being gay are about 15 percent, compared to the 1 percent to 5 percent of the general population.

The puzzle of sexual orientation is still a mystery, but recent studies suggest it is something we discover about ourselves, not something that we choose. Think about your own sexual orientation. When did you first know you were attracted to men or women? Homosexuals and heterosexuals alike say their sexual orientation was present in their childhood thoughts and fantasies, typically by age 10 or 11.

Did you consider all the alternatives and then consciously choose the one that felt right to you? Did you ever think you made a mistake or that you should give a different sexual orientation "a chance"? Chances are, at some point you just knew your sexual orientation, probably long before you understood it. Whatever its cause or causes, sexual orientation is a deeply rooted and early emerging aspect of ourselves.

In Search of Higher Ground

Sex is a lot of fun, but we can't spend all of our time doing it. In fact, in the late 1960s Abraham Maslow proposed the revolutionary idea that people are ultimately motivated to grow and reach their potential. At a time when most psychologists thought motivation was driven by a need to make up for some physical or psychological deficit, Maslow's optimistic view of human motivation was a breath of fresh air.

Beginning with Basics

Maslow would certainly agree that we have to put first things first—basic needs have to be met before we search for higher ground. If we're starving, worries about our self-esteem take a back seat. That fight you had with your best friend pales in comparison to the rumblies in your tummy. If you're hungry enough, even concern over whether you reset the house alarm might be forgotten in your race to the refrigerator. Let's face it: If you're hungry enough, you'd consider selling your firstborn for a hamburger.

Don't feel ashamed. Maslow would say your feelings are completely normal. How can you even think about anything else if your basic hunger drive is not being satisfied? Missionaries around the world often feed and clothe people before they try to convert them. They may not be licensed psychologists, but they understand at least one thing about human nature: The need for knowledge and understanding is not a priority until we're fed and clothed. It's impossible to climb to higher ground when we're stuck at the bottom of the ladder.

Moving On Up

Maslow believed our basic needs naturally formed a hierarchy, from primitive to more advanced goals. At the very bottom are our most basic biological needs, like hunger and thirst. The next rung up the ladder is our need for safety and security. In the middle are our needs for knowledge and a sense of belonging and, at the very top, are the spiritual needs that allow us to identify with all of mankind.

Of course, not all of us get to the top of the ladder before our time on earth runs out. If you were raised in the ambitious United States, chances are you got far enough up to reach a need for achievement. Let's take a look at a motive that, for better or worse, has made our country what it is today.

Brain Buster

Believe it or not, it's possible to be too motivated. While motivation energizes us on simple tasks, it can quickly disrupt our performance on difficult or more complex ones. A student who is highly motivated to do well on a test might perform better if she spent the last 30 minutes listening to a relaxation tape rather than studying.

The Need to Achieve

If you had to predict who would be a success in life, would you take the person with the highest IQ score, the best grades, or the strongest need to achieve? Personally, I'd pick the person motivated to do well. We all know bright people who chronically underachieve. And we also know some high school graduates who tanked the SATs and could now afford to buy the company that publishes them. In the long run, desire and perseverance exceeds talent or brains.

The "need for achievement," first identified by Harvard psychologist David Murray, refers to differences between individuals in their drive to meet a variety of goals. When your need for achievement is high, you're energized and focused toward success and motivated to continually evaluate and improve your performance. When channeled properly, this can be an organizing force in linking your thoughts, feelings,

Insight

The fastest way to turn play into work is to reward someone for something he already enjoys doing. Children who enjoyed reading were given gold stars as an added incentive, and the experiment backfired! It seems that being handed external rewards for doing something we genuinely like shifts the motivation outside of ourselves. As a result, when the reward is withdrawn, our enjoyment dwindles, too.

and actions. Taken to extreme, it can be a monkey on your back. Perfectionism is a need for achievement that has run haywire.

One of the most interesting ways the need for achievement influences us is in the way we approach a challenge. For instance, a group of subjects were presented with an impossible task that could not be solved. When people were told the task was difficult, those who had a high need to achieve kept trying longer than those who had a low need to achieve. Low-need achievers also kept at it, but only when they were told the task was easy. When the low-need achievers were told the task was difficult, they either didn't think it was worth the effort or weren't willing to spend it.

What Motive Works for You?

All of us work better when our jobs match our personal motivation. Psychologists David McClellan and John Atkinson studied motives that drive people in work situations. They found that all people have three motivational characteristics, and that their behavior is likely to be determined by the degree to which each is present. These three motives are:

> ➤ a need to achieve
> ➤ a need for power
> ➤ a need for affiliation

Let's take a brief look at each of these three in action. See if your motives would most likely steer you into politics, business, or nonprofit work.

Achievement in Action

At work, you appreciate a supervisor who gets down to business and lets you work independently. You hate for people to waste your time, and prefer to focus on the "bottom line" of what needs to be done. When you daydream, you are most likely to think about how to do a better job, how to advance your career, or how you can overcome the obstacles you are facing. You can motivate yourself well and like to succeed in situations that require outstanding performance.

The Thirst for Power

You want a supervisor who's a mover and shaker and can serve as a role model. You are good at office politics and know the best way to get to the top is by who you know and who they know. You have strong feelings about status and prestige and are good at influencing others and getting them to change their minds and/or behavior. When you daydream, you are most likely to think about how you can use your influence to win arguments or improve your status and/or authority. You like public speaking and negotiating.

The Team Player

You are a "people" person. You want a supervisor who is also your friend and who values who you are and what you do. You are excellent at establishing rapport with others and enjoy assignments that allow you to work within a group. You are very loyal and get many of your social needs met in your job. You are well liked; people may come to you with their problems and value your advice. You are great at planning company social functions and are often recruited to serve on the hospitality or banquet committee.

Human motives are fascinating, ranging from basic, universal needs for shelter, food, and clothing to complex, unique drives for self-esteem and achievement. Richard Nixon and Mother Theresa may have both needed to eat, but their "higher" motives led them down vastly different career paths. Whether you're a born Richard Nixon or Mother Theresa, though, there's one motivator that lights a fire under all of us. In the next chapter, we'll take a look at the motivational power of emotions.

The Least You Need to Know

➤ Our bodies seek to maintain homeostasis, or balance—if our equilibrium is off, our body signals us to take action to fix it.

➤ The hunger drive is a strong part of our body's balancing act, but not all hunger is based on bodily needs—strong food cues from the environment can cause physical hunger even if we don't need food.

➤ Human beings are the sexiest creatures on the planet, with a wider sexual repertoire and an ability to respond to a number of physical and psychological stimuli.

➤ Sexual orientation is much more of a discovery about oneself than a conscious choice. It is determined early and is very rarely changed.

➤ Until basic survival needs are met, it's hard to be concerned with love, self-improvement, or spirituality.

➤ At work, people may be motivated by a need for power, achievement, or affiliation, or a combination of the three.

Chapter 10

Emotions in Motion

In This Chapter

➤ Finding the source of your feelings

➤ Tuning in to your body

➤ Who's in charge here?

➤ What's your emotional IQ?

➤ Managing your everyday moods

The movie *October Sky* tells the true story about a small coal mining town and an exceptional boy who lived there. The threat of injury or death in the coal mines was constant. Whenever the siren sounds, the townspeople know that someone, perhaps a loved one, has been seriously injured. You could feel the constant strain the wives faced as they spent their lives waiting for tragic news.

The mine foreman repeatedly places himself in danger as time and again he rushes to the rescue of his coworkers. In one poignant scene, his wife, with a look of fear, exhaustion, and anger on her face, turns to her son and says, "Your father always has to be a hero. If he dies, I swear I won't shed a tear."

How do couples maintain their love in the face of constant danger? How do the spouses of firefighters and police officers kiss them good-bye every day, knowing each time that this could be the last time they see them? In the face of stress, do we learn to ration our emotions? Do we gradually lose our ability to feel? This chapter explores the psychology of emotions; how we feel and express them, how our culture influences them, what purpose they serve, and how we can handle our own moods more effectively.

Hooked on a Feeling

The powerful love between Romeo and Juliet. The bitter rivalry between Caesar and Mark Anthony. The passion of Martin Luther King Jr. When it comes to human beings, emotions move us. Whether we admit it or not, our emotions guide much of what we do; they focus our attention, help us record experiences more strongly in our memory, and arouse us.

Most of us equate emotions with feelings. We feel angry, sad, afraid, or happy. But, in reality, emotions are much more complicated. When we feel an emotion, we experience a complex pattern of physical arousal, feelings, and thoughts in response to a personally significant situation. Imagine your boss humiliating you in front of your coworkers. Not only would you feel angry, you would think angry thoughts. You might find yourself plotting revenge or obsessing over why he or she did that. And, while your blood wouldn't literally boil, your heart would beat faster and your blood pressure would rise.

Your emotions would stimulate you to take action. You might yell or cry in the privacy of your office. You might spit in his or her coffee cup when he or she wasn't look-

Insight

Think you can hide your feelings from your children? Think again. By age five, children can recognize surprise, disgust, happiness, sadness, anger, and fear about as well as most college students.

ing. If it happened often enough, you might quit your job. Or you might decide to reframe your boss' rude behavior as his or her problem, and not take it so personally. No matter what you do, you are responding to your emotions; they have signaled danger and geared you for action.

How angry you get about your boss' rude behavior will depend on how personally significant the situation is to you. Situations that are perceived as highly threatening or highly rewarding will be highly emotional. If your boss's opinion is important to you, or if his or her comments challenge your sense of self-worth, you'll feel much angrier than if you discount what he says or refuse to take it personally. Similarly, if you had a great time on a first date, you're going to be much

more disappointed if he or she never calls you again. You've had a taste of the rewards, and now they've been taken away!

Adjust Your Attitude and Improve Your Love Life!

For many of us, adjusting our attitudes about emotions would greatly enhance our relationships. For example, one of the easiest mistakes to make in your interactions with other people is assuming that there's a "right" amount of emotional intensity for any situation—that the only "right" amount is the amount you personally feel. So it's easy to think that someone who feels more strongly than you do is "overreacting." And, of course, when you try to "help" him by pointing this out, he blows a fuse!

Certainly, some people are hotheads and some people are unusually sensitive. However, most of the time, people have emotional reactions that are consistent with the importance of the topic. You might not mind being called "Baldy," but to someone who invests a lot of self-esteem in his physical appearance, that teasing comment can be highly threatening and provoke strong feelings. So, the next time someone "overreacts," don't waste your energy trying to change his feelings. Try changing your *own* attitude!

Psychobabble

There are no Mr. Spocks on this planet. Humans are amazingly emotional creatures, and we're all surprisingly similar in the way we feel and express our emotions. But if you've ever behaved irrationally in the grip of a strong emotion, you might be wondering what evolutionary purpose emotions ever served.

Where Did These Feelings Come From?

Let's face it. Love may not make the world go 'round, but it sure helps people put up with each other. It gives us rose-colored glasses in the beginning of a relationship. It gets us through the hassles of meeting someone, courting them, getting married, and fighting over the remote control. Could parents put up with all the sleepless nights, poopy diapers, and Barney movies without that incredible emotional bond with their child? Apparently, evolution thought not.

In fact, our emotional capacity may have been naturally selected. Ancestors with the strongest feelings may have been more motivated to defend their turf, protect their young, and impress their mate than those who were less passionate. Emotions aren't just feelings; they are feelings associated with tendencies to behave in certain ways. They are inherited, specialized mental states designed to deal with recurring situations in the world.

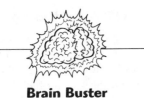

Brain Buster

Don't underestimate the importance of your emotions. Without the glue of emotional bonds, human relationships would be difficult to maintain in the face of hardship.

From an evolutionary perspective, sexual jealousy can be viewed as a special switch that is "turned on" to deal with an unfaithful mate. When a partner is unfaithful, this emotion energizes us for possible conflict. It may have motivated our ancestors to either eliminate the rival or punish or leave the mate. In modern times, it often triggers memories that cause us to reassess the relationship. Luckily for all of us, evolution also gave us some "control" buttons that prevent us from acting impulsively on our feelings!

Seen this way, emotions evolved to stimulate whatever biological or psychological processes were needed to deal with a given situation. They may also help us use our energy most effectively. For example, happiness and sadness are moods that regulate your energy in opposite directions. When you're "on a roll" and things are going well, you feel happy. When you're happy, you're more optimistic, active, and energetic which, of course, helps *keep* you on that roll.

Sometimes, though, the best thing to do is nothing. When you lose a loved one, there's not much you can do to change it. Emotions like sadness are passive; they tend to slow you down and allow you to conserve your energy—which may be why they evolved in the first place.

Body Feelings

Your emotions aren't all in your head—they're whole body experiences. People who are anxious say their heart is racing, they can't breathe, they feel jittery, and they can't sit still. People suffering from depression lose their appetite and can't sleep. Your body and your mind are constantly interacting with each other, and the messages your body sends can either magnify or inhibit your emotions.

Psychobabble

Think animals don't have emotions? Think twice before you tease one. A young killer whale in captivity pushed an oceanarium worker to the floor of the tank and briefly held him there. When aquarium managers investigated, they learned that this particular worker had a history of secretly teasing the killer whale.

This emotional connection between your "mind" and your body is formed in your brain. While certain parts of your body respond to different emotions, your brain is the matchmaker that coordinates these bodily changes and emotional feelings. Specifically, the amygdala in the limbic system, and the frontal lobes in the cerebral cortex act as your emotional regulators.

Shrink Rap

Somatization is the tendency to channel emotions into physical complaints; instead of feeling angry, you might get a headache. A hypochondriac is an extreme example of somatization.

Are you a quick judge of character? Can you leap tall buildings at the first sign of danger? Thank your amygdala—your own, personal crisis manager. It does a quick survival check by assessing the emotional significance of a situation and generating some of your immediate responses. Through connections to the hypothalamus, your amygdala gears your body for action by stimulating the hormones that produce the physical responses (like increasing your heart rate and blood pressure) that accompany strong emotions.

Animals become pretty whacked out when their amygdalas are removed. For example, monkeys whose amygdalas have been removed demonstrate a fascinating phenomenon known as *psychic blindness*. They can still see objects, but they seem to be completely indifferent to the psychological significance of them. Nothing scares them. Nothing angers them. And they become pretty indiscriminate in their search for pleasure; some of them attempted to eat and/or have sex with just about anything—alive or not!

Humans aren't quite that indiscriminate, even without their amygdalas. Among humans, the amygdala keeps us from getting suckered by allowing us to interpret the emotions of others. People who have suffered brain damage to the amygdala lose that ability. It's a subtle version of psychic blindness in which they lose the ability to detect fear or anger in the voices or faces of others.

You can't blame (or credit) *all* your emotions on your amygdala, however. Your frontal lobes are also critical in your conscious experience of feelings, and they help you get a grip on the way you express them. Your frontal lobes help you plan, and initiate, your responses to your feelings. You probably don't have any fewer emotions than your most primitive ancestors; you've just developed the brakes—your frontal lobes—to help control them. Without our frontal lobes, we'd still be bopping each other over the head with clubs!

What We Think About Feelings

In Chapter 3, "The Chicken or the Egg?," we talked about the debate of child development. Here's another chicken or egg argument, and this is an emotional one: Which comes first, your emotional feelings or your bodily sensations? In other words, does your body react to your feelings or are your feelings an interpretation of your bodily sensations?

Insight

If you're about to fall on your head, you might want to turn to your right. Damage to the left frontal lobe typically lowers positive emotions (like happiness), while damage to your right frontal lobe produces a decline in negative ones (like anger).

Common sense argues for the first explanation. First you get angry and then your body responds to that anger by getting all fired up. William James, however, was never one to succumb to common sense. He thought the reverse was true. In his view, we don't cry because we're sad; we're sad because we cry.

James's beliefs arose from a single research subject: himself. When he analyzed his own feelings, he concluded that they really began as sensations in his body. For instance, when he really stopped to think about what "fear" was to him, he concluded that it was the sensation of pounding heart, shallow breathing, and shaky limbs. Anger, he believed, came from the physical jolt of temperature and blood pressure rising.

James thought there were predictable bodily changes for each emotion and that, without these bodily changes, there would be no feeling. Interestingly, people throughout the world report amazingly consistent bodily changes with different emotions.

The essence of James's theory is that our initial assessment of a situation (that snake is poisonous) and the subsequent physical arousal occurs quickly, automatically, and without conscious thought. But since, in James's view, emotion was always a conscious experience, it could not be part of the initial process. Instead, the emotions came later, as a result of the physical sensations. The sequence went like this:

1. You get punched.
2. Your body responds to the punch automatically.
3. Your mind registers your bodily response and interprets it to mean you're angry.

Once again, it was up to the cognitive psychologists to shed some light on things. Stanley Schachter recognized that emotions are dependent on more than feedback from the body. In his view, our perceptions and thoughts about what's happening influence what kind of emotion we feel (anger, fear, joy), and sensory feedback from the body influences how intensely we feel it (very joyful or mildly happy). If you see a snake, for instance, your belief that snakes are dangerous will cause you to feel fear, and if your body gets all fired up (you start sweating, your heart starts pounding), your fear might turn to terror.

Psychobabble

When are emotions "real"? In one study that measured brain waves, the auditory hallucinations of schizophrenics actually stimulated the parts of the brain that involve motivation and emotion. In addition, there was no corresponding activity in the part of the brain that checks out reality. This brain pattern suggested that there would be no way of knowing whether these voices were real or whether an emotional response to them was reasonable.

Schachter came to his conclusions after playing around with people's emotions. He injected some of his subjects with adrenaline and then exposed them to emotion-eliciting stimuli, like a sad movie or an angry story. Adrenaline itself did not produce any particular emotion; the subjects might have felt jittery or jazzed up, but they didn't associate it with a feeling. When the drug was combined with an emotional situation, however, their emotions were stronger. They felt angrier in response to the angry story and sadder over the tear-jerking movie. I wonder if a little coffee drinking with a new flame would make the love bug bite a little harder?

Touchy-Feely Psychology

Adrenaline isn't the only thing that can jumble up your feelings. Apparently, so can wishful thinking. Listen to this: A few years ago, a friend of mine told me he was attracted to a new co-worker, Linda. He was convinced she felt the same way. "She's so cute. Whenever I go into her office, she seems so nervous. She gets so distracted when I talk to her; she stumbles over her words, and yesterday, she dropped her pencil. I know she likes me."

Recently, at a dinner celebrating their wedding anniversary, Linda was talking about their early courtship. "I don't know why Rob was attracted to me. I was a nervous wreck over having my first job. I was so preoccupied with doing well, I barely even noticed Rob's existence until he asked me out." What Rob had optimistically interpreted as a sign of Linda's interest in him was a bad case of first-job jitters!

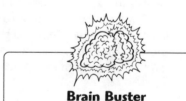

Brain Buster

Having a few drinks to cure the blues can actually leave you feeling more depressed! When your body is in a physically depressed state from alcohol, it intensifies your emotions and, in turn, this emotional intensity influences your interpretation of the situation. A fight with a friend would be a bummer; under the influence of alcohol, it can feel devastating.

Emotions—our own or others—can be hard to figure out. The physical arousal that accompanies different emotional states can be similar. For example, your heartbeat will speed up and your blood pressure will climb whether you're feeling angry or afraid. Our mental processes go far beyond fitting a label of "sad, mad, or glad" onto our feelings. We also try to figure out why we feel a certain way and what our reaction means.

The Mind and Body, Working Together

Because of the strong link between physical arousal and emotional arousal, we sometimes misinterpret physical cues as emotions. Being overheated can be interpreted as feeling anxious. Being tired can feel like depression. And being physically charged can be misinterpreted as sexual arousal.

This has some practical utility. First of all, it suggests that taking care of your body is one of the best paths to good mental health—being tired or hungry, for example, makes you much more vulnerable to mood swings. In the romance department, a scary movie or roller coaster ride might be the activity of choice if you want to pique your date's sexual interest. However, given that your window of opportunity lasts only as long as the person is physically aroused—less than 10 minutes—you'd better strike while the iron is hot and make your move right after the show is over!

Are You Cultured?

All human beings are remarkably similar with regard to the kinds of emotions we feel. We also speak and understand the same emotional language; the facial expression of a sad New Guinean is similar to your sad face. But if you've ever traveled in another country, you'll have noticed that culture sets the standard for when to show certain emotions and for the social appropriateness of various emotional displays, and those standards vary from one place to the next.

Psychobabble

In one fascinating study, a female experimenter showed two groups of men a picture of a woman and asked them to tell a story about her. Half of the men had just crossed a rickety, wobbly bridge, and half had just crossed a safe bridge. The rickety-bridge crossers were much more likely to use sexual themes than the men who had just crossed a safe bridge. They were also four times more likely to call the researcher later!

Cross-Cultural Confusion

I've done quite a bit of work with a Finnish-owned company that has a huge headquarters in the United States. The communication glitches that occur between the Finns and the Americans are quite amusing. One of the biggest cultural differences is in the expression of emotion. In fact, early on, I was given a cartoon that was titled "The Finnish Expression of Emotions." Underneath it was a list of numerous emotions—sad, happy, afraid, surprised, afraid, angry—and above each emotion was a picture of the exact same stone face!

From an American perspective, the Finnish culture seems to breed a bunch of Mr. Spock clones. From a Finnish perspective, Americans probably seem like a bunch of impulsive, irrational children! While Americans and Finns feel the same feelings, their culture sends very different messages about what you can do and say about them.

Insight

Believe it or not, the old advice to "fake it till you make it" has some merit, at least as far as our feelings go. Several experiments have found that smiling, whether you feel like it or not, actually makes you feel happier. In fact, the facial expression of smiling triggers the physiological response to happiness just as much as reliving a pleasant experience does.

Guilt Trippin'

In addition to the cultural influence on emotional expression, some feelings may have a social motive behind them. Guilt, for example, may have evolved as a form of social control that motivates people to be nice to each other. For example, to avoid guilt, we're likely to act in ways that enhance our relationships with others. If someone has ever laid a guilt trip on you, you know it can be a powerful social influence; when I miss a lunch date with my son, the guilt he can induce suddenly gives this four-year-old a tremendous amount of power!

And, last but not least, guilt is a way for partners to restore justice in their relationship. If you lie to a friend, you might benefit in the short run, but you'll feel bad about the consequences to the relationship. One hopes you'll feel bad enough to regret your mistake, 'fess up, and make amends.

Coding and Decoding

Recently, I watched a *60 Minutes* episode featuring a woman who was conned out of thousands of dollars by a man pretending to love her. This brave woman went public with a humiliating tale of a con artist who not only manipulated her feelings, but who did a remarkable job of disguising his own. Experiencing your own feelings is one important survival skill, but communicating them is another. And, as this woman learned the hard way, decoding the way others are feeling can help us more accurately predict whom to approach and whom to avoid.

Apparently, evolution thought human beings would benefit more from the ability to hide their emotions than from the ability to detect a lying salesperson or a con artist. Most people I know, though, think they can have it both ways. Most of us think we are good judges of character, and we're sure that we'd never have been as gullible or naive as that woman on *60 Minutes*. If that's what you think, it's time to be honest with yourself.

Most of us are very poor lie detectors. The key to deception detection lies in having perceived patterns of the liar's behavior and facial expressions over time. Once you've established a baseline of how he normally behaves, you're more likely to smell a rat. Without the chance to observe that person in different situations over time, you're unlikely to accurately judge his honesty.

Psychobabble

You experience emotions spontaneously, but you can learn to control their expression. You're often better off masking your feelings than expressing them: For example, if you dislike your boss, you may be smart to keep those feelings to yourself. If you're wild about someone you've just met, wearing your heart on your sleeve can make you vulnerable. And you'd be a pretty poor poker player if every feeling immediately showed up on your face!

Smart Feelings

Eleanor Roosevelt was known as "First Lady of the World" decades after her husband, President Franklin D. Roosevelt, died. Biographers, determined to uncover how this plain, modest housewife became one of the world's most influential women, spent years interviewing her closest friends and family. What they discovered was that Eleanor possessed an uncanny understanding of people, an endless compassion for the underdog, and an incredible ability to motivate and channel her emotions into purposeful goals. In pop psychology terms, Eleanor Roosevelt was a genius of emotional intelligence.

Emotional intelligence teaches us that, in the contest of life, we're much better off being Miss Congeniality than Miss America. Interpersonal relationships, we're finding, hold the keys to much of what life has to offer, and our ability to understand ourselves and others are the skills that get us the key. In his groundbreaking book *Emotional Intelligence,* psychologist Daniel Goleman outlines interpersonal skills that he believes greatly enhance, or hurt, our quality of life:

➤ Self-awareness—knowing what you're feeling when you feel it

➤ Managing your emotions—knowing what to do with your feelings

➤ Motivating yourself—channeling your feelings in the right direction without acting impulsively

➤ Empathy—feeling for others and accepting their feelings, too.

➤ Handling relationships—having good interpersonal skills so others feel good about you.

The phrase *emotional intelligence* was first coined by Yale psychologist Peter Salovey and the University of New Hampshire's John Mayer to describe qualities like understanding one's own feelings, empathy for the feelings of others, and the ability to use one's emotions in a helpful way. An *emotional quotient (EQ)* is not the opposite of IQ; some of us are blessed with a lot of both, some with little of either. Researchers are now trying to understand how the two complement each other; how our smarts about our feelings help us put our intelligence to better use.

We already have some clues. Students who are depressed or angry literally cannot learn. Children who have trouble being accepted by their classmates are two to eight times more likely to drop out. And the manager who answers his e-mails and is a good collaborator with colleagues is far more likely to be successful than the lone-wolf genius.

Why are some people more "emotionally intelligent" than others? Emotions might be built-in, but they can be shaped by experience. Infants as young as three months old show empathy—they get upset at the sound of another baby crying. Even very young children develop a repertoire of sensitive responses when they see others acting compassionately.

If, on the other hand, the feelings a child expresses are not recognized and reinforced by the adults in his or her life, the child will gradually become less able to recognize them in himself or in others. Not only will this cause problems in his or her relationships, he will have lifelong trouble with something we all struggle with now and then—managing his everyday moods.

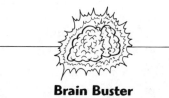

Brain Buster

Dwelling on anger actually increases its power. Contrary to popular wisdom, the best way to handle anger is not to "let it all hang out"; the body needs a chance to process the adrenaline that anger generates. So, before you say something you regret, get some exercise, plug in a relaxation tape, or count until you cool down.

Managing Your Everyday Moods

Do you ever wake up on the wrong side of the bed? Do you sometimes get in a bad mood for no reason? Do you have a temper that's hotter than a jalapeño? If you answered yes to all three questions, here's your diagnosis: You're moody!

Moods aren't the same as emotions, although they do have a great deal in common with them. First of all, moods are often less intense and longer lasting than emotions, although this isn't true in the case of a clinical depression. And, unlike most emotions, moods don't seem to have an identifiable cause; we can't pinpoint the reason we are in a bad or a good mood.

So, where do moods come from? Many people think our routine activities, relationships, successes, and failures create our moods. But, as it turns out, that's only partly correct. Your health, sleep, food, amount of recent exercise, and even the time of day are contributors to your mood, too. In fact, moods are crucial indicators of your physiological functioning and your psychological experience at any given moment. Your mood is like a clinical thermometer, reflecting all the inner and outer events that affect you.

Meet the Mood Managers

Whether you're consciously aware of it or not, you continually sense your moods and try to improve them. In fact, you spend more time than you might think trying to regulate your moods. You might eat chocolate to feel better, call a friend to cheer you up, or zone out in front of the TV after a hard day at work. Each of these behaviors is in some way an attempt to manage your mood.

Here's a way to see how good you are at managing your own moods. Check the three techniques you use most often to get yourself out of a funk:

___ listen to music

___ exercise (including taking a walk)

___ watch television

___ have sex

___ eat something

___ use a relaxation strategy

___ call or talk to someone

___ be alone

___ avoid the person or the thing that's getting you down

___ use humor

___ get lost in a hobby

___ try to think about the problem differently

If you use physical exercise as one of your mood management strategies, go to the head of the class. Studies show that regular physical exercise is one of the most effective mood regulators we have. Even a 10-minute walk can beat the blues and raise your energy level. Other effective mood managers are: listening to music, relaxation techniques, challenging negative thoughts, using humor, and getting lost in a hobby or productive activity.

On the other hand, avoidance, isolating yourself from others, and behaviors such as eating, smoking, and drinking reduce tension in the short run, but may increase tension over time. Talking things over with a friend is a good strategy as long as you end your conversation with an action plan and don't get stuck wallowing in your emotions! And if coming up with action plans is a problem, no sweat! You'll learn all about them in the next chapter, when we talk about problem solving.

Psychobabble

Believe it or not, your problems seem different at different times during the day, depending on your mood and your energy level. See for yourself; write down a personal problem you're having and then make a journal entry about it at four separate times during the day. Don't be surprised if the same problem that looked so grim late at night seems less troublesome at midmorning.

The Least You Need to Know

➤ Evolution apparently gave us emotions to motivate us to take care of ourselves and to stick with the people we love.

➤ Emotions are whole-body experiences, combining feelings, thoughts, and bodily sensations.

➤ There are six universal emotions: sadness, anger, disgust, fear, happiness, and surprise. Culture, however, determines how and when these are expressed.

➤ Emotional intelligence is the ability to be aware of, and effectively use, our own feelings and the emotions of those around us.

➤ Your moods are like clinical thermometers that tell you how you're doing physically and psychologically. Physical exercise is perhaps the best way to regulate them.

Think Before You Speak

Long before serial killer Wayne Williams was caught, psychologist John Douglas described him as a 20-something black male and a police buff. He described another serial killer, known as the Trailside Murderer, as a stutterer. And he pegged the Unabomber as a highly intelligent white male with an obsessive-compulsive personality and a previous university affiliation. In all three instances, he was right.

How can someone like Douglas come up with accurate profiles of murderers he's never even met? In this chapter, you'll find out.

Get ready to explore the way people think—how we form our thoughts. Along the way you'll learn how people use mental scripts and schemata to figure out the mysteries of daily life. You'll learn about common problem-solving strategies, and how mental shortcuts can help you solve problems more efficiently (and, sometimes, lead you astray).

Getting into Another's Mind

Profiling is hot stuff these days. There's even a popular TV series about this arcane skill. But people like John Douglas aren't psychic. They just truly understand the criminal mind. Douglas spent 25 years working as a behavioral profiler with the investigative support unit for the FBI, spending hundreds of hours in prisons getting inside the minds of convicted serial killers. Using what he learned there, he has developed behavior profiles of criminal offenders. John Douglas may have more insight into the thoughts that drive criminal behavior than anyone else.

Mind Detectives

The human mind is uniquely suited to solving mysteries, to going beyond the evidence to find a solution that seizes new insights, opportunities, and interpretations. Sometimes the results are as impressive as Douglas's profiles of killers he never met. Other times the mysteries we solve are more mundane. In every case, the tools your mind uses in problem solving are called *cognitive processes*.

Shrink Rap

Cognitive processes are the mental abilities that allow you to know and understand the things around you. They include attending, thinking, remembering, and reasoning.

When I was 16, I took one of those high school vocational tests that are supposed to help you figure out what you want to be when you grow up. When mine came back, the advised career was "private investigator." Given that I had never met a private investigator and grew up at a time when it wouldn't have been the kind of career my guidance counselor would have picked out for a female, this was not the most useful psychological test I've ever taken. My only consolation was that my best friend's ideal career was funeral director.

Years later, I realized that vocational test was smarter than I thought. I did become a private investigator—of the mind. Psychologists are, in essence, mind detectives. We are constantly looking for clues about human nature by examining thoughts, feelings, and behaviors. When I am doing therapy, my client and I are trying to solve the mystery that brought him or her to my office.

Solving problems is what we all do, every day. Our ability to go beyond the surface of things—to make sense of clues and solve mysteries—are the gifts of our cognitive processes. Our thoughts allow us to carry around mental representations of our physical and social worlds wherever we go. They allow us to look back and investigate why we behaved in a certain way, and they allow us to look ahead to predict what might happen. Our cognitive processes are our detective tools; we use them to explore, and improve, the world around us.

Some of your cognitive processes mentally represent the world around you. They classify information and interpret your experiences. These are like the evidence files detectives gather, organize, and review when they're working on a case. And just as a detective might have a map of the scenes of a series of crimes, you have a mental map of how to get to work every day. Other cognitive processes, like your dreams and fantasies, are internally focused; they help you solve your future mysteries more effectively.

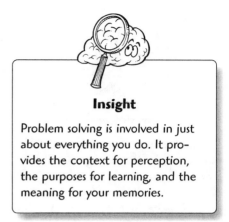

Insight

Problem solving is involved in just about everything you do. It provides the context for perception, the purposes for learning, and the meaning for your memories.

Models of the Mind

Cognitive psychology is the "science of the mind." It was born in the 1950s, partly as a reaction to the behaviorist perspective. However, technology also had a lot to do with enabling this new branch of psychology to grow. Ironically, the computer helped scientists become more interested in human beings, particularly in how the human mind compared to computer hardware.

In 1945, a mathematician named John von Neumann compared the electronic circuits of a new digital computer to the brain's neurons and the computer program to the brain's memory, introducing the human computer analogy for the first time. Psychological researchers Herbert Simon and Allen Newell continued von Neumann's research. They were able to develop computer programs that mimicked human problem solving, thereby giving us new ways to study mental processes.

The idea of creating models of the mind caught on. Today, researchers build conceptual models to help them understand the processes involved in information processing. These *cognitive models* are metaphors to explain how information is detected, stored, and used. The most popular model today, not surprisingly, is the information-processing model.

Information Overload!

The information-processing model suggests that thinking can be broken down into component parts that work together to create a system of information flow. According to this model, the key to understanding cognition is by examining these parts and how they work together. It's similar to the strategy an auto mechanic might take when working on a car.

If that mechanic *really* wanted to understand cars, though, he might even take a trip to the Ford Motor Company and spend a few days watching the assembly line put one together. Then he'd see firsthand how complicated automobile making really is—the hundreds of parts that go into one and the choreography involved in getting all those parts in the right places. The human mind would make car building look like a Mickey Mouse operation.

Shrink Rap

A **cognitive model** is a hypothetical representation of how cognitive processes work. Just as a model airplane is a small replica of a real one, cognitive psychologists build cognitive models to explain how the human mind takes in, and uses, information.

Your mind has *many* assembly lines, all operating at the same time. Each one works with the rest, taking raw material (like basic sensations and perceptions) to more complex stages such as naming, classifying, reasoning, and problem solving.

And, unlike mechanical assembly lines, your mental assembly lines are a lot more flexible. "Workers" on one assembly line might notice a piece of information that relates to another assembly line—and pop it right on over to where it belongs. In fact, your mind frequently makes new associations among thoughts, and often comes up with creative "products" that haven't been "ordered."

Investigating Thoughts

The human mind is pretty complex. Cognition is an active process; when you think, you aren't just taking information in, you're sorting through it, making sense of it, and transforming it—all at the same time. This transformation of basic input into news you can use involves a number of sophisticated tasks—judging, problem solving, planning, reasoning, imagining, and, sometimes, creativity.

As complex as it is, though, thinking is also practical. If you think about it, you'll realize thinking is *always* some form of problem solving. Just about everything you think is directed toward making things better or different. It's your built-in self-improvement program!

You might be wondering how we know so much about thoughts, since they can't be observed directly. Cognitive psychologists had quite a problem themselves when they began studying human cognition. Undaunted, they came up with some pretty clever investigative tools to measure the mind. Let's take a look at some of the most popular mind measures:

➤ introspection

➤ behavioral observation

➤ error analysis

➤ brain scanning

Introspection

In the late 1800s, psychologist Wilhelm Wundt taught people to study their own minds. Using a self-report method called *introspection,* he encouraged them to write down their sensations, images, and feelings *as they were having them.* By getting people to record their mental processes as they were occurring, Wundt hoped to break them down into their smallest unit.

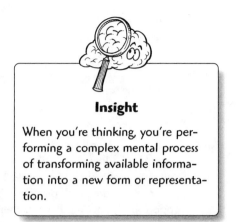

Insight

When you're thinking, you're performing a complex mental process of transforming available information into a new form or representation.

Wundt's project was based on this theory: If people can dissect their mental processes into their most basic units, we can begin to create a structure of human thought. If enough people do it, we should begin to see patterns of sensations, images, and feelings emerge. Over time, we should be able to present various individuals with certain stimuli and generate the same images, thoughts, and feelings in all of them. His ultimate goal was an admirable one—he felt that, if we can understand human thought, we can predict it and, when it's not working properly, we can change it.

Ring a bell? Just as Pavlov thought certain stimuli would produce predictable behavior, Wundt believed that human thoughts could be controlled by systematically changing the environment. In that respect, Wundt believed thoughts developed in a manner similar to classically conditioned behavior.

Alas, he was dead wrong. People are much more complicated than early psychologists thought, which makes them much more interesting, unpredictable, and, alas, much harder to study. And which is why introspection, as a research tool, is basically extinct today.

Behavioral Observations

People's thoughts and actions don't always match up. Nevertheless, we can get clues about what people think by observing what they do and the context in which they do it. Observing what a person is doing, and the situation in which it occurs, can help us figure out the thoughts, feelings, and motivations guiding them. If someone is crying at a funeral, I can infer that the person is feeling sad and probably having thoughts about their deceased loved one. On the other hand, if the newly crowned Miss America is crying on stage, I am more likely to infer happy thoughts and joy (although I might infer grief from the first runner-up).

Although Wundt was disappointed in achieving his goal, he did have a few successes. One such useful observation is that reaction time can be used to measure the complexity of thinking required for any given task. The longer it takes to perform a task, the more complex its solution is likely to be. Today, cognitive psychologists use reaction time to gauge mental flexibility and quickness. Let's take a look at two psychological tests, the Trail Making Tests, as examples of how they do it.

Psychobabble

Think-aloud protocols add a new twist to the old introspection studies. In these protocols, subjects are asked to describe the strategy they use to solve a problem as opposed to a description of the problem itself. These studies indicate that people's problem-solving strategies in action are much different than they think. For example, shoppers are much more opportunistic and impulsive in their trip planning than they believe themselves to be. Of course, that's no great surprise to us impulse buyers!

Trail Making Test A looks a lot like one of those connect-the-numbers pictures you used to do as a child. It doesn't take a mental giant to be pretty good at this test, but it does help to be pretty quick with your pencil. Trail Making Test A provides a baseline of your motor speed.

Trail B, however, requires you to alternate between numbers and letters in order—you must draw a line from the letter A to the number 1 to the letter B and so forth. This obviously requires more thought. If you do okay on Trail A but bomb Trail B, the examiner will start wondering a little bit about the flexibility of your frontal lobes.

Analyzing Errors

Ever make the same mistake over and over again? Well, we all do and cognitive psychologists are pretty darned happy about it. It helps them get to know us better. In fact, cognitive psychologists study errors in thinking about as much as they do anything else.

What cognitivists have learned is that people don't just jump to the wrong conclusion—they often jump to the same wrong conclusion, over and over again. This is why, as you'll see later in this chapter, there are some thinking errors that we all make, and some of them suggest that people make pretty poor jurors.

Brain Scanning

When Benjamin Franklin discovered electricity, he had no idea what he was doing for the human brain. Not only did his discovery allow us to see the light outside, he ultimately allowed us to measure the light bulbs inside your head. It has helped researchers see the different brain waves that you produce when you sleep (see Chapter 5, "Come to Your Senses"), and to measure changes in activity related to a particular mental event; a pattern known as an *event-related potential* (ERP).

In fact, with electrical measurements, researchers can even tell which light bulbs are going off in what part of the brain. For example, while you're reading these pages, lights are going off in the part of your brain that perceives the words, the part that compares them to other words you've read, and the part that organizes their individual meanings into coherent thoughts. Even the sentences themselves can cause different ERPs; the part of the brain that gets excited over an unfamiliar word is different than the part of the brain that tries to untangle a confusing sentence structure.

Shrink Rap

An **event-related potential (ERP)** is the measurable change in brain waves in response to a particular stimulus.

Clearly, mind detectives use a variety of tools in their exploration of the mysterious human mind. But what are they looking for? What are these tools actually going to help them find? Let's take a look at how thoughts are structured. As you're about to see, it's a lot harder to get lost in thought than you might think.

Jeopardy of the Mind

If your brain were a game show, it would be *Jeopardy*. It loves categories—creating categories, putting information into categories, and fitting new stuff into old categories. Your brain is a categorizing machine.

It's also a tiny bit lazy. It would rather put information into existing categories than build new ones. As a result, your brain looks for similarities among individual experiences—it prefers to treat new information as instances of familiar, remembered categories. "Been there, done that" is a concept with which your brain is very familiar. Maybe that's why boredom is such a part of the human condition!

I'll Take "Building Blocks" for $200, Alex

The categories are the building blocks of thinking—we call them *concepts*. *Animal*, for example, is a concept that conjures up many related creatures that we have grouped together in a single category. *Dog* is another concept, although the category it refers to is a smaller one. Concepts can also represent activities (your idea of exercise may be a lot different from mine), relationships (an apple and a banana are both fruit), and abstract ideas (truth, justice).

In relationships, concepts can cause trouble. Here's an example. If, on our first date, I asked you if you thought honesty was important, you'd probably say yes. Social pressure aside (who would go out with someone who said no), you'd probably mean it. However, your understanding of the concept of *honesty* might be entirely different from mine, and the concepts *important* and *relationship* can muddy the waters even further. Your definition of honesty might mean outright lying is off limits, but it's

Brain Buster

Think you know what your sweetheart thinks? Don't be too sure! We don't all mean the same things by the words we use. One of the slipperiest concepts that we all talk about all the time is love. We all say the word, but each of us has our own, uniquely personal understanding of what it means.

okay to leave a few things out. Or, I might agree that honesty is important, but not as important as staying out of trouble!

Ask any two people what love is and you'll find different ideas grouped in the same category. If I am loving you according to my concept, without understanding what love means to you, you still might feel unloved. The best way to understand what a person's concept of honesty or love really means is to see whether he or she acts in ways that are loving or trustworthy. If there's a discrepancy between someone's words and actions, believe what he does, not what he says!

Building the Building Blocks

Just as relationships involve finding people with whom we have a lot in common, a basic task of thinking is concept formation—identifying what objects or ideas have in common and grouping them accordingly. "How are they the same?" is a fundamental question your mind is always asking. Psychologists still aren't exactly sure, though, what features the mind considers when answering this question.

In other words, when your mind asks this question, what does "the same" mean? Do the objects need to look similar, do similar things, or what? If concepts are the building blocks, what are the blocks made of? Let's take a look at two schools of thought that attempt to solve this riddle—the *critical features* theory and the *prototype hypothesis*.

Insight

To understand the difference between *necessary* and *sufficient* features, think of the birds and the bees. Both have wings—a necessary feature to define either one. But wings alone are not sufficient to tell the two apart.

Don't Criticize My Prototype

According to critical features theory, your brain stores mental lists of important characteristics that define concepts. If the concept is *bird,* then *feathers* and *beaks* would be critical features. These critical features are qualities or characteristics that are both necessary and sufficient for a concept to be included in a category. A concept is a member of the category if (and only if) it has every feature on the list.

The second school of thought, the prototype hypothesis, is based on building a mental model of your conceptual category—an ideal or representative example that all other members of the category must resemble. This ideal is called a prototype.

Lists or Likeness?

Here's how the two schools of thought differ. Let's say you're trying to define the concept "potential marriage candidate." According to critical-features theory, you'd make a list of characteristics: handsome, funny, intelligent, ambitious, generous, and empathic. Then you'd spend your time looking only for those individuals who meet all these criteria.

The prototype hypothesis, however, suggests you would be more likely to build a mental model of your ideal mate. If you worship the ground your opposite sex parent walks on, you're likely to use him or her as the prototype of the perfect wife or husband, and date only those individuals who are similar to that parent in significant ways.

The critical-features approach is rigid. If a person doesn't live up to all the features on the list, he or she simply doesn't count as a member of the category. The prototype approach is a little more flexible about its categories. If a person does not exactly match the ideal model, he or she can still be classified as belonging to the same category. There will never be anyone just like Mom or Dad, but we look for someone who is close enough.

One from Column A, One from Column B

Recent research suggests these two schools of thought are both right, although for different kinds of concepts. When it comes to concepts such as mammals, the critical features approach works well; all mammals are warm-blooded, have vertebrae, and nurse their young. Other concepts, though, are harder to peg.

Take birds, for example. *Wings, flies,* and *feathers* seem like pretty safe critical features, but what about penguins and ostriches? They're birds, but they don't fit neatly into our critical features category. Bird is a blurry category; it has no clear boundaries between members of its class that fly and do not fly. To correct this fuzziness, you probably define the concept not only by critical features (feathers) but in relation to your ideas about typical members of the category—your prototype.

Psychobabble

Every fan of television cop shows has seen a prototype—police use them all the time when they help witnesses identify criminal suspects. They prepare a prototype face made of plastic overlays of different facial features taken from a commercially prepared Identi-Kit, then they ask the witness to modify the prototype model until it is most similar to the suspect's face.

Concepts are often organized from the general to the specific. The broad category of vegetation has several subcategories, such as flowers, trees, and plants, which lead us to smaller categories like azalea, live oak, and cactus. Going back to our more interesting relationship category, "men" might be our broad category that leads to dates, that leads to potential marriage candidates. And, ideally, that category eventually branches off into a one-member category: spouse.

Great Expectations

Tell me 10 things you associate with having a picnic. Here are the 10 that come to my mind; sunshine, a blanket, a picnic basket, fried chicken, hard-boiled eggs, potato salad, salt, relaxing, sand, and ants. That's my schema for picnic. Understanding the concept "picnic" is nice, but schemas really give us the scoop on what to expect if we're going on one.

Schemas are packets of information that help us expect what we'll find when we encounter a certain concept, category, person, or situation. These expectations come from our understanding of, and experience with, this person, place, or thing. For example, I've certainly had my picnic rained out, but that's not what usually happens—so rain is not part of my picnic schema. On the other hand, I've never been able to prevent a certain number of ants from sharing my lunch. (Now that I've seen *A Bug's Life,* at least I feel better about it!)

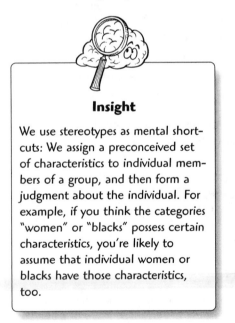

Insight

We use stereotypes as mental shortcuts: We assign a preconceived set of characteristics to individual members of a group, and then form a judgment about the individual. For example, if you think the categories "women" or "blacks" possess certain characteristics, you're likely to assume that individual women or blacks have those characteristics, too.

New information is easier to handle when you can relate it to existing knowledge. If you ask me if I want to go on a picnic, I can quickly review my picnic schema and compare the costs (ants, sand) to the rewards (fried chicken!). But schemas do more than help you make quick decisions. They also help you fill in the gaps when something is missing. If I overhear part of a conversation that includes "bummed out," "opened the basket," and "forgot the salt," I'm likely to realize the person is talking about a picnic basket, not a flower basket.

Danger, Danger, Danger

Your mind is constantly drawing on old information to make sense out of new data. If you find a discrepancy between new input and already stored schemata, you adjust by either changing what you know or ignoring the new input. Unfortunately, as you might imagine, this strategy has a downside.

If we approach new information with an already-formed idea of how it's supposed to fit into our grand conceptual schema, we are likely to tune in to information that confirms our expectations and tune out the information that doesn't fit—it's easier to think information that doesn't fit neatly into a category is the "exception to the rule" rather than to take a second look at the rules. For example, people who are told they are about to meet someone with schizophrenia often "see" these characteristics in their new acquaintance, even when the information is completely false. Our schemata may make it easier for us to understand information but, if we're not careful, they can also distort it.

We're All Actors Following Scripts

I just read that Julia Roberts got $20 million for her last movie. Too bad we can't all capitalize on our acting ability. After all, we've been reading *scripts* since we were small. From a psychological standpoint, a script is a special name for a schema about how things are supposed to happen. And, as long as everyone knows his part, everything is fine.

We follow scripts for just about every common experience in our lives. While we each have our own ideas about how people should behave on first dates, most of us would agree that making a good impression is part of that script. We have scripts for marriage proposals and birthday celebrations. We have expectations (scripts again) about how our boss should behave. These scripts help us know what actions and events are appropriate for a particular setting; they help us decide what to expect or how people should behave under certain circumstances.

When everyone is following similar scripts, everyone is comfortable, because we understand the "meaning" of that situation in the same way and have the same expectations of each other. When people do not follow the same script, though, it can be pretty uncomfortable. If your script for a first date includes being wined and dined by someone eagerly picking up the tab, you are not going to be happy when your date asks you to split the check.

Brain Buster

Scripts have the same risks that schemata have—in both cases, we tend to see information that confirms our expectations and discard information that challenges it. When we're following scripts, we tend to hang around with people who follow the same lines as we do, and to ignore or feel uncomfortable around people who seem to be reading from a different page.

One reason why people tend to stick with their own ethnic group is that they're more likely to share common scripts. If you've ever worked for an international company, you've experienced a degree of "culture shock" when someone from another country did business in a way that was completely foreign to you. Adjusting to different scripts can be frustrating and uncomfortable. At the same time, while it might be more comfortable for people to stick with what's familiar, it's also limiting. If you aren't exposed to new ways of being, you have less opportunity to reexamine old schemata or scripts and see if they're still relevant. And you have virtually no opportunity to learn new ones.

If that doesn't seem like such a big deal, think back to a time when your parents treated you like you were still 16 years old. Many of us gripe about our parents' occasional tendency to forget we're past driving age; we complain that they're "stuck in the past" or "trying to keep us from growing up." It is a frustrating experience to feel that every minor slip up is viewed as an indicator of immaturity and that all of our newfound adult wisdom is overlooked.

This situation is a common one, where parents don't reexamine their scripts for how to relate to their (now adult) children. However, as always, there's more than one side to this story. It may be that we haven't reexamined our own scripts for our parents, so that we're still relating to *them* in ways that were more appropriate to our more youthful selves. And dare I mention how easy it is, after a few days of this treatment, to start acting like a teenager again?

Be Reasonable

What do Sherlock Holmes, Albert Einstein, Marie Curie, and Jonas Salk have in common? They each used the power of logic and reasoning to transform information and solve problems. Whether the task was solving a crime or finding a vaccine for polio, these people had incredible minds that allowed them to see bits of data in unique and revolutionary ways.

Now that we've examined the basics of thinking, let's take a look at the really fascinating, creative stuff our minds do with all these concepts, schemata, and scripts. When you think of our mind's tendency to get stuck in a groove and lazily file information into existing categories, the voyage of discovery is amazing indeed.

Shrink Rap

Reasoning is a process of realistic, goal-directed thinking in which conclusions are drawn from a set of facts.

Cognitive psychologists are fascinated by the way people use their mental building blocks to solve problems and achieve new insights. This creative process begins with *reasoning*. We are reasonable *before* we're creative.

There are two types of reasoning: inductive and deductive. Deductive reasoning starts from the "big picture" and uses it to see if it applies to the current situation. Let's say your theory is "all bosses are out to get their employees." What you're really trying to figure out is whether your boss is out to get you. If you were using deductive reasoning, you might generate several hypotheses that, once tested, should confirm or discount your somewhat paranoid theory about bosses.

So, you start generating hypotheses about conniving bosses. Conniving bosses might take credit for your work. (And just last week, your boss got a pat on the back for the filing system *you* devised!) Conniving bosses might say one thing and do another (your boss promised you a raise a week ago, but you're paycheck isn't any bigger!). Conniving bosses might give you a lower performance evaluation than you deserve (wasn't there a note about your coming in late a couple of times?). Obviously, there's evidence to support the validity of applying your general "conniving boss theory" to your current boss.

Psychobabble

How'd you like to buy eye protectors for your pet chicken? Always wanted a nose job but can't afford it? Try a nose shaper—a device that allegedly works much like a dental retainer! Visit http://colitz.com/site/wacky.htm and discover some of the zaniest inventions ever made. I'm not sure how reasonable they are, but they sure are fun!

But what if, after comparing your boss's behavior to your general theory, you find the opposite? You not only got credit for that filing system, you also got a bonus in your paycheck and a rave review at evaluation time. Evidence no longer supports the idea that your boss is a conniver. At first, you might cling to your general theory (all bosses are out to get their employees), but decide that your boss is that one-in-a-million exception to the rule. Over time, however, especially if you encounter several benevolent bosses, you might begin to reexamine your general theory. But there's no guarantee! Human beings are tricky; we hold fast to existing beliefs and are most likely to judge as true the conclusions with which we already agree!

Sherlock Holmes was a lot better at solving a mystery than explaining the logic behind his solution. He frequently attributed his brilliance and insight to the powers of observation and deduction, when, in fact, inductive reasoning deserved the credit. Inductive reasoning starts with *specific* observations and clues. Once we begin to detect patterns and regularities among those observations, we formulate some tentative hypotheses to explore, and end up developing some general conclusions or theories.

Let's see how that would work with the conniving boss example. Your boss "forgets" to give you credit for an idea at a staff meeting. At first you shrug it off as a mere oversight, but then it happens again. Later, your boss encourages you to apply for a higher position in another department, and then you learn he sabotaged your candidacy. You don't have to be Ace Ventura to see a pattern of deception emerging. This pattern might lead you to the wise conclusion that your boss is conniving. If you're smart, you'll watch your back.

Problem Solving

What's the fastest way to get to work in the morning traffic? How are we going to get a 24-hour project done in 8 hours? And, how can we get that cute guy or girl in cubicle number 27 to acknowledge our existence? Problem solving is the space between what we know and what we need to know. Any time our thinking is directed toward solving specific challenges, we're doing it.

Try This at Home

Everybody can improve his skills at problem solving. Here are just a couple of ways you can hone your abilities:

➤ If you want to rev up your brain power, play with toys. Adult puzzles and games encourage problem solving much like children's toys do. Don't get trapped by the rules of the game; after you've whipped your friend at backgammon, make up another game with the backgammon board and pieces.

➤ Having trouble finding a solution to a problem? Just before going to bed, think about your problem and the various choices you could make. Think about each choice clearly in your mind. Tell yourself you're going to make the decision while you're sleeping. You may not get the solution the next morning, but if you keep trying, within a few days you'll wake up with your mind made up.

Insight

Which kind of logic would you use to find your lost keys? Most of us would use inductive reasoning to search our memory and review the evidence. By mentally replaying what was going on when you first came in the house, and retracing your steps, you'd eventually solve the mystery of the missing keys.

Working Things Through

In some respects, solving a problem is like walking through a maze; you start at the beginning (facing the problem), then, through a series of twists and turns (problem-solving strategies), you end up where you want to be (the solution). Sometimes you get lost and have to back up and figure out where you took the wrong turn—maybe you started out in a different place than you had originally thought or maybe you got sidetracked along the way. Figuring out why your problem isn't solved requires problem solving, too.

Defining Your Puzzles

Sometimes it's hard to know what your problem really is. For example, an unhappily married friend of mine wanted to try and "fix" her marriage. She and her husband had been growing apart for some time, and he didn't seem happy either. However, when she tried to discuss it with him, he repeatedly said he was happy, nothing was wrong, and they didn't need any professional help. For months, my friend defined their problem as a breakdown in communication, and tried many times and many different ways to get her message across.

When that didn't work, she had to rethink the problem. Maybe it wasn't a communication issue at all. She began to think maybe her unhappiness was her problem alone. This started her wondering if, rather than investing more energy in her marriage, she should first take care of herself.

Once she identified her problem this way, she solved it. She quit trying to arm wrestle her husband into couples' therapy. When her husband came home from work, she told him that she was going to get some therapy on her own, and she made an appointment to get her own life back on track.

You know what happened? Within a month, her husband was sitting on the couch right beside her. He later said he had been terrified to go to therapy, but more terrified of losing his wife. What his wife had initially interpreted as disinterest was really fear, and it was only the even greater fear of losing his wife that allowed him to overcome his resistance to therapy. To this day, he says it was the best thing to happen to their marriage, and all because his wife redefined the problem. Sometimes, if we just can't come up with the right solution, it pays to take a second look at the problem.

Desperately Seeking Solutions

Of course, even when we know what the problem is, we still have to solve it. We all have a variety of search strategies we can use as we attempt to find our way through life's maze. Two such strategies are *algorithms* and *heuristics*.

Psychobabble

A 1991 national poll calculated that 31 percent of adult respondents said yes to at least one of these indicators of alien abduction: being lost for at least an hour without remembering why; flying through the air without knowing why or how; waking up paralyzed with the sense of a strange presence in the room; seeing unusual lights in a room without understanding what caused them; or discovering puzzling scars on one's body with no memory of what caused them. Strange beliefs might not be reasonable, but they sure are common.

An algorithmic approach to solving problems involves thinking through every possible solution. A step-by-step approach. A heuristic approach, on the other hand, is a "rule of thumb" that serves as a shortcut to solving complex problems. Heuristics are general strategies that have worked in similar situations in the past. When I was getting married, one of my friends had all the married women write down "words of wisdom" for a happy marriage. Heuristics like "never go to sleep mad" have helped thousands of couples; if only I could stick with them!

Shrink Rap

Judgment is the process of using available information to form opinions, draw conclusions, and evaluate people and situations. Our decision making is based on our judgment.

Guilty Until Proven Innocent

The step-by-step diligence required by algorithms can be terrifically time-consuming, so it's no wonder that people use heuristics a lot of the time. And sometimes these shortcuts can be pretty useful. It's probably hard to go wrong with the "never go to sleep mad at each other" heuristic. However, our use of mental shortcuts can result in *cognitive bias,* errors in thinking that impact our judgment and ability to make effective decisions. Humans seem to have a number of built-in biases.

For example, remember that your mind tries to find connections between events and concepts. This means that it will look for connections even between random events, and see events that occur together as somehow causing each other. For instance, many medical professionals will tell you that a full moon "makes people crazy" and will give you anecdote after anecdote about wild experiences in the ER on full-moon weekends in the face of clear evidence to the contrary.

We also want to believe we control our fate. This might be a generally healthy belief, but it can hurt other people. All too easily, cognitive bias leads us to faulty *judgments,* such as blaming the victim, somehow believing that he caused whatever misfortune he experienced. The "she asked for" it attitude toward rape is an extreme example of human logic gone astray.

When used excessively, two mental shortcuts can lead us down blind alleys. One of these is the *availability heuristic.* This cognitive strategy encourages us to estimate probabilities based on our personal information or knowledge. If we have experienced it, or know about it, we will overestimate the frequency of its occurrence.

Take sexual harassment, for example. Here are the facts: The number-one reason people file complaints is to get the offensive behavior to stop, most complaints are settled through company policies and procedures, and few cases ever end up inside a courtroom. Yet, because of the media hype around this hot topic, people often think the fastest way to vacation in Tahiti is to sue for sexual harassment.

Another shortcut that can do some social damage is the *representativeness heuristic.* Think of this as confusing the part with the whole (or, referring back to Chapter 1, "A Little Psychological Insight," defining the whole elephant by its legs).

How would you like to be the official representative of your entire race or gender? Well, to some people, you are. The representativeness is based on the idea that people and events can be grouped into categories; once you've been categorized, the assumption is that you share all the features of other members in that category—and they share all your features, too.

The danger in this strategy is that it oversimplifies things. People, places, and things do not neatly fit into categories simply because we lazily assign them to certain groups. We're also likely to ignore or underestimate the complexity and diversity of unique individuals.

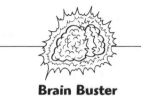

Brain Buster

The penalty for judging people or events by what seems to be their "type" is the Archie Bunker syndrome: We develop set ideas about people based on our preexisting notions and we spend the rest of our lives gathering evidence that confirms them.

Controlling the Winds of Change

If you're faced with the need to make a major decision, here's your chance to put all your new knowledge into action. We'll call this the "wind analysis"—a decision-making strategy that lets you control the winds of change and get them blowing in your favor—no matter what you ultimately decide.

To carry out a "wind analysis," take the following steps:

1. List all forces for a change in one column, and all the forces against change in another.

2. Assign a score to each force, from one (weak) to five (strong).

3. Draw a picture showing the forces for and against change. Be sure to illustrate the size of the forces.

Let's see how these steps work in a real decision-making context. Let's say you're deciding whether or not to switch careers from law to a community relations position for a nonprofit agency.

Forces for Change	Forces Against Change
Hate your job (5)	Used to your current position (2)
May be layoffs soon (3)	Are starting a family soon (4)
Have two months rent saved up (2)	Like the status of being an attorney (2)
	May be a promotion coming up (2)
	Parents might be disappointed (5)

Right now, your forces against change outweigh the forces for change (count up the points). A sketch illustrating the relative forces for and against change will help you clarify just how important each item is to you.

If you would like to make the change, but see that the forces of nature seem to be holding you back, brainstorm about how you can reduce the forces working against change and increase the forces in change's favor. For example, you might talk to your parents about how much the career move means to you—that might be enough to eliminate their disappointment. Give yourself a deadline to put your plan into action, and sail ahead!

Arguably, cognitive psychology is the most influential branch of psychology today. After reading this chapter you can see why. Our cognitive processes have an impact upon every single aspect of our lives. Not only do they enable us to solve life's mysteries, they strongly influence how we feel about them. "I think, therefore I am," may be somewhat of an overstatement, but not by much!

The Least You Need to Know

➤ Psychologists are detectives of the mind—by observing human behavior, analyzing errors, and scanning our brains, they gather clues about the way our minds work.

➤ Thinking is like a highly sophisticated assembly line made up of concepts, schemata, and scripts.

➤ There are two types of reasoning: inductive (which moves from general principles to specific cases) and deductive (which moves from specific clues to general conclusions).

➤ All thinking is geared toward solving problems, and uses either algorithmic or heuristic strategies.

➤ Algorithms consider every possible solution, while heuristics rely on shortcuts that have worked in similar situations.

➤ Heuristics save time, but they can also lead to cognitive errors.

Chapter 12

Get a Grip!

In This Chapter

➤ Stress is just a *GAS!*

➤ The difference between coping and moping

➤ The top-10 stress busters

➤ How your mind controls your matter

One joke, three times a day. A diet of *Candid Camera* clips. Ten minutes of laughter. These aren't the kinds of prescriptions we're used to our doctor prescribing, but research suggests maybe they should be. The link between our mind and our body is a powerful one. If negative emotions can cause physical distress, then positive emotions can enhance the healing process.

This chapter focuses on one of the greatest mental health challenges facing Americans today: stress. You'll find out what stress is, what causes it, and, most importantly, what coping strategies can best help you deal with it. We'll also take a look at other mind-body connections: the psychological effects of physical illness, how psychological illnesses can cause physical symptoms, and the complex interaction between our brain, body, emotions, and immune system. Follow the advice in this chapter and, by the end, you'll be an official stress buster—not to mention a workout fiend and comedy club groupie!

Shrink Rap

Stress is a general term that includes all the physical, behavioral, emotional, and cognitive responses we make to a disruptive internal or external event. **Stressors** are the events that trigger a stress response.

Stressed or Stressed Out?

Writer Norman Cousins was suffering from a debilitating, and generally incurable, connective tissue disease. Along with his traditional medical treatment, he routinely watched Marx Brothers movies of the 1930s and 1940s. Surprisingly, Cousins' doctors found that his tissue inflammation went down after only a few minutes of hearty laughter. He was eventually pronounced "cured" of his illness. Cousins was really onto something; laughter, as it turns out, is strong medicine, and humor a wonderful coping strategy.

Stress Is All Around

Have you ever heard anyone say he needed *more* stress in his life? I haven't. There are literally hundreds of stress-management tapes, books, and courses on the market, and not one of them offers strategies for increasing it. In the high-powered era in which we live, stress reduction has become a part of the American dream.

Given that we're constantly trying to get rid of stress, wouldn't we all be better off without any? Not really. Without stress, we would have no problems to overcome, goals to reach, or inventions to create. Pretty soon, we'd wind up as lazy couch potatoes with dull wits and no motivation. Even if we didn't, life would be pretty boring, which can be pretty stressful itself!

Stress and the Individual

Stress is a part of being alive. Being stressed out, however, isn't. Stress becomes a problem for us when we have too much stress and not enough resources to cope with it. Yet what is "too much" stress?

We've all known people who bounce back from even the toughest challenges, while others seem to have trouble coping with life's daily hassles. People also respond differently to the same stressor; the next time you're stuck in traffic, take a look around. You'll see some people calmly bebopping to the radio while others are frantically pulling onto the shoulder and craning their necks to look for a break in the traffic.

The difference between the beboppers and the neck craners is how the stressor is interpreted and the coping resources that are available to deal with it.

Psychobabble

Want to see a dramatic portrayal of what can happen when, over time, a person's stress overwhelms his ability to cope with it? Check out *Falling Down,* starring Michael Douglas. I don't want to spoil the ending for you, but let's just say that, given the outcome of the movie, stress-management strategies might look a little more appealing to you, too!

What Determines Your Stress Level

Stress is uniquely personal. Our response to stress is a unique combination of bodily reactions, thoughts, feelings, and behaviors. Take a look at all the factors that determine your stress level, and you'll understand why one person's pleasure is another person's poison.

Factors Affecting Your Personal Stress Level

Internal Factors	External Factors
physical health	medical care
genetic vulnerabilities	finances
mental health	skills and training
self-esteem	support systems
temperament	counseling
self-confidence	predictability of stressor
cultural expectations	frequency of stressor's occurrence
cultural definitions	intensity of stressor's occurrence

Your unique combination of personal factors, externally available resources, and certain attributes of the stressor itself are what determine just how much stress (if any) you'll feel in response to a given stressor.

Making Change

Evolution gave us stress to keep us on our toes, and we're still trying to keep our balance. Historically, changes in food supply, weather, or safety were the stressors our human ancestors faced. While today's challenges are more likely to challenge our self-esteem than our physical safety, they still involve coping with change.

Brain Buster

Too much change can be hazardous to your health. Recent widows and widowers are much more vulnerable to all types of disease in the six months following the death of a spouse. Losing someone close to you is a red flag to take extra good care of your mental and physical health.

When you think about it, change is the culprit in much of our stress. Whether it's the loss of a loved one or the birth of a baby, adjustment to a new situation requires a lot of energy and, sometimes, different coping strategies. Having a "good" change can be especially difficult because our expectations don't match reality.

For example, society tells expectant parents that the birth of a child is an utterly joyful event. When a new parent is less than thrilled with the reality of existing on two hours of sleep and changing diapers every 10 minutes, he or she can easily interpret the resulting stress as a sign of bad or incompetent parenting. This, of course, only adds more stress. If new parents can see their stress as a normal reaction to a dramatic lifestyle change, they might applaud themselves for surviving rather than berate themselves for feeling grouchy and tired!

Sometimes, stress appears before change even takes place. The "cold feet" many people get before their marriage is an example of the anticipatory stress of getting hitched. Change may put the spice in our life, but it also burns some calories!

How Do You Know If You're Stressed Out?

"I'm stressed out," you tell your best friend. But how do you know? Since people experience stress differently, it is important to know what being "stressed out" feels like to you. What did you do, how did you feel, and what were you thinking? When you're stressed, write down what you do, how you feel, and what you're thinking—and use the answers to these questions to conduct regular stress checkups. To get you started, here are some of the most common symptoms of stress:

➤ Feeling on edge, frustrated, easily annoyed

➤ Having trouble concentrating or making decisions

➤ Finding even simple things to be burdensome or difficult

➤ Eating more or less than usual

➤ Experiencing mood swings

➤ Feeling distracted—having a hard time keeping track of little things

➤ Being irritable or impatient

➤ Overreacting with strong feelings to minor events

➤ Not getting as much pleasure out of things that you usually enjoy

➤ Drinking more to relax or feel less tense

Burning Out

I once read that the average career life of a therapist was seven years. After seven years, most psychotherapists who are on the "front lines" dealing with clients every day go AWOL. They quit. They change careers. They burn out.

Burnout is a combination of emotional exhaustion, personal detachment, and a reduced sense of accomplishment that most often plagues professionals in the service industries—doctors, lawyers, psychologists, teachers. Anyone who has high-intensity contact with other people on a daily basis is at risk for job burnout. Not only does the professional suffer, the person on the receiving end gets shortchanged by inadequate or impersonal care. Perhaps the fire and enthusiasm that motivate people to choose a helping profession gradually gets extinguished by problems, paperwork, and too much people contact.

Shrink Rap

Burnout is a unique pattern of emotional symptoms often found in professionals who have high-intensity contact with others on a daily basis. It is a form of emotional fatigue characterized by exhaustion, a sense of failure, and a tendency to relate to others in a depersonalized and detached manner.

The Fires of Burnout Build over Time

Burnout is the end result of chronic, interpersonal stress. And it can happen in our personal lives, too. Ever had a friend whose life was one crisis after the next? With the first crisis, you probably mobilized all your resources to help your buddy out. With the second, you also responded to the "fire alarm." By the tenth or eleventh, however, your attitude may have been a little more cynical and your offer to help a lot slower. Your friend has cried wolf one too many times and burned your caring right out of you!

Know Your Stress Signs!

Chronic stress can cause serious physical and mental problems. Most of these problems can be prevented, and burnout is one of them. Health care professionals who regulate the amount of face-to-face patient contact, who take regular vacations and mental health days, who schedule in leisure activities, and who get support from work colleagues and family members are much less likely to burn out. How many times do we have to hear "an ounce of prevention is worth a pound of cure" before we listen to this good advice?

Brain Buster

Don't sweat the small stuff. There is a clear relationship between hassles—those small, everyday irritations like time pressure, money problems, or annoying neighbors—and health problems. If your life is filled with hassles, take care of them or, at the least, change your attitude toward them.

I Feel Like Fighting or Flying Away

You and a close friend are having lunch with a new work acquaintance. As you go through the normal get-acquainted chitchat, the conversation gradually turns to your love lives. While your friend is spilling her guts about her romantic history, she suddenly begins to tell your acquaintance about your recent breakup with a mutual work colleague. With you sitting right there, she goes on and on about your lingering feelings and your discomfort at seeing this person at work every day. Shocked, your blood pressure starts to rise and you're suddenly torn between punching your friend in the mouth or running out of the restaurant.

Punching out your friend might feel good for a few minutes, but you know it would only make matters worse. And running from the restaurant would not only make you feel foolish, it might confirm your new acquaintance's view of the emotional instability your friend's words seem to imply. So, why do you feel like running away or striking out?

Remember the endocrine system from Chapter 2, "Bio Psycho What?" This communication system helps regulate things like blood pressure, metabolism, and heart rate. As you sit there in the restaurant, clenching your fist and tightening your jaw, you are experiencing the *fight-or-flight syndrome,* a sequence of internal processes that are triggered by your endocrine system when it prepares for a threatening situation. This syndrome is not to be taken lightly; at least 15 bodily changes are triggered all at once.

Unfortunately, it's very rare these days for your built-in ability to become an instant lean, mean, fighting machine to pay off. Certainly, when it comes to relationships, your best bet is to stay calm, listen, and respond rationally. For example, if you logically think through your friend's breach of confidence, you might interrupt tactfully and let her know you don't want to talk about these things. And you can make your boundaries clear for the future. This may not be as immediately gratifying as a kick in the pants, but it's a lot more effective in the long term!

It's a GAS, GAS, GAS

Of course, the long term isn't necessarily our strong suit. In some respects, human beings are better equipped for the short run than the long haul. We get tired of the same foods. We get bored with the same activities. We get burned out on our jobs and, yes, sometimes we do punch out our friends! Even our stress responses work better in the short term; if we have to fight or flee too much, our emergency response system breaks down.

Hans Seyle was a man with great endurance and a psychologist's interest in the effects of chronic, severe stress on the body. He started wondering what would happen if the body were in a constant state of alarm. He got his answer—nothing good. Over time, chronic stress can tear us down and wear us out.

Shrink Rap

The **general adaptation response (GAS)** is a pattern of general physical responses that are triggered by any stressors, no matter what kind.

GASsing Up

According to Seyle, one of the reasons life stressors have a cumulative effect is that our bodies can't distinguish between them. Instead of generating different physical reactions to different life events, our bodies have a general physical response to any stress. Seyle called the pattern of bodily reactions to an ongoing, serious threat the *general adaptation response (GAS)* and identified three stages that make it up. Let's take a look at each stage:

1. alarm
2. resistance
3. exhaustion

All Stations on Alert!

The alarm stage is the "fight-or-flight" response in action. The body mobilizes energy to deal with a specific stressor, such as a near car accident, making a public speech, or getting married. Adrenaline is released into the blood stream; commonly causing sweaty palms, a pounding heart, rapid breathing, increased blood pressure, and slowed digestion. Although these symptoms can be uncomfortable, your body returns to normal fairly quickly once the stressor is alleviated. No harm done.

Fighting Harder

If the stressor continues, the body tries to compensate by kicking into overdrive. Temporarily, it works harder to resist the stress—hormones continue to pump adrenaline, physical arousal remains high, and the immune system works harder. Of course, you might not feel any of these things. What you may feel, though, is anxiety and a sense of being pressured or driven. You may begin having problems remembering details and you may start to feel fatigued. If you find yourself drinking more coffee, smoking more cigarettes, or boozing more than normal, your body may be trying to cope with too much stress.

Psychobabble

Post-traumatic stress disorder (PTSD) is a delayed, recurring stress reaction to a life-threatening event. During the reaction, victims involuntarily relive the past trauma, feel emotionally numb to everyday events, and often feel alienated from other people. In every war, soldiers have suffered similar symptoms, but they have been known by different names such as "combat fatigue" and "shell shock."

Ending in Exhaustion

Chronic stress often beats the body. Over time, it consumes more energy resources than your body can produce. Your hormones "burn out," leaving you with less resistance to emotional stress and physical illness. The emotional "burn out" that chronic stress produces is often known by another name: depression.

You'd save your body a lot of wear and tear if you could just switch your stress response on and off as needed, or if you could teach it the difference between a life-threatening event and a stressful, but happy, occasion. Unfortunately, you can't. What you *can* do is work with your stress response by building up your emotional "muscles" to handle stress more effectively.

Stress Busters

We can't always control what happens to us, but we can change how we respond to it. People who handle stress well have a healthy lifestyle that builds up their "stress resistance." They also develop some good crisis management techniques for those particularly difficult times. These 10 "stress busters" combine these strategies. The more you can incorporate into your life, the less likely it is that stress will get you down.

1. Exercise three to five times a week for at least 30 minutes.
2. Work off your anger by doing something physical (gardening, running, hitting a punching bag).
3. Use relaxation techniques—yoga, meditation, deep breathing.
4. Watch one funny movie a week, more during especially stressful times.
5. Maintain a regular sleep schedule—sleep deprivation is a big contributor to emotional stress.

6. Don't procrastinate.

7. Avoid caffeine, alcohol, sugar, and tobacco when you are stressed.

8. Volunteer once a month—helping others is an incredible stress reliever.

9. Set priorities weekly and make sure to schedule in leisure time.

10. Talk with others. A support system is one of the greatest stress busters. If you are going through a severe stressor (divorce, death in the family, serious medical illness) it can be helpful to be with others who have been through the same thing.

Coping or Moping

I once had a client who was a young, single mother of two very active sons. One of her sons had been diagnosed with attention deficit disorder and a learning disability, and needed extra attention and support. This woman received no financial or emotional support from her ex-spouse, who had left her for a younger woman and quit his job. Week after week, she worked full time, juggled her bills, and did a pretty darned good job of single parenting.

Yet she often came into my office in tears, berating herself for being unable to "cope" with her situation. In her definition, occasionally losing her temper or feeling stressed out was "not coping." In my professional opinion, the fact that she got through each day was a miracle and was worthy of an Olympic gold medal in the coping department.

Insight

Stress is one example of the mind-body connection. According to a recent study, nearly half of people with chronic tension headaches may also have anxiety and/or depression. Researchers don't know which comes first, headaches or the blues, but it's clear that for some chronic headaches, therapy might bring more relief than Motrin.

Developing a lifestyle that enhances your physical or mental well-being is a good strategy. Who could argue with advice such as don't procrastinate, eat healthy food, and get plenty of sleep? But a good lifestyle can't keep bad things from happening. When they do, the way you cope with them can mean the difference between bouncing back and getting knocked on your behind.

Coping is any strategy you use to deal with a situation that strains or overwhelms your emotional and/or physical resources. For example, if you get laid off of your job, you might feel angry and hurt, fantasize about revenge, and then polish your resumé and hit the pavement. Different stressors require different coping strategies; grieving the loss of a child would require different coping strategies than putting up with a chronically nagging spouse.

All Coping Is Not Created Equal

Let's say you applied for your dream job three months ago. You believe you were qualified for the job and were sure you'd get it. However six weeks ago, harsh reality knocked on your door—you found out someone else was hired. Now, all you can think about is how it should have been. Even though you know you should pick yourself up and start job-hunting again, you find yourself daydreaming about what would have happened if you'd been hired. You spend hours plotting revenge on the company official you're sure gave you the thumbs down. Are you coping?

Therapists would say no. Instead, they'd say you're defending against the pain of rejection by escaping into fantasies. Coping, on the other hand, involves identifying and eliminating the source of your problem—your lack of a job and your disappointment over not getting the job of your dreams.

Psychobabble

The next time you find yourself worrying, channel your stress into anticipatory coping. Mentally review similar past experiences; these will reacquaint you with what mistakes to avoid repeating, what reactions to expect, how you will feel, and what resources can help. Plan what you will do to cope with this stressor more effectively than you have in the past. While worrying can increase stress, anticipatory coping can help you prepare for a stressful event.

The difference between coping and defending can be tricky to understand and even harder to detect in our own lives. As a rule of thumb, defending ourselves merely lessens the symptoms of the problems, often only temporarily. Coping, on the other hand, gets to the root of the problem and focuses on changing what we can change and making peace with what we can't.

What Are You Coping With?

Life would be a lot easier if the perfect solution to every argument was to look your opponents in the eye and tell them your honest thoughts and feelings. This coping strategy might work well with your spouse, but there aren't many job supervisors who want to hear that you think they're incompetent boobs. Psychologists would agree that facing up to a stressful situation is always a pretty good idea, but finding the best way to face up to it depends on the situation.

Categories of Coping

In general, coping strategies fall into two categories—problem-focused coping and emotion-focused coping. Each has it's strengths and weaknesses, and each is best suited to particular categories of stressors.

Focusing on the Problem

With problem-focused coping, you deal directly with the stressor to change or eliminate it. You confront your teenager about running up your long-distance phone bill or, more realistically, you put on a block so she can't dial out. You take a self-defense class to cope with your fear of being victimized. Problem-focused coping works best when the stressor is controllable—when you can actually do something to change it.

Gaining the Emotional Edge

With emotion-focused coping, the goal is to change the way you feel and think about whatever is stressing you. For example, unless you can afford to quit your job, it might not be a good idea to confront a critical or controlling boss. You can, however, get emotional support from coworkers in the same boat. You can also use self-talk that lessens your boss's impact on you: The next time he or she criticizes you, you can mentally remind yourself that it's your boss's problem and he or she is the one who should be embarrassed by such behavior, not you.

Emotion-focused coping works best for stressors that you can't control. They don't eliminate the source of the stress, but they can change what the stressor means to you. It's a lot more stressful to think of divorce as a personal failure than to think of it as a painful learning experience.

In reality, of course, many stressors in our lives have both uncontrollable *and* controllable parts. A person who has cancer can seek the best medical care and take control of his or her illness. At the same time, however, that person can't change the diagnosis and will have to find ways to cope with the fear, anger, and sadness that accompany such a scary illness.

Identifying Your Stressors

If you frequently feel victimized by life's events, you may be using emotion-focused coping to deal with situations you can change. One of the complicated parts of coping is identifying which

Insight

For years, research concluded that men used problem-focused coping while women more often used emotion-focused coping: Men "took action" while women "wallowed in their feelings." Recent research disagrees. Gender differences in coping are limited to what events are considered to be most stressful. Women say relationship hassles, while men complain about work-related problems.

events are controllable and which are not. How many times have you heard a friend complain about her boyfriend over and over, yet never tell him what was bothering or hurting her? It's fine that she's dealing with her emotions by complaining to her friends, but she should have an action plan in place before she hangs up the phone!

Stressful Thoughts

Oh, no, I just have seven more weeks to finish this book. That's not enough time! What if I miss my deadline? I've heard Macmillan is really strict about deadlines; they will never ask me to write another book if I turn this one in late. Maybe they won't even publish this one!

Do those thoughts sound like a good general coping strategy to you? Probably not; in fact, you may have started getting nervous about my deadline, too. The way we think about the stressors in our lives influences both the emotions we have about them and the solutions we come up with. To some extent, they're the key to both emotion-focused *and* problem-focused coping.

For example, before you can decide what to do about whatever event is stressing you out, you have to identify it and evaluate its severity. This is called *cognitive appraisal*, a highly subjective and amazingly powerful process. As you can see from my frantic thoughts above, the time pressure (the stressor) of writing this book sometimes became much greater because of the catastrophic thoughts (the cognitive appraisal) that went with it. Even psychologists have trouble coping sometimes!

Humor Helps

Clearly, one powerful way to handle stress more adaptively is to change the way we think about the stressors in our lives and to prevent self-defeating thoughts about how to deal with them. A commonsense way to reduce speech anxiety is to mentally make the audience less threatening—by imagining them in their underwear or wearing clown noses. Even hard-driving pro quarterback Joe Montana used humor to relieve pressure; he often made jokes in the huddle while he led his team to yet another Super Bowl victory!

I Think I Can, I Think I Can, I Think I Can

And it helps to believe that you can cope with your stressors. People often underestimate their ability to cope with life's curve balls. Even though they've survived relationship breakups, career disappointments, physical illnesses, and many other stressors, the minute a new stressor comes along they start thinking that they can't cope with it.

One of the most powerful stress-busting strategies is to keep track of your coping history. Seeing your impressive track record helps you keep at bay any untrue negative self-statements like, "I'll never get this right" or "I just can't stand this."

Psychobabble

In 1974, bank employees in Stockholm, Sweden, were imprisoned in a bank vault for five days during a robbery. Upon their release, the employees expressed warmth—and even attraction—for the men who had taken them hostage. This bizarre emotional response became known as the Stockholm Syndrome, a coping pattern in which hostages and prisoners identify and sympathize with their captors. Sometimes, extreme situations trigger extreme forms of emotion-focused coping.

Mind over Matter

The boundary between our minds and our bodies is so thin that it's practically non-existent. Thinking differently about a stressful event can actually help your body relax. Psychological stress leads to bodily arousal. Depression lowers your immune system. And as you saw in the beginning of this chapter, positive emotions can even speed up the healing process.

This shouldn't be all that surprising. After all, your brain is responsible for your thoughts and feelings as well as for the regulation of many of your bodily functions. No wonder experiences that have an impact on your thoughts and feelings can also affect your physical functioning.

In fact, sometimes the body expresses what the mind can't. One example of this is when a person experiences bodily ailments in the absence of any physical illness. Psychologists call these *somatoform disorders.* The most dramatic of these disorders is *conversion disorder,* in which the person temporarily loses some bodily function in ways that cannot be explained by physical illness.

A less dramatic example is *somatization disorder,* which is characterized by a long history of vague and unverifiable medical complaints. Most typically, the person complains of symptoms of several disorders; so, for example, the person might complain of headaches, dizziness, heart palpitations, and nausea. While a certain

Shrink Rap

Somatoform disorders are mental disorders in which the person experiences symptoms of physical illness but has no medical disease that could cause them. **Conversion disorder** and **somatization disorder** are included in this category.

percentage of people with these diagnoses turn out to have underlying medical conditions, a significant number have an underlying psychological condition—depression.

Seeking Immunity

At the beginning of this chapter, you met Norman Cousins. Through his use of laughter to cope with a life-threatening illness, he reawakened Western medicine's interest in the positive relationship between our mental and physical health. We now know that laughter brings oxygen to the blood very quickly by increasing respiration, heart rate, and circulation. People who must cope with devastating illness or trauma may find humor a therapeutic way to respond to their difficult circumstances.

The field of *psychoneuroimmunology* is the study of the interactions between the brain, the body, the emotions, and the immune system. It's common sense that anxiety or depression would make us more susceptible to physical illness. We now have scientific confirmation; an increasing number of studies show that emotional distress shuts down some of the body's defenses against viruses and, in that way, makes us more vulnerable to infectious diseases.

It seems that evolution had to make a tradeoff. When the emergency stress response is triggered, the body mobilizes all of its resources for action. Functions that are not on the emergency team are temporarily shut down. While hormones are raging around preparing for battle, energy-consuming aspects of the immune system, like the production of white blood cells, are temporarily suppressed. Alas, modern stresses don't go away as quickly as a charging tiger, and the immune system sometimes takes a back seat long enough for a few bugs to crawl in.

Psychobabble

How many horrible things can a person bear to see? Cambodian women who immigrated to the United States after the Khmer Rouge reign of terror show a high rate of psychological blindness. Many of them had seen their children tortured and killed. There's nothing physically wrong with their vision, but they're literally blind to further atrocities.

We started off this chapter looking at the evolution of our "fight-or-flight" response to emergencies. In some respects, our bodies have not caught up with the times. They're still using the same old emergency system our ancestors used to fight off bears and defend their territory. Luckily for us, our brains have given us the ability to develop some nifty coping strategies to handle the stress in our lives. If we use them, we can help the evolution of our own body—that is, the aging process—go more smoothly.

The Least You Need to Know

➤ Stress is a normal response to overwhelming internal or external events.

➤ Common symptoms of stress include feeling irritable and on edge, overreacting to minor events, mood swings, and difficulty concentrating.

➤ While stress initially energizes your body to take action, over time it is physically exhausting and your immune system is weakened.

➤ We handle threatening situations by coping—either through changing the situation or by altering the ways we think and feel about it.

➤ Psychological difficulties can get channeled into physical symptoms—psychologists call these "somatization disorders."

Part 4
Self and Otherness

What is it that makes us feel as if we belong? And what makes us feel like outsiders? Each of us possesses a unique mix of personality traits, values, behavioral styles, and beliefs—a combination of elements that makes for the incredible diversity of humankind. Here's where you'll learn all about these building blocks of the individual personality, and about the factors that shape each of us as we experience our way through life. You'll learn what is meant by "intelligence" and how it's measured, and you'll explore the murky area between eccentricity and abnormal behavior.

Chapter 13

Me, Myself, and I

In This Chapter

➤ We're *all* "material girls" (or guys)

➤ Teenage angst and other postpubescent blues

➤ Getting in touch with your masculine and feminine sides

➤ Making your midlife crisis–free

➤ Seeing how far your gender bends

➤ Exploring the gentle art of self-defense

Who are you? What are you? *How* are you? These are all aspects of a larger question: How is your identity formed?

In this chapter, we'll help you answer that question. We'll explore how people develop their self-concept, and straighten out that overused but frequently misunderstood thing called self-esteem. And last, but certainly not least, we'll talk about the ways we protect our good opinion of ourselves, and how we dissociate ourselves from bad experiences.

Gender and Selfhood

What if someone told you that you had to live the rest of your life as a member of the opposite sex? You'd still think of yourself as a man (or a woman) and have the same

Insight

Check out the movie *Tootsie,* in which Dustin Hoffman plays an unemployed actor posing as a female to get a part in a soap opera. During the filming, Hoffman was so concerned with his performance that he got into arguments defending his femininity. Even more confusing was Julie Andrews's character in *Victor, Victoria:* a female singer playing a man playing a woman.

feelings and behaviors. Nothing about you would change, but from this day forward, the world would treat you as if you were of the opposite gender.

That's how Canadian Michelle Josef, born as Bohdan Hluszko, has felt all her life. Since the age of seven, Michelle thought of herself as a girl and was often mistaken for one. But Bohdan was biologically a man. Over the years, he tried everything to cope with his ongoing sense of being a woman trapped in a man's body: drugs, therapy, marriage, and cross-dressing. Four years ago, he reached the end of his rope, called a friend, and said he was going to shoot himself.

That was the day Bohdan Hluszko died and Michelle Josef was born. Rescued from the brink of suicide, Michelle began years of psychotherapy and hormone treatments. She began living as a woman and is working toward sex reassignment surgery. While Michelle has finally achieved self-acceptance, the Canadian government has not been so open-minded. It refused national health insurance payment for Michelle's surgery, and as a result, she is suing.

Josef/Michelle had a particularly difficult time figuring out who he/she was. After all, gender is the most fundamental characteristic of who we are. But it's not easy for many of us, either. And there are other, important aspects of selfhood, beyond gender, that we need to consider.

Insight

The only other animals beside ourselves who have passed the rouge test of self-recognition are the other great apes: chimpanzees, bonobos, orangutans, and at least one species of gorilla. Other animals continue to treat the mirror image as another animal and try to threaten or chase it away.

Know Thyself

In ancient Greece, worshipers who wanted to know the future would consult the oracle at the Temple of Apollo in Delphi. At the Temple entrance, a stone inscription counseled visitors to "Know Thyself"—something psychologists counsel their clients about today. Apparently, good advice is timeless.

Self-awareness is one of the hallmarks of human nature, and it starts early. By about 15 months of age, infants understand that they are separate from other people and things in their lives. Around this time babies stop reacting to their image in a mirror as if it were another child and begin to see it as their own reflection. If a researcher places a bright red spot of rouge on an infant's nose while she's watching in a mirror, the 15-month-old responds by touching her own nose to feel or rub off the rouge. A younger child will touch the mirror or look behind it to find the funny-looking, red-nosed baby.

But Who Is Thyself?

Just who is the self and how do we know about it? If psychologist William James had known Madonna, he would have said she was right on when she sang about being a "material girl." James believed we're all partly material girls, or guys. In his view, the "material" self is an essential part of who we are; the other two parts are the social self and the spiritual self. Each of these is essential to the way we experience ourselves.

Our Toys "R" Us

For James, just about everything we came into contact with on a regular basis became part of our identity. For example, James believed the "material me" is the part of the self that is concerned with the body and with material possessions. He wouldn't bat an eye at a car buff's need to wash and polish his new Jaguar every weekend. Why not? James would argue that the Jag is an extension of its owner's identity.

It's Who You Know

A second part of James's self, the "social me" revolves around our interactions and reputation with others. James believed that our relationships with other people were a strong part of our identity. If you got upset when someone hurt your feelings, your therapist might recommend you read the book *Codependent No More*, but William James would say your feelings are perfectly normal. After all, when your family or friends are hurt, hasn't part of your "self" been threatened?

That's the Spirit!

The "spiritual me" is the one that holds your private thoughts and feelings. You don't have to go to church to get in touch with your spiritual side, but you do have to spend time alone getting to know yourself. If you don't, you may rely on your social and physical sides to make up for your underdeveloped spirituality—and, heaven forbid, you might turn into a money-grubbing social climber!

Reflections in a Looking Glass

Many years ago, sociologist Charles Cooley coined the phrase "looking-glass self" to describe the influence that others' opinions have on our self-concept, especially when we're young. He believed that we defined ourselves, in part, by what others "reflect" back in response to who we are and what we do. In Cooley's opinion, we use the inferences and images other people have of us to build our own self-concepts.

Shrink Rap

Your **self-concept** is your awareness of your identity as a distinct and unique individual.

Mirror, Mirror on the Wall

The implications of Cooley's theory are clear. If a child is treated lovingly, she believes she is lovable. If he is told he is handsome (and treated handsomely), he comes to believe that, too. To a child, the difference between being "good" and "bad" is not so much how he behaves, but how he is treated. What awesome power (and responsibility) grownups have!

The impact that your perceptions can have on a child's sense of self has been widely documented. Children really do live up to our expectations and opinions of them—for better or worse. The good news is that you can put your influence to good use. If you want a child to develop a certain quality, treating him or her as if that quality is already present can actually shape the child in that direction. Telling a child "you are" has a much greater impact than saying "you should be."

Reflections in a Golden Eye

Studies clearly illustrate that a child's self-concept changes in accordance with feedback from teachers and peers. In experiments where children were told they were a certain kind of person, they responded by behaving in a way that was consistent with this feedback. For example, one group of children was told they were neat and tidy, another was told they *should be* neat and tidy, and a third group was given no direction at all. Those who had been told they were neat and tidy became neater and tidier, while the others pretty much stayed the same.

Psychobabble

Is your self-concept realistic? Here's a test to help you find out. Write down the top-10 adjectives that you believe most fully express who you are. Now, ask five of your closest friends or family members to do the same thing. (Make sure you're getting along with them when you ask.) How closely does your own description match up with the others? Could you be wrong about yourself? Could your friends be wrong about you?

Of course, most people aren't as easily manipulated as the children in this experiment. However, adults can be amazingly vulnerable to the whims and feedback of others if they haven't developed a strong sense of identity. If you don't know who you are, you may change your self-perceptions every time someone misperceives you; if your sense of self is strong, however, you're more likely to correct the misperceptions of others than to change your self-concept to fit them.

It's Like, You Know, a Teen Thing

While your self-concept begins at birth, it's during the teen years that your identity really takes shape. According to psychologist Erik Erikson, between ages 12 and 18 we begin to discover who we are, and, as many parents know firsthand, who we don't want to be. In fact, much of adolescents' "rebellion" against parents and other authority figures is a healthy attempt to get some space and figure out the lay of the land for themselves.

Insight

Were your teenage years lonely? Between 15 percent and 25 percent of all teenagers report feeling very lonely. The intensity of a search for identity, and the need for a good support system, can be a difficult balance, indeed.

Adolescent Angst

While we often associate identity crises with midlife, Erikson believed that the first identity crisis happens in adolescence. This very necessary crisis involves discovering one's true identity among the many different roles we play for different audiences: parents, teachers, and friends.

In Erickson's opinion, resolving this crisis is both a uniquely personal process and a shared social experience. While teens are going through it, they're struggling to find themselves without losing the comfort of belonging with friends and family members. Some of us would say this struggle never ends.

The Power of the Peer Group

Peers are especially important to a teen's identity formation. As teens move away from their parents, they spend less time at home and more time with peers. They also use peers to try out different social behaviors. One compromise between a teen's need for independence and desire for interdependence involves experimenting with different norms, such as clothing or hairstyle, within the security of a peer group, a clique, or a romantic partner.

Ironically, while new norms may establish a teen's separateness from the family, they simultaneously establish conformity with his or her peers. (In Chapter 24, "You Can't Live with 'Em," you'll find more about giving up the "norms" of one social group for another.)

Psychobabble

Famous psychologists can have identity crises, too. Erik Erickson had a hard time forming an identity that was uniquely his. His biological father, who left before Erik was born, was Nordic but his mother and stepfather were Jewish and he was raised in that culture. Because he looked Nordic but had a different upbringing, he did not fit in either culture.

The Family Circle

While a teenager's major source of approval and acceptance comes from the peer group, teens still rely on their families for structure and support. Teens spend a lot of time talking about their parents, even if that talk isn't very flattering. Trying to be different from your parents requires a lot of involvement and attention, because you have to consider what your parents are before you decide what you are not.

Going through an identity crisis can be painful at any age, and it's no fun for most teens. The rewards, however, are great. Teens who face identity issues head-on develop an identity that remains stable regardless of the setting or the social group in which they find themselves. They have a clearer sense of who they are and they're better able to make independent decisions and choices about their career, sexual orientation, and life in general.

In Defense of the Midlife Identity Crisis

Surviving adolescence gives most of us a couple of peaceful decades before the next identity crisis hits. This is the one you've surely heard about: Your friend turns 40, ditches her vice-presidency and six-figure salary, and buys a cabin in the backwoods of Montana. Or the straightlaced accountant suddenly starts wearing leather and espousing new age mysticism. The stable family man buys a red Porsche and finds a girlfriend half his age. The midlife crisis has become so well known that people who don't have one may feel they're missing out!

But is it real? Studies say yes, but it appears to be less common than we think. Only one in 10 midlifers goes through a true crisis, where their world suddenly turns upside down and they consider radically changing their lifestyle. However, while most 40-somethings don't find their identities completely off-center, many are likely to experience a midlife review of their accomplishments and make some adjustments to their expectations and goals.

When mortality rears its threatening head, many people find themselves thinking about spirituality as well as the legacy they'd like to leave behind. In fact, a midlife review may be the process by which people not only evaluate the first half of their lives, but also figure out the pleasures of the second.

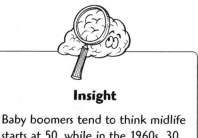

Insight

Baby boomers tend to think midlife starts at 50, while in the 1960s, 30 was considered the beginning of middle age. So even if you're headed for a midlife crisis, you get to put it off for a decade or so longer than your parents' generation did!

Avoiding the Comparison Trap

You've just gotten ready for a night on the town. You took a leisurely bath, put on your makeup, and are wearing your favorite outfit. For once, when you look in the mirror you feel pretty satisfied with what you see. Until you step out of your apartment. There, waiting in line for the elevator, is the clear winner of the Supermodel Look-Alike contest. Suddenly, you feel like running back into the apartment and pulling the covers over your head until the next eclipse of the moon.

Keeping Up with the Joneses

For better or worse, we all compare ourselves to the people around us. This cursed tendency probably has its origins in Cooley's "looking-glass self." While we're busy building models of ourselves from the feedback others give us, part of that work is comparing our models of ourselves to the models we observe of other people. As we grow older, this comparison becomes an internal frame of reference through which we see ourselves.

The evaluation part of such a *social comparison* can be very emotional. You feel good when you think you measure up to others, and bad when you don't. Some people might argue that every adjective we use to describe ourselves is secretly a comparison. If I describe myself as "tall," the implicit question is "tall in comparison to whom?" The answer to that question depends upon who is your *reference group*.

Shrink Rap

The process of comparing ourselves with others to identify our own unique abilities is called **social comparison**. A **reference group** is any group I am using to compare and evaluate myself, from age-related peers to supermodels on the covers of fashion magazines.

Referentially Speaking

The reference group is any group you use for social comparison. At work, it might be your coworkers or, if you have a competitive streak, your boss. For teenagers, it's almost always their peers. Sometimes a shift in your sense of self-worth can occur with a new job or a move to a new school; such a move entails a change of reference group that can have a dramatic impact your self-esteem.

Beautiful teenage girls often see themselves as ugly, and the more often they read fashion magazines, the more likely they are to do so. Girls who compare themselves with airbrushed supermodels are bound to feel bad about themselves because they are comparing themselves to a fantasy reference group. Even the models themselves don't look like that when they wake up in the morning, so how can any normal teen hope to do so?

Hello, Your High Esteemness!

The number-one, most popular psychology buzzword today is *self-esteem.* I've heard the low self-esteem "diagnosis" used to explain everything from a car that won't run to a boyfriend who won't commit. Low self-esteem, it seems, is either a worldwide epidemic or a popular excuse for bratty behavior—maybe both!

Self-esteem is a particular way of experiencing the self. While we most frequently think of it as a feeling ("I don't feel good about myself," or "I need to feel better about myself"), it is much more. It is a way of thinking and acting and feeling. For example, self-esteem is your tendency to experience yourself as being capable of coping with life's challenges and of being worthy of happiness and love. The two components most often linked to self-esteem are self-confidence and self-respect.

Self-esteem is not the same as being conceited or having a "big ego." In fact, people you might call vain or selfish generally have low self-esteem. Here are a few other myths and realities of this important, but misunderstood, concept:

Myth: If your self-esteem is too high, you will be self-absorbed and selfish.

Reality: It is impossible to have too much self-esteem. Self-absorption comes from not having enough self-esteem.

Myth: If you want to raise your child's self-esteem, praise her for whatever she does.

Reality: Children quickly realize when parents' praise is not based on their efforts or accomplishments. Too much praise can feel like "pressure" and unconditional praise (which is different than unconditional love) isn't credible. It can actually *lower* a child's self-concept.

Myth: If you want to solve your problems, raise your self-esteem.

Reality: The myth has it backwards. Self-esteem is often raised by meeting your problems head-on and treating yourself with respect.

Myth: Your self-esteem is determined by your childhood.

Reality: Self-esteem is something that can be raised or lowered at any point in life. Your parents can give you a boost, or throw you some curve balls, as can your peers, teachers, and others.

Myth: If you have good self-esteem, nothing bothers you.

Reality: Struggle is a part of life and sooner or later, we all feel anxiety and sadness, and go through tough times. Self-esteem won't protect you from pain, but it can help you bounce back faster and believe that you'll make it through.

Psychobabble

While the term *is* certainly overused, there's no doubt that self-esteem *is* important. And, as it turns out, you have as much to do with your self-esteem as your parents, teachers, and peers. While your self-concept is heavily influenced by others, your self-esteem is equally dictated by your own thoughts and actions. It is built, or rebuilt, according to the way you treat yourself and the way you talk to, and about, yourself.

"High self-esteem" is something you earn; it is an active process of treating yourself (and others) well, and replacing negative or self-critical thoughts with acceptance and realism. The good feelings you associate with self-esteem are often the result of hard work. Luckily, you have some built-in mechanisms that protect your self-esteem from your own misdeeds as well as your daily trials and tribulations. One of the most fascinating is the self-serving bias.

Safeguarding Self-Esteem

You consider yourself a principled, loyal person who would never cheat on your spouse or loved one. Yet, at a recent work conference, you gave in to temptation and hit the sack with a colleague. Now what do you do?

Chances are the first thing you'd do is try to get rid of the emotional turmoil your actions have created. We're uncomfortable when our actions don't match our self-perceptions, beliefs, and values. According to cognitive theorist Leon Festinger, we experience an internal tension he calls *cognitive dissonance.*

Festinger's theory of cognitive dissonance says that we all have a strong need to perceive a consistency between our thoughts, words, actions, and values. When we do something we think we "shouldn't" have, we search for some viable explanation that will make our emotional discomfort go away.

213

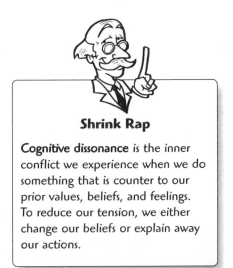

Shrink Rap

Cognitive dissonance is the inner conflict we experience when we do something that is counter to our prior values, beliefs, and feelings. To reduce our tension, we either change our beliefs or explain away our actions.

Cognitive dissonance motivates us to try to rationalize our contradictory behaviors so that they seem to follow naturally from personal beliefs and attitudes. For your conference fling, you might try denial ("it wasn't really sex"), or you might revise your attitudes to make them fit your actions ("as long as my spouse doesn't find out, no harm was done" or "I'll make it up to him in some way"). You then might internalize your attitude to make acceptable what otherwise appears to be irrational or wrong.

To some extent, this self-justification is the gentle art of verbal self-persuasion. You're actively using your communication skills to convince yourself that your actions were justified—or at least understandable. If this sounds like plain old excuse making to you, it is—except that you're making convincing excuses to yourself!

Sex Roles and Designated Gender Drivers

When did pink and blue become the designated drivers of our gender identity? Why wasn't it yellow or green? I know women who hate pink for what it implies (and some who love it for the same reason). Even today, with more gender equality, we have trouble giving up our stereotypes. The helpful clerk in the toy store asks if you're buying for a girl or a boy. Unisex clothing is blurring the gender lines a bit, but there is still that holdover for "frilly" versus "rugged."

Puppy Dogs' Tails or Sugar and Spice?

One reason we may never settle the nature-nurture debate of male-female differences is that parents begin interacting differently from birth depending on the sex of the child. We focus on different behaviors and we interpret the same behavior differently. If you follow traditional thinking, you are much more likely to believe your bawling six-month-old boy is angry but your squalling six-month-old daughter is sad or afraid. Such gender imprinting shapes our identities from birth.

Gender, Worth, and Self-Worth

In many cultures there is great celebration at the arrival of a new son, while plans for the daughter include selling her off in marriage for a good price. Imagine what that does to a girl's self-esteem from day one. Even *here* it persists. A couple who had planned to adopt a baby from a pregnant Chicago teenager had their hopes dashed when the baby turned out to be a boy—the teenager's boyfriend decided he would keep it. He would give up a daughter, but not a son.

Gender is a fundamental part of your self-concept. From birth, a boy and a girl will have a dramatically different experience—just because they are of different sexes. And gender does more than shape who we are. It can have a profound influence on what we, and others, think we're worth. Luckily, gender identity is much more complicated than mere biological sex. And it's this fact that can even the odds for women.

Call It Gender, Not Sex

Your gender identity is your personal sense of maleness or femaleness, and it isn't fully established until you're about three years old. Until that age, gender reassignments can occur fairly easily; after that, children think of themselves as either permanently male or permanently female. While your genes determine your sex, your gender identity may be like language—easily acquired, but only in a critical "window" during early childhood.

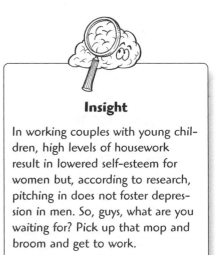

Insight

In working couples with young children, high levels of housework result in lowered self-esteem for women but, according to research, pitching in does not foster depression in men. So, guys, what are you waiting for? Pick up that mop and broom and get to work.

Your gender identity is much more complicated than your sexual identity—it's your total pattern of traits, tastes, and interests. In the past, masculinity and femininity were thought to be polar opposites (pink or blue, passive or aggressive). Men were thought to have instrumental qualities (to take action) and women were believed to have expressive qualities (nurturant, gentleness). There were often dire consequences for failing to conform to these gender norms.

Psychobabble

Your gender may be more flexible than you think. Due to a circumcision accident, a Canadian boy was reassigned a new gender and raised as a girl. An operation at seven months removed the testicles, and female hormones were given to help the child develop breasts and other female traits. The child, now an adult, lives happily as a woman and describes herself as bisexual.

Oddly enough, the birth control pill was the impetus for challenging traditional gender roles. Women were freed to choose the number of children they had, and therefore could enter the workforce in greater numbers. Voilà! They got in touch with their "masculine side," and proved that sex roles could be transformed.

Gender Bending

Do you consider yourself feminine, masculine, or somewhere in between? How do you think others see you? What are your earliest memories of being aware that you were a boy or a girl? The answers to all of these questions provide clues about your gender identity.

Not so long ago, many people (including a fair number of psychologists) assumed that the "proper" personality for a man did not include nurturant behavior, and that women should be compliant and nurturing and essentially passive. In fact, if you asked a man if he was in touch with his feminine side he might have punched your lights out!

We now know that women who get in touch with their masculine side, and men who discover the "woman" within, are better off for doing so. Men and women with androgynous personalities are far more successful (and happier) than are people with stereotypically masculine and feminine personalities.

Meet Mr. and Ms. Androgyny

The androgynous personality incorporates both the positive feminine or expressive qualities of nurturing, kindness, and an ability to listen to others, with the positive qualities stereotypically associated with masculinity—such as self-assurance, decisiveness, and leadership ability.

It's a widespread phenomenon these days. We see it with the melding of roles in two-income families. Men travel around with baby carriers on their backs, or pushing strollers, and doing grocery shopping with the toddler sitting in the cart. And these men don't look any less masculine to me (and their wives look a whole lot happier). Another sign of progress is the increasing opportunity for women to play team sports; anyone watching the U.S. women's soccer team win the world cup got a first-hand glimpse of female competitiveness and power.

In other words, anyone can have the tastes, abilities, and temperaments of both a male and a female. The androgynous person has a healthy mix of masculine and feminine qualities—the best of both worlds.

Do you? See how androgynous you are. Rate the traits in the three columns with the number that best fits you according to the following scale, and see if your world needs to be expanded.

1 = never true

2 = rarely true

3 = sometimes true

4 = often true

5 = always or almost always true

Column 1	Column 2	Column 3
Loyal	Moody	Act as a leader
Cheerful	Happy	Forceful
Compassionate	Secretive	Assertive
Warm	Reliable	Independent
Shy	Tactful	Willing to take risks

Scoring: Add up your scores in each column. In column 1 are stereotypically feminine traits, in column 2 are neutral traits, and in column three are stereotypically masculine traits. Subtract column 1 from column 3; the higher the score, the more "masculine" you are; the lower the score (including negative numbers), the more feminine you are. The neutral column is neither stereotypically masculine or feminine; it is there as a "control" to prevent expectations about which adjectives are masculine or feminine from completely dominating your scores.

The Big-Time Gender Blues

Remember Josef/Michelle at the beginning of the chapter? He/she is a transsexual, a condition technically referred to as *gender dysphoria*. Gender dysphoria affects one out of every 20,000 to 50,000 persons in the United States, and each one has the biological makeup of one sex but the psychological makeup of the other. The transsexual truly feels trapped inside the wrong body.

Boys with gender dysphoria are typically preoccupied with traditionally feminine activities. They may prefer dressing in girls' or women's clothing or may improvise such items from available materials when clothes aren't available. They show a strong attraction for the stereotypical games and pastimes of girls, may express a strong wish to be a girl, and, when young, may express the belief that they will grow up to be a woman. Girls with

Insight

If it's still around, go through your childhood toy box. What's in it? Boy toys like little soldiers and train sets? Girl toys like baby dolls and cooking utensils? See which toys were gender-specific and which were neutral. Do you anticipate your own children playing with similar toys?

Shrink Rap

Gender identity disorder, or **gender dysphoria,** is a clinical illness characterized by a desire to be, or insistence that one is, of the opposite sex. Men have this disorder two to three times more often than women.

gender dysphoria display intensely negative reactions to parental expectations or attempts to have them wear dresses or other feminine attire, have powerful male figures as fantasy heroes, and may dress and act like boys.

Children do not "grow out of" gender dysphoria. Oftentimes, they become socially isolated and, like Josef/Michelle, spend years trying to come to terms with their gender dysphoria and confusion. Sex-change surgery, considered the best treatment for those who qualify, is a gradual and strict process. The individual must live as the other gender for two years before surgery, undergo a rigorous battery of psychological tests, and undergo a lot of hormone replacement treatment before the final decision is made. While only a handful of patients qualify for sex reassignment surgery each year, most transsexuals are much happier with their new lives.

Sacrificing Identity to Escape Pain

Your identity is, fundamentally, who you are. From birth, you struggle to define the boundaries between yourself and the people around you. You develop a sense of your gender, and work hard to decide what it will say about who you are. And you use built-in strategies to protect your "self" from your own behavioral errors and to buffer you from hurtful feedback from others. In short, you work hard to build, and then protect, your identity.

If your emotional pain is great enough, however, you might sacrifice parts of who you are to get away from the hurt you feel. This is what happens with *dissociative* disorders; people escape from their conflicts by giving up parts of themselves, sacrificing a consistent and continuous identity to get away from intense psychic pain. Dissociative disorders are involuntary psychic tradeoffs. Let's take a look at three of them:

➤ psychogenic amnesia

➤ dissociative fugue states

➤ depersonalization

Dissociative (Psychogenic) Amnesia

Psychogenic amnesia is a psychological disorder in which a person loses the memory of important (usually stressful or traumatic) personal experiences for no apparent physical reason. For example, an uninjured driver in a serious car crash in which a friend was killed may not recall anything that happened from the time of the accident until a few days later. Understandably, in that tragic situation, the psyche may decide that it's worth losing a few days of one's identity to avoid the pain of remembering such a sad experience.

Dissociative Fugue States

The fugue state is a fascinating and rare phenomenon in which someone suddenly leaves home but doesn't remember how or why, loses his or her identity, and sometimes actually develops a new identity. Often, the person's new identity contrasts sharply with his or her original identity. For example, a timid man might turn into a fast-talking hustler. While soap opera plots may try to convince you otherwise, most fugue states involve brief, apparently purposeful travel with only partial construction of a new identity. In fact, about half of all fugues last less than 24 hours.

Shrink Rap

A **dissociative disorder** is a psychological disorder characterized by a disturbance in the integration of identity, memory, or consciousness. Psychogenic amnesia and fugue states are examples of dissociative disorders.

Psychobabble

In 1980, a woman dubbed "Jane Doe" was found wandering in a park in Florida. She was emaciated and near death, had no memory of her name or her past. She even lacked the ability to read and write. After a national search, an Illinois couple recognized Jane Doe as their daughter. This girl had moved to Florida four years earlier and not contacted them again. They were confident that she was their daughter, but Jane Doe was never able to remember her past or what had happened to her.

Depersonalization

Ever feel like you're walking around in a dream? If you suffered from depersonalization you'd feel like that a lot. Depersonalization disorder is characterized by an ongoing and persistent sense of feeling detached from yourself. It's as if there's an invisible wall or shield that is between you and your feelings, thoughts, and experiences. "I feel like a robot walking around," or, "I feel like I'm just observing myself" are common complaints. Extreme stress can bring this feeling on for all of us, but for the clinically depersonalized individual, this is an ongoing, distressing part of everyday life.

Dissociative disorders are identity disorders; they disrupt our ongoing and stable sense of who we are and they break up our integration of thoughts, feelings and behaviors. You've probably noticed, however, that I haven't mentioned the most famous dissociative disorder of them all—multiple personality disorder. Don't worry, we'll discuss it at length in our personality chapters. But, there's another group of "multiples" that affects our sense of who we are—multiple roles.

The Days of All Our Lives

When you think about it, you'll see that we're *all* multiples, in a way. I am a mother, a daughter, a sister, a writer, a psychologist, a friend, and a wife, and who "I" am differs a little in each role. I interact differently with my son than I do with my close friends.

If the raw material for self-understanding lies in our relationships, it seems like we have a tough row to hoe. I mean, how can we develop a stable self-concept when we play such different roles with such unique people? And, indeed, with all the different traits and attitudes that various roles require, to some extent we all develop multiple personalities.

The Many Faces of Me

Research has shown that you don't just have one self-concept—you have many, depending upon the social role in which you are engaged. Ask me what kind of mother I am, and I will say "playful, loving, and a student in the art of patience." As a writer, I define myself as "committed, passionate, and outspoken." In some respects, then, self-concept is like a spider web; some self-perceived traits are attached to specific roles (the knots in the web), while others are attached to several roles. These are the strands that tie our identities together.

You might think that juggling multiple self-concepts would be psychologically stressful. But the reverse is actually true. Having multiple roles seems to keep us from putting all of our psychological eggs in one basket. Having multiple roles and lots of traits provides a buffer against becoming depressed when one role is lost or diminished in importance. For example, when a woman's only role is the care of her family, then when the kids leave home she feels she has lost her identity and suffers what is known as the "empty nest syndrome." Role jugglers of the world, unite!

As you've seen throughout this chapter, self-concept gets set pretty early in life. While our identities are formed in our teen years, our self-esteem, and ability to play many roles, continues to evolve. By the time we're all grown up, most of us have a good idea of who we are. In the next chapter, we'll take a close look at a trait that, in the United States, has a lot of influence over our sense of identity—intelligence. You'll find out how smart human beings really are as we explore intelligent life (on this planet).

The Least You Need to Know

➤ We develop our self-concept, beginning at about age 15 months, by relating to the world and internalizing feedback from the people around us.

➤ Self-esteem has a lot to do with self-worth and self-respect. We can grow it by changing our attitudes and behavior.

➤ Our gender has a strong influence on our identity formation. If we can develop our masculine and our feminine traits, we're likely to be happier.

➤ A transsexual has the psychological identity of one sex and the body of the other.

➤ We all have multiple roles to play in our lifetime, and the more we have, the happier we'll be.

Chapter 14

The Search for Intelligent Life

> ### In This Chapter
>
> ➤ Getting smart about intelligence
>
> ➤ Your IQ, and what it means
>
> ➤ Understanding why smart people sometimes fail
>
> ➤ Raising your IQ
>
> ➤ Tracing the bell curve from edge to edge

If you've always been a little insecure in the brains department, you might be reassured to learn about the role intelligence plays in getting what you want out of life. Don't think a person with a low IQ score can't be a whiz in some areas. In this chapter, you'll discover different theories of intelligence, and get the lowdown on how intelligence is measured. You'll get the good, the bad, and the ugly about intelligence—even what we think about intelligent life on other planets!

He'll Never Amount to Anything!

Imagine moving to a new town in Italy back in the fifteenth century. As you're sitting at a sidewalk cafe, sipping espresso with your new neighbors, a young man walks by and suddenly gossip begins to buzz around. "He's illegitimate, you know. His mother should be ashamed of herself." "He's never going to amount to anything if he doesn't pick a profession." "Of course, with his peasant blood, he can't amount to anything anyway."

Believe it or not, the subject of this malicious gossip could very well have been Leonardo da Vinci. Born out of wedlock to a peasant woman and notary, he became a master painter, sculptor, architect, musician, engineer, inventor, and scientist. Leonardo da Vinci was a true genius—one of the brightest minds to ever live.

But how did it happen? Did da Vinci inherit some smart genes or was his genius nurtured along during the uniquely intellectual and creative Renaissance into which he was born?

The First Intelligence Agent

The main man behind modern views of intelligence testing is Sir Francis Galton. In some ways, Sir Francis was ahead of his times. For example, he was the first to believe that differences in intelligence were normally distributed among people, with most people bunching in the middle and only a few at the extremes. He was also the first person to believe these differences could be measured, and he set out to do so.

Since his concept of intelligence was basically a combination of sharp ears, good vision, and fast fingers, Galton's early tests measured things such as how fast a person could react to a signal and his or her ability to detect the difference between two similar sounds. Interesting experiments, perhaps, but not exactly what we think of as critical life skills.

Unfortunately, some of Sir Francis's ideas weren't so great and some were downright self-serving. For example, he thought genius was passed down through families (what a coincidence that one of his family members was the esteemed and highly intelligent Charles Darwin). He also drew the incorrect assumption that a person's intelligence was somehow related to his or her moral worth. Not only did Sir Francis think stupid people were more likely to engage in immoral or criminal behavior, he attempted to influence public policy based on the concept of genetically superior and inferior people.

Some of Sir Francis's ideas clearly illustrate the fact that intelligence and common sense don't always go hand in hand. Equating intelligence with well-developed physical senses overlooks the fact that many people with disabilities are brainy—how about Helen Keller, for example?

And, while someone who's committed a crime has done something dumb, he or she isn't necessarily stupid. Criminality and intelligence are two different concepts. The serial killer Ted Bundy is a prime example of how a man with superior intelligence can be an amoral psychopath. Intelligence comes with the good, the bad, and the ugly and, as you're about to see, so do intelligence tests.

Psychobabble

Sir Francis Galton was a man of many talents. Not only did he think about intelligence, he invented a periscope that allowed him to see over the heads of taller people. And, he was no dummy when it came to making money. For a small fee, you could enter his lab, have various measures taken, and receive an intelligence test report.

Intelligence Tests—The Good, the Bad, and the Ugly

Clearly, intelligence is not based on how quick you can tap a button or how clearly you can see the warning light on the dashboard of your car. So what *is* it? Ask 1,000 psychologists and you'll get almost as many different answers, but most of them will include a few of the same abilities:

➤ the ability to adapt to new information and situations

➤ the ability to profit from experience

➤ the ability to think abstractly

Simply put, intelligence is the ability to learn.

Of course, intelligence can't be seen with the naked eye. It must be measured, usually through intelligence tests. In fact, intelligence and IQ tests are so closely linked that you might say intelligence is the stuff intelligence tests measure. And, indeed, intelligence tests do a pretty good job of measuring specific intellectual abilities. Historically, their problems have been elsewhere.

On the good side, intelligence tests have leveled the playing field for those of us who didn't grow up with silver spoons in our mouths. They've indirectly provided academic and career opportunities for people who score high on them; they've probably helped some people get into Yale or Harvard who otherwise wouldn't have. In theory, intelligence tests allow schools and employers to select individuals based on *what* they know instead of *whom* they know.

Shrink Rap

Intelligence is a general ability that allows us to learn from experience and go beyond given information to create new ideas and solutions.

The bad side of intelligence tests includes the argument that intelligence tests only level the playing field for people who are already on the same team—white, middle-class Americans. Individuals who didn't grow up in the United States or who were raised in a minority subculture have sometimes performed poorly on standardized intelligence tests—perhaps because they weren't included in the "standard" to begin with. While this criticism is much less true today, the influence of cultural biases in psychological testing is hard to completely erase.

Psychobabble

Sir Francis Galton invented eugenics, a movement advocating family planning based on genetic superiority. According to this view, biologically superior people should interbreed and biologically inferior people should be discouraged from having children. Adolph Hitler is infamous for carrying the idea of eugenics to the extreme with his ideas about the Aryan super race.

And the ugly side of intelligence tests? Their results have been used to contribute to elitism and to justify discrimination among disadvantaged groups. Sir Francis Galton isn't the only "intelligence agent" to use theories of intelligence for political or self-serving means. However, just because tests can be misused doesn't mean the tests themselves are bad. In fact, the first intelligence tests were developed with the best of intentions.

Benevolent Binet

The first intelligence test was published in 1911 by Alfred Binet. Binet was about as far from an elitist as you can get; in fact, at the time, he was trying to get the French school system to become more child-friendly. Binet had the radical idea that education should fit the child's competence level and not the other way around. If I can define our children's competence levels, he optimistically thought, maybe the school will wake up and smell the coffee.

Binet had another agenda as well. He knew that teachers could be biased in their evaluations of students. By coming up with an objective test that measured kids' abilities, he hoped to take the bias out of the evaluation.

Binet was particularly interested in helping children who were struggling, and wanted to identify areas in which special training and opportunities could help children catch up. He thought scores on an intelligence test could measure current performance (not inherited ability) and that learning problems identified by the test could be fixed.

The road to intelligence testing was paved with good intentions!

Act Your (Mental) Age

Binet started out by developing a series of problems and giving them to hundreds of children at different ages. He then compared the performance of groups of children at the same age, and came up with average scores for different age levels. Test results were expressed in terms of the average age at which normal children achieved a particular score.

If, for example, your child performed on the test at the same level as the average 12-year-old, Binet would say your child has a *mental age* of 12. This would be good news if your child was 10 years old and alarming news if he or she was 14. In addition to a child's overall mental age, Binet looked at his or her overall performance to identify strengths and weaknesses that could be used to develop a curriculum for that student.

Binet's concept of mental age, of course, had nothing to do with emotional maturity—we've all known virtual geniuses who acted like temper-tantruming three-year-olds. But the idea quickly caught on. In fact, it may have caught on a little too fast with parents, who, I'd bet, immediately started comparing their children's scores to other kids in the class!

Insight

Want a smart dog? Check out Stanley Coren's book *The Intelligence of Dogs*. You'll find his definitions of dog intelligence as well as intelligence tests you can give your own pooch. If you're looking to buy a smart dog, he includes ranked lists of the smartest breeds (hint: steer clear of Afghans).

Brain Buster

If you think you're smarter than your children are, I've got some bad news. In the years since World War I, IQ in the United States has risen about 20 to 30 points. And the average score keeps rising for each successive generation! People are getting so smart that intelligence testers must keep making the tests harder.

What's Your IQ?

Here's a new diagnosis for you: post-traumatic intelligence test disorder. I've had it. When my mom was studying to be a school psychologist, I became the guinea pig for all her psychological testing practice. You think the SATs are stressful? You ought to have your mom standing over you while the clock is ticking, saying, "I know you know the answer to this." "Don't give up, keep trying." These comments are not part of the usual test instructions and are one of many good reasons why psychologists should never evaluate their relatives.

Of course, growing up in the United States, it's hard not to be competitive. It probably won't surprise you that an American developed the really competitive part of intelligence tests—IQ scores. In 1916, Louis Terman adapted Binet's intelligence test for U.S. school children and published the Stanford-Binet Intelligence Scale. He kept the basic concept of mental age, but altered it to fit into an intelligence quotient.

Here's how it worked. To calculate a person's intelligence quotient, Terman simply divided his mental age (MA) by his chronological age (CA), then multiplied the answer by 100:

$$IQ = MA/CA \times 100$$

If a chronological 10-year-old performed intellectually like a 12-year-old, here's what his IQ score would be:

12 divided by 10 = 1.2

$1.2 \times 100 = 120$

IQ = 120

If you think it through, you'll see that the average IQ score would be 100 (10 years in mental age divided by 10 years in chronological age = 1, $1 \times 100 = 100$). So, just as we expect, our 10-year-old with an IQ of 120 is smarter than his peers.

IQ scores are no longer calculated by dividing mental age by chronological age. Today, your score is totaled and the sum compared directly with other people your age. That's because, although the concept of mental age worked with children, it gave pretty strange results when applied to adults. Imagine being 20 years old and performing like an 80-year-old! You'd have an IQ of 400!

Insight

Nurture can raise IQ, but it has to start from birth. Researchers now believe that early educational intervention programs failed because they weren't started early enough. If intellectual stimulation starts in the first few months of life, infants' scores on intelligent tests can be raised by 15 to 30 points.

Intelligent Theories

By themselves, IQ scores don't tell us as much as you might think. A tenth grader with an IQ of 95 can do more than a second grader with an IQ of 120. Two people with the same IQ score can have amazingly different skills and abilities. And people labeled developmentally disabled from their IQ scores show a remarkable range in what they can do and how much they can learn.

Intelligence is much more than what intelligence tests measure. Psychologists pretty much agree that intelligence is a group of abilities rather than a single trait or skill; the jury is still out on how many and which traits form intelligence. Let's take a brief look at three theories of intelligence.

Spearman's "G" Spot

Charles Spearman, the leading IQ assessment theorist of the 1920s, noticed that individuals who performed highly on one test also tended to perform well on others. He found, for example, that people who did well on memory tests also tended to score higher on perceptual tests, logic tests, and verbal tests. He thought this common level of performance was due to a single common factor of general intelligence: People were either doomed or gifted by their degree of general intellectual ability—the "g" factor—from birth.

But why didn't the scores on the various tests perfectly match each other? If someone was a genius in logic, why were they "only" above average or gifted on verbal tests? Spearman thought that people had individual abilities on various tests, and this accounted for the variability across tests.

Spearman called these abilities "s" factors—specific *kinds* of intelligence. For example, you might be a gifted person overall (there's your "g" factor) but have a real knack for logic ("s") and a relative weakness ("s") for verbal tests. Spearman thought "s" factors could be learned but "g" factors could not.

Cattell's Crystals and Fluids

Raymond Cattell agreed with Spearman that there were many "s" factors, but he thought that Spearman's "g" factor was too big. So, he divided it into two independent categories—crystallized intelligence and fluid intelligence.

According to Cattell, your crystallized intelligence is the knowledge that is already "set" into your brain; it is the knowledge you've acquired through learning and past experience. Your vocabulary, math skills, and general store of facts and knowledge are examples of crystallized intelligence. From a psychological standpoint, you rely on your crystallized intelligence to deal with recurring, concrete challenges in life, such as knowing what to do on a first date or what conversation topics are good ice breakers.

Fluid intelligence, on the other hand, helps you deal with new problems. Your fluid intelligence allows you to see complex relationships and come up with novel, abstract solutions. On formal intelligence tests, a test that requires you to make complex designs out of simple blocks would measure fluid intelligence. In the real world, comparing your new boyfriend with your past relationships might require fluid thinking.

Fluid ability typically peaks between the age of 20 and 25 and declines gradually after that, while crystallized intelligence continues to increase until about 50 (most of us know these "crystals" by another name—wisdom).

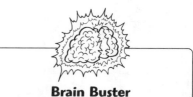

Brain Buster

Believe it or not, the average student takes as many as 20 intelligence tests before he or she graduates from high school! Most of these measure a narrow range of intellectual ability, often called school ability or aptitude.

While Cattell thought these two forms of intelligence were different, he didn't think they were entirely independent of each other. Noting the obvious relationship between the two, he guessed that it might be because people who are able to skillfully handle novel situations and new relationships (fluid intelligence) are the same folks who learn and remember more from their experiences. In other words, if we have more fluid to start with, we wind up with more crystals!

Gardner's Seven Wonders of the Mind

Howard Gardner could be nicknamed the "Mr. Diversity" of the intelligence field. A professor of education at Harvard University, he thinks American psychologists are too narrow in their thinking about intelligence—and, perhaps, somewhat snobby to boot.

In Gardner's view, there are at least seven kinds of intelligence, and each one is equally important. However, cultures often value one or two over the others because these are the abilities that are most useful to that society. And, of course, individuals who grow up in a particular culture learn that being "smart" is having those culturally selected abilities. That might be fine if you have them, but it can be a real bummer if you don't.

According to Gardner, the seven intelligences are:

1. linguistic (language) ability
2. logical-mathematical ability
3. spatial ability (navigating in space, using mental imagery)
4. musical ability
5. bodily kinesthetic ability
6. interpersonal ability (understanding others)
7. intrapersonal ability (knowing ourselves)

Psychobabble

Want to see how your IQ measures up to geniuses like Einstein, Mozart, and Confucius? Visit http://home8.swipnet.se/~we-80790/Index.htm. Not only will you find estimated IQs of some of the world's greatest geniuses, you'll see which intellectual clubs you are qualified for!

Most people are stronger in some of these intelligences and weaker in others—Mozart certainly had a knack for music, while Leonardo da Vinci may have covered all seven bases. While American culture doesn't tend to recognize the abilities numbered 6 and 7, we've all suffered from relationships with people who lack interpersonal skills, and we've all felt the pain of not being sure of who we are. And while U.S. culture traditionally favors language and math, the salaries of recent pro athletes may make you wonder if the fifth intelligence, bodily kinesthetic ability, isn't the best way to earn a living.

Why Smart People Fail

Do you know people who have a lot of potential, but never live up to it? They're smart as a whip and have a lot going for them; unfortunately, they never seem to get it going in the right direction.

There are lots of reasons why smart people fail. In fact, if you've always felt a little insecure about your smarts, you will be relieved to know that there is no demonstrable relationship between IQ test scores and life success, whether it's measured as college performance, job success, or achieved income level. An IQ score is better at predicting what we're capable of than what we'll actually do.

Here are some of the more common blocks to success.

Mental Mistakes	Emotional Blocks
Lack of concentration	Fear of failure
Using the wrong abilities	Blaming others for mistakes
Can't see the forest for the trees	"Poor me" attitude
Spreading oneself to thick or too thin	Untreated depression or anxiety
Inflexible thinking or problem-solving	Excessive dependency on others

Behavior Problems
Lack of motivation
Procrastination
Inability to focus or follow through
Lack of impulse control
Inability to translate goals into action

Did any of these hit a little too close to home? If so, don't worry too much; insight is the first step to a more productive life. And, unlike intelligence, all of these are things that can be changed!

How Honest Are IQ Tests?

We've already established that IQ scores are poor predictors of where we'll end up on the success ladder. However, if they really measure intellectual ability, they should at least be consistent with other indicators of a person's smarts. And they do—at least throughout elementary and high school. IQ scores have a moderate relationship with grades in school; if you're a straight-A student, you're likely to score high on an IQ test and vice versa.

How well they predict achievement outside of school is more difficult to measure. Intelligence scores are not correlated with employment in prestigious occupations such as doctor, lawyer, or business executive. In fact, the best predictor of these is the socioeconomic status of your parents; if your parents are bigwigs, you'll have more access to education and more personal connections. Alas, who you know really does matter!

Intelligence test scores also don't measure job success once you've been hired. While they're pretty good at predicting how well someone can learn a new job, they don't know beans about how well someone will do once they've mastered it. If you're interviewing potential employees, look for someone who's smart *and* motivated, experienced *and* conscientious. These latter three abilities might serve you better over the long haul.

It's Not Black and White

Americans have a lot of things to be proud of, but our legacy of slavery isn't one of them. Given our heritage of prejudice and discrimination, it's no wonder IQ differences among ethnic groups have been a political hot potato. And, historically speaking, IQ scores have been used to justify excluding certain immigrant groups, to maintain status quo policies, and even to sterilize people.

The political hot potato began when it was discovered that comparisons of racial and cultural groups routinely reveal average differences in IQ scores. In the United States, blacks, on average, score 15 points lower than whites on standardized intelligence tests.

But why? For lots of reasons, many people have assumed that if IQ is inheritable within a group, then differences between the two groups must also be due to genetic differences. But that assumption appears to be wrong.

To start untangling this complicated issue, consider the way we classify people as "black" or "white." In the United States, we have traditionally classified a person as "black" if he or she has *any* detectable black African ancestry, no matter how small the percentage is. So, a person who is half Swedish, one-fourth French, and one-fourth African is called black; a person who is half Swedish, one-fourth French, and one-fourth English is called white. While some average genetic differences exist between "blacks" and "whites," such as the amount of skin pigmentation, obviously the amount of genetic variation within each group is far greater than the average difference between them.

Brain Buster

The Baruka, a cultural class in Japan whose ancestors were tanners and butchers, have been discriminated against for hundreds of years. The gap in school achievement and IQ scores in Japan between the Baruka and the majority is similar to blacks and whites in the United States; but when the Baruka relocate to the United States, it completely disappears.

Contrary to some theories, the amount of African ancestry cannot predict intelligence. There is no evidence that blacks with more African ancestry have lower IQs than blacks with European ancestry. When it comes to understanding average black-white IQ score differences, the social label of "black" is most likely the critical variable.

A researcher by the name of Ogbu has found that involuntary minorities (groups that do not choose their minority status) in every culture perform more poorly in school than members of the majority group do, and they score an average of 10 to 15 points lower on IQ tests. Involuntary minorities are routinely discriminated against by the majority, and often see little hope of improvement through the traditional routes open to the majority. These groups face challenges that other minority groups do not. And these social and emotional challenges, he believes, often take an intellectual toll.

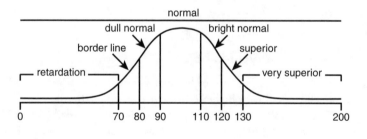

When measuring intelligence test scores, the shape of a bell appears because most of the scores bunch up in the middle of the chart and taper down on each side toward retardation or genius. Most of us are in the middle of the "bell."

Islands of Genius

What intelligence test could adequately measure Dustin Hoffman in the movie *The Rain Man*? Playing an autistic savant, the actor's portrayal of the lightning calculations and exceptional memorization skills made the savant syndrome a household word. Anyone who has ever wrestled with math felt a tinge of envy.

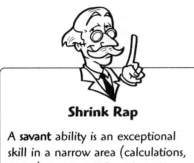

Approximately 10 percent of all people with autistic disorder have some *savant* abilities. This percentage is much higher than any other developmental disability. However, not all persons with autism have savant abilities and not all savants are autistic.

Savant syndrome is a rare but spectacular condition in which persons with various developmental disabilities have islands of genius that stand in stark contrast to their overall handicap. Sometimes, the savant skill is remarkable just because the talent so contrasts with severe handicaps in other areas. However, in rare situations, a handicapped individual has a special ability that would be spectacular in anyone. This person is known as a *prodigious* savant; there are only 25 prodigious savants alive today and fewer than 100 ever reported.

The most common savant skill is musical ability; other skills include calendar calculating, lightning mathematical skills, art, mechanical skills, and spatial skills. The special skill is accompanied by phenomenal memory, but this memory is limited to the savant skill. No one knows what causes savant syndrome, but recent theories have suggested it is a result of left hemisphere brain damage before, during, or shortly after birth.

Psychobabble

In May 1998, Robert Plonin of London's Institute of Psychiatry reported the discovery of a gene variation that is statistically linked with higher intelligence. The variation lies in chromosome 6, within a gene that may influence the brain's metabolic rate. Actually, given that his subjects were 50 students with high SAT scores, he may have discovered a gene for SATs!

Life on the Edge

When it comes to intelligence, most of us are pretty normal. A normal IQ score ranges from 85 to 115 with the average, of course, being 100. Only 1 percent of the people in the world have an IQ over 135, and we can barely measure it if it exceeds 200. In fact, the highest measurable scores to date have been between 210 and 220. Of course, at that level, the person can afford to give or take a few IQ points!

Here's what it looks like at upper edges of the bell curve:

Genius is defined as an IQ of 145 or higher.

Highly gifted: 135 to 145

Gifted: 125 to 135

Above average: 115 to 125

Average IQ: 85 to 115

Mental retardation is at the other "edge" of intelligence. Perhaps because of all the name-calling we suffer when we're children, the term *mental retardation* is often misunderstood or seen as derogatory. In reality, it's a specific diagnosable disorder that affects one out of every 10 families.

A diagnosis of mental retardation is partly based on a subaverage intelligence score (75 to 50), but it also requires that the person have significant problems adapting in everyday life. It can be caused by any condition that impairs development of the brain before birth such as a genetic defect, infections, or maternal drug use. Severe environmental deprivation or toxins such as lead paint can also cause retardation. About a third of the time, the cause is never known.

Shrink Rap

Mental retardation is diagnosed when a person has significantly impaired intelligence in combination with problems in living (taking care of oneself, getting along with others, and/or doing other age-appropriate tasks).

Can You Boost Your Brain Power?

We all want to be better looking, make more money, and have a great relationship. Why wouldn't we want to be smarter? Companies are banking millions on our endless quest for perfection—and that they can convince us that, in the smart department, their "smart drugs" are the answer.

Unfortunately, all the buzz about "smart drugs" is just hype. For instance, package labels on the popular herb gingko biloba exaggerate its usefulness—while it does have some modest benefits in Alzheimer's patients, it doesn't do much for the healthy individual. For other drugs, like modified estrogen, the research isn't far enough along for us to tell how useful it might be. For now, the best smart drug may be in your kitchen: sugar, the energy source of neurons.

After all is said and done (and tested), we are intelligent in more ways than one. While a genius may be superior in music and math, he or she may lack common sense or interpersonal skills. We also know that intelligence is part biology and part what happens to us after birth. Some intelligence is set by an early age, but much of it can grow with nurture and education.

Psychobabble

Enough about intelligent life on earth. What about intelligent life "out there"? Astronomer Guillermo A. Lemarchand's review of the search for extraterrestrial intelligence suggests that other advanced civilizations exist. So why haven't we found them? Our sky is so big that astronomers have only looked at a fraction of it. We probably haven't explored enough yet. And, of course, there's the chance that we've already received alien greetings but haven't been smart enough to recognize them!

The human mind is capable of many surprises; just as a high IQ score doesn't guarantee life success, we can never count anyone out who has a lower one. In the next chapter, we'll explore a part of the human mind that, ultimately, may have much more influence on happiness and well-being than our IQ score. We'll explore the human personality.

The Least You Need to Know

➤ Definitions of intelligence vary, but most theorists include the ability to profit from experience and the ability to think abstractly.

➤ Most psychologists believe there is more than one kind of intelligence; some say as many as seven, and these reflect different abilities such as linguistic, mathematical, musical, physical, and social abilities.

➤ High intelligence does not guarantee success in life—emotional blocks, behavior problems, and mental lapses are all factors that may hinder us in getting ahead.

➤ Intelligence values may vary with culture, but there is no genetic racial difference in intelligence.

➤ Mental retardation, which is fairly common, and savant syndrome, which is extremely rare, lie at the lower edge of the bell curve.

Chapter 15

He's Got ...
Personality!

In This Chapter

➤ How stable *are* you, really?

➤ Unlocking the secrets of your personality

➤ Why Minnesota is the personality state

➤ Discovering the state your traits are in

➤ Spotting the "sick" personality

Like many nurses in the early 1900s, Margaret Sanger saw some harsh realities. She watched countless women, desperate to avoid having yet another mouth to feed, die from illegal abortions. Unlike other nurses, Margaret Sanger decided to find an answer to her patients' pleas for safe contraception no matter what the cost. She left nursing and put her husband and three children in the background—and ultimately changed women's lives forever.

For 40 years, Margaret Sanger challenged the laws that made contraception a criminal act, insisting that women take control of, and responsibility for, their sexuality and childbearing. She lost her husband and was jailed several times for illegally distributing information about birth control. And, she won! In 1960, the "pill," a contraceptive Sanger co-sponsored, was approved by the U.S. Food and Drug Administration.

What drove Sanger in her crusade? What personality qualities empowered her to endure such personal sacrifice and punishment? In this chapter, you'll find out what made Margaret Sanger the person she was—and what makes you the person you are.

We'll explore all the ingredients that go into personalities; how much depends upon genes, hormones, environment, or birth order. You'll see how psychologists test personalities, and how stable our personalities really are. And you'll learn the difference between an offbeat personality and a serious personality disorder.

Shrink Rap

Personality is the unique bundle of all the psychological qualities that consistently influence an individual's behavior across situations and time.

Finding the Person in Personality

How would you describe your personality? Are you fun-loving? Patient? Shy? When we describe ourselves, we tend to think of certain traits or qualities that have been around for a long time and that seem to hold true in a number of circumstances. For example, if you describe yourself as "patient," you might be remembering how you interact with your children, how you generally listen to others without interrupting them, and how you stick with a difficult task until it's finished.

In the study of personality, psychologists try to study how individuals differ from each other yet are the same within themselves. They tend to focus on two qualities: uniqueness and consistency. *Personality* is the sum of all the unique psychological qualities that influence an individual's behavior across situations and time. Someone who is shy may blush easily, avoid parties, and wait for other people to take the initiative in conversation. On the other hand, a person who is reticent about public speaking but is the life of the party in other situations wouldn't be classified as having a shy personality.

Psychobabble

Wouldn't it be nice if we could size up a person's insides by looking at his outsides? William Seldon thought you could. According to his theory of personality, a long, thin (ectomorphic) body type signaled an artistic, introverted temperament. A muscular (mesomorphic) frame was occupied by a courageous and assertive personality, and a person with a fat, soft (endomorphic) body type displayed a relaxed and sociable demeanor. Interesting, but completely wrong.

The fact that personality traits are somewhat consistent across time and settings is comforting to everyone. It gives us a stable sense of who we are, and it helps us (to some degree) predict the behavior of the people around us. And, through personality testing, it gives psychologists an x-ray of our psyches.

X-rays of the Psyche

As you now know, IQ tests are designed to measure how much intelligence you have. Personality tests, on the other hand, don't measure *how much* personality you have but rather *what kind*. You can't be diagnosed with a lack of personality! Personality tests, then, describe personalities rather than measure them.

There are two kinds of personality tests: objective and projective. Objective personality tests are paper and pencil "self-report" tests with true-or-false questions. That is, you answer questions about your thoughts, feelings, and actions by checking *true* if the statement is generally or mostly true and *false* if it is false most of the time. Projective tests, including the well-known "inkblots," are more subjective—they're subject to interpretation by the person giving them.

Personality testing scares a lot of people, usually because they misunderstand what it can and can't do. First of all, personality testing is more like taking an x-ray than looking into a crystal ball: The results can suggest what's wrong, but they can't tell you how it got broken or to what extent it's affecting your life. The same test results that indicate antisocial behavior might show up in a politician *and* a convicted felon!

Second, personality test results are practically useless when taken out of context. They must always be evaluated in terms of the test subject's current life situation. Someone who is usually reticent may become very effusive if she just won the lottery. And a person who's just lost a loved one might look seriously depressed on a personality test when, in fact, he or she is just experiencing the normal throes of grief.

I found this out the hard way when, as a psychology graduate student, I was blindly given the Rorschach inkblot test as part of my personality assessment class. What did I see in those inkblots? Well, let's just say I saw quite a few teddy bears. Imagine my humiliation on my professor's casual comment that "seeing" too many furry animals suggested someone was excessively needy! Okay, I had just broken up with the love of my life and moved 500 miles away from home!

Insight

People who score as extroverts on personality questionnaires choose to live and work with more people, prefer a wider range of sexual activities, and talk more in group meetings, when compared to introverted personalities.

Minnesota, the Personality State

When you think of Minnesota (if you ever do), what images pop up? Snow? The movie *Fargo*? How about the pool hustler Minnesota Fats? Well, here's another little bit of trivia to store in your Minnesota memory bank. The most popular objective personality test was developed at the University of Minnesota.

The Minnesota Multiphasic Personality Inventory, or MMPI, first appeared in the 1940s. It originally consisted of more than 500 true and false questions that asked about your mood, physical symptoms, current functioning, and a whole lot more. In the late 1980s, the original version underwent a significant revision (MMPI-2) because some questions were deemed inappropriate, politically insensitive, or outdated.

The MMPI-2 has 10 *clinical* scales, each designed to tell the difference between a special clinical group (like people suffering from major depression) and a normal group. These scales measure problems like paranoia, schizophrenia, depression, and anti-social personality traits. The higher a person scores on a clinical scale, the more likely it is that he or she belongs in the clinical group.

Psychobabble

Hippocrates may have developed the first personality theory. He thought the body contained four essential fluids—blood, phlegm, black bile, and yellow bile—and that a person's temperament was a result of the differing combinations of these humors. In his theory, a surplus of blood makes you cheerful and active, phlegm makes you sluggish and apathetic, black bile puts you in a sad and brooding mood, and yellow bile leads to a quick temper. This may be where the term *bad blood* comes from!

The MMPI-2 also has 15 *content* scales. These measure various mental health problems that aren't, in and of themselves, diagnosable psychiatric disorders. There are content scales that measure low self-esteem, anger, family problems, and workaholism, among other problems. Low self-esteem is not a clinical diagnosis, but it certainly contributes to a number of psychological disorders, such as depression and psychasthenia (discussed later in this chapter). The job of the content scales is to pinpoint specific problems that either contribute to, or put someone at risk for, a full-blown psychological disorder.

Can You Pull the Wool over Your Psychologist's Eyes?

Since objective tests like the MMPI-2 are self-reporting, you might think they'd be easy to fake. If, for example, you were faced with the choice of either going directly to jail or looking "crazy" and stay out, surely you'd fake the results, right? Well, you could, but the odds are you'll get caught!

That's because the MMPI-2 has built-in "lie detectors." Psychologists weren't born yesterday—or maybe we're just a little paranoid—but the tests have safeguards that detect lying, carelessness, defensiveness, and evasiveness. So, while you're free to answer "true" or "false" however you please, it's almost impossible to convince the test that you're answering honestly if you're not.

Brain Buster

Let's say you want to take a vacation from work and think "depression" might be a good excuse for a little R-and-R. If you answer yes to every "depression" question on the MMPI-2, you'd certainly look depressed. In fact, you'd look so depressed that the results would indicate that you're exaggerating (or outright lying) about your level of emotional distress!

Projecting Your Personality

It'd be even harder to fake a projective test like the Rorschach, because there are thousands of possible answers. How could you know what answer would give the results you wanted? And even if you tried to second-guess the test, the answers you gave would still provide valuable clues about your true personality.

Projective personality tests are based on the theory that your inner feelings, motives, and conflicts color your perception of the world. The less structured your world, the more likely your psyche will spill over onto what you see. This is what happens when you look at clouds. The next time you're outside with a friend, look at the sky and tell each other what you see. You might see a dancing clown while you're friend spies a rocket poised for blast off. Both of you are right—the cloud shapes are ambiguous and open to several interpretations.

In some respects, you and your friend have just participated in a projective "test." You have both used your senses and personalities to make meaning out of relatively shapeless clouds. Psychologists rely on this same process when they give you those famous ink blots known as Rorschach cards.

Ink Blots of the Mind

The Rorschach was developed by Swiss psychiatrist Hermann Rorschach (pronounced *raw*-shock). While working with teenagers in a psychiatric hospital, Hermann watched them playing a popular game called "Blotto." Certain children, he observed, gave different answers to questions posed by the game, and he surmised that these different answers might provide clues into the minds, and personalities, of the players. Using this premise, he fooled around with a bunch of ink blots, and published the Rorschach in 1921.

When you take the Rorschach test, the examiner gives you 10 cards, each with an inkblot on it, and asks you to describe what you see. You will be assured that there are not right or wrong answers and, if you're like most people, you will immediately think the examiner is pulling the wool over your eyes.

Such skepticism is partially valid—yes, there technically *are* "wrong" answers to the Rorschach (and no, I'm not going to tell you what they are!). However, there are literally hundreds of *right* answers, and a tremendous amount of room for creative responses as well, so your examiner is not pulling the wool over your eyes too much.

Psychobabble

Want a partner who'll be faithful and stay away from the booze? Rate your mate! Go to http://members.aol.com/HOON4VR/personality.html for a virtual bonanza of personality quizzes. Hint: You've struck gold if he or she scores high on the conscientious scale.

Is Your Personality Stable?

Even if it doesn't always feel like it, most of us have remarkably stable personalities. You have many of the same quirks and qualities you did 10 years ago, and you'll probably have them 20 years from now. Go to a high school reunion, and you'll see what I mean. Your former tennis team buddy may have put on weight and gained a few wrinkles, but after 30 seconds of catching up you'll find the funny, free-spirited charmer who used to beat you all over the tennis court. Even after 30 or 40 years, adults have remarkably consistent personalities.

Personality tests are pretty stable, too. They do a pretty good job at describing the individual qualities that make each of us unique. A person who is assessed as "extroverted" at age 20 is likely to be extroverted at age 50. And while they're not perfect at predicting a person's behavior, the tests are certainly better than chance.

The Theories Behind the Tests

What are the three most important personal qualities you'd like to see in a mate? What about the three worst qualities? Answer these two questions and you've formed a theory of personality.

In fact, you're already a seasoned personality theorist. Chances are you choose your relationships based on a theory about what personalities make good friends, how you can tell who is untrustworthy, and what qualities would make a person a good role model. We all naturally assume that certain personality characteristics will lead to certain behaviors, and we try to associate with people who will do things that make us happy (and vice versa). In other words, every single one of us is a personality theorist.

Shrink Rap

A **trait** is a stable characteristic that influences your thoughts, feelings, and behavior. A **state** is a temporary emotional condition.

Through observations, interviews, biographical information, and life events, researchers in personality theory have developed beliefs about the structure and functioning of individual personalities. Their goal is to understand the personality and to predict what a person will do based upon what is already known about him. The tricky part is in separating out the traits from the states. In other words, in discovering if people act in a certain way because of who they are or in response to a sticky situation in which they've landed.

What State Are Your Traits In?

From a psychologist's point of view, a personality trait is a relatively stable tendency to act in a certain way. Generosity, shyness, aggressiveness—these are all examples of traits. Traits are considered to be ongoing parts of the person, not the environment; they follow us wherever we go.

That's not to say that the situation, for better or worse, doesn't influence our expression of the traits we have. Let's say you're hot-tempered by nature: You have a pretty stable predisposition to lose your cool. If someone runs into your car in a parking lot, you're more likely to fight or yell than someone who doesn't have as much built-in aggression. However, in many other situations, such as sitting in a classroom, you'd probably be much less likely to get into a screaming match, even though you still have an aggressive temperament. For a hot-blooded temperament, then, the environment provides the spark that sets it afire.

When psychologists are trying to figure out personalities, however, a psychological state can throw a monkey wrench into the works. Unlike traits, states are temporary conditions. Hunger is one such temporary state—it can be powerful when it's there, but it goes away after we eat.

Often, your emotional responses to situations are temporary states and when you get away from the situation, or when circumstances change, your feelings do, too. If someone comes to therapy complaining of depression, a psychologist has to figure out if that person is in a state of sadness or has a depressive personality trait. And, of course, there's some relationship between the two—an aggressive personality trait will lead to more angry states!

243

Insight

How many personality traits can one person have? What would you say, if you had to guess? If you looked in the dictionary, you would find 18,000 adjectives that could describe individual characteristics! A psychologist could spend his or her entire career just evaluating one person.

Psychologist Walter Mischel thinks there may be a "happy medium" between states and traits, which he calls *situation-specific dispositions*. He believes that people are likely to be highly consistent over time in response to the same situation, but that their behavior may not generalize across settings. For example, if you were a cheater on tests in high school, chances are that you'll also cheat on tests in graduate school. This doesn't necessarily mean, though, that you'd cheat on your taxes or on your spouse.

Allport's Search for Personality

The jury is still out on exactly how many personality traits we really have. Psychologist Gordon Allport considered personality traits to be the building blocks of an individual's overall personality. He also thought that some traits were big blocks, some were medium-sized, and some were smaller. These three different-sized blocks represented the varying degrees of influence the trait had on a person's life.

The building blocks of personality.

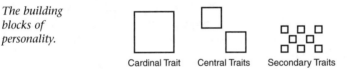

Cardinal Trait   Central Traits   Secondary Traits

According to Allport, a *cardinal trait* is a single giant-sized trait around which someone organizes his or her life. Martin Luther King Jr. may have organized his life around social conscientiousness, seeking to improve the quality of life for African Americans. Not everyone has a cardinal trait.

A *central trait* represents a major characteristic of a person, such as honesty or optimism. Surely Gloria Steinem's outspokenness is a central trait that enables her to withstand criticism and controversy and speak before large audiences about women's rights. People can have more than one central trait.

A *secondary trait* is an enduring personality trait, but it doesn't explain general behavior patterns. Personal styles (being a "sporty" dresser) and preferences (I like tall, blue-eyed men) might be examples of secondary traits. We all have a lot of secondary traits.

Apparently, patience was a central (if not cardinal) trait in Gordon Allport's personality—he spent his entire career working to make sense of personality traits. He began by boiling down all of the dictionary's 18,000 personality-related adjectives into 200 clusters of synonyms (groups like easygoing, lighthearted, and carefree), and then formed two-ended trait dimensions. For example, on one such dimension, "responsible" might be at one end, and "irresponsible" would be at the other. In our daily lives, all of us would fall somewhere on the continuum between these two adjectives.

Psychobabble

It's a guy thing! According to personality tests, men in every country of the world are more antagonistic, while women are more agreeable. Could this explain why we continue to have wars?

After having countless people rate themselves on these 200 dimensions, Allport looked at the relationships between the synonyms. To his astonishment, he found there were only five basic characteristics underlying all of the adjectives people used to describe themselves. These became known as the "Big Five" dimensions of human personality—the five categories into which Allport organized all of our traits and behaviors. To help remember them, think of the acronym *OCEAN*:

➤ *Openness* to experiences. At one end would be individuals who are creative, intellectual, and open-minded versus people who are shallow, simple, and less intelligent.

➤ *Conscientious.* Here would be organized, responsible, and cautious persons as opposed to those who are irresponsible, careless, and frivolous.

➤ *Extroversion.* These people are assertive, outgoing, and energetic rather than quiet, reserved, and shy.

➤ *Agreeableness.* Here individuals who are sympathetic, kind, and affectionate are contrasted with those who are cold, argumentative, and cruel.

➤ *Neuroticism.* Here we contrast an anxious, unstable, and moody personality with one that is emotionally stable, calm, and content.

The Eysenck Alternative

Another psychologist, Prof. Hans Eysenck of the University of London, used some different numbers to measure personality. On the basis of his research, he came to believe there were 21 personality traits that were consistent with three major dimensions of personality. If you ever take his personality assessment, the Eysenck Personality Profiler, your scores will fit into three categories:

➤ *Extraversion:* measures traits including activity level, sociability, expressiveness, assertiveness, ambition, dogmatism, and aggressiveness.

➤ *Neuroticism:* measures traits like inferiority, unhappiness, anxiety, dependence, hypochondria, guilt, and obsessiveness.

➤ *Psychoticism:* measures traits such as risk-taking, impulsivity, irresponsibility, manipulativeness, sensation-seeking, tough-mindedness, and practicality.

You've probably noticed some overlap in the two personality theories we've discussed. Each emphasizes the ability to get along with others, general emotional adjustment, and flexibility and open-mindedness as key parts of a person's personality. But, how do people become more open-minded or outgoing? Are we born with pizzazz or do we have to go to charm school to get it?

Programmed for Pizzazz or Charm School Graduate?

Who in your school was voted "Best Personality?" Who was most popular? What do we mean when we say someone has "personality plus"?

These questions bring us right back to the "nature versus nurture" debate you learned about in Chapter 3, "The Chicken or the Egg?" When it comes to personality, most people vote for nurture as the primary influence—we tend to credit, or blame, our upbringing and life experiences for the good and bad traits we wind up with. But, as the song says, it ain't necessarily so.

The traits singled out by personality tests appear to be at least moderately inheritable. Identical twins share about 50 percent of the same personality traits, the same percentage that they share when it comes to measuring intelligence. And identical twins who are reared apart are more similar in personality to one another than are siblings or fraternal twins who are raised together. In fact, people raised in the same family are just about as different as any two people picked at random off the street. If you have brothers and sisters, you know what I mean.

But why would upbringing have so little an effect on personality? One reason is that siblings have very different experiences growing up within the same family. For example, my sister, who is 10 years younger than me, felt like an only child growing up.

On the other hand, my two-years-younger brother and I felt like the dynamic duo. And my sister and I have very different experiences relating to my parents' divorce. I was 20 when it happened; my sister was only 10.

You can see how my sister's childhood experiences were dramatically different from my own. I grew up in a four-member, two-parent family. She grew up as an only child (since her siblings were so much older) in a single-parent family. In addition, personal temperament has an effect on how we experience our upbringing. Each sibling in a family comes into the world with a unique temperament, which may lead us to choose very different friends, activities, and life experiences. With all these variables, maybe no two people ever grow up in the "same" family!

Personality by Birth Order

If you aren't like the other members of your family, then who are you most like? Well, for starters, numerous studies suggest you're likely to share some of the same personality traits with other people who share the same birth order. If you were the firstborn in your family, for example, you're probably like other kids who entered their families first—you're a member of the family of firstborns!

Because firstborns are older, they're likely to be bigger, stronger, more knowledgeable, and more competent than later-born children. They're first to receive privileges, first to grow up, and, alas, the first to be asked to take care of younger siblings.

The firstborns' privileged position makes them special, and at times, burdens them—and their personalities are likely to reflect this mixed bag. For example, they tend to be leaders, but they also may be hard to get along with and are most likely to feel insecure and jealous. Perhaps that's because they never get over their younger siblings invading their territory! More U.S. presidents have been firstborns than any other birth order, and, as we all know, some of them (who shall remain nameless) have had some unresolved personality issues.

Insight

It's no coincidence that Evil Kneivel is a man. Men consistently score higher on sensation (or "thrill") seeking. This is true for every society that has been studied.

Later-born children are the rebels—with or without a cause. Having been picked on and dominated by firstborns, later children are more likely to support liberal causes, be open to new ideas and experiences, and support innovative ideas in science and politics. Later-born children are also more agreeable and more sociable—firstborns may be most likely to achieve, but later-borns are clearly most popular.

Personality by Gender

No, men do not have personalities from Mars and women personalities from Venus. The uniqueness of our own personalities, and the diversity of personality traits within each gender, far outweighs any personality differences based on gender. However, numerous cross-cultural studies suggest that members of each gender are more likely to share a few common personality traits and, well, guys, it doesn't look good.

The most consistent difference by far is that women are easier to get along with (this appears to be a universal truth and not just your own personal experience). In every study in every country, women score higher on agreeableness, and less on antagonism, than men. To be specific, about 84 percent of women score higher on measures of the ability to get along with others than the average man (and, guys, its just your bad luck if you married into the other 16 percent).

Disturbing Personalities

So far, we've spent our time talking about normal personalities and how we get them. We know, for instance, that there is an incredible range of "normal" personality traits, that we inherit certain traits from family members, and that, as a general rule, first-born women are likely to share more personality traits than a middle-born man or a last-born female. But how does an *abnormal* personality develop? And when does an eccentric personality become a personality disorder?

We're All a Little Bit "Off"

Personality disorders are chronic mental disorders that affect a person's ability to function in everyday activities. While most people can live pretty normally with mildly self-defeating personality traits (to some extent, we all do), during times of increased stress the symptoms of a personality disorder will gain strength and begin to seriously interfere with their functioning. Personality disorders are at the extreme end of the continuum.

Shrink Rap

A **personality disorder** is a long-standing, inflexible, and maladaptive pattern of thinking, perceiving, or behaving that usually causes serious problems in the person's social or work environment.

For example, just about everyone enjoys attention. And we all know someone who hogs the limelight or seems to be constantly seeking approval or recognition. But while we might not like such people or find them pleasant to be around, their personality traits don't necessarily indicate a clinical disorder. Sure, they might be self-centered or have a narcissistic view of the world, but that's not the same as having narcissistic personality disorder.

But It's All About Me and My Needs!

People with narcissistic personality disorder have a grandiose sense of self-importance, a preoccupation with fantasies of success or power, and a constant need for attention and admiration. They might "overreact" to the mildest criticism, defeat, or rejection. In addition, they're likely to have an unrealistic sense of entitlement and a limited ability to empathize with others. This lack of empathy, tendency to exploit others, and lack of insight almost always results in serious relationship problems. As you can see, these are not people who are merely "selfish"; they're people who genuinely can't relate to others.

Before you start diagnosing friends and family, however, keep in mind that true personality disorders are usually severe enough to interfere with a person's life in some way. A hunger for the limelight can be healthy if it's channeled in the right direction; without it, many of our greatest actors might not have chosen acting as a profession. And some of our greatest inventors, artists, business leaders, and reformers could be considered quite eccentric if you take a closer look at them—people who take a stand often don't conform to the norm. Think of Margaret Sanger, whom you met at the start of this chapter. Her personality was considered to be disturbed because of her views on "free love." Today, she's a hero.

Insight

Want to see what someone is really made of? Take him or her on an extreme sports adventure, or, if that's not practical, get stuck in an elevator together. Personalities are most clearly revealed in new, ambiguous, and stressful situations, where there are no clues about how we are supposed to behave.

Ten Personality Disorders and How They Grew

Mental health professionals disagree about the prevalence and makeup of personality disorders, and they can be pretty darned hard to treat. But there are a few things that are generally accepted as true on the subject.

For one thing, it's largely accepted that personality disorders are recognizable by the time a person reaches late adolescence or early adulthood—and that there are no "personality disorders" among children because their personalities are still being shaped. It's also true that no one knows exactly what causes personality disorders. It may be a combination of parental upbringing, one's innate personality, and social development, as well as genetic and biological factors.

For example, while we know there was no obvious physical abuse in serial murderer Ted Bundy's childhood, some form of emotional abuse that contributed to his antisocial personality disorder could perhaps be traced to the lies perpetrated by his family: His "parents" were actually his grandparents and his "sister" was, in fact, his mother.

Psychobabble

Do plastic surgery candidates have more personality disorders? According to a recent study, up to 70 percent of plastic surgery candidates meet the criteria for at least one personality disorder—most commonly, narcissistic personality disorder and obsessive compulsive personality disorder.

The *Diagnostic and Statistical Manual of Mental Disorders* (*DSM-IV*) recognizes 10 types of personality disorders. Here's a glimpse at how the manual describes them. Keep in mind that these are only thumbnail descriptions; they don't include all the symptoms for each personality disorder, only some of the more common ones.

1. **Antisocial personality disorder** (this cannot be diagnosed until age 18):

    repeatedly breaking the law

    deceitfulness, including lying, using aliases, conning others for profit

    impulsivity, aggressiveness, and consistent irresponsibility

    reckless disregard for the safety of oneself or others

    lack of remorse

2. **Schizotypal personality disorder**:

    acute discomfort in and reduced capacity for relationships

    suspiciousness toward others

    odd, eccentric, or peculiar behavior

    odd beliefs that influence thinking and are inconsistent with social norms (for example, strange superstitions, the belief that one has a "sixth sense")

    emotions that are inappropriate for the situation, or a lack of emotions

3. **Avoidant personality disorder**:

    long-standing and complex feelings of inadequacy

    extreme sensitivity to what others think and say about them

    social inhibition (avoiding occupations with a lot of interpersonal contact, unwilling to get involved with others unless certain of being liked)

    a belief that one is unappealing or inferior to others

4. **Borderline personality disorder:**

   very emotional and unstable relationships with others (I love you, I hate you)

   recurrent suicidal threats or self-mutilation

   extreme, short-term mood swings (lasting a few hours, rarely more than a few days)

   intense anger or difficulty controlling anger

   unstable self-image or sense of self

5. **Dependent personality disorder:**

   intense need to be taken care of and a fear of being abandoned by others

   "clinging behavior" such as difficulty making any decision without an excessive amount of advice and reassurance from others

   difficulty expressing disagreement or anger because of fears of abandonment

   uncomfortable or helpless when alone

   goes to excessive lengths to obtain nurture and support from others

6. **Histrionic personality disorder:**

   excessive emotionality and attention-seeking

   discomfort when not the center of attention

   dramatic, and at times inappropriately seductive, behavior

   highly suggestible, easily influenced by others

   considers relationships to be more intimate than they actually are

7. **Narcissistic personality disorder:**

   requires excessive admiration

   has a grandiose sense of one's own importance (believes he or she is special or unique and can only be understood by others of high status)

   is preoccupied with fantasies of unlimited success, beauty, and/or brilliance

   has a sense of entitlement (unreasonable expectations of especially favorable treatment)

8. **Obsessive-compulsive personality disorder** (not to be confused with an obsessive-compulsive anxiety):

   is preoccupied with orderliness and perfectionism

is excessively devoted to work and productivity to the exclusion of leisure activities and friendships

displays rigid and inflexible thinking

displays a preoccupation with lists, details, and schedules to the point that the big picture is lost

9. **Paranoid personality disorder** (not to be confused with paranoid delusions):

has a pervasive distrust and suspiciousness of others

has recurrent, unjustified suspicions of a partner's infidelity and similarly questions the loyalty of friends and associates

perceives personal attacks that are not obvious to others and is quick to react angrily or counterattack

persistently bears grudges

10. **Schizoid personality disorder:**

displays a pervasive pattern of detachment from social relationships

shows a limited range of emotions in interpersonal settings

appears indifferent to the praise or criticism of others

almost always chooses solitary activities

has little, if any, sexual interest in others

In this chapter you've learned how difficult it can be to predict someone's behavior no matter how well you think you know them. However, personality tests are one tool that can help us understand how traits lead to behavior patterns. In the next chapter you'll learn about the methods people use to protect their personalities and defend themselves emotionally.

Insight

If you want to change your personality, you'd better hurry. Personalities become much more stable after age 30. Don't sweat it too much, though—it appears that we naturally get better with age. Between their late teens and early 30s, most people become less neurotic, more conscientious, and more agreeable.

The Least You Need to Know

➤ Your personality is a complex assortment of unique traits that are stable over time and across settings.

➤ Psychologists use both objective and projective personality tests to figure out who we are and sometimes (but not always) predict what we will do.

➤ We all have traits (characteristics of personality that are stable and consistent over time) and we all have states (temporary emotional responses to specific situations).

➤ Personality development is influenced by a number of things, including genetics, environment, birth order, and gender.

➤ There are 10 diagnosable personality disorders. They are complex, somewhat fuzzy, and often difficult to treat.

Chapter 16

Psychic Self-Defense

> ## In This Chapter
>
> ➤ The personalities behind the personality theories
>
> ➤ Understanding your hidden motives and urges
>
> ➤ Strategies for psychic self-defenses
>
> ➤ Exploring the person you were born to be
>
> ➤ Do you believe in destiny?

Joyce is a shy, exhausted-looking young woman who has come to you, a psychologist, for help with her frequent headaches. For the past hour, she's been telling you about her complete devotion to her husband and child, but at a stressful moment in the conversation, she closes her eyes.

When she reopens them, the expression on Joyce's face is completely transformed. She sits up, squarely facing you, and speaks in a confident voice. Suddenly she has become a vivacious and talkative woman who jauntily calls you "Doc." When you ask about her headaches, she looks bewildered and says she's never had a headache in her life. This woman calls herself "Joanna" and says she's single and "a little bit wild." Yes, she knows Joyce; in fact she feels sorry for her, being saddled with that boring husband and bratty child.

This anecdote illustrates a rare, and somewhat controversial, form of psychological self-defense—multiple personality disorder. It's an extreme example of how a person

Shrink Rap

A psychodynamic personality theory is a model of personality that assumes inner forces (needs, drives, motives) shape personality and influence behavior.

defends herself against emotional pain, but we all have less dramatic ways of defending and protecting our psyches. In this chapter, we'll look at various theories of personality development; how our conflicts and needs shape who we are; how we protect our psyches; and how our backgrounds and beliefs influence our everyday lives.

Ulterior Motives

You might call Sigmund Freud the personality pioneer. As a young physician in the late nineteenth century, Freud came to believe that many of his patients' complaints were not due to physical illnesses but to mental conflicts of which they were unaware. On the basis of this insight, he ultimately developed an elaborate model of the mind that he believed explained why, and how, people cope with the psychological stresses of their daily lives.

Freud's theory was the first of the *psychodynamic personality theories*—theories that emphasize the interplay of mental forces (the word *dynamic* refers to energy or force). While each of these theories emphasizes different influences on personality development, they share two beliefs:

➤ that people are often clueless about their real motives

➤ that our minds develop self-protective strategies called defenses, which keep unacceptable or distressing motives, thoughts, and feelings out of our awareness.

When Freud talked about hidden motives, he wasn't kidding around. Freud believed that the main causes of behavior lie buried in the unconscious mind. That is, the part of your mind that affects your conscious thought and action but is not itself open to conscious inspection. The differences between my personality and yours, Freud thought, were variations in our unconscious motives, in how these motives pop up in our daily lives, and in the ways you and I protect ourselves from emotional pain and/or anxiety.

At center stage in his human drama, Freud put the concept of the unconscious, a kind of psychic storehouse of primitive and repressed impulses. This is not an actual place in our psyches, but rather an important process we learn as a child. The unconscious helps us deal with all these inborn drives and raw psychic energy so we can grow up to be respectable, law-abiding citizens.

But if people themselves don't know why they do the things they do, how can a psychologist ever hope to help them? Freud was a big believer in the "believe what they do, not what they say" approach to therapy—he thought that by sifting through his patients' behavior he could make inroads into their unconscious. Because the conscious mind always attempts to act in ways that are logical and rational, Freud did a lot of digging for clues through his patients' most irrational thoughts and behavior—which he felt were generated by the unconscious, or subconscious, mind. Thus, slips of the tongue or the pen, dreams, and random thoughts were the grist for Freud's mill.

According to psychoanalytic theory, at the root of your personality are powerful inner forces that drive your behavior. Personality problems, according to Freud, aren't caused by a lack of motivation. In fact, they're much more likely to be caused by too much motivation—for sex, pleasure, and aggression.

Sex in Overdrive

Some people think Freud was hung up on sex. There's no doubt that Freud thought about sex

Insight

Freud thought physical and behavioral symptoms were meaningfully related to significant life events. If you are constantly late for a date, or always miss your appointment with your therapist because you "forgot," Freud would say these represent unconscious conflicts that are playing with your conscious life.

a lot, wrote about sex a lot, and believed that the sex drive had a powerful influence on the personality. But before you start wondering if Freud had a few skeletons in his sexual closet, it's important to realize that he believed the sex drive to be much more than the simple desire to have sex. He saw it as the human drive toward pleasure-seeking and life-creating activities. He also believed that there were differences in how people channeled their sex drives. Since the most direct ways to express this drive were often unacceptable to the straight-laced Viennese society of his day, people had to channel its energy into something less dangerous.

Psychobabble

If you're clueless about the opposite sex, don't feel too bad. Even Freud had trouble with male-female relations. In fact, reflecting back on his illustrious career, Freud concluded, "The great question which I have not been able to answer, despite my 30 years of research into the feminine soul, is 'What does a woman want?'" (Most men are still asking this question.)

Freud believed that most of us channel our sex drives into a wide range of thoughts and actions that on the surface are not sexual at all. This idea of channeling sexual energy is reflected in the belief, held by some athletes, that they must abstain from

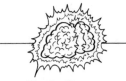

Brain Buster

Television advertisers use psychoanalytic theory against you all the time. They often promote their products by arousing your fears of inadequacy or failure, then promise you relief if you buy their product.

sex while training or before a competition—they need that energy to win. Some creative people also believe their creativity is channeled directly from their sex drive. (This may be true for erotic art.) But if this theory were true, you'd think our personalities would have gotten to be much simpler now that we're more free to express our sex drives more directly!

As if constantly reining in our sexual impulses wasn't work enough, Freud also believed that human beings were naturally aggressive, and that this aggression, like the sex drive, had to be channeled into more acceptable forms of behavior, or else we'd commit more murders than we already do. In Freud's view, then, people were pretty asocial, forced into society more by necessity than desire and interacting principally in terms of sex, aggression, and various squashed versions of these drives. And, to Freud's way of thinking, it all begins in childhood.

Urges "R" Us

Freud believed that a person's personality is shaped most strongly during infancy and early childhood. Each of us, he thought, progresses through a series of predictable stages in which we associate pleasure with the stimulation of certain body areas at certain times in our early lives. If we get through them unscathed, we have a chance of turning out okay. However, according to Freud, we can get stuck in any one of these stages because of too much or too little stimulation during that critical time period. This would lead to problems in adult life.

The three stages in Freud's personality play are:

➤ **The oral stage.** In the first year of life, the mouth is the center of pleasure. A baby sucks, drools, and mouths objects like crazy. If the baby gets just enough mouth stimulation, he or she will move on to other pleasure centers. However, babies who are under- or overfed might grow up to be needy, dependent adults. In addition, they may develop some bad habits—overeating, for example, might be a result of getting stuck at the oral stage.

➤ **The anal stage.** From ages one to three—prime toilet training time—babies feel good about the process of elimination, but they also learn there are pretty strict social rules about bodily functions, self-control, and personal hygiene. Freud would say that people who are stingy and obsessively neat got stuck here. (Whenever I look around my office, I wish I'd gotten stuck here at least for just a little while!)

➤ **The phallic stage.** From the ages of three to six, a child's genitals become the major focus of his or her pleasure. Freud believed that this was the age when boys wanted to marry their moms and kill their dads (the Oedipus complex) and girls wanted to kill their moms and marry their dads (the Electra complex). The way we resolve this conflict, according to Freud, is by identifying more with the same-sex parent.

On the Mat with Freud

Freud thought childhood was no picnic. We have all these inborn drives and urges we have to tame. We have psychosexual minefields we have to navigate. And we have mental forces that are constantly warring with each other. These warring parts of our personality are the id, the ego, and the superego.

Shrink Rap

In Freudian terms, your **id** is the uninhibited pleasure-seeker in your personality, your **superego** is your social conscience, and your **ego** is the part of your personality that focuses on self-preservation and the appropriate channeling of your basic instincts.

What's Id to Ya?

The id is the primitive "want it, gotta have it" part of your personality. It acts on impulse and pushes for immediate gratification—especially sexual, physical, and emotional pleasures—and it wants to worry about the consequences later. (Actually, the id never worries about the consequences at all. That's the superego's job.)

It's a Bird, It's a Plane, It's Superego!

Your superego is the storehouse of values and moral attitudes you've learned from society as you were growing up. This is your conscience. It develops as you internalize the "no's" of our parents and other grown-up do-gooders who preach against socially undesirable behaviors.

Think of your superego as your inner voice of "oughts" and "should nots." Your superego also includes your *ego ideal*—your view of the person you should try to be. It's that nagging inner voice that constantly critiques your actions and compares them to perfection.

And in This Corner

Your ego is your psyche's referee. It tries to find that happy medium between getting what the id wants and doing what the superego thinks is right. When your id and your superego are fighting, your ego looks for a compromise. For example, if you're unprepared for an exam, your id might want to cheat, your superego would worry about the consequences of cheating, and your ego might ask the teacher if you could take the test at a later date.

Given the "personalities" of your id and superego, it's no wonder they don't like each other. The id wants to do what feels good, while the superego wants to put a lid on your id and do what's right. Your ego is the part of your personality that tries to make peace between the other two. It represents your personal view of the way things are; your physical and social reality. Its job is to try to pick actions that will satisfy the id without getting you into big trouble. Sometimes it succeeds and sometimes it doesn't.

Post-Freudian Dynamic Personalities

Not all psychoanalysts share Freud's grim view of human nature. While most agree that the personality battle is won or lost during childhood, not every psychodynamic theorist believes that the battle itself was quite as primordial as Freud would have it. In fact, a lot of neo-Freudians see people simply as social beings just trying to get along with themselves and others.

Forever Jung

Swiss psychologist Carl Jung and Sigmund Freud had a complicated relationship. For many years, Jung was thought to be the heir apparent to the Freudian throne. However, Jung eventually got fed up with Freud's pessimism about human nature and developed a few ideas of his own. Some people think the reasons behind their eventual breakup went even deeper—like maybe their eventual dispute was their own miniversion of *Oedipus Rex*!

Jung contributed many new and enlightening ideas about personality development. For example, he thought the unconscious was not limited to one person's unique life experiences but was filled with universal psychological truths shared by the whole human race. This *collective unconscious,* in Jung's view, is an inherited storehouse of unconscious ideas and forces common to all human beings.

Shrink Rap

According to Carl Jung, an **arche-type** is a universal symbol of human experience that is stored in our **collective unconscious,** the storehouse of ideas and forces shared by every human being who ever lived.

Jung was also interested in the creative parts of the personality. Sure, he thought sex and aggression were powerful motives, but he also thought that people have an instinctive need to create and self-actualize. And, while we might not all be Van Gogh or Cessna, Jung thought we were all predisposed to at least appreciate and intuitively understand myths, art forms, and symbols.

In particular, Jung zoomed in on certain universally recognizable symbols he labeled *archetypes*. Each archetype is associated with an instinctive tendency to feel and think in a special way. Borrowing from history and mythology, Jung named many images and characters that can be found in ancient and diverse cultures—the hero, earth mother, the sun god, and the trickster. These, he believed, are archetypes that reside in the collective unconscious of us all.

Horney's Need for Security

While Jung was preoccupied with the creative side of human nature, Karen Horney took a look at our relationship needs. In particular, Horney, a German psychiatrist who settled in the United States, focused on the need for security as a driving force in blossoming personalities. This inborn human need for security can only be filled by other people and if it isn't filled when we're little, Horney believed that we'll spend the rest of our lives looking for it.

Horney thought the most fundamental human emotion was anxiety—a child's feelings of being isolated and helpless in a potentially hostile world. In Horney's view, parents shape a child's personality by their success or failure in relieving this basic anxiety and helping the child feel secure.

Children who find security with their parents will continue to find security with others later on in life. And children who fail to find security with their parents will grow up feeling insecure and distrustful of others. This distrust will show up in any of three unhappy personality styles of relating or not relating: avoiding others, always giving in to others, or dominating others.

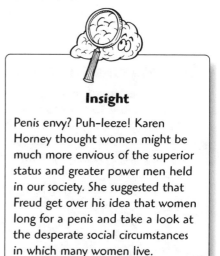

Insight

Penis envy? Puh-leeze! Karen Horney thought women might be much more envious of the superior status and greater power men held in our society. She suggested that Freud get over his idea that women long for a penis and take a look at the desperate social circumstances in which many women live.

Adler's Quest for Competence

Perhaps Alfred Adler had an inferiority complex. We don't know for sure, but we do know that he thought a lot of other people had one! Alfred Adler, a contemporary of Freud and Horney, thought that one of the biggest struggles people face throughout their lives was the need to feel competent. And he believed that we start out with at least one strike against us because of the helpless and dependent state of early childhood. In his view, that helplessness means that we all begin life feeling pretty inferior. The manner in which we learn to cope with or overcome this feeling provides the basis for our life-long personality.

Adler believed that personal achievements are important because they boost our sense of competence. Psychologically healthy people have a mature sense of their own abilities and worth (self-esteem) and they direct those abilities toward useful achievements.

On the other hand, people who are overwhelmed by a sense of inferiority will constantly think that other people are better than they are and wind up as frustrated underachievers. Or, they may go through life masking their feelings of inferiority behind a snobby attitude and an endless need to prove that they are better than others.

In Adler's view, the first reaction is a classic case of an inferiority complex, the second is a classic example of a superiority complex, but both are the opposite sides of the same coin!

The Well-Defended Mind

Whew! If you add up Freud's sex and aggression, Jung's creativity, Horney's security, and Adler's competence, one thing becomes quickly apparent—we've all got a lot of needs to meet! And, it's not like the rest of the world is cooperating with us as we go about the business of meeting them. Society says that we can't have sex whenever we want to; we're likely to find out that the relationship we were counting on wasn't as secure as we thought; and the boss doesn't give us the promotion we think we deserve! How do we keep our personalities from getting beaten down while we're building them?

Your Psyche to the Rescue

Defenses, my dear Watson. You have them and so do I. I can't tell you how often people, upon learning I'm a psychologist, start monitoring their every move. There is usually an abrupt and noticeable change of expression when they are told my profession, as if I'm some superpsych who has x-ray vision into their secrets! "Are you going to psychoanalyze me?" they frequently ask in half-jest and half-concern. Believe me, psychologists have all the normal defense mechanisms working and I, for one, am more than happy to suppress my clinical skills in social settings.

Shrink Rap

A **defense mechanism** is a mental process of self-deception that reduces our awareness of threatening or anxiety-producing thoughts, wishes, or memories.

The theory of defense mechanisms was most thoroughly developed by Freud's daughter, Anna, who became a psychoanalyst herself. You might think of defense mechanisms as doing for anxiety what endorphins do for physical pain—they reduce its impact.

Anxiety frequently promotes survival, by spurring us to action to overcome a threatening situation. But in some situations it does us more harm than good. Our defense mechanisms are a way to reduce the amount of anxiety we feel, and—to the degree that they help us worry less about things that aren't worth worrying about, or that we can't do much about anyway— defense mechanisms are helpful. But sometimes they distort reality or keep us from taking action to improve a situation, and that's when they hurt us.

Among the most common defense mechanisms are repression, projection, reaction formation, rationalization, displacement, and sublimation.

Out of Sight, Out of Mind!

Freud believed repression was the mind's first line of defense—it lays the foundation for the other defense mechanisms. When painful memories or anxiety-producing thoughts occur, repression is the process of pushing or keeping them out of the mind. Repression is often called a "primitive" defense mechanism because we aren't aware that it's happening. (If we were, that would be *sup*pression.)

Freud visualized repression as the damming-up of a pool of mental energy. And, just as water will leak through any crack in a dam, repressed wishes and memories will leak through the barriers that separate the unconscious from the conscious. But sometimes repression isn't enough, and that's when the other defense mechanisms kick in.

Insight

The "serenity prayer" used in alcohol recovery programs is an example of getting the balance right between using defenses to worry less, but not letting them hold us back from progress. It asks for "the serenity to accept the things I cannot change, the courage to change the things I can, and the wisdom to know the difference."

It's Your Problem, Not Mine!

Projection occurs when someone consciously experiences an unconscious drive, wish, or feeling as though it belongs to someone else. For example, a person with intense, unconscious anger may project that anger onto her friend and think it is her friend who is angry.

My husband and I have used this one so often we eventually developed a code word, "Hello, Mr. Projection," when one of us realizes our emotional boundaries have gotten confused. If he's in a bad mood or overly stressed, he sometimes thinks I'm mad at him—and vice versa. The teasing statement, "Hello, Mr. Projection," has become our signal to encourage the other to look deep within and see if maybe the source of irritation is really coming from inside ourselves. (Naturally, this kind of humor would only survive in the home of a psychologist!)

The Devil Made Me Do It!

The late comedian Flip Wilson made this line famous. But the devil is not involved in the use of conscious reasoning, or rationalization, to explain away anxiety-provoking thoughts or feelings. A man who cannot face his own violent tendencies may rationalize the beatings he gives his children by convincing himself that his children "asked for it" and that he is only carrying out his fatherly duty. The sexual abuser may rationalize that his four-year-old is "coming on" to him. More recently, this has become known as the President Clinton defense, as in, "It wasn't really sex."

Always Keep 'Em Guessing

Reaction formation is an interesting defense mechanism, and it illustrates the paradox of human nature. With reaction formation, the person does or says exactly the opposite of how he or she really feels. The true feelings or wishes are so unacceptable that they are turned into their safer opposite. An example of this mechanism would be a woman who has an unwanted child but who feels so guilty about her feelings that she becomes an overprotective and smothering mother.

Kick the Dog Instead of the Boss

When an unconscious wish or drive is unacceptable to the conscious mind, it is frequently redirected toward a more acceptable alternative. A person who wants to have an affair might spend time looking at pornography instead so as not to "cross the line" into infidelity. A man who discovers his beloved wife has a terminal illness might yell at the garage mechanic for not taking better care of his car because he'd be considered a heel if he yelled at his dying wife.

On a conscious level, punching your pillow is an often-used "displacement" remedy to get rid of anger and hostility. It's also a pretty good idea, since by venting your anger that way you're less likely to hit anybody else.

Psychobabble

Norman Cousins's book *Anatomy of an Illness* was not only a best-seller, but a great example of the way suppression can work. Stricken with a terminal illness, Cousins diverted his fear and anger about an early death into watching movies that made him laugh. Then he wrote a book about it, which not only helped others, but extended his life far beyond what the doctors had predicted.

If You Can't Beat 'Em, Join 'Em

Sublimation is a little like displacement, but instead of turning unacceptable urges into their opposites, it seeks to find an acceptable use to which those urges can be put. Martin Luther King channeled his anger into political activism against discrimination and racial injustice and had a worldwide impact. Orson Welles channeled his narcissism into a phenomenally creative acting and directing career. Each of these men directed their aggressive or otherwise unacceptable energies into activities that are valued by society.

What's *Your* Defense?

Time for a pop quiz to see how savvy you are about emotional defense mechanisms. Match up each of the defense mechanisms listed below to the statements that follow. This is not a trick test—there is only one answer for each statement. (The answers appear at the end of the chapter.)

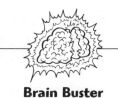

Brain Buster

There's a dangerous difference between looking on the bright side and denying that a dark side exists. Driving recklessly because you believe that you would never get into a car crash or having unprotected sex out of a sense of invulnerability are examples of unrealistic, self-deluding optimism. And no, teenagers aren't the only ones who have it.

A. Projection

B. Repression

C. Rationalization

D. Reaction Formation

E. Displacement

F. Sublimation

___1. As an aggressive child, Steven frequently got into scrapes with other children. Now that he's an adult, he's a million-dollar earner with the World Wrestling Federation (WWF) and frequently sends his former schoolteachers free tickets as a "thank-you" for putting up with him until he found his niche.

___2. The CEO of a large company has multiple affairs but insists that they "don't count" since they happen during business hours and "satisfy his customers."

___3. Jared expresses such hatred and fear toward homosexuals that he constantly tells gay bashing jokes and has occasionally gone into gay bars and picked fights. His friends are starting to wonder if Jared is protesting a little too much.

___4. Janine is constantly talking about the conniving and manipulative ways of company employees. It is obvious to people who know her that any knife that lands in their back is likely to be hers.

___5. When Serena, eight months pregnant, nearly had a head-on collision during a multicar pileup, she was terrified by the thought of losing her baby. Later, when asked to testify at the trial, she realizes she was so traumatized by the event that she can't remember the details (not to mention the trauma of labor and delivery!).

___6. Molly is so frustrated by her dietician that she feels like punching her out. Instead, she comes home after a session and beats up her refrigerator.

The Best Defense

You might be interested to know which of these defense mechanisms works best. Lots of studies have been done with this goal in mind. While the effectiveness of the defense mechanism somewhat depends upon the situation you're in, there do seem to be some that generally promote more effective coping than others.

Projection, not surprisingly, is one of the least effective defense mechanisms. Not only does it block self-awareness, it often interferes with interpersonal relationships. For instance, you'd tire pretty quickly if your partner always thought relationship conflict was *your* problem. Repression and reaction formation distort reality less than projection does, and they can lead to somewhat more effective coping but they still use up unnecessary amounts of psychic energy.

Two of the best defenses are suppression and humor. Suppression—the conscious avoidance of negative thinking—is different from repression. Unlike repression, you're still aware of negative information and can think about it whenever you choose to do so. And humor relieves anxiety and simultaneously allows us to face feared ideas because we're poking fun at them.

Ultimately, however, the best defense is no defense at all. Many people learn that once they face a painful memory or a fearful situation, the reality is not as bad as it first seemed.

Psychobabble

Robbie Robertson, rock-and-roll songwriter and guitarist with *The Band,* suffered from stage fright before each performance. He even wrote a song about it called "Stage Fright." This is one good way to practice sublimation! Robertson's fear never prevented him from being one of the most acclaimed guitarists in rock history.

Free the Psychic Balloons!

While psychodynamic theorists see personality development as a battle, the humanists think of it as a natural, free-flowing process that is sometimes weighed down by outside forces. The humanists are much more optimistic about human nature than the Freudians. To them, we're not so much driven by unconscious conflicts and defenses against anxiety, as we are inspired to adapt, learn, and grow. Free the psychic balloons, they proclaim, and our personalities will fly!

Humanists focus on the innate qualities within us that influence our behavior, while they view environmental influences as barriers or blocks, like strings tying down balloons. Once people are freed from their negative situations, humanists would argue, their natural tendency to learn and grow (the actualizing tendency) should actively guide them to choose life-fulfilling situations.

Shrink Rap

Self-actualization is the constant striving to realize your full potential.

Humanistic personality theorists believe that the motivation for behavior comes from a unique blend of biological and learned tendencies to develop and change and grow positively. *Self-actualization* is a constant striving to realize your full potential, to fully develop your abilities and talents. This innate quest for self-fulfillment and the realization of your unique potential is a useful guiding force that moves you toward generally positive behaviors.

Problems arise, however, when your drive for self-actualization conflicts with your need for approval—from yourself and from others—especially when you feel that certain obligations or conditions must be met in order to gain that approval. For example, if you're a natural-born artist, your drive for self-actualization might be sabotaged if you fear disapproval from one of your parents. Or, you might take up sports, not because you wants to play but because you need approval from your father.

The Personality Habit

All this stuff about free-loving balloons is a bit much for social-cognitive psychologists. And, their view of psychodynamic theories might be that the theorists have watched one too many episodes of *All My Children*! According to the social-cognitivists, personalities are shaped by beliefs and habits of thought acquired through each individual's unique experiences in the social environment.

These learned beliefs and habits may be conscious, but they're tricky. In fact, over time, they may be so ingrained and automatic that they exert their influence without us even realizing it. To social-cognitive theorists, "unconscious" refers only to automatic mental processes, not to thoughts that are barred from consciousness by our defense mechanisms. The self-talk we engage in every day is a good example of automatic ways of thinking that influence how we feel and what we do—until we stop and listen to ourselves, we might now even know what's being said.

Learned beliefs and habits of thinking either increase or decrease our ability to take control of our lives and accomplish the tasks we wish to accomplish. If, for instance, I kept telling myself I could not write this book because I have too much else to do, I might have given up before I got started. Instead, I told myself I *could* write it—if I reorganized my life to make room for it. Voilà! The book *did* happen!

Let's take a look at three of our thinking habits that have a tremendous impact on our lives:

➤ locus of control

➤ self-efficacy

➤ optimism

Psychobabble

Just because you became more practical with age doesn't mean you can't keep your dreams alive. Childhood dreams can provide valuable clues to long lost parts of ourselves. Take a minute and think back on the first three things you wanted to be when you grew up. Former vet-wanna-bes make great pet owners or animal activists. And, if you wanted to be a ballerina, are you still dancing? If not, why not give it a try?

Who's in the Driver's Seat?

Clinical psychologist Julian Rotter was a major player in developing the social-cognitive school of psychology. Influenced by Alfred Adler's interest in competence and achievement, Rotter found that people behaved differently on tests or games depending upon whether they believed success depended on luck or skill. If you believe your success depends on your skill, you're likely to work harder and get better. To the degree that you believe success depends on luck, you're less likely to work hard.

Rotter found that people's beliefs about their control over the rewards depend on the situation—and they should. At an early age, you figured out that in some situations you could control what happened, and in others you couldn't. You learned that saying please and thank you usually made people like you better, but that no matter *what* you did, your third-grade teacher had in it for you.

However, in some situations, the degree to which your reward depends on your own efforts is not readily apparent. If you bomb a test, for example, it could be that you didn't study hard enough, or maybe it was because the test was unfair and biased. Rotter found that in these situations, people behave differently according to their general disposition, acquired from their personal experiences, to believe that rewards either are or are not *usually* controlled by their own efforts. He called this disposition the *locus of control*.

People who believe they can control their own fate are said to have an internal locus of control. People who believe life is essentially a crapshoot have an external locus of control. Not suprisingly, when tested, people who score toward the internal end on locus of control try to control their own fate more often than those who score at the external end. Let's see where you measure on the locus on control scale. (Answers to the quiz are at the end of the chapter.)

Shrink Rap

A **locus of control** is a person's perception of the usual source of control over rewards. An internal locus of control means we believe our behavior determines our fate; an external locus of control means we think our fate is controlled by external forces (destiny, luck, or the gods).

The Locus of Control Quiz

1. Living in the tornado belt, you would be most likely to:

   A. dig your own tornado shelter just in case.

   B. rent *The Wizard of Oz* to see what might be in store for you.

2. In general, your attitude toward your health is:

   A. An ounce of prevention is worth a pound of cure.

   B. Eat, drink, and be merry, for tomorrow we shall die.

3. If a group of your friends were playing the drinking game "Alabama Slammer" and you didn't feel like boozing, you would:

   A. rather be a hung-over friend than a sober party pooper.

   B. roll the dice for your friends but stick to your Diet Coke.

4. If you had an hour to kill, you'd rather spend it:

   A. on the tennis court.

   B. playing Yahtzee.

5. If you had to sum up your life philosophy, it would be:

   A. He that is born to hang shall never be drowned.

   B. Fate doesn't fall on men however they act; it falls on men who fail to act.

How Good a Driver Are You?

Albert Bandura's self-efficacy is not the same as Rotter's locus of control (although it sounds similar). Self-efficacy refers to your sense of your ability to perform a particular task. If you *think* you can do it, you have high self-efficacy. If you don't, then you have low self-efficacy for that particular task. Locus of control, on the other hand, refers to your belief about whether or not your ability will do you any good.

Insight

The children's story *The Little Engine That Could* is a wonderful self-efficacy fable. This little engine, smaller and weaker than the others, just kept insisting it could pull the train. "I think I can, I think I can." It kept on trying, and believing, and ultimately, it succeeded!

Take singing, for example. You might believe that your voice is so fabulous that Barbra Streisand could learn a few things from you. At the same time, you might believe that your chances of "being discovered" as a singing talent are determined by some cosmic roll of the dice. In this situation, you have high self-efficacy but an external locus of control.

Bandura's self-efficacy concept certainly has educational and child-rearing implications. For example, some studies suggest that improving self-efficacy actually improves performance—students who are told they are good in math do better even when their original scores were no higher than their peers. And parents know that highlighting a child's abilities and effort leads to greater long-term achievement than using methods that point out inability or failure. But, then, you don't need a Ph.D. to realize that!

Handling Your Speed Bumps and Roadblocks

If you were looking into your future through a crystal ball, would you predict sunshine or thunderstorms? Psychologist Martin Seligman has spent years looking inside a lot of people's crystal balls, as well as the impact pessimism has on them. People who are pessimistic tend to believe statements like, "In times of uncertainty, I usually expect to fail." Perhaps the first genuine pessimist was Chicken Little, who always expected they sky to fall.

Shrink Rap

Optimism is the tendency to believe in a bright future. **Pessimism** is the tendency to believe that things are bound to turn out badly.

In general, optimistic people tend to cope better with life's stresses than their pessimistic counterparts. Optimists recover faster from surgery, even when their medical problems are equal to ones faced by pessimists. No one knows exactly why. It may be that optimistic thinking leads people to devote attention and energy to solving their problems or recovering from their disabilities, which in turn leads to positive results. Pessimistic people, with their attitude that things are likely to turn out badly, may see no need to even try.

Being of Two Minds

We started out this chapter with Joyce/Joanna, a make-believe example of dissociative identity disorder, commonly called multiple personality disorder (MPD). A person with MPD has two or more distinct personalities ("alters") that coexist and control his or her behavior. The "alters" occur spontaneously and involuntarily, can be male or female, and operate more or less independently of each other.

There are plenty of mental health professionals who don't believe MPD actually exists, but those who do agree on some common themes. First of all, it's agreed that a person develops multiple personalities when still a child—any time between birth and about 12 years of age. It's also generally accepted that while the child is still in the process of mapping out his or her collection of beliefs, morals, and experiences, severe trauma can cause parts of the psyche to split off from each other, forming alternative personalities, or alters. Memory and other aspects of consciousness are divided up among the "alters" at the time of such splits.

Shrink Rap

Dissociative identity disorder (better known as multiple personality disorder) is a psychological disorder in which two or more distinct personalities coexist in the same person at different times.

No one knows why some people form multiple personalities and others don't, but when it does happen, it's usually in response to severe, repetitive physical or sexual abuse—more than 80 percent of all documented multiple personalities appear to have been created in response to such traumatic events. Continuous emotional abuse or neglect may also be a cause.

Multiple personality disorder is a very confusing problem to have. Any dissociative disorder disrupts the continuity of life—people report "missing time." They are unable to account for certain times of the day, or they are told they've done things they don't remember. If you've ever been awakened while sleepwalking, you've had a glimpse of how frightening it can be to come to your senses and not know where you are or how you got there—something that people suffering from MPD have to deal with regularly.

Psychobabble

Sybil, starring Sally Field, was one of the first movies to claim to look at a real-life example of multiple personality disorder—but was it true? Dr. Herbert Spiegel, who also treated "Sybil" (Shirley Ardell Mason) believes the therapist featured in the film, Cornelia Wilbur, actually suggested the personalities as part of Shirley's therapy and that the patient adopted them with the help of hypnosis and sodium pentathol. Shirley apparently had no MPD symptoms before her therapy began.

Human beings have amazing ways of expressing their personalities and coping with the curve balls life throws at them. And, just as our personalities are always changing and growing, our theories about how personality develops continue to evolve. Freud was certainly right about one thing—we'll probably never uncover all the layers of the human psyche. In the next chapter, we'll take a look at the various ways human psyches can get out of whack. We'll talk about what's normal, what's not, and who decides which is which.

The Least You Need to Know

➤ Freud, the father of psychoanalysis, believed that personalities developed through a battle between primitive urges and the need to get along with others.

➤ According to Freud, children pass through three predictable stages of psychosexual development—the oral stage, the anal stage, and the phallic stage.

➤ Freud identified three parts of the personality: the id, the superego, and the ego.

➤ Jung, Horney, and Adler believed that humans are driven by needs for creativity, security, and competence.

➤ Defense mechanisms help us cope with unbearable thoughts, feelings, and wishes. Some of these are repression, projection, rationalization, reaction formation, displacement, and sublimation.

➤ Humanist psychologists believe we are born with healthy personalities that sometimes get stifled by the needs of others and the demands of our environment.

➤ Social-cognitive psychologists believe our personalities arise out of the beliefs and attitudes we develop through our unique life experiences.

Answers to the Defense Mechanisms Quiz

Statement	Answer
1	F
2	D
3	C
4	A
5	B
6	E

If you got all these questions right, you are not easily fooled by someone's defense mechanisms.

Answers to the Locus of Control Quiz

The answers indicating you chose internal locus of control are these:

Question	Answer
1	A
2	A
3	B
4	A
5	B

If you answered at least three questions toward internal locus of control, you believe you have control over your own destiny. If you answered fewer than three, you probably believe you cannot control your destiny.

Part 5

Just What *Is* Normal, Anyway?

Get ready for a wild ride! This section deals with the tricky question of what's normal and what's not. How do clinical psychologists identify mental illness? And how do they determine the best way to treat it? In these chapters, you'll learn all about psychological diagnoses—how they're made and what they mean. You'll also learn about the politics of mental illness, and how the labels of mental illness can often do more harm than good. In the end, you'll have a good idea of what you can do to take charge of your own life—you'll learn when and how self-improvement techniques can make a positive difference in your life!

Chapter 17

Are You Out of Your *Mind?*

In This Chapter

➤ What's normal, and what's not

➤ MUUDI-ing the waters of the mind

➤ Why labels should come with warnings

➤ A "classy" diagnosis

➤ The perils of pleading insanity

In 1973, psychologist Dr. David Rosenhan and seven other sane individuals faked mental illness to gain admission to a total of 12 different psychiatric hospitals. It wasn't hard; they all complained of hearing voices that said "empty, hollow, thud." Other than this one symptom, they answered every question honestly. Once in the hospital, they behaved normally—just as they would have outside the hospital. When asked about "the voices," they said they no longer heard them.

You'd think the hospital's staff would have soon realized that these individuals had never been "crazy" or, if they had been, they weren't any longer. But you'd be wrong. The only people who suspected anything were the other patients, who'd say, "You're not crazy. I bet you're a reporter doing research on the hospital."

Worse still was the way the staff consistently responded to these men. They talked about the patients in front of them, as if they couldn't hear or understand what was being said. And, in the hospital notes, normal behavior was often written up as symptoms of emotional instability. For example, the pseudopatients each kept a journal of

Brain Buster

Warning! Don't succumb to the "psychology student's disease"—a tendency to discover in yourself the symptoms of every disorder discussed in the book. By the time I had finished my first abnormal psychology course, the only mental illness I could rule out for sure was anorexia (I weighed too much and love to eat!). Forewarned is forearmed.

Insight

A major National Institute of Mental Health study found that, in any given month, about 15 percent of the population is suffering from a diagnosable mental health problem, and almost one out of every three people will suffer from one in the course of a lifetime.

his experience. No one on staff asked about it, but they'd make notes on the patients' charts about "excessive writing."

In this chapter, you'll learn how psychiatric labels are made—what psychologists define as abnormal, how diagnoses are classified, and the pros and cons of our current classification system. And you'll learn how difficult it is to get rid of the label "mentally ill" once it's been applied. You'll get a sense of the "politics" of mental illness, and its implications for anyone trying to overcome mental illness. You'll know not only know what psychiatric diagnoses are currently in use, but also why you should use them with caution.

Meet Abby Normal

In a hilarious scene in the movie *Young Frankenstein*, Igor mistakenly chooses a physically abnormal brain for Dr. Frankenstein's experiments. The resulting "monster" looks physically abnormal, is intellectually impaired, and certainly doesn't know how to win friends and influence people.

If this movie were coming from a psychological framework, then the underlying message would be that the monster's abnormal behavior came about as a result of his abnormal brain. This biological perspective of mental illness has dominated research on mental illness for the past 10 years.

But, what exactly *is* abnormal? Have you ever worried excessively, felt depressed for no apparent reason, or felt afraid of something that you knew couldn't really hurt you? I certainly have—I have been known, to mow people down in my frantic need to get away from a harmless cockroach. A few irrational fears, and occasional periods of worry or sadness, seem to be part of life. The challenge is in knowing how many are too many, and how long is too long.

Mental health professionals face a difficult task when they try to come up with a definition of mental illness. It is hard to determine at what point eccentric or free-spirited behavior becomes a marker of mental illness. But when a person begins to behave in a way that causes significant personal distress and disrupts his or her ability to function effectively at work or at home, it seems obvious that something must be done.

So, mental health professionals need to designate some point at which a person's behavior crosses the (imaginary) line between health and illness. This cutoff point is called a diagnosis.

Psychological diagnoses are interpretations based on a person's behavior. In order for someone to receive a psychological diagnosis, that person must have had the problem for some time—to make certain that it's not just a temporary state (see Chapter 15, "He's Got … Personality!"). For some diagnoses, like clinical depression, the minimum time period could be as short as two weeks; for personality disorders, the time frame must be at least two years.

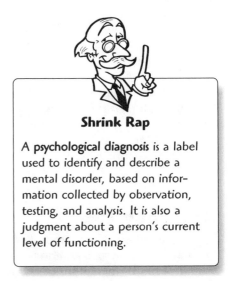

Shrink Rap

A **psychological diagnosis** is a label used to identify and describe a mental disorder, based on information collected by observation, testing, and analysis. It is also a judgment about a person's current level of functioning.

In addition, the person's behavior problems must be bad enough to disrupt normal daily activities. Maybe you've started waking up in the middle of the night and you can't go back to sleep. Maybe you're calling in sick at work a lot, or maybe you're drinking too much. Whatever the problem is, to warrant a psychological diagnosis, it must be severe enough that you would function a lot better without it.

How Psychologists MUUDI the Waters

Clinical psychologists generally evaluate a person's behavior according to five basic criteria: is it maladaptive, unpredictable, unconventional, distressing, and/or irrational. If at least two of these criteria are present, it sets off a warning bell for the psychologist to look more closely at the person's symptoms. In the world of diagnosis, this is how mental health professionals often **MUUDI** the waters of the mind.

➤ *Maladaptive:* The person fails to adapt to the demands of everyday life, either by acting counter to his or her own well-being or against the goals and needs of society.

➤ *Unpredictable:* The person loses control or acts erratically from one situation to another. For example, the child who suddenly smashes a toy for no apparent reason is behaving unpredictably.

➤ *Unconventional:* Behavior that psychologists define as unconventional is both rare and undesirable. Geniuses may be eccentric, but a psychologist wouldn't apply the term *unconventional* unless their behavior violates social standards of what is morally acceptable or desirable.

➤ *Distressing:* The person is suffering from severe personal distress or intensely negative emotions. If a person is nervous before an exam, it's normal; if he or she throws up, can't concentrate, and eventually gets up and walks out, that's abnormal.

➤ *Irrational:* The person acts in ways that are incomprehensible to others. Hearing voices or believing that you're overweight at 95 pounds are examples of "irrational" behavior.

Of course, there's another factor involved in any psychological diagnosis—the level of discomfort in the person making the judgment! Certainly, what is defined as "abnormal" partly depends on the comfort level of the society in which we live. A person who hears voices in the United States is much more likely to be labeled "mentally ill" than someone who lives in a culture that views hallucinations as a form of spiritual guidance.

Sick Societies

For hundreds of years, most societies have had a "sick" view of mental illness—they saw abnormal behavior as a sign of evil. Throughout the Middle Ages, for example, concepts of mental illness were intertwined with superstition and religion, and the outcome wasn't pretty: How'd you like having holes drilled in your head to let the evil spirits out?

Psychobabble

In Salem, Massachusetts, in 1692, several young girls began experiencing convulsions, nausea, and weakness. They reported sensations of being bitten or pinched, and some became temporarily blind or deaf. Believing that the girls' symptoms were the work of the devil, a witchcraft panic led to the execution of more than 20 men and women believed to be witches. These "bewitched" young women may have been suffering from ergot poisoning, a fungus that grows on rye and is a source of LSD.

Until the end of the eighteenth century, the mentally ill in Western cultures were viewed as mindless beasts who could only be controlled with chains and physical discipline. "Psychiatric hospitals" were nothing more than jail cells.

In the late eighteenth century, however, Phillipe Pinel began preaching that the mentally ill were neither immoral nor demonically possessed—they were simply suffering from a sickness. Believing that disorders of thought, mood, and behavior were similar to physical illnesses, he developed the first system to classify psychological disorders. His classifications were a huge step forward because they made it easier for clinicians to identify and design treatments for common disorders.

It wasn't until 1896, however, that the first truly comprehensive system of classifying psychological disorders was created by German psychiatrist Emil Kraeplin. When psychiatrists today speak of "mental illness" and talk of treating "patients," they are borrowing from Kraeplin's medical view of the origins of mental illness. While Kraeplin's medical approach helped reduce the stigma of mental illness, it also slowed down the discovery of the psychological, social, and environmental influences on mental health problems. It took Sigmund Freud to swing attention back in that direction.

Insight

Beware the power of labels. One in three applicants with severe mental illness have been turned down for a job for which they were qualified—because of their psychiatric label. Seven out of ten have been treated as less competent when their illness was disclosed. It makes you wonder if honesty is always the best policy.

Psychology Today

Well, today's psychologists have ruled out evil spirits as the source of mental illness—but that's just about as far as we've come. The search for the causes of mental illness is still alive and well, and it's currently led by teams divided into two camps: the biological team and the psychological team.

Walking the Biological Beat

The biological team follows the medical model in assuming that psychological problems are directly attributable to underlying brain or nervous system disorders. As you saw in Chapter 2, "Bio Psycho What?," the brain is a complex and delicate organ; subtle alterations in its tissue or its chemical messengers can have a dramatic influence on a person's mental health. For example, tumors in certain areas of the brain can cause extremely violent behavior. And having too little or too much of even one neurotransmitter can mean the difference between happiness and despair.

Shrink Rap

Psychopathology is the clinical term for an abnormality or disorder in thought, emotion, or behavior.

The biological approach to mental illness is responsible for developing the powerful psychiatric medications that are available today, some of which enable people to live normal, satisfying lives. Years ago, those same people would have spent their lives chained to the wall of an insane asylum.

Pulling for the Psychological Team

The psychological team, of course, focuses on the causal role of social or psychological factors in the development of *psychopathology*. They search for the personal experiences, traumas, conflicts, parenting styles, and so forth that lead to psychological disorders. A therapist relying on the psychodynamic perspective, for example, might focus on a person's past actions and relationships and the conflicts in these. Behaviorists would examine problem behaviors and the conditions in the environment that keep them in place, while therapists using the cognitive approach would investigate unhealthy reasoning or poor problem solving and its impact on our lives.

Putting It All Together

Luckily for all of us, the biological and psychological camps are beginning to work together. Both are becoming increasingly aware that psychopathology is the product of a complex interaction between biology and psychology. A person might have a genetic susceptibility for depression (biology), but doesn't get depressed until his or her divorce (psychology). In fact, many mental illnesses seem to work this way; a person is vulnerable to a mental illness because of faulty hormones or neurotransmitters, but certain stresses or maladaptive coping strategies are necessary for the illness to fully develop.

Of course, it's pretty useless to argue about what *causes* mental illness unless you are in agreement about what it *is*. To create greater consistency among clinicians with various theoretical backgrounds, psychologists and psychiatrists have developed a system of diagnosis and classification that provides precise descriptions of symptoms. At its best, our classification system provides an objective framework for evaluating a person's behavior and picking the most effective treatment. At its worst, it promotes labeling and focuses on the illness rather than on the person who has it.

DSM-IV: The Mental Health Catalog

Without an agreed-upon system to identify people whose disorders are similar to each other, the accumulation of knowledge about causes and effective treatments would be impossible. The system that is currently in vogue is the *DSM-IV*. The "DSM" stands for *Diagnostic and Statistical Manual of Mental Disorders,* and the "IV" means this is our fourth attempt to get it right. Diagnosis is always a work in progress.

The first version of *DSM* appeared in 1952, and listed several dozen mental illnesses. In 1968, *DSM-II* was published. One of the improvements of this new version was to make the diagnoses more compatible with the international classification system, the World Health Organization's International Classification of Diseases. The *DSM-IV* appeared in 1994.

Psychobabble

Early classification systems divided mental illnesses into two categories: neurosis and psychosis. *Neurosis* referred to a relatively common pattern of distress or self-defeating behavior (like chronic worrying or mild depression) that did not show signs of brain abnormalities or grossly irrational thinking. *Psychosis* referred to profound disturbances in rational thinking and a lack of touch with reality. Because they were so general, they were discarded in 1980.

As classification systems go, *DSM-IV* isn't too shabby. First of all, it's pretty reliable: The agreement among diagnosticians as to who has or does not have a particular disorder is pretty high. And that's an important point—after all, we must be able to agree on the diagnosis before we compare the individuals who have it.

But is the *DSM-IV* clinically meaningful? That's still a matter of debate. Critics argue that two people with the same diagnosis may suffer in very different ways and respond to different treatments.

Shopping in the *DSM-IV* Catalog

The *DSM-IV* lists more than 200 mental illnesses, grouped under 16 diagnostic categories, summarized below. As you review these categories, remember that, in order for a diagnostic decision to be made, classification systems must designate some arbitrary cutoff point; below that point you don't have a disorder, and above it you do. In real life, though, mental health and emotional challenges are on a continuum.

➤ *Anxiety disorders:* A group of disorders in which either fear or anxiety is a major symptom. Examples: panic disorder, phobias, obsessive-compulsive disorder, post-traumatic stress disorder.

➤ *Mood disorders:* Disorders characterized by depression and/or mania. Examples: major depression, bipolar disorder (formerly called manic-depression), dysthymia, and cyclothymia.

➤ *Somataform disorders:* Disorders in which physical symptoms arise from psychological problems. Examples: somatization disorder, conversion disorder.

➤ *Substance-related disorders:* Disorders caused by drugs, including alcohol, cocaine, amphetamines, or opiates. Examples: amphetamine withdrawal, alcohol dependence.

➤ *Dissociative disorders:* Disorders in which a part of one's experience is separated off from one's conscious memory or identity. Examples: dissociative identity disorder, psychogenic amnesia.

➤ *Psychotic disorders:* Disorders characterized by a loss of contact with reality, either through hallucinations, delusions, and/or inappropriate emotions. Examples: schizophrenia, delusional disorder.

➤ *Sexual and gender identity disorders:* Sexual disorders are disorders of sexual functioning. Examples: fetishism, exhibitionism, psychosexual dysfunction. Gender identity disorders involve a persistent desire to be, or appear to be, a member of the opposite sex.

➤ *Eating disorders:* Disorders marked by excessive concern about weight gain accompanied by extreme undereating, overeating, or purging. Examples: anorexia nervosa, bulimia nervosa.

➤ *Sleep disorders:* Disorders involving disrupted sleep, sleepwalking, fear of nightmares, or fear of sleep. Examples: insomnia, sleep-wake disorder.

➤ *Impulse control disorders:* Disorders in which impulsive behaviors harm the self or others. Example: intermittent explosive disorder, kleptomania, or pathological gambling.

➤ *Disorders usually first diagnosed in infancy, childhood, or adolescence:* A wide range of disorders that appear before adulthood. Examples: mental retardation, learning disorders, and language development disorders.

➤ *Adjustment disorder:* An extreme emotional reaction to a stressor that occurred within the previous month (much greater than most people would experience).

➤ *Personality disorders:* Long-term disorders characterized by rigid, maladaptive personality traits. Examples: antisocial personality disorder, histrionic personality disorder, narcissistic personality disorder.

➤ *Delirium, dementia, amnestic and other cognitive disorders:* A diverse group of disorders of memory and cognition that is caused by identifiable brain damage. Examples: Alzheimer's disease, intellectual impairment due to stroke or head injury, and delirium (change in consciousness) as a result of a drug overdose.

➤ *Mental disorders due to a general medical condition:* A group of mental disorders that can be directly traced to a medical cause. Examples: personality changes due to frontal lobe injury, psychotic disorder due to epilepsy, and depression secondary to diabetes.

➤ *Factitious disorders:* Physical or psychological symptoms that are faked in order to assume the "sick" role. Examples: making up physical complaints, exaggerating genuine medical symptoms, or self-inflicting wounds and then seeking medical treatment.

Warning: Labels Can Be Hazardous to Your Health

Pretend you and I are getting ready to go out with another friend of mine, Jan. You've never met Jan, so you're asking me for a little bit of information about her in preparation for our dinner together. I'm singing her praises: "She's really smart, she's headed up the corporate ladder, she's funny, generous, and attractive. Oh, and by the way, she suffers from depression and is on Prozac." Did your level of enthusiasm drop a little with that last remark?

If so, you're like most of us. Diagnosing and labeling may be essential for the scientific study of mental illness. Insurance companies may require them. However, they should be used with caution—studies have shown that labels can be harmful to your mental health.

The Trouble with Tunnel Vision

When we meet a person who is labeled as having a mental disorder, we're often blinded to the qualities of the person that aren't captured by the label. For example, now that Jan has the label "depressed," you're less likely to notice her sense of humor.

Unfortunately, this tunnel vision isn't limited to the lay person—psychotherapists are as susceptible to it as anyone else. In one study, a group of psychotherapists watched a videotape of a man talking about his personal problems. The ones who were told he was a patient rated his mental health far more negatively than those who were given no such information. Even children treat each other based on labels; a child labeled as having attention deficit disorder, for example, is often ostracized even if he or she doesn't really have the disorder.

That's a Person Under That Label!

Worse still, these labels can hurt the people who carry them. In another experiment, former patients in a psychiatric hospital were found to be much more socially inept if they believed their psychiatric treatment was known to the person with whom they were interacting.

Obviously, mental health professionals should continually evaluate the pros and cons of psychiatric labels. And both professionals *and* lay persons should work hard to use language that distinguishes the person from his or her diagnosis. It is dangerous and damaging to call someone "an anorexic" or "a schizophrenic." Such language implies that the diagnosis sums up the entire person. If I truly had my way, we'd say, "Joni has received the diagnosis of anorexia nervosa from a mental health professional." That way, the person is distinct from the illness, *and* we'd be acknowledging that the diagnosis itself is a judgment made by a fallible human being. It's subjective and never completely reliable.

The Gender Politics of Mental Illness

Before I get completely off my soapbox, I should tell you a story. In the 1970s, a study asked a number of mental health professionals to describe a mentally healthy man. Adjectives like *assertive* and *confident* were used. These same people were asked to describe a mentally healthy woman. This time words like *warm, sensitive, nurturing* appeared. Then came the biggest challenge: describe a mentally healthy *person*. Want to know what happened? The mentally healthy person had the same traits as the mentally healthy man. So, where does that leave those of us of the female persuasion?

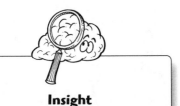

Insight

The movie *Frances* is a disturbing and controversial look at the life of actress Frances Farmer and her involuntary commitment to a mental hospital. Not only will you see a stunning performance by Jessica Lange, you'll be a mental health activist for life.

Brain Buster

Different roles may have an influence on mental health. Analysis of mental health data collected between 1950 and 1980 found that, as employment for men and women became more similar, the gender gap in anxiety and mood disorders declined.

Gender differences in mental health diagnoses exist and their causes have been debated ever since they were noticed. While there is little difference between men and women in the overall prevalence of mental illness, large gender differences are found for specific disorders. Women are much more likely to be diagnosed with anxiety and mood disorders, and men are more likely than women to be diagnosed with substance abuse problems and antisocial personality disorder.

Without getting dragged into the nature-nurture debate again, let's consider a few explanations for why this might be so. It is possible that such differences might directly come from biological differences between the sexes. Most attention, though, has been paid to the sociocultural explanations for these differences, such as self-reporting differences, biased observers, and gender-based differences in life experiences.

Generally speaking, men are much less likely to seek treatment for emotional problems and more reluctant to admit to psychological distress. For instance, experiments have shown that when men and women are subjected to the same stressful situation, such as a final exam, men show physical signs of distress equal to or greater than female peers but are much less likely to admit to them during interviews or on questionnaires. In addition, women receive more social permission to express sadness and fear, while men have more freedom to express anger.

Psychologists are people too, with their own biases, opinions, and values. These biases may at times influence their clinical decisions. For example, studies suggest that diagnoses may sometimes be circular; because some diagnoses occur more frequently in men and women, clinicians may expect to find them. And, not surprisingly, they find what they are looking for!

Psychobabble

In the nineteenth century, Samuel Cartwright argued that slaves were suffering from two forms of mental illness: 1) drapetomania, an uncontrollable urge to escape from slavery, and 2) dyasthesia aethiopica, which included symptoms such as being disobedient, talking back, refusing to work, and fighting back when being beaten. I can think of a few labels that might fit Mr. Cartwright; how about you?

Are You Insane?

On March 30, 1981, John W. Hinckley Jr. shot President Ronald Reagan. His defense attorneys did not dispute that he had planned and committed the act. Instead, they argued that he was not guilty by reason of insanity. Specifically, they argued that Hinckley's life was controlled by his pathological obsession with the movie *Taxi Driver,* starring Jodie Foster. In that movie, Foster's character is terrorized by a stalker, who eventually gets into a shoot-out. The defense attorney argued that Hinckley was schizophrenic, and that the movie was the force behind his assassination attempt against the president. The jury believed it.

Mental Illness vs. Insanity

Mental illness is a medical decision. Insanity, on the other hand, is a legal one. To be insane, a person must be unable to control his or her behavior and be unaware that his behavior is wrong. If Mr. X, on trial for shooting his boss, truly believed he needed to defend himself against a corporate conspiracy that was ruining his life, he might honestly think that his actions were justified; in fact, he might believe that his actions would protect others from receiving similar treatment. Serial killers like Ted Bundy, on the other hand, do bizarre things but have a clear awareness that their behavior is morally and socially wrong.

The insanity defense is based on the principle that punishment is justified only if the defendant is capable of understanding and controlling his or her behavior. Because some people suffering from a mental disorder are not capable of knowing or choosing right from wrong, the insanity defense prevents them from going to prison.

The Perils of Pleading Insanity

Despite popular belief, the insanity defense is not the easy way out. Defendants rarely enter pleas of "not guilty by reason of insanity," probably because it works less than

287

1 percent of the time. Also, defendants who are successful may, over time, wish they hadn't been. Their "successful" defense gets them confined to a mental institution until their sanity is established. Some of these defendants spend more time in a mental institution than they would have served in prison.

Stigma Is a Dirty Word

In a recent *People* magazine article, a celebrity was talking about the birth of her child and the joys of being a new mom. She made the passing comment that she "just didn't have time" to have the blues after the baby was born. Numerous readers wrote in, hurt and incensed that this naive star could honestly believe that postpartum depression was a matter or choice or a result of having too much time on one's hands.

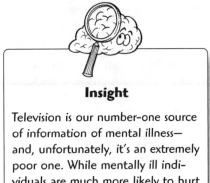

Insight

Television is our number-one source of information of mental illness—and, unfortunately, it's an extremely poor one. While mentally ill individuals are much more likely to hurt themselves than others, mentally ill characters on prime-time television are portrayed as violent 70 percent of the time.

In spite of numerous public education campaigns, you can still find major American newspapers running articles that advise the depressed to "buck up," "throw away your antidepressants," or "go away and sulk until you're ready to be sociable." Such stigmatizing attitudes lead many who would benefit from treatment to avoid getting it and to hide their pain from friends and family members. Tipper Gore, who recently went public about her own experience with depression after her son's near-fatal car crash, probably thought long and hard about the possible impact of her disclosure on the Gore campaign. No one, it seems, is immune from the stigma of mental illness.

These attitudes ignore the fact that many mental illnesses have a biological basis. Nearly 25 percent of us see mental illness as a personal shortcoming, and 60 percent of employers say they would "never" hire a candidate who had been diagnosed with depression for an executive job. It seems that, so far, psychology has done a better job at diagnosing individual problems than "treating" the society that condemns them.

Five Things You Can Do to Fight Stigma

You might not be a psychologist, but there's a lot you can do to improve our *society's* mental health. Here are five:

➤ Wise up. Mental illness is not a character flaw, a lack of willpower, or a luxury. People with mental illness are much more likely to be victims, not perpetrators of crime. And people who suffer from a mental illness can be just as effective as people with a physical illness. (Do the names Winston Churchill and Abraham Lincoln ring a bell?)

➤ Avoid using slang like "crazy," "loony," or "nuts" to describe people or situations, even if you're just kidding around.

➤ Be a media watchdog—fire off letters to editors, writers, and producers who include demeaning expressions or inaccurate descriptions of mental illness in their work.

➤ Don't be afraid to tell someone if you're concerned about his emotional well-being or if you know he's received psychiatric treatment. Asking about someone's mental health problems does not make them worse.

➤ Take charge of your own mental health. If you've struggled with depression or anxiety for a while, get some help.

The Least You Need to Know

➤ Many mental illnesses are a complex interaction between a biological predisposition and stressful life events.

➤ Diagnoses are labels mental health professionals use to group together people who have the same symptoms and behaviors.

➤ The most popular classification system in the United States is the *DSM-IV*. It lists more than 200 mental diagnoses, which can be grouped into 16 categories.

➤ While mental illness is a medical decision, insanity—the inability to control one's behavior and distinguish between right and wrong—is strictly a legal determination.

➤ The stigma of mental illness is one of the greatest barriers people face in finding the courage to get help for mental problems.

Mood Swingers and Scaredy-Cats

"I'm afraid the black dog has really got me .... It crouches in the corner of the room, waits for me to make a move. Or lies at the foot of the bed, like a shadow, until I try to get up. Growls and will not let me up ....

"Little things overwhelm me ... My baby gives me one of those dazzling you're-the-only-one-in-the-world smiles—so what? ... I'm one beat off, one step removed from all around me ... I don't shower, brush my hair, or make the bed. I cancel appointments or don't show up ... I stand for a moment too long in front of the cabinet staring at the Drano and thinking I wonder what will happen if I drank it?"

So begins the prologue of Cathy Kronkite's candid book, *On the Edge of Darkness: Conversations About Conquering Depression* in which she talks about her own experience with depression and shares countless interviews with other celebrities who've had similar experiences. They're not hard to find: Queen Elizabeth, Elton John, Patti Duke, Tipper Gore. Not to mention one out of every 20 regular U.S. citizens.

Shrink Rap

Affective disorders comprise a family of illnesses in which the primary symptom is a disturbance of mood. "Mood disorder" is another name for the same group of illnesses.

In this chapter, we'll explore mood and anxiety disorders. You'll discover the difference between a bad mood and major depression and you'll see where you fall on the mood continuum. You'll learn about the mood swings in manic depression, the low-level sadness of dysthymia, and the gentler ups and downs of cyclothymia. You'll also meet the four anxiety disorders, discover what "panicking" really means, and learn what to do when obsessive thoughts won't go away.

Be Psychologically Correct

You may or may not be politically correct but please, as a personal favor to me, try to be psychologically correct. When you have a bad day and are sharing it with a friend or loved one, try to say you are "in a funk," "have got the blues," or are in a "bad mood." Please, oh please, don't call it *depression*.

While it might not seem like a big deal to use the word *depression* to describe a temporary funk, it is. When the word *depression* is used to describe everything from a passing mood to a chronic illness, it creates confusion for all of us.

Bad moods or grief over a loss are normal parts of life; they aren't pleasant, but we get through them with time. Clinical depression, also called unipolar disorder, is a different animal altogether. Depression can kill you.

As long as we use the terms interchangeably, when someone tells you she is suffering from depression, you're likely to misunderstand what she's saying. "So what?" you think. "I was depressed yesterday, too, and I snapped out of it." Not if you were experiencing a major depression, you didn't. Episodes of untreated depression typically last several months, and invade every part of your life. Let's take a look at what clinical depression really is.

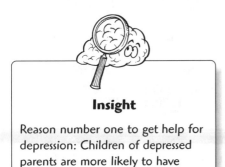

Insight

Reason number one to get help for depression: Children of depressed parents are more likely to have medical problems and to be depressed themselves.

In a Major Funk

You don't feel hopeful or happy about anything in your life. You feel like you're moving in slow motion. Nothing tastes good. Getting up in the morning requires a lot of effort. You find yourself crying over nothing, or at something that wouldn't normally bother you. These are the faces of clinical depression.

Major depression, the common term for clinical depression, is an equal opportunity illness. It affects one in 20 Americans every year, about twice as many women as men. It hits people at all socioeconomic levels and ethnic backgrounds. It can creep up on you or grab you by the throat. Major depression is debilitating and dangerous—an overwhelming sadness that lasts at least two weeks and is severe enough to interfere with a person's life.

When mental health professionals assess someone for depression, they look for specific signs that differ from the blues everyone feels at one time or another, or the grief we experience over the loss of a loved one. If you went to your physician and complained of depression, he or she would look for five or more of the following symptoms.

Loss of interest in things you used to enjoy, including sex.

Feeling sad, blue, or down in the dumps.

Feeling either slowed down or so restless you can't sit still.

Changes in appetite.

Thoughts of death or suicide.

Problems concentrating, remembering, or making decisions.

Loss of energy or feeling tired all the time.

Feeling worthless or guilty.

Trouble sleeping or sleeping all the time.

One of the first two symptoms is mandatory—the depression must cause significant emotional distress and/or disrupt your daily life.

The problem with lists of clinical symptoms is they sound so clinical. A list of symptoms can't capture the personal experience of living with depression. Here are some real-world examples of what a depressed person might say:

"I just don't want to be around anyone. I keep making excuses to my friends. I know I'm hurting their feelings, but I don't want to be a downer to them and I just can't pretend anymore that I'm up."

"I can't remember the last time I laughed. I have so much to be thankful for, so why can't I just snap out of it?"

"It takes me a week to do what I used to do in a day. Some days I don't get out of bed until noon."

"I feel so bad that sometimes I wish I were dead. Yeah, I guess I've had thoughts of killing myself; anything would be better than this."

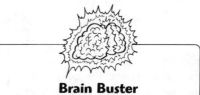

Brain Buster

Untreated depression is one of the top three workplace problems. Fifty percent of people with depression report work-related problems, and it costs the United States 200 million sick days each year.

"I wake up in the middle of the night and can't go back to sleep. I try not to think of the future, because I can't imagine feeling any better."

As you can see, these thoughts and feelings are not typical of being down in the dumps. You might want to pull the covers up over your head when you're in a bad mood, but you don't think about suicide. Why do some people bounce back from a minor funk, while others slide into a downward spiral that takes months to crawl out of? Let's take a look at what causes depression and who's likely to get it.

Why Me?

Depression runs in families. There are some people whose brain chemistry is vulnerable to a depressive response, and others who won't get clinically depressed even in the face of serious physical or psychological stress. However, depression can occur in people whose family history is clean of depressive genes, and we may all be vulnerable to depression if our life circumstances are tough enough.

Most people with depression can point to an incident or situation which they believe has triggered their unhappiness, although this is not true for everyone. While the specific life events vary, they almost always involve loss—loss of physical health, loss of a loved one, loss of a job, or loss of self-confidence or self-control. Obviously, not everyone who goes through a divorce or loses a job becomes depressed; most often, it's the double whammy of depressive genes and a stressful life event that triggers the first clinical depression.

As you can see, the question "is depression mostly physical or psychological?" is a moot one. Clinical depression can be triggered by either physical or psychological events. Most commonly, both seem to be involved. And, however it begins, depression can quickly develop into a set of physical and psychological problems that feed on each other and grow.

Brain Buster

Severe depression heightens the risk of dying after a heart attack or stroke, and reduces the quality of life (and possibly the survival time) for cancer patients. And a majority of depressed people who go untreated seriously consider suicide, with up to 17 percent eventually succeeding in killing themselves.

How Bad Is Your Mood?

You might think a person would know if he or she is depressed, but that often isn't true. Depression can develop gradually, so a person may slip into a clinical depression without fully realizing how far down he's fallen. If you've ever had a cold that gradually turned into bronchitis or pneumonia, you've experienced the medical version of this phenomenon—you knew you didn't feel well, but because the progression from cold to pneumonia was gradual you may not have appreciated exactly how bad you really felt until you finally felt better. Depression can be like that, too.

Here's a handy quiz to assess your own mood. Place the number that most accurately reflects your responses to the following statements in the blank.

Mood Assessment Quiz

1 = never   4 = often
2 = rarely   5 = always
3 = sometimes

_____ I have been more unhappy than usual over the past month.

_____ I don't seem to have much energy.

_____ I don't get very much pleasure from anything.

_____ It is hard to get things done that I used to accomplish easily.

_____ I have been more angry and/or irritated over the past few weeks.

_____ I feel worse in the morning than in the afternoon.

_____ Lately, I feel like crying at the drop of a hat.

_____ I have been sleeping poorly for the past month.

_____ I feel pretty hopeless about my life getting any better.

_____ I can't seem to concentrate like I usually do.

Now let's total up your score and see what kind of mood you're in. Here's how to interpret your score:

20 or less. You seem to be on the "happy" end of the mood spectrum. Rarely does a bad mood get you down for long, and when it does, it usually doesn't keep you from doing the things you need to do. What's your secret?

21–30. While life is manageable, you may find that your moods are a little more volatile than usual. Maybe you're going through a stressful time or a bumpy relationship. Whatever the reason, take good care of yourself, get regular exercise, and try some of the depression buffers.

31–40. Bad moods seem to grip you more often than most people. If some of the depression buffers aren't working, or if you're having trouble getting your normal activities done, consider talking to a professional. It can't hurt!

41–50. While this is not a professional tool, your score worries me. Life is much harder than it has to be, and it seems like depression has you pretty firmly in its grasp. There is no need to suffer needlessly; depression is much more treatable than many physical illnesses. It's time to find that out for yourself.

Depression Buffers

Whether you're in a really bad mood or a major depression, there are things you can do that will help you ride the situation out. These ten depression buffers can be useful either as a bad mood buster or as some additional self-help strategies while you're getting the professional help you need.

➤ Don't hide out in your house or apartment for more than a few hours. Depressive thoughts can worsen when no one else is around.

➤ Don't make major life decisions until you feel better. If you have to make one, talk it over with at least two people you trust.

➤ Structure your mornings as much as possible. Get up and take a shower every day, even if you don't feel like it.

➤ Avoid drugs and alcohol. They can make depression worse.

➤ If you've lost your appetite, eat small snacks during the day rather than trying to force yourself to eat a big meal.

➤ Take notes and make lists. Having trouble concentrating is common with depression, so don't trust your memory even if it's normally better than an elephant's.

➤ If you wake up during the middle of the night, get out of bed and do something (read inspirational material, for example).

➤ At the minimum, go for a 20-minute walk every day. Exercise can be helpful in reducing mild depression.

➤ Give yourself a break. Don't expect to do all the things you normally do.

➤ Make a date to get some help. If you've been depressed for two weeks or more, talk to someone—your physician, your minister, or a therapist.

We'll explore medication and psychotherapy in detail in later chapters, where you'll get the straight scoop on antidepressants and psychotherapy. For now, however, it's enough to know that antidepressants work about 70 percent of the time, and the most effective kinds of psychotherapy for depression are cognitive behavioral therapy and interpersonal therapy. Cognitive behavioral therapy focuses on changing the way a depressed person thinks about failure and loss, while interpersonal therapy takes a here-and-now look at social relationships and the impact they can have on mental health. Some of these are tools we could all use!

When Someone You Love Is Depressed

When someone you love is depressed, you worry. You probably also feel frustrated, overwhelmed, and confused. You may find yourself asking, "Why can't he or she just snap out of it?" Or you may think there's something you should be able to do to cure your loved one's problems.

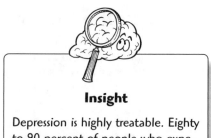

Insight

Depression is highly treatable. Eighty to 90 percent of people who experience a clinical depression can be effectively treated and resume their normal and productive life.

Sadly, no one can "cure" someone else's depression, but there are things you can say that will help and things you can say that will hurt. Even if you've got the best of intentions, telling someone, "Don't worry, be happy," or "Just get over it" is not going to earn you brownie points—plus it trivializes a serious illness. Would you tell someone with cancer to "just get over it"? I don't so.

There are much more useful things you can say to help someone who's suffering from depression. Here are a few:

➤ I care about you.

➤ You're not alone in this. I'll help any way I can.

➤ I'm sorry you're hurting so much.

➤ You're not "crazy."

➤ I can't understand exactly how you're feeling, but I can offer my support and compassion.

On the other hand, here's a handful of things you want to avoid saying to a depressed loved one:

➤ What do you have to be depressed about?

➤ It's all in your head.

➤ Pull yourself up by your bootstraps.

➤ I know just how you feel.

➤ You're just feeling sorry for yourself.

➤ You have so many things to be thankful for!

➤ Happiness is a choice.

➤ You think *you've* got problems.

➤ There is always somebody worse off than you are.

➤ Lighten up!

Low-Level Sadness

I had my first ear infection when I was 25, but for six weeks, I didn't know it. Gradually, I got more and more fatigued. I didn't feel "right." My ears didn't hurt, I ran little if any fever, and by looking at me, you would never have known I didn't feel well. But every day, I dragged myself to work.

Shrink Rap

Dysthymia is a psychological disorder in which the feelings of depression are less severe than those in major depression, but last for at least a two-year period.

Of course, I psychoanalyzed myself; was I depressed? I didn't think so, but what else could be causing this incredible fatigue and the vague physical symptoms I was feeling? For me at least, one of the perils of being a psychologist is that I can easily be a reverse hypochondriac—I tend to think every physical symptom is due to some emotional block!

When I finally saw the doctor, he took one look in my ears, diagnosed my infection, and after five days of antibiotics, I was back to my rambunctious self. But my instinct to look for a psychological cause for my distress wasn't entirely misplaced. *Dysthymia* is like having a low-grade emotional "infection" that saps your mood, drains your energy, and takes a lot of life's pleasure away.

Dysthymic disorder, or dysthymia, is a mild to moderate level of depression that lasts at least two years. It often causes a poor appetite or overeating, difficulty sleeping or sleeping too much, low energy, fatigue, and feelings of hopelessness. But people with dysthymic disorder may have periods of normal mood that can last up to two months. Even though this type of depression is mild, it's kind of like carrying around a ball and chain; you're still able to do what you have to, but it sure makes it harder.

Insight

If you're into alternative treatments, some studies suggest that acupuncture can relieve symptoms of depression for some people. If you're seeing an acupuncturist for back pain, though, don't expect relief. The treatment must be specifically designed for depression—nonspecific acupuncture doesn't work.

No one knows what causes dysthymic disorder, but it's fairly common. Up to 3 percent of the U.S. population suffers from dysthymia. It can begin at anytime, from childhood to adulthood, and it seems to affect more women than men. Although the cause is unknown, there may be changes in the brain that involve the neurotransmitter serotonin. In addition, personality problems, medical problems, and chronic life stresses may also play a role.

While we don't know what causes it, we're getting some good ideas about how to get rid of it. Dysthymic disorder can be effectively treated like major depression—with antidepressants, psychotherapy, or a combination of the two.

Riding the Mood Roller Coaster

Bipolar disorder, commonly called manic depression, is a psychological disorder that affects about 1 percent of the population of every country in the world, including the United States; this distribution is very different from major depression, which varies remarkably from country to country. And, unlike major depression, men and women are equally likely to get it.

Bipolar disorder is characterized by extreme mood swings. While all of us have "up" days and "down" days, individuals with bipolar disorder will be severely up sometimes, severely down sometimes, and in the middle some or most of the time. The hallmark of the disorder is the alternation between periods of mania and periods of depression.

The depressive end of bipolar disorder looks much like it does with major depression. For this reason, it's the manic part of bipolar disorder that determines the diagnosis. While there are a few cases of mania without depression, there is no current formal diagnosis of mania alone. Apparently, the mental health community embraces the "what goes up, must come down" philosophy. Anyone who has a manic episode will be diagnosed with bipolar disorder.

Psychobabble

Check out Kay Redfield Jamison's book *Touched With Fire* to get a fascinating look at the link between creativity and mood disorders. And for an up-close-and-personal encounter with bipolar disorder, read her autobiography, *An Unquiet Mind*.

When mania first starts, it can be productive and fun. Imagine being in a great mood, full of energy and inspiration. Dr. John Kelso, one of the leading researchers in bipolar disorder, suspects the reason evolution has passed along the bipolar gene is the increased creativity and energy that a mild level of mania (hypomania) bestows on us. The problem is, of course, the person can't stay at the level forever. In a full-blown manic episode, the person may:

➤ become so restless that he or she can't sit still;

➤ be unable to concentrate on anything, going back and forth from one thing to another without finishing anything;

➤ have racing thoughts and rapid, disconnected speech;

➤ develop paranoid ideas and/or extremely religious ideas and thoughts;

➤ be extremely impulsive and put him- or herself at risk through increased sexuality, financial extravagance, or an obsessive interest in some venture or hobby;

➤ become highly irritable or easily excitable;

➤ have grandiose delusions;

➤ suffer profound weight loss;

➤ stay awake for days and be unable to sleep.

Shrink Rap

Cyclothymia is a disorder in which a person experiences the symptoms of bipolar disorder, but in milder form. The symptoms are not severe enough to disrupt normal functioning and don't include hallucinations or delusions.

Cyclothymia is similar to bipolar disorder because it is characterized by mood swings from mania to depression. However, there are important distinctions between the two. A person with cyclothymia experiences symptoms of hypomania but never a full blown manic episode. Hypomanic symptoms are exactly the same as the symptoms of a manic episode, but milder. A hypomanic episode does not disrupt the person's ability to function, doesn't require hospitalization, and doesn't include hallucinations or delusions.

Likewise, while depression is a part of cyclothymia, the symptoms are never severe enough to meet the criteria for a major depressive episode. For cyclothymia to be diagnosed, hypomanic and depressive symptoms must alternate for at least two years. Treatment depends upon the severity of the disorder—mild symptoms may respond to psychotherapy and more severe mood problems may need lithium and/or antidepressants.

Moody Children

All children are happy. Children have nothing to worry about. Childhood is the best time of your life. These statements may seem absurd to you, but, for years, they reflected the attitudes of the mental health community. It was only in the 1980s that mood disorders in children were included in the category of diagnosed psychiatric illnesses.

There's a Lot of Troubled Kids out There

There is increasing evidence that major depression can develop in children—and that it occurs in teenagers much more often than we once thought. Seven to 14 percent of children will experience an episode of major depression before age 15; 20 percent to 30 percent of adults with bipolar disorder have their first episode before age 20; and an estimated 2,000 teenagers commit suicide each year.

The major ingredients of mood disorders are the same in children and adults, although children may express their symptoms differently. Unlike adults, children may not have the words to accurately describe how they feel, and therefore may exhibit more behavioral problems. In other words, children are more likely to "show" you their problems than talk about them.

Is It Moodiness or Depression?

While most preschoolers are unhappy when their wishes aren't granted, there are definite signs when the problem is more than simple disappointment or moodiness. Depressed preschoolers may be frequently tearful or irritable for no apparent reason. They may seem unusually serious and lack the bounce of their peers. And, of most concern, they may make frequent negative self-statements ("I hate myself," "I wish I were dead") and do things that are self-destructive (such as hitting themselves).

Depressed older children and teenagers often display behavioral problems. They may be irritable and aggressive, disruptive at school, and have declining grades. Parents may complain that nothing pleases the child and that he or she seems to hate himself and everything around him or her. A teenager who isolates himself in his room, has deteriorating grades, and few friends is not just going through a stage; he or she may be clinically depressed.

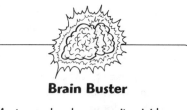

Brain Buster

Most people who commit suicide talk about it first. Talking or joking about suicide, acting in a reckless or dangerous manner, giving away possessions, or expressing feelings of hopelessness are common signs of suicidal plans.

I'm Always Anxious, About *Everything*

If you've ever found yourself unable to relax or get to sleep at night because of worries, you know some of the toll anxiety can take. Everyone experiences anxiety or fear in certain life situations, but 15 percent of the population has, at some point in their lives, experienced anxiety that was severe enough to disrupt their lives.

When a person feels anxious or worried most of the time for a period of at least six months, it's quite possible that he or she is suffering from generalized anxiety disorder. The anxiety might focus on a specific circumstance, such as unrealistic money worries or an inexplicable fear that a loved one will die or be injured. Or it might be a general apprehension that something bad is about to happen. For example, a person suffering from generalized anxiety disorder might start calling the emergency rooms if his or her spouse was late coming home from work.

In addition to the emotional discomfort, a person with generalized anxiety disorder often experiences a number of physical symptoms. He or she feels tense all the time,

Insight

While suicide is most commonly associated with depression, studies show that severe anxiety often leads to suicidal thoughts. They also show that when panic attacks occur along with depression, a person may be at high risk for suicide.

is easily startled, is unusually attentive to the cause or source of the anxiety, and may lay awake at night worrying. You can imagine what an energy drain this would be over time, and people who suffer from generalized anxiety disorder often report fatigue and tiredness. They literally wear themselves out with worry.

Luckily, generalized anxiety disorder is highly treatable. It appears to respond best to cognitive-behavioral therapy (CBT). In CBT, a person gradually learns to see situations and problems in a different perspective and is taught methods and techniques that can help alleviate anxiety. Medication can be a useful adjunct to therapy, but it's not always necessary. Generalized anxiety can usually be overcome in about three to six months, if the person is motivated and works toward recovery.

Hit-and-Run Fear

With generalized anxiety disorder, a person worries about everything. With panic disorder, on the other hand, the person never knows when an attack will occur. Panic disorder is one of the most confusing and terrifying psychological disorders.

In the Path of an Onrushing Train

People who've had panic attacks often say it feels like a train is bearing down on them at top speed and they can't move out of the way. They know there's no train in their heads, but their body responds as if there is—their hearts race, their mouths get dry, their blood pressure rises, and they feel as if they're going to die—or at the very least, lose their minds.

Sufferers of panic disorder experience unexpected but severe bouts of anxiety, from out of the blue, at least several times a month. They can happen anywhere; during a romantic dinner with your spouse, at the grocery store, or in the middle of an aerobics class. And, wham! There you go again.

Panic-Attack Pile-Up

As you might imagine, it wouldn't take too many of these emotional whacks upside the head before you started worrying about when the next one will happen. For many people with panic attacks, this anticipatory anxiety is as bad as the panic attack itself. They can never relax because there's always a chance that the next terrifying fear will be triggered out of the blue. They may avoid anyplace where they've had an attack, in hopes that this will cut down the odds of having another one. But this can lead to even worse problems, as you'll see when we talk about agoraphobia.

Panic disorder has a strong biological component. For some reason, the normal "fight-or-flight" response begins misfiring. And the disorder tends to run in families. Once it starts, the frightening physical symptoms snowball into a psychological nightmare characterized by constant worry (when will it happen again?), catastrophic thinking (what if I go crazy?), and self-doubt (I can't handle another one).

While medication can certainly help panic disorder, learning cognitive behavioral techniques that modify the frightening thoughts that accompany panic can also be extremely effective. For example, responding to a panic disorder with calm, reassuring self-talk ("I've been through this before and I'll get through it again") can actually extinguish the physical arousal of the attack over time. Apparently, if panic can't hit hard enough, it eventually runs away.

Shrink Rap

Panic disorder is an anxiety disorder during which the person experiences recurrent episodes of intense anxiety and physical arousal that lasts up to 10 minutes.

Stuck in the House All Day

To look at Kim Bassinger, it's hard to imagine she has a care in the world. She's beautiful. She's smart. She's an Academy Award winner. She's married to a hunk—Alec Baldwin. And, she's a recovering agoraphobic.

Individuals with agoraphobia experience anxiety in public places where escape might be difficult or embarrassing. They are controlled by the fear that, if they panic or become frightened outside the home, they'll either embarrass themselves or become paralyzed with their fear. As a result, they may gradually narrow their world until they literally become prisoners in their own homes. They cannot hold a job or carry out normal daily activities because their fear limits their ability to maintain contact with the outside world.

People don't just wake up one day with agoraphobia. It often starts out with panic attacks that are terrifying and random. Maybe someone is shopping at the mall and has a panic attack. She leaves immediately and feels better. But the next time she needs to go to the mall for something, she starts to feel a little anxious. "What if it happens again?," a little voice whispers. The mere thought of going through another panic attack—or the fear of public humiliation—sends chills up her spine. Maybe she decides go to a *different* mall, just in case. Everything is fine, but a few weeks later she has a panic attack there, too.

Over time, you can see how a person might become more and more afraid to venture out. After all, if a panic attack could happen anywhere, no place is 100 percent safe. At least at home no one will see it happen.

Psychobabble

Charles Darwin's theory of evolution may have been partly inspired by a psychological disorder. According to an article in the *Journal of the American Medical Association*, at least two psychiatrists think the "strange illness" that led to Darwin's famous reclusiveness, which focused his time and energy on his studies, was, in fact, panic disorder and agoraphobia.

Meet the Phobia Family

If your house is on fire or you're being mugged, fear is a rational reaction. It gives you an edge to get out of the house or away from your attacker. In contrast, a person with a phobia suffers from an ongoing, irrational fear of something that is so strong it creates a compelling desire to avoid it. Common phobias include the fear of heights (acrophobia), the fear of cramped spaces (claustrophobia), and the fear of snakes (ophidiophobia).

The Five Most Common Phobias

Name	Percentage of Phobias
Agoraphobia (fear of crowds or public places)	10–50%
Social phobia (fear of embarrassing oneself in public)	10%
Fear of inanimate objects (heights, storms, closed spaces)	20%
Illness-injury (death, cancer)	15–25%
Animals (snakes, dogs, insects)	5–15%

In addition to phobias that center on places or things, there's also social phobia. Social phobia is a pervasive and ongoing fear of social or performance situations in which the person might either be under scrutiny from others (public speaking, speaking to authority figures) or around strangers (going to parties, striking up conversations, dating). The sufferer will generally experience a lot of anxiety in these situations, and the fear of embarrassment and humiliation can lead him or her to avoid having to face such situations. Unlike a simple phobia, which is limited to specific objects such as dogs or flying, social phobias are more complex because the fear of embarrassment or humiliation can lead to an avoidance of numerous situations and settings.

Do you have a phobia? One out of every eight Americans will develop a phobia at some point in their lives. Some of them gradually go away by themselves and some of us just live with them. One way to reduce the power of phobias is systematic desensitization (you learned about that in Chapter 7, "Get *That* Through Your Thick Skull!"). This can be effective, and it usually works in just a few hair-raising sessions.

Most people, however, just live with their phobias, unless the fears begin to interfere with their lives in some way. For example, if you were considering a run for public office, a fear of public speaking (one form of social phobia) would be a real drag. It would also be a bummer if your fear kept you from going for a promotion because you knew you'd have to speak before a group.

On the other hand, if you're a computer programmer, the fear of public speaking might be a nuisance, but it wouldn't necessarily interfere with your life in any way. My fear of insects is a lot less cumbersome now that I live in California—with those Texas-sized cockroaches in Dallas, I would have either had to face up to my fear sooner or later, or risk my husband tiring of being stuck with endless pest control duty and squirting *me* with the bug spray!

This Can't Be As Good As It Gets

You know the feeling. You've just locked the door and gotten in your car to head to the movie. You're running late and you don't want to miss the beginning. But, just as you're backing out of the driveway, an unwanted thought creeps in. "Did I turn off the stove?" You mentally retrace your movements and you're 95 percent sure you did. But, horrible images of your house in flames still dance through your head. What if you forgot? What if your house burns down while you're watching *Star Wars*? Odds are you'll give up and run back in the house to check—or spend much of the movie wishing you had.

We all have moments like this—it's pretty normal. But, what if you ran back in the house, saw that you turned off the stove, got back in your car—and had the exact same level of

Insight

Okay, you movie fans, check out Jack Nicholson in *As Good As it Gets*. For once, the person with a psychiatric disorder is not portrayed as "crazy or violent." He isn't cured by the love of a good woman, although she does inspire him to get help. And, at the end of the movie, he's taken charge of his obsessive-compulsive disorder—and gets the girl to boot! Hooray for Hollywood!

doubt and fear about burning the house down? And, what if that fear surfaced every single time you left the house, even though you knew it was irrational and illogical. What if these fears made you so miserable if you didn't check that you often gave in? Welcome to obsessive-compulsive disorder (OCD).

My Obsessions Compelled Me to Do It!

Obsessive-compulsive disorder is an illness that traps people in endless cycles of repetitive thoughts (obsessions) and behaviors (compulsions). We all have habits and routines that help us organize our daily lives; people with OCD develop patterns of behavior that take up too much time and interfere with their daily lives. This could mean checking to make sure the stove is off 100 times before leaving for work, or washing your hands for hours after using a public toilet because of a profound fear of germs.

These behaviors are prompted by obsessive thoughts—unwanted and intrusive ideas, images, and impulses that run through your mind over and over again. When you're in the grip of such obsessive thoughts, you're likely to respond with compulsive behaviors that are intended to control or alleviate the obsession. You might perform these compulsive behaviors—often called rituals—according to "rules" you make up to try to control the nervous feelings that come along with the obsessive thoughts. Rituals like this do make the nervous feelings go away, but usually only for a short while. Then fear and discomfort return, and you find yourself repeating the routine all over again.

The Neurochemical Connection

No one knows why 3 million people in the United States have OCD or exactly what causes it. OCD may be connected with an imbalance in a brain chemical called serotonin, a neurotransmitter that is involved in regulating repetitive behaviors. The fact that most people with OCD respond to medication argues for a neurochemical involvement. Anafranil, for example, helps 60 percent of people with OCD; other medicines that may help include Prozac, Zoloft, and Paxil.

Psychotherapy is also important. Behavioral therapy is often used to weaken the power of unwanted compulsions. Sufferers of the disorder are first exposed to a situation that produces the obsessions and anxiety, and then they are encouraged to resist performing the behaviors that they normally use to control their discomfort. While this treatment takes guts, it works. Over time, the symptoms gradually fade.

In this chapter, we've examined the range of mood disorders. While most of us haven't been clinically depressed or anxious, we all know what it feels like to have the blues or feel nervous. In the next chapter, we'll take a look at a mental illness whose symptoms—hallucinations, disorganization, delusions—most of us will never experience. We'll explore the fascinating, complex, and misunderstood condition known as schizophrenia.

The Least You Need to Know

➤ Clinical depression is a psychological disorder that lasts for at least two weeks, causes significant emotional distress, and interferes with a person's ability to conduct normal activities.

➤ The best treatments for depression are a combination of antidepressant medication and psychotherapy.

➤ Dysthymia is a low-grade sadness that lasts for at least two years and responds well to antidepressants.

➤ Bipolar disorder—commonly called manic depression—is characterized by extreme mood swings of "highs" and "lows." Cyclothymia is a milder version of the disorder.

➤ Children can get depressed too, and are more likely to "show" their illness through behavior problems and a declining school performance.

➤ Anxiety disorders generally respond to cognitive behavioral psychotherapy and/or medication.

Chapter 19

Postcards from the Edge of Reality

In This Chapter

➤ Scoping out schizophrenia

➤ Curious conditions: Hallucinations, delusions and other strange things

➤ Learning about the family tie

➤ When you think they're out to get you

Thirty years ago, Frederick Frese was locked up inside an Ohio mental hospital. A college graduate and Marine, Frese had been guarding atomic weapons in Jacksonville, Florida when he developed the belief that enemy nations had hypnotized American leaders in a plot to take over the U.S. atomic weapons supply. He was diagnosed with paranoid schizophrenia.

Twelve years later Frese was the chief psychologist for the same mental health system that had once confined him. He was also happily married and had four children. Despite 10 further hospitalizations, Frese had earned a master's degree and a doctorate. Moral of the story: A mental illness is not a death sentence.

This chapter is about one of the most challenging, illusive, and maligned mental illnesses: schizophrenia. Here you'll learn about the different types, their symptoms and causes, and new groundbreaking treatments for this difficult condition. And you'll learn about paranoia in all its forms and why you can't just talk someone out of his suspicious beliefs. Finally, you'll see why anatomy is never destiny: Someone with a biological vulnerability to schizophrenia can take steps to minimize the risk of getting it.

Shrink Rap

Schizophrenia is a severe mental disorder characterized by a breakdown in perceptual and thought processes, often including hallucinations and delusions.

The General Scoop on Schizophrenia

Schizophrenia is the disorder people usually mean when they talk about "crazy," "psychotic," or "insane." It is probably the most famous mental illness, or at least it runs a close second to multiple personality disorder. It's also not very well understood by the general public—when it's portrayed in the media, it's often linked to a violent crime. While violence by a mentally ill person is rare, it is most likely to happen with someone with a diagnosis of paranoid schizophrenia.

Schizophrenia is also the most costly of all mental illnesses. People with this illness make up the majority of all patients hospitalized with mental disorders. It strikes approximately 1 percent of the U.S. population, generally in adolescence and young adulthood, and this percentage rate holds true for many other countries as well.

Schizophrenia is not a rare mental disorder. In the United States alone, there are as many people with schizophrenia as the combined populations of Wyoming, Vermont, Delaware, and Hawaii. It is equally common in men and women, although, for some reason, it tends to hit men earlier (between the ages of 18 and 25) and women later (26 to 45).

It is also a scary diagnosis to receive. While the treatment for schizophrenia has improved dramatically over the past 30 years, it is often a tough battle to win. Mental health professionals often talk about the "one-third" prognosis for schizophrenia: one-third make a full recovery and lead a normal life; one-third make a partial recovery; and one-third of the time, the person with schizophrenia is faced with a slow, downhill spiral of the disease throughout the rest of his or her life.

The Split Personality

Much of what is known about schizophrenia comes from the Swiss psychiatrist who "discovered" it: Eugen Bleuler. He was the first person to use the label *schizophrenia* to describe the devastating symptoms he saw in the people who suffered from this illness. The term comes from the Greek words *schizo*, which means "split" and *phrenum*, which means "mind." Bleuler observed that patients with schizophrenia often acted as if different parts of their minds were split off from each other, and each part was just doing its own thing.

For example, patients with schizophrenia might be listening to auditory hallucinations and thus unable to attend to anything going on around them. Or, they might talk about the recent death of a loved one—but smile or laugh as they're doing so.

This "splitting" of the various functions of the brain can lead to bizarre and disorganized thoughts and actions. Our sense of who we are depends on our attention, emotions, thoughts, behaviors, perceptions, and motivations all working in harmony with each other—or at least being on the same page.

Unfortunately, while many of Bleuler's insights still apply today, his choice of names leaves a lot to be desired. Many of us commonly confuse schizophrenia with multiple-personality disorder, although the two have very little in common. Someone in the acute stages of schizophrenia has one mind that may not be in touch with reality. A person with multiple-personality disorder, on the other hand, sees reality pretty clearly, but has at least two distinct personalities that compete for dominance.

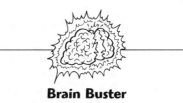

Brain Buster

Don't believe what you see in the movies and on television! You are not going to get ambushed by a homicidal stranger suffering from schizophrenia. When violence *does* occur, which is rare, it's almost always directed at a family member—not at strangers.

Schizophrenia from the Inside Out

Schizophrenia can literally put a person in another world. In the acute stage of the illness, the differences in thinking, altered sensory experiences, and disruptions in the ability to relate to others gives the person a drastically different experience of the world than you or I have. The essence of schizophrenia is *impaired reality testing:* The person is unable to tell the difference between fact and imagination or fantasy.

What's Real?

So, how do you tell the difference between fantasy and reality? How do you normally tell the difference between your wish that a coworker had the "hots" for you and the harsh reality that, in fact, she's happily married? Or how about dreams? When you wake up from a dream in which you vacationed in Tahiti, how do you know you weren't really there? If these sound like silly questions, it's because you take for granted the mental processes on which you rely to make sense of the world every day. You can trust yours; someone with schizophrenia sometimes can't.

Most of us evaluate the reality of our inner worlds against the outer one. You notice that, despite your fond daydreams of office romance, your coworker is merely cordial and polite to you, and frequently talks about her fabulous husband. Or, you wake up in your bed with no sunburn, and can easily calculate the odds against the likelihood that you traveled to and from Tahiti overnight.

When the Dream Defeats Reality

Someone with schizophrenia reverses this procedure. Inner experiences are the criteria against which they test the validity of their outer world. So, for example, if a person with schizophrenia hears a voice within his head, he believes it is real even though he can't see the speaker anywhere nearby and there is no other evidence that this voice is real. The voice is more real than the external evidence that suggests it is imagined. And if that voice orders him to go out into the street to alert people that enemy missiles are about to strike the city, he will do so. To him, this voice is as real as your boss's voice on Monday morning.

Delusions and Hallucinations: The Dynamic Duo

No two sufferers of schizophrenia have exactly the same symptoms. In fact, many mental health professionals believe schizophrenia is a cluster of several distinct illnesses. However, there are some similarities that these illnesses all share, and it's these similarities that professionals look for when they're trying to figure out what the problem is and how to help.

To receive a diagnosis of schizophrenia, a person has to have a serious, long-lasting decline in his or her ability to work, care for him- or herself, and connect with other people. In addition, he or she must have at least two of the five following symptoms: delusions, hallucinations, disorganized speech, extremely disorganized behavior, and what clinicians call "negative" symptoms. Let's take a look at the first two.

Insight

The person most at risk for schizophrenic violence is the person who suffers from it. Forty percent of people with schizophrenia attempt suicide, and 10 percent succeed in the attempt.

Delusions

Delusions are basically false ideas a person believes to be true. These ideas cannot be verified objectively, but the person suffering from schizophrenia believes them in the face of all reason. Delusional beliefs can be outlandish (such as believing you can control the space shuttle) or they might just be unrealistic or untrue (such as believing your partner is being unfaithful to you even though he or she is home every night and has given you absolutely no reason to think this). If you've ever been extremely jealous, you can see how easy it might be to slide down the slippery slope into delusion.

Some common types of delusions in schizophrenia are:

➤ *delusions of persecution*—beliefs that others are plotting against you, that you are being watched, followed, persecuted, or attacked.

➤ *delusions of grandeur*—beliefs in one's own extraordinary importance. If you think you're Jesus Christ or the Queen of England, you're suffering from a delusion of grandeur.

➤ *delusions of being controlled*—belief that your thoughts or movements are being controlled by radio waves or by invisible wires, like a puppet.

Hallucinations

As you learned in Chapter 6, "It's Consciousness-Raising Time!," hallucinations are imagined sensory perceptions that are thought to be real. The most common hallucinations with schizophrenia are auditory—the hearing of voices. For example, a person might hear a running commentary on his or her behavior, or several voices having a conversation.

Hallucinations and delusions can occur together, as can several different *types* of delusions. For example, a person who believes she's the Queen of England might also believe that others are plotting to overthrow the throne. Or a man who has delusions of persecution may also hear the voice of his imagined persecutor threatening or insulting him. Clearly, these symptoms severely impair a person's ability to function in the day-to-day world. They are what psychologists call symptoms of *psychosis*.

Shrink Rap

Psychosis (also called "psychotic disorder") is a general term for a severe mental disorder that prevents an accurate understanding and interaction with reality due to impaired thoughts, inappropriate emotions, and distorted perceptions.

Handling Hallucinations

All psychology students have at least one story that illustrates just how naive we are at the beginning of our training. Here's mine: I once had a 15-year-old patient who believed voices were talking to him through the television. I fell prey to the strange (and rather grandiose) belief that I could convince him that these hallucinations did not exist.

In my defense, I was motivated by a genuine liking for this young man, and he had come to trust me. So I gently asked him to tell me when the voices were talking to him. Pretty soon, he did—and I told him I did not hear them. At first he was puzzled—he tried to help me hear them by continuing to point out when they were talking. When it was clear that I still did not "get it," no matter how much he tried to help me hear them, he didn't know what to think. Since he trusted me, he chose not to believe that I was deliberately lying to him about my inability to hear the voices, and after a while he came to a rather creative conclusion. He decided that, since the voices were talking specifically to *him*, perhaps they were able to conceal themselves from other people.

Brain Buster

Sometimes a person in the midst of psychosis needs to be hospitalized until his or her symptoms are under control. While people can be hospitalized against their will, they must present a clear danger to themselves or to others and refuse voluntary admission before involuntary commitment is considered.

Rituals and Rationalizations

Sufferers of schizophrenia can be pretty creative in their battle against hallucinations and often develop elaborate rituals to control them. Some can stop the voices by humming to themselves, counting, or holding their mouth in a certain way.

Interestingly enough, auditory hallucinations in schizophrenia occur through the same mechanism that produces vividly imagined speech sounds in everyone. For example, if you "rehearse" an argument before you face the person you're angry with, or if you imagine how your boss's voice will sound after you ask her to double your salary, you're generating the imagined sound by the same means that is used to create auditory hallucinations. And the same tricks a person with schizophrenia might use to quiet his or her voices will impede your *own* efforts at imagining sounds. You'll never learn Italian if you're humming or counting the number of books on your shelf while listening to your language tapes!

Getting More and More Disorganized

If you're hearing voices that aren't there, you might have a little trouble focusing on the ones that are. Over time, a person in the "acute" stage of schizophrenia has more and more trouble responding to the outside world, and less and less ability to organize his behavior. As the internal stimulation escalates, behavior deteriorates, and the person will exhibit three other symptoms:

1. disorganized speech
2. grossly disorganized behavior
3. changes in emotions

Disorganized Speech

The speech of people with schizophrenia often reflects the level of disorganization in their thinking. They may jump wildly and illogically from one idea to another, a phenomenon known as a *flight of ideas.* Or they may suddenly start rhyming. For example, a person may begin talking about the school bell ringing and suddenly jump to "sing, fling, wing, ding, the school bells always ring." Such speech patterns represent a disturbance in the logical thought processes.

Grossly Disorganized Behavior

We're not talking about something as minor as wearing messy clothes or forgetting to write things down so you'll remember them. Grossly disorganized behavior is behavior that is completely inappropriate for the situation, such as wearing layers of wool clothes on a hot day or behaving in a silly manner at a funeral. Other examples of grossly disorganized behavior are the failure, or inability, to prepare a simple meal or to dress oneself.

Changes in Emotions

The earliest emotional changes seen in schizophrenia are rapid changes in mood and an exaggeration of normal feelings, particularly of guilt and fear. As the schizophrenia gets worse, the person may exhibit strange or bizarrely inappropriate emotions. For example, he or she might burst into laughter at news of a death, or burst into tears at a joke. Or the person may seem to lack emotions at all, and gradually become more detached and apathetic toward other people.

There Are No "Good" Symptoms of Schizophrenia

Psychologists often talk about "positive" and "negative" signs of schizophrenia, but don't confuse these terms with "good" and "bad." While there are a lot of good—that is, helpful—treatments for the disorder, there simply aren't any "good" symptoms associated with schizophrenia, except the absence of any symptoms at all.

When psychologists speak of a positive sign of schizophrenia, they're referring to a symptom that most people do not display, unless they're suffering from the disorder. Delusions, hallucinations, and disorganized speech and behavior are all positive signs of schizophrenia. When they are present, the illness is said to be in the acute (or psychotic) phase. When such symptoms subside, the illness is said to be in the residual phase.

Negatively Speaking

In addition to positive symptoms of schizophrenia, people suffering from this disorder also exhibit negative signs—they lack certain behaviors, thoughts, feelings, and drives that most people have. They may move more slowly than

Shrink Rap

Positive signs of schizophrenia—like delusions or hallucinations—are actively manifested symptoms that rarely occur in persons without the disorder. **Negative signs** are normally expected behaviors, emotions, and the like that the person with schizophrenia fails to exhibit: a lack of emotion, for example, or a failure to register hunger or thirst.

their peers do. Their speech may lack spontaneity and their range of emotional expression may be restricted. They may lose touch with basic drives such as hunger or thirst, and lose the normal pleasure that comes from satisfying them. For the person with schizophrenia, these symptoms cause real problems in coping with day-to-day life. To date, psychiatric medications have been much more effective at eliminating the positive signs of schizophrenia than at alleviating the negative signs.

The Faces of Schizophrenia

One of schizophrenia's challenges for psychologists is that it appears in many different guises. Two people with the same diagnosis may share very few of the same symptoms. One might hear taunting voices and attribute them to a very specific (delusional) source. Another may just seem to indulge in silly and inappropriate behavior and not make a lot of sense. Researchers have tried to determine which symptoms are most likely to go together, and have come up with three different clusters of symptoms:

➤ Clusters of positive symptoms—usually a combination of delusions and hallucinations

➤ Clusters of disorganized symptoms, for example, a combination of illogical speech and disorganized behaviors

➤ Clusters of negative symptoms

According to the *Diagnostic and Statistical Manual of Mental Disorders (DSM-IV)*, here's how mental health professionals classify the diverse symptoms of schizophrenia:

The Many Faces of Schizophrenia

The Type of Symptoms	What It Looks Like
Disorganized	inappropriate behavior and emotions, incoherent speech; delusions or hallucinations are random
Catatonic	bizarre movements, either a frozen or rigid posture or very excitable movements
Paranoid	behavior is more organized, delusions and hallucinations centered around a theme of persecution or grandiosity
Undifferentiated	a grab bag category, mixed set of symptoms, unusual thinking with features from other categories
Residual	no positive symptoms appear, but the person still shows some signs like flattened affect and social withdrawal

Psychobabble

Never bet against the power of the human spirit. When John Nash received the 1994 Nobel prize for economics, no one would have known that he had been diagnosed with paranoid schizophrenia more than three decades earlier, or that he had spent some 20 years of his life in and out of psychiatric hospitals.

What Causes Schizophrenia?

Ever since it was discovered, scientists have been on the warpath trying to figure out why people get schizophrenia. In fact, because of its seriousness, schizophrenia has been more fully studied than any other mental disorder. But while we've ruled out some possible causes—for instance, we know that poor family communication does *not* cause the disorder—we still haven't gotten to the root of the problem. Probably because there's more than one root.

The Biological Connection

In the early 1970s, neuroscientists thought they were onto something—they thought schizophrenia might be caused by having too much of the neurotransmitter dopamine in the brain. There was sound reasoning behind this logic. Researchers had discovered that when a psychiatric drug blocked the release of dopamine in a patient's brain, schizophrenic symptoms appeared to be reduced—the more dopamine that was blocked, the greater the reduction in symptoms.

Also, quite by accident, it was discovered that an overdose of L-dopa, a drug used to treat Parkinson's disease, produced schizophrenia-like symptoms. Parkinson's disease is a disorder in which a patient does not naturally produce enough dopamine. L-dopa is used to replenish deficient stores of dopamine in the brain and increase dopaminergic activity; if Parkinson's patients are given too much, it has the same effect as if the brain is overproducing the neurotransmitter—a situation that appears to be the case for schizophrenia sufferers.

Alas, while dopamine is involved in schizophrenia, we now know it's not simply a matter of how much or how little you have—in fact, the way dopamine is distributed and what it does are far more important factors. Unusual patterns of dopamine activity, perhaps including overactivity in some areas and underactivity in others, may be partly responsible for schizophrenia. (For a refresher on the role of neurotransmitters, return to Chapter 2, "Bio Psycho What?")

One thing we do know for certain is that schizophrenia is as much a medical illness as diabetes, multiple sclerosis, and cancer. And, like cancer, it probably has more than one cause. Let's take a look at the extent to which four other factors play a role in the onset of schizophrenia:

➤ genes

➤ prenatal development

➤ home life

➤ cultural influences

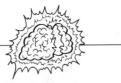

Brain Buster

Approximately one-third of the 600,000 homeless people in the United States have been diagnosed with a serious mental illness, including schizophrenia and other psychotic disorders.

Family Links

If someone in your family has schizophrenia, you're about four times more likely to get it than someone who doesn't have schizophrenia lurking in the family gene pool. If one identical twin has schizophrenia, the other twin has a 50-50 chance of getting it, too. The siblings of a non-twin or fraternal twin with the disease have a 9 percent chance of developing the illness, while the child of one parent with schizophrenia has a 13 percent chance. And a child whose parents both suffer from the disease has a 46 percent chance of developing it.

However, the fact that even people with the exact same genes (identical twins) share it only half the time also points out the obvious fact that our genes don't necessarily "make" us get schizophrenia. If the disease were completely genetic in origin, both twins would always get the disease. Obviously, therefore, other factors must be involved.

Prenatal Effects

Prenatal or birth trauma may stack the deck against someone with a genetic vulnerability to schizophrenia. When one identical twin develops schizophrenia, it is more likely to be the one who had the more difficult birth. Prenatal viral infections or lack of nutrition also put a baby at risk. But even here, the sequence of cause and effect isn't completely straightforward—trauma alone is not enough to cause the problem. According to one long-term study, prenatal and birth traumas were related to the later development of schizophrenia in babies whose mothers had schizophrenia but *not* in the babies who weren't genetically at risk.

Oddly enough, two risk factors for schizophrenia are place and season of birth. Babies born in February and March have a 10 percent above-average risk for schizophrenia, while babies born in August and September have a 10 percent lower risk. And here's a reason to move out of the city—an urban birth puts a child at twice the risk for schizophrenia, compared with babies born in rural areas.

Effects of the Home Environment

A chaotic family environment can contribute to schizophrenia but it doesn't cause the disease. A study of adopted children in Finland found that when high-risk children (whose biological mothers had schizophrenia) were adopted by parents with poor communication skills, they had more bizarre or unusual thoughts than did high-risk children whose parents communicated in a calmer, more organized fashion. There was no such difference found for low-risk children, however, so communication styles alone can't account for the onset of schizophrenia.

Other research has focused on the effects of criticism and negative attitudes or feelings expressed about and toward a person with schizophrenia by his or her family members. Other things being equal, the greater the expressed anger and hostility toward someone with schizophrenia, the more likely his or her symptoms will worsen and the person will require hospitalization. So these factors can intensify the symptoms of the disease, but once again, they don't appear to be the cause of it.

Psychobabble

For a while, some psychologists held to a strange idea about the cause of schizophrenia—it was called the "double bind" theory. A "double bind" is giving someone simultaneous but mutually exclusive messages. For example, a mother might complain to her child that he's never affectionate, then slap him when he tries to give her a hug. This theory held that such sick communication patterns could cause *anyone* to slip over the edge. While this communication style would upset anyone, it takes a lot more than poor communication to cause psychosis.

Cultural Influences

You can't blame American culture for causing schizophrenia—the disease looks remarkably the same across cultures. The prevalence of symptoms, the average age of onset, and the sex difference in age of onset (men getting it earlier than women) are similar despite wide variations in the ways people live.

However, Western culture may make it harder to get well. Patients in developing countries get better much faster than they do in developed countries like the United States, and this holds true for every category of schizophrenia, using every measure of recovery. In fact, in one study of 1,379 patients across 10 countries, 63 percent of the patients in developing countries, compared with only 37 percent in the developed countries, showed a full recovery within a two-year period.

One possible explanation for this difference in recovery patterns is the different cultural attitudes toward mental illness. Family members in developing countries are more accepting of a family member with schizophrenia—and so is the culture in which the family lives. They are much less likely to label the person as "sick" or to think of schizophrenia as a permanent condition. They may call it "a case of nerves," which sounds more benign, and they may be more likely to tie it to experiences that everyone has had.

Perhaps more importantly, the social organization common to non-Western cultures provides more support for a person suffering from schizophrenia and for his or her family. Extended families provide more resources and care, which helps caregivers be more nurturing and tolerant. And nonindustrialized, more agriculturally based cultures can be more flexible in allowing a person with schizophrenia to play a useful role in the family economy by performing chores on the family farm. These social factors are generally unavailable in highly individualistic, non-agricultural societies like the United States.

When Schizophrenia Happens in Childhood

The appearance of schizophrenia before age 12 is rare—less than $1/60$ as common as adult-onset schizophrenia. Some children who develop the illness seem to be different from their peers at an early age; about 30 percent have on-and-off symptoms in the first years of life. As a group, they are more anxious and disruptive than their peers, and are more likely to exhibit behaviors frequently seen in pervasive developmental disorders such as autism—rocking, arm flapping, or other unusual, repetitive behaviors. Most of them also show delays in learning language and other skills.

Childhood schizophrenia tends to develop gradually, without the sudden onset of psychotic symptoms—called a psychotic break—that we see in adults and adolescents. Hallucinations, delusions, and disorganized thinking almost always occur after age seven. Once the schizophrenia starts, its symptoms often parallel those seen in adults and older adolescents.

A significant drop in IQ during early childhood (between ages four and seven) may signal an increased risk of psychotic symptoms in adulthood. The *American Journal of Psychiatry* reported a study of 547 Americans born between 1959 and 1966. A decline in IQ between ages four and seven was associated with psychotic symptoms 16 years later. This was seven times higher than for individuals whose childhood IQ did not decline.

The treatment for childhood schizophrenia is also similar to adults. Standard antipsychotic drugs appear to be effective for most children and adolescents with schizophrenia, although concerns about the effects of medication on growing children require that such medication be carefully monitored.

Who Gets Better?

One thing should be clear by now: The human spirit is stronger than any psychiatric illness. But as a clinician I know that some people with a serious mental illness get better, some coast along, and some get worse. My job is to push my clients into the first category as hard as I can.

Studies of the outcome of treatment suggest some things that make a good recovery more likely, and a few others that work against a happy ending. A person with little or no family history of schizophrenia—as was true for Mr. Frese at the start of this chapter—is more likely to have a better treatment outcome than someone whose family genes are stacked against him or her. Another good sign is having lived a normal and productive life before the onset of schizophrenia. And early intervention is critical: The sooner someone gets help for his first psychotic episode, the more likely he is to avoid future crashes.

On the downside, if schizophrenia strikes at an early age and there's a strong family history of the disease, the person may have a tough road to recovery. The sex of the patient makes a difference too: For some reason, men tend to do worse than women. In addition, patients who have a lot of *negative* signs—such as apathy and

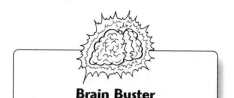

Brain Buster

While the term *nervous breakdown* was once commonly used by physicians as a generic term for any acute mental problem, in reality it is so vague as to be meaningless as a description of a psychological disorder. The term has been used to describe emotional problems ranging from a severe stress reaction (like post-traumatic stress disorder) to debilitating depression or psychosis.

withdrawal from others—often have a harder time than those who do not. Last but not least, the greater the number of relapses a patient suffers, the lower his chances for complete recovery. And, of course, while getting effective treatment for schizophrenia is the first step, sticking to it is the rest of the game.

Zapping Schizophrenia

Schizophrenia tends to scare everyone—the person who has it, the family that hears the diagnosis, and the mental health professional who's treating it. Fortunately, we have a whole new arsenal in our war on schizophrenia and, finally, it's a war we're starting to win.

The Pharmaceutical Approach

When schizophrenia is treated right from the start, remission rates are as high as 80 to 85 percent. And without question, the treatment of choice is medication. As with diabetes, medication is used to control the symptoms, not to cure the disease itself. But when the symptoms are under control, a person with schizophrenia can lead a normal life. The sooner treatment is begun after the first psychotic episode, the greater the chance that medication will get the symptoms under control.

The medications used to treat schizophrenia are called antipsychotic or neuroleptic drugs. These drugs help restore the function of the brain to normal levels. And they have an encouragingly high success rate: On average, a person with schizophrenia who takes medication has a 60 percent chance of not being rehospitalized. Without medication, those odds drop to 20 percent.

The Couch Trip

Psychotherapy alone doesn't work at all when someone is having a psychotic episode, and traditionally it hasn't been considered an important part of the treatment for schizophrenia. However, according to a 1998 study in the *British Medical Journal,* cognitive behavior therapy can be helpful if used in conjunction with medication. Useful therapy focuses on helping the person deal with his or her symptoms and on devising problem-solving strategies that reduce the risk of relapse.

Clearing Up Any Remaining Confusion

We've already cleared up the confusion between schizophrenia and multiple-personality disorder. However, because of the common use of generic words like *nervous breakdown* and *psychotic break,* schizophrenia is often confused with a number of other, very different mental illnesses. Let's clear up the confusion once and for all.

Schizophrenia is *not:*

➤ *Bipolar disorder* (manic depression). Bipolar disorder is a periodic, recurrent mood disorder of extreme highs and lows interspersed with periods of complete normalcy. It does not involve the negative signs (like blunted affect and social withdrawal) associated with schizophrenia, nor does it usually involve hallucinations and fixed delusions.

➤ *Schizoaffective disorder.* This disorder has symptoms of schizophrenia and bipolar disorder and often responds to lithium. Schizoaffective disorder involves a disturbance of mood (depression, anxiety) that lasts for a major portion of the acute phase of the illness, on top of the usual signs (hallucinations, delusions) of schizophrenia. In schizophrenia, mood symptoms are either brief or do not meet the full criteria for a mood disorder.

➤ *Brief reactive psychosis.* While this disorder has symptoms similar to schizophrenia, it lasts for less than two weeks and is generally brought on by extreme stress. An example is postpartum psychosis.

➤ *Personality disorders.* Schizoid and schizotypal personality disorders share some of the odd behaviors and impaired relationships as are found in schizophrenia, but there are no breaks with reality and the person who has such a disorder can still function more or less competently in society.

➤ *Creativity.* Extremely creative people may have unusual thoughts and views and may behave in ways that other people consider to be eccentric, but the creative person is in control of his thought processes, while a person with schizophrenia is not.

➤ *Diseases afflicting the brain.* Hallucinations or delusions can be caused by brain infection or tumors. But once the infection is treated or the tumor is removed, these symptoms will end without the need for continued medication.

The Perils of Paranoia

One of my all-time favorite bumper stickers says, "Just because I'm paranoid doesn't mean they're not out to get me." This humorous bumper sticker illustrates how often (although certainly not always) there can be a grain of truth in the most irrational beliefs.

Dealing with Distress

Suppose Mr. Smith worked for a national pharmacy chain for 30 years, was an exemplary employee, and never missed a day's work. One day he comes to work to discover that the pharmacy chain has been bought out and he's abruptly laid off from work. Understandably, he feels hurt and betrayed. He spends hours thinking about what's happened to him and how, after all his years of service to the company, something like this could have happened to him.

From Distress to Delusion

So far, Mr. Smith's reactions are perfectly normal. But what if, after a while, his thoughts take a stranger turn? Unemployed and isolated in his apartment, he begins to believe that his layoff has nothing to do with the company buyout and begins to wonder if his former employer was engaged in a systematic plot to destroy his life and take away his sanity. He begins to believe that company agents are tampering with his mail, following him, even tapping his phone. He is as puzzled by their torture as you or I would be, but he's also convinced that it is, in fact, happening. And no amount of persuasion or evidence to the contrary will persuade him that its not.

Insight

Here's a good reason to lay off "uppers" such as cocaine and amphetamines. They can greatly increase the symptoms of schizophrenia in people who already have them and, at high doses, can even induce those symptoms in people who do not. And the abuse of drugs like amphetamines, LSD, and PCP can also cause paranoid thinking and behavior.

Mr. Smith has developed a paranoid delusion. This is a serious psychological diagnosis—it's not what most people mean when they use the term *paranoid* casually, to refer to simple suspiciousness. When a person is suspicious based on past personal experience or observation, it is inappropriate to call him or her paranoid. In fact, mental health clinicians only use the term when a person's suspiciousness or mistrust is either highly exaggerated or completely unwarranted.

Because paranoia is common in many psychiatric disorders, it can be difficult to fit the symptoms to the right diagnosis. We've already explored one diagnosis in which paranoia plays a part—paranoid schizophrenia. Now let's talk about another disorder in which paranoia reaches delusional proportions.

Paranoid Delusional Disorder

Someone with a paranoid *personality* might frequently suspect colleagues of making jokes at his or her expense. Persons with paranoid *delusions,* on the other hand, might believe their colleagues are poisoning them, drugging them, spying on them, or plotting a grand conspiracy to smear their name. There's a big difference between the two.

The Green-Eyed Monster

Not all people who suffer paranoid delusions are convinced that they're going to be harmed or killed. Jealousy can become delusional, for example. I once knew a man who truly believed his wife had gotten into an automobile accident deliberately—in an attempt to cover up her rendezvous with her lover. This is more than a simple fear that a loved one might find somebody new—this man took *everything* as a sign that his partner was unfaithful. While his beliefs might sound almost comical, the genuine emotional distress his delusion caused both him and his partner was no laughing matter.

The Strange Psyche of the Stalker

On rare occasions, you read about a celebrity whose life is plagued by a stalker. Late-night talk-show host David Letterman was stalked for years by such a woman. She phoned him, she wrote him love letters, and she became a constant and unwelcome presence in his life. Despite Letterman's consistent failure to respond to her proclamations of love, she continued to believe he really loved him. She was arrested, hospitalized, and eventually killed herself.

This woman was in the grip of a powerful form of paranoia—an erotic delusion. No amount of external evidence could shake her in her belief that Letterman returned her love. A paranoid delusion like hers is an extreme example of the power our beliefs can hold over our entire lives.

The Origins of Paranoid Delusions

Families of people with paranoid delusional disorder do not have higher than normal rates of schizophrenia or depression. A person suffering from the disorder, however, is more likely to come from a family in which other members have the same problem: Twins are more likely to share paranoia than non-twins, and paranoid disorders are more common among relatives.

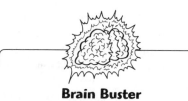

Brain Buster

Don't confuse paranoid schizophrenia with paranoid delusional disorder. The latter is not accompanied by hallucinations or generally disorganized behavior. In fact, except for actions and thoughts that center around the specific delusion, the person with paranoid delusional disorder can often function normally.

Although we don't know exactly what causes paranoia, we do know that certain drugs make it worse. And, there's bad news for *all* of us these days—some studies show that paranoia has become more common since the start of the twentieth century. Just being alive at the start of the new millennium puts some of us at risk!

There are other factors at work as well. Stress, for example, can trigger paranoia or make it worse. Prisoners of war, immigrants, and other people living under extreme stress all show a higher likelihood of developing paranoid delusions. Even "normal" people can suffer from a short-lived form of paranoia, called acute paranoia, when they are thrust into highly stressful new situations. The relationship between stress paranoia is complex, but it appears that a person can be genetically predisposed to paranoia and that stress is likely to trigger it.

Putting Paranoia to Rest

Let's keep our terms straight—there's more than one condition covered by the term *paranoia*. There's paranoid schizophrenia, paranoid delusional disorder, and paranoid personality disorder. The best treatment for any of these illnesses depends upon the nature of the underlying disorder.

The best treatment for paranoid schizophrenia, for example, is medication—because the schizophrenic responds so well to that type of treatment. But antipsychotic medication for paranoid delusional disorder has had only mixed results; it seems to help the person function better but does not necessarily get rid of his or her paranoid ideas. And someone with a paranoid personality disorder would benefit most from psychotherapy—a form of treatment that has little or no utility for paranoid schizophrenics—but the patient has to stay with the therapy long enough to establish a trusting relationship with his or her therapist.

And that can be a problem: If paranoia is a primary symptom, it can provide a powerful barrier against getting the help that's needed. A person with paranoia may understandably try to avoid medication or hospitalization for fear of losing control or other imagined, or real, dangers. A therapist often will avoid alienating the paranoid patient by completely denying the reality of his fears. Instead, the therapist may focus on helping to keep the paranoid fears and beliefs from completely disrupting the patient's life.

In the past couple of chapters, we've been looking at some pretty extreme forms of mental illness. But those are not the only kinds of psychological trouble people can face. In fact, we all fall somewhere along the mental health continuum—at different times during different parts of our lives. In the next chapter, we'll take a look at an aspect of mental health that's particularly fuzzy: the borderline between "normal" and "abnormal" behaviors, and what happens when the "normal" ones get out of control.

The Least You Need to Know

➤ Schizophrenia is a serious medical illness that affects about 1 percent of the global population, strikes men earlier (ages 18 to 25) than women (ages 26 to 45), and on rare occasion affects children as young as seven years of age.

➤ Common symptoms of schizophrenia are delusions, hallucinations, disorganized speech, disorganized behavior, and inappropriate emotions.

➤ Schizophrenia is a disease of the brain—much as diabetes or cancer are diseases of the body—and its symptoms can be controlled with medication.

➤ The odds of getting schizophrenia are greater if one or more members of your family have it. Prenatal birth trauma and living in a chaotic home may also contribute.

➤ Paranoia is a symptom found in many psychiatric disorders, including paranoid schizophrenia, paranoid delusional disorder, and paranoid personality disorder.

➤ Paranoid delusional disorder is characterized by a highly exaggerated and unwarranted mistrust and suspicion of others, but it does not involve hallucinations or other psychotic symptoms.

Outta Control!

In 1983, 32-year-old singer Karen Carpenter died from heart failure, the result of complications she had sustained during her eight-year battle with anorexia nervosa. Millions of shocked and saddened fans asked how a young, beautiful, talented woman could starve herself? Why couldn't she "see" that she was dangerously thin?

Back then we didn't understand the seriousness of anorexia nervosa. Today, the news of another death from anorexia still saddens us, but isn't such a shock. Anorexia, the most lethal psychiatric disorder, ultimately kills 10 to 20 percent of the people who have it.

In this chapter, we'll look at a group of disorders that share a common theme: they all start out with normal or common behaviors. Most of us have dieted, drunk alcohol, or gambled—but most us don't develop an eating disorder or an addiction to alcohol or gambling. Similarly, while young children are often fascinated by fire and, at least once, take something that doesn't belong to them, they rarely grow up to become fire setters or kleptomaniacs. In this chapter, we'll explore when, why, and how these behaviors get out of control, what can be done to prevent it, and how people with addictions or impulse control disorders can kick the habit.

What's Eating You?

Many people think of eating disorders as stemming from an unhealthy desire for a perfect body. If that were true, the disorders would be a lot easier to get rid of. You might be surprised to know that eating disorders are not about vanity and not really about weight at all. They are complex, psychological illnesses in which people try to control the conflict and stress in their lives by controlling their food intake. The food, weight, and body-image issues are obvious symptoms of deeper problems.

Insight

A person with an *eating disorder* develops a pathological relationship with food—she may eat extreme amounts of food in a single sitting, she may starve herself, or she may prevent her body from digesting her food through purging or using laxatives.

Shrink Rap

Anorexia nervosa is a pattern of self-starvation that occurs primarily in young girls in Western cultures from middle and upper socioeconomic classes.

Typically, people who develop an eating disorder are at a difficult time in their lives. Let's use a fictitious person, whom we'll call Suzanne, as an example of how the eating disorder ball gets rolling. Suzanne came from a family in which a slim physique was a prized attribute. Luckily, she had "thin" genes and never had to worry about her weight—until she graduated from college.

Suzanne's first job was with a small company that was planning to go public soon, so she was expected to work longer-than-normal hours. To take the position, she had to move to a new city where she had no friends and no family—no emotional support system to rely on. She had to travel three out of every four weeks and do a considerable amount of business entertaining, so she had little time to make new friends, no time to exercise, and her meals were dictated by her work hours and business appointments.

At 23, Suzanne was lonely, homesick, and terrified of failing at her first job. After about six months, she stepped on the scale at her doctor's office and was horrified to learn that she had gained 10 pounds. Her life already felt out of control, now her weight was out of control, too!

Over time, all of her anxiety, self-doubt, and feelings of failure and inadequacy became tied to her weight. She began making herself vomit after her business dinners and started bingeing as a way to comfort herself in her lonely apartment on weekends. What would have been a difficult time in anyone's life gradually turned into an anorexic nightmare. If it had lasted long enough, Suzanne could have died.

Wasting Away to Nothing

Anorexia nervosa is hard to understand because we relate it to dieting. Think back to a time when you were on a diet. Maybe you crash dieted to get ready for the senior prom. Maybe you shed a few pounds for your tenth high school reunion. Most of us think *diet* is truly a four-letter word. Sure, you'd have sympathy for anyone who had trouble sticking to a diet, but most of us find it less easy to see how it could be hard to *quit* one!

Anorexia is a lot more complicated than an out-of-control diet. With anorexia, the strong desire to be thin, which plagues most American women, turns into an obsession. Someone with this disorder is terrified of becoming obese. The problem is compounded by the fact that people with anorexia have lost their ability to see themselves objectively. You or I can look at a person and tell if he or she is plump or skinny, but people with anorexia feel fat no matter what their actual weight is. Even when they're close to death, they'll point out areas of their bodies where they "need" to lose weight.

A person with anorexia may also be trying to cope with feelings of powerlessness: She may feel that if she can't control what is happening around her, at least she can control her weight. Each morning, the number on the bathroom scale determines whether or not she has succeeded or failed in her goal for thinness. She feels powerful and in control when she can make herself lose weight.

And sometimes, focusing on calories and losing weight is a way of blocking out feelings and emotions. It's easier to diet then it is to deal with problems directly. In addition, people with anorexia usually have low self-esteem and sometimes feel they don't deserve to eat.

Psychobabble

Most of us grew up with the mantra that thinness is next to godliness. Apparently, this is nothing new; a form of anorexia nervosa was seen in the Middle Ages, at least 500 years ago. It was called anorexia mirabilis, a term meaning loss of appetite caused by a miracle. In those days, when women would refuse to eat, their fasting was considered miraculous and they were thought of as very holy people.

A person with anorexia will often deny that anything is wrong. She might say she doesn't get hungry. If you try to get her help, she'll fight you, because she is likely to see therapy as a way to force her to eat. There is hope, however: If she can see she has a problem and is willing to get help, she can be treated effectively through a combination of psychological, nutritional, and medical care. But the big battle is getting there.

Before getting help, a person with an eating disorder can do some significant damage to herself—in ways you might never have imagined. For example, parents of young children often keep syrup of ipecac around the house in case of accidental poisoning, because it causes immediate vomiting. About 300,000 people with anorexia and bulimia, however, use it for another reason—to get rid of unwanted food. Some physicians believe that many mysterious heart failures in patients with anorexia and bulimia may actually be due to ipecac abuse.

The Food Roller Coaster

Have you ever overeaten because you were stressed? Then, consumed with guilt, you pulled yourself up by your bootstraps and dieted like crazy the next day? Maybe you even consciously added up the extra calories you ate the day before and made sure you deprived yourself of the same amount. Welcome to food games.

To some extent, we play that kind of give-and-take all the time. We "splurge" at birthdays and we "cut back" after the holidays. These are miniversions of the big eating-disorder roller coaster: *bulimia nervosa*. Bulimia takes the "splurging" and "cutting back" to extremes.

Bulimia nervosa is a cycle of binge eating followed by some method of trying to rid the body of unwanted calories—through fasting, vomiting, laxatives, diuretics, diet pills, or even excessive exercise. People with bulimia are amazingly different in how they define a binge; while most of us have the image of a young woman locking herself in her apartment and eating her way through her entire refrigerator, another person may define a "binge" as eating foods that are normally prohibited from her diet.

Shrink Rap

Bulimia nervosa is a disorder in which a person binges (overeats) and purges (attempts to get rid of the food).

The psychological dynamics of bulimia nervosa are different from those associated with anorexia. In bulimia, food often becomes a person's only source of comfort and a way to hide or suppress uncomfortable feelings. Unlike many people suffering from anorexia, people with bulimia are often well aware that they have a problem, but they may be too ashamed or scared to get help.

Perhaps the best-known sufferer of this eating disorder in recent years was Princess Diana. In the 1990s, she brought much-needed attention to the emotional and physical costs of bulimia nervosa when she publicly divulged her own struggle with this illness.

I Just Can't Quit Eating

Compulsive overeating, or as professionals call it, *binge eating disorder*, is the other side of the eating-disorder coin. It's characterized by uncontrollable eating and consequent weight gain. A person who compulsively overeats uses food as a way to cope with stress, emotional conflicts, and daily problems. The food blocks out feelings and emotions, but at a price—compulsive overeaters usually feel out of control and are aware that their eating patterns are abnormal. Like people with bulimia, people who compulsively overeat recognize they have a problem, but are often too ashamed of their "lack of discipline" with regard to food to seek help with the problem.

Shrink Rap

Binge eating disorder is the official diagnosis given a person who eats a large amount of food within two hours at least two days a week for six months without purging in any way to lose or maintain her weight. This disorder is commonly called compulsive overeating.

"Comfort" Food Gone Wrong

Compulsive overeating usually starts in early childhood, when eating patterns are formed. Perhaps a child watches a parent overeat in response to stress. When she falls and skins her knee, she is treated to an ice cream sundae. When she feels mad, a grandparent suggests she "treat herself" to a special food. Over time, the child learns that food is useful for a lot more than helping you grow—it can soothe hurt feelings, melt away loneliness, and push down unpleasant feelings.

Most people who become compulsive eaters have never learned the proper way to deal with stressful situations, and so they use food instead as a way of coping. In addition, while a person with bulimia is terrified of getting fat, people who compulsively overeat often find comfort in their excess weight. They use fat as a barrier that protects them from other people getting too close. This is especially common in people who have been victims of sexual abuse.

The Vicious Binge-Diet Cycle

But no matter how much emotional protection a large body size may provide for someone who compulsively overeats, she's likely to be disgusted by her excess weight and undisciplined eating habits. So her binges are usually followed by feelings of powerlessness, guilt, shame, and failure. The more weight she gains, the harder she diets, and her drastic dieting usually leads to the next binge. This vicious cycle can go on and on—unless she gets help or begins to address the underlying emotional issues that trigger her out-of-control eating.

Many people with binge eating disorder complain that their problem isn't taken seriously enough—and rightly so. Most people who have an overeating problem are

331

directed to diet centers and health spas, where they lose weight and then regain it—but that only addresses a part of the problem. It does nothing to help them overcome the emotional issues underlying the overeating in the first place.

And it's important that those issues be addressed. While most eating-disorder fatalities are due to starvation, bingeing itself can be fatal. A 23-year-old model, who had starved herself down to 84 pounds, died in London after gaining 19 pounds in a single binge. Clearly, compulsive overeating can be a serious problem with life-threatening medical complications, just like anorexia and bulimia. And, with a combination of therapy and medical and nutritional counseling, it *can* be conquered.

We Might Look Different, but We Have a Lot in Common

A woman who weighs 210 pounds looks dramatically different than a woman who weighs 75 pounds—on the outside, at least. But put these two women in a dark room and listen to them talk, and you might not be able to tell them apart. They share a pathological relationship with food and eating, no matter which eating disorder they're struggling with. And there are other common elements shared by anorexia, bulimia, and binge eating disorder, as well. Some of these are psychological, such as:

➤ low self-esteem

➤ an obsession and preoccupation with food

➤ depression

➤ a distorted body image

➤ feelings of powerlessness—that life has gotten out of control

➤ a "secret life" in which eating habits are kept from others

➤ mood swings

➤ the use of food to "solve" other problems (feel more in control, get nurtured, escape from or soothe feelings)

These disorders are also similar in the kinds of physical dangers they can cause for their sufferers, including:

➤ disruptions in blood sugar levels

➤ kidney infection and failure

➤ liver failure

➤ bad circulation

➤ slowed or irregular heartbeat

➤ vitamin and mineral deficiencies

➤ weakness and fatigue

➤ infertility and/or problems during pregnancy

➤ digestive problems

➤ osteoporosis and/or arthritis

An Ounce of Prevention Is Worth a Pound of Cure

There is an environmental factor that plays a role in the development of eating disorders: family attitudes toward food and eating. If one or both parents are stressed about how to deal with their own anxieties about their body or weight, they can unintentionally pass them along to their children. Conversely, parents can provide a healthy, balanced role model for their children.

If you're committed to teaching healthy eating habits and a positive body image to your children, you need to know that you're swimming upstream—just look at all the media messages that bombard us every day. By the time your child is six, she will have formed a definite prejudice against obesity and a clear idea that thin is in. Throw in a few fashion magazines and, by the time she reaches adolescence, she's a lucky girl indeed if she's managed to escape our culture's beauty obsession unscathed.

Shrink Rap

Your **body image** is the subjective way you view your physical appearance. It consists of a complex array of thoughts, feelings, and behaviors.

There are things you can do, though, to at least buffer your children against this culture's bondage to beauty and to decrease the risk that they'll develop eating disorders. For example, you can teach your children to eat healthy and to view food as nothing more than an enjoyable source of energy for their bodies. And you can teach your children to appreciate all the things their bodies can do—and not just to obsess about how they look.

Ten Seeds That Grow Healthy Eaters

Here are 10 do's and don'ts that you can use to help prevent your child from developing an eating disorder. Warning: These tips are not for the faint-hearted—and they may require you to do a little body image work of your own!

➤ **Don't** make disparaging comments about your child's weight or body size. Parents' comments about their children's weight plays a direct role in the number of times a child tries to diet, their self-esteem, and their concern about weight gain.

➤ **Don't** soothe your child with food. If she's hurt, let her cry, put a Band-Aid on it, or give her a punching bag to work her feelings out on. Just don't give her a cookie! One of the easiest mistakes we make is to teach our kids to equate food with emotion. Food is not love, pride, sadness, or a friend. It is something our bodies need for fuel to keep us healthy and strong.

➤ **Don't** use food as a regular reward. If your children do something good, give them hugs, kisses, and praise, or spend special time with them. Don't however, use a trip to McDonald's or a hot fudge sundae as a regular reward.

➤ **Don't** withhold food as punishment or force your children to eat when they're not hungry. This teaches them not to trust their own bodily cues for hunger and fullness.

➤ **Do** engage in fun physical activity as a family and limit the amount of television your family watches.

➤ **Do** provide structure for your child's eating. Eat around the same time each day and provide a well-balanced meal. Let your child determine how much he or she eats.

Insight

While the reasons an eating disorder develops are complex, we can justifiably point a finger at our culture's beauty ideal. The dramatic rise in the prevalence of bulimia directly parallels the Western preoccupation with female thinness. Anorexia and bulimia are extremely rare in non-Western countries.

➤ **Don't** forbid any foods. "Junk food" in moderation is fine. Restricting sweets from your children's diet will only backfire and make them want them more, especially as they approach school age and see other children eating and enjoying candy, cookies, and chips.

➤ **Do** set an example. Kids learn their lifestyles from the people around them, and thinking "do what I say, not what I do" will not get you very far.

➤ **Don't** *ever* put your child on a diet unless it is for medical reasons. While most teenagers who diet don't develop an eating disorder, dieting during adolescence is the best predictor of whether any one teenager will subsequently develop a problematic relationship with food. If your child is complaining about feeling "fat," encourage her to become more physically active and to feel better about her body image.

Winning Food Battles

The road to recovery for someone with an eating disorder is often bumpy. Unlike alcohol or drugs, we can't just quit eating "cold turkey." For better or worse, we have to have a relationship with food for the rest of our lives. In addition, because there is no one cause for eating disorders, there isn't one cure. Whether you're suffering from anorexia, bulimia, or binge eating disorder, the best treatment is often a team of professionals who work together to tackle all of the different parts of the illness.

Bring in the Professionals

For example, because of the serious health complications associated with eating disorders, it's critical to have a physician as part of any treatment team. In fact, hospitalization or inpatient psychiatric treatment may be helpful if the person's weight is dangerously low or if she just can't stop the self-destructive behaviors on her own.

Nutritional counseling can also be helpful, as can support groups—especially if you can find members of the group who are farther down the road to recovery than you are. Because of the many complex psychological issues that often go along with eating problems, therapy is a critical part of any recovery. Studies show that cognitive-behavioral therapy and interpersonal therapy are particularly effective.

Do Drugs Help?

The jury's still out on the effectiveness of antidepressant medication to treat eating disorders. Some studies show an impressive link between depression and bingeing disorders—especially bulimia and, to a lesser extent, compulsive overeating. In fact, some studies have suggested that between a third and a half of women with bulimia also have a problem with depression. Several studies have also shown that drugs like Prozac, in combination with psychotherapy and nutritional counseling, can help prevent relapse.

While a subset of individuals with anorexia may also be suffering from depression, as a group they tend to have more problems with obsessive-compulsive symptoms. Some studies have shown that antidepressants can help, while others are more pessimistic. The jury is still out on the effectiveness of medication to treat anorexia.

When Someone You Love Has an Eating Disorder

Eating disorders don't just hurt the people who have them. It also makes life hard for their families, who spend a lot of time worrying about them, trying to get help, and, oftentimes, getting into energy-draining food battles in an attempt to "fix" their loved one's eating problem. When someone has an eating disorder, it can be hard to know when to step in and where to draw the line.

And if you *do* step in to help a family member with an eating disorder, your help is often unappreciated. That doesn't mean, however, that you shouldn't try. Silence can be deadly, and a compassionate talk with your troubled loved one about worrisome behaviors can at least plant seeds that could later blossom into the recognition of the need for treatment. Here are eight ways to help someone with an eating disorder and still keep your sanity:

➤ Know your limits. You can be a friend and you can be supportive. You can encourage the person to get help. But you cannot make the person get help or change before he or she is ready. You are not responsible for his or her recovery.

➤ Provide information and encourage the person to get help. Offer to go along for the first visit to a therapist or doctor.

➤ Refrain from comments like "you're too thin" or "you don't have to worry about your weight." Do not give advice about weight loss. And, whatever you do, *never* say, "I'm glad you've put on a few pounds."

➤ Do not ignore behavior that concerns you. If you see clear signs that someone has been purging (for example, they always head to the bathroom right after a meal), tell him or her in a nonjudgmental way and express your concern.

➤ Avoid power struggles over food—you will never win them.

➤ Do not let the person control when, where, or what *you* eat. For example, if you live together, don't quit buying certain foods if he asks you to, or change your eating schedule in the hope that he will eat more.

➤ No matter how tempting it is, don't nag, beg, bribe, threaten, or manipulate.

➤ Get support for yourself. Being in a relationship with someone who has an eating disorder can take its toll.

Eat, Drink, and Be—Addicted?

"First the man takes the drink, then the drink takes a drink, then the drink takes the man." This Japanese proverb applies to at least one out of every 10 people in the United States. Four out of 10 Americans have alcoholism in their family. Odds are you personally know someone who is addicted to alcohol—a friend, a family member, or a coworker. While tens of thousands of people attend Alcoholics Anonymous every week, there are a lot more alcoholics secretly drinking their lives away.

Of course, not all drinking is problem drinking. The National Institute on Alcohol Abuse and Alcoholism defines moderate drinking as an average of 2 drinks a day or less. But 15 million Americans exceed this drinking limit. And the 15 percent of men and 3 percent of women who drink more than four drinks a day are on the slippery slope to alcohol dependence.

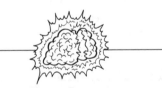

Brain Buster

Booze might make you the life of the party, but it can end lives, too. The use of alcohol is involved in half of all murders, accidental deaths, and suicides in the United States. It's also involved in half of all crimes, and nearly half of all fatal automobile accidents in this country.

The Road to Alcoholism

There are many different ways that a person might wind up with an addiction to alcohol. Some people drink till they're drunk from the time they take their first drink—immediately acting in ways that are destructive to themselves and their relationships. Others start with acceptable social drinking that gradually spirals out of control. But no matter how they start, alcoholics end up at the same place—with their lives revolving around booze.

Alcoholism is not always progressive, although it usually is. And it generally takes some remarkably predictable steps in its development:

➤ Step One: Quickly or gradually, the drinker comes to depend upon the mood-altering qualities of alcohol. Drinks perk him up, relieve anxiety and stress, make special occasions more fun, and temporarily take away the blues. Maybe the drinker gulps a few drinks before the party or has a double before dinner. The drinking might still be under control, but the amount of alcohol consumed gradually increases.

➤ Step Two: The drinker's life starts to revolve around alcohol. The urge to drink starts earlier in the day, and the person begins to prefer alcohol-related activities and to hang around with friends who drink. An increasing tolerance for alcohol is accompanied by *blackouts* and an increasing loss of control.

During the middle stages of alcoholism, some drinkers may try to stop on their own. Before the "denial" sets in, they may begin to be secretly ashamed of their behavior and may be aware that life is getting out of control. They may try to monitor their alcohol consumption, switch brands, or limit drinking to a certain time of day. As their strategies fail, they may begin to deny their powerlessness and instead rationalize that they could quit if they "really wanted to." Relationship problems, financial difficulties, and work problems all provide excuses for having a drink.

Shrink Rap

Blackouts are a type of amnesia in which the person can still function (drive or make dinner) but later can't remember what happened.

➤ Step Three: The later stages of alcoholism are often characterized by an obsession with alcohol—to the exclusion of almost everything else. As relationships and financial responsibilities deteriorate, guilt and remorse are alleviated with more alcohol. The person in the late stages of alcoholism may drink around the clock despite an inability to keep down the first drinks in the morning. Without help, the alcoholic may eventually drink him- or herself to death.

Are You Hitting the Booze Too Hard?

Even today, when people think of alcoholics, they tend to picture a wild-eyed, disheveled bum. But they'd be wrong. Alcohol abuse can sneak up on anyone. You can be a problem drinker and still not drink more than the people you hang out with. You can be the life of the party, and let no one know that you keep drinking when you go home. You can have a problem with alcohol and still get up and go to work the next day.

Assessing Your Intake

Because of the misguided stereotypes we have of what alcoholics are like, it can be difficult to identify the point at which "normal" social drinking becomes problem drinking. The following quiz may help you assess your own alcohol use, or abuse.

Respond to the following questions using the number key below:

1 = never   4 = often
2 = rarely   5 = almost always
3 = sometimes

1. Have you ever awakened the next day after partying the night before and not been able to remember part of the evening? _____
2. Is it hard to stop drinking after you've had one or two drinks? _____
3. Does someone you care about worry or complain about your drinking? _____
4. Do you ever feel guilty about your drinking? _____
5. Have you ever gotten in trouble at work because of your drinking? _____
6. Has your drinking caused problems between you and your spouse, parent, or other friend/relative? _____
7. Have you ever blown off your responsibilities for two or more days in a row because you were drinking? _____
8. Do you drink before noon? _____
9. Do people close to you say you have a problem with alcohol? _____
10. Do you drink more than most people you know? _____

Now, total up your answers. Here's how to assess your score:

10–15: We all have problems, but alcohol probably isn't one of yours. When it comes to booze, you can usually take it or leave it—and most of the time, you leave it before it takes hold of you.

16–20: It might surprise you that, despite your relatively low score, I'm urging you to take a close look at the role alcohol plays in your life. Even if it "rarely" causes blackouts or arguments, the numbers show that you're experiencing negative consequences from drinking, and that's enough for me to consider raising a red flag.

21–30: Consider the red flag truly raised. Remember the Japanese proverb at the beginning of this section? If your score is over 25, you are at least at the "drink takes a drink" stage half of the time you use alcohol.

31 or higher: I am worried about your alcohol use. And, judging by your answers, you are worried about it, too. Why not err on the side of caution and talk to a professional—or attend an AA meeting just for kicks?

Why Can't I Handle My Liquor?

Alcoholism isn't fair. Some people can drink like a fish and never develop a drinking problem. For others, alcohol is like a hypnotic poison—it quickly puts them under its spell, dramatically changes their behavior, and causes blackouts and other physical problems. Why can some of us handle liquor so much better than others do?

To some extent, the answer may lie in our genes. There's no question that alcoholism runs in families. Identical twins reared apart are more likely to share alcoholism than fraternal twins living in the same family. A child of an alcoholic has four times the risk of becoming an alcoholic than the a child of a nonalcoholic—even when raised by teetotalers. At the very least, some of us inherit a predisposition to alcoholism.

Psychobabble

Have you got an alcohol problem? The best way to find out is to get input from friends, family members, and/or coworkers. Their input is important because it is hard to objectively assess the pros and cons of a behavior that you've found to be very enjoyable or that you've used to cope with problems in your life. And in addition to asking the people around you, remember that having blackouts, doing things while drinking that caused you to lose your self-respect, and thinking about drinking a lot are other red flags.

Alcoholism is not like a cold, however—you can't catch it from your family. Most people who develop an addiction to alcohol start out with a genetic predisposition, but the actual progression of a drinking problem is triggered by stressful life events. Developing effective stress management strategies is one way to buffer yourself

339

against life's tornadoes. And, there's no two ways around it, it pays to stay away from the booze. No matter how many studies you read touting the heart benefits of a glass of wine a day, you're better off exercising regularly than risking addiction.

On the Road to Recovery

When I was in graduate school many moons ago, addictions were not a popular specialty. Professionals often didn't know what to do with them and what we *did* do with them often didn't work. Professionals on the alcohol ward of the V.A., where I did my internship, cynically referred to the "seasonal cure" for alcoholism: When it got cold enough outside, the homeless drunks would come in to dry out and keep warm. Spring, of course, was the backsliding season.

As with any addiction, recovery is often two steps forward and one step backward. The picture of alcohol recovery is not as grim as my colleagues at the V.A. may have thought. Just ask the people in Alcoholics Anonymous (AA). AA is a worldwide self-help support group of individuals recovering from alcohol addiction. It was started in 1935 by two alcoholics, Bill W. and Dr. Bob, after all of their professional treatment programs had failed. Neither one of them ever drank again.

In an informal survey of AA members, 29 percent said they had remained sober for more than five years, 38 percent for one to five years, and 33 percent for less than a year. Overall recovery rates suggest that between 20 percent and 35 percent of alcohol-dependent adults will completely recover, another third of them will struggle, and the rest are likely to die prematurely or remain alcohol-dependent.

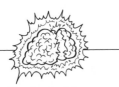

Brain Buster

Depression and alcohol don't mix. While most people with alcohol problems are not clinically depressed, the substantial minority who suffer from depression are much more likely to relapse if they don't get treatment for the depression along with treatment for alcoholism. And substance abusers who are depressed are much more likely to commit suicide.

Like eating disorders treatment, there is no single treatment for alcoholism. Physical withdrawal from alcohol can be fatal if not closely supervised, so some professionals routinely recommend inpatient treatment for detoxification (detox). Psychotherapy and AA are the treatments of choice, and the combination of a support group and psychotherapy is probably ideal. Perhaps even more significant than the type of treatment is the alcoholic's commitment to sticking with it. The motto "if you at first don't succeed, try, try again" is likely to help the person in therapy—and the therapist.

Helping a Loved One with a Drinking Problem

Most people have heard about 12-step programs—there's one for just about every compulsive behavior out there, from narcotics abuse to gambling. And, of course, there's the granddaddy of all 12-step programs:

the one that AA introduced. Here's my own recommended 12 steps for coping when someone you love has a drinking problem.

1. Don't try to control your loved one's drinking. Don't hide or get rid of the booze—he or she will only replace it and feel justified in his or her anger.

2. Don't bail your loved one out of trouble or lie for him to cover up his drinking. Let him suffer the consequences.

3. Don't blame yourself. You didn't cause your loved one to start drinking, and you can't make him or her stop.

4. Don't make threats unless you've thought them through and intend to carry them out.

5. Don't try to be your loved one's therapist. Express your concern about his or her alcohol use in terms of the problems you see it creating, not by labeling him or her with the term *alcoholic*.

6. Don't nag, preach, or lecture. You'll only wear yourself out and your loved one won't appreciate it, anyway.

7. Take care of yourself. Read as much as you can about alcoholism and the traps that family members can fall into.

8. Don't drink with your loved one in the hope that he or she will drink less.

9. Support any and every attempt your loved one makes to get help—even if it's not the method you would choose.

10. Offer as much love and support as you can without sacrificing yourself or neglecting your own needs.

11. Give Al-Anon a try. It's a self-help group for the friends and families of alcoholics. You'll find that it's helpful to be around other people who are dealing with the same issues you are.

12. Don't give up. Contrary to popular belief, not everyone with an alcohol problem has to hit bottom and lose everything before he sees the light.

Insight

Does AA work? No controlled study of AA has ever been done. What we do know, however, looks promising: of the third of alcoholics who have a good treatment outcome, most rate regular attendance at AA meetings as "very important" to their recovery.

I Can't Control My Impulses

Okay, admit it. At some time in your life, you've behaved impulsively. Most of us have said or done something in our lives that, looking back, seems completely out of character. Something we regret. Maybe you blamed your behavior on the full moon or your first love. However you tried to explain it to yourself, the fact is that we all commit impulsive actions once in a while.

People suffering from impulse control disorders, however, have to live with the consequences of their rash actions *all the time*. They repeatedly fail in their attempts to resist temptation and wind up doing something that could be harmful to themselves or others.

The immediate payoff for impulsive behavior is usually a release of tension: by acting impulsively, you can "blow off steam" or feel an immediate sense of pleasure and gratification. Later, however, you're likely to feel regret or guilt or, if the behavior has gone on over time, you may find yourself constantly having to rationalize or justify your actions. The long-term consequences, whether it's jail or financial ruin, are much harder to escape.

Let's take a look at three impulse control disorders that can get people into a lot of trouble: kleptomania, pyromania, and compulsive gambling.

I Just Had to Take It!

Kleptomania is a psychological disorder whereby a person literally cannot resist the impulse to steal objects that are not needed for personal use or for their monetary value. We're not talking about a plain old shoplifter or common criminal. In fact, the stolen objects are often discarded or given away or, if the person suffers enough remorse, returned surreptitiously at a later date. It is the act of stealing that is the "goal," not the object that is stolen.

For people with kleptomania, stealing provides a relief of tension. They'll report feeling increasingly tense before the theft and an immediate sense of relief or pleasure after the act is committed. They don't really want to steal—they know that stealing is wrong and senseless, and they often feel depressed and guilty afterward. However, when tension builds, they can't resist.

Pyromania

My four-year-old son is fascinated with fire; he loves watching the flames dance in the fireplace and wants to be a firefighter when he grows up. While I don't mind his career choice, I'm counting on his fascination with fire to die down as he grows older. For people with pyromania, however, it never does.

Pyromania is characterized by well-planned fire setting on at least more than one occasion. Like all impulse control disorders, the fire setting is a response to emotional tension and serves as a way for the person to find relief. In addition to setting actual fires, people with pyromania often set off false alarms, hang out around fire stations, follow fire trucks, and watch neighborhood fires.

Pathological Gambling

There's a big difference between taking a trip to Las Vegas and developing a problem with compulsive gambling. Social gambling typically occurs with friends or colleagues, lasts for a fixed amount of time, and results in affordable (although unwelcome) financial losses.

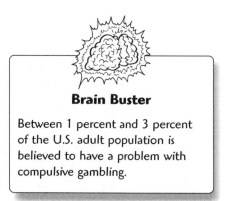

Brain Buster

Between 1 percent and 3 percent of the U.S. adult population is believed to have a problem with compulsive gambling.

Compulsive gambling, on the other hand, is out of control. Compulsive gamblers are obsessed with gambling. They gamble with money they can't afford to lose and use gambling either to escape from problems or to get a "high." People who compulsively gamble truly feel compelled to roll the dice. They'll lie to friends, family members, or therapists to conceal the extent to which their behavior is affecting their job or their relationships. As with other addictions, the disorder tends to run in families, is tough to treat, and responds best to a combination of psychotherapy and frequent attendance at a support group for problem gamblers.

The use of medication is still up in the air. While most people rely on therapy and peer support for their recovery, some clinicians believe compulsive gambling should be treated exactly like any other addiction—such as alcoholism—and that, like alcoholism, a significant subset of gamblers may have an underlying mood or anxiety disorder that may respond to antidepressant medication.

There's Hope and Help out There

In this chapter, we've explored a number of behaviors that, when taken to excess, can become serious psychological disorders. Whether the "addiction" is food, alcohol, or setting fires, these disorders can have serious psychological, physical, and, sometimes, legal consequences. With the right treatment, they can also get better.

As you can see, many psychological problems fall on a continuum; between normal eating and bulimia, for example, lies dieting and occasional overeating. As we saw in Chapter 18, "Mood Swingers and Scaredy Cats," between happiness and major depression lie bad moods, grief, and mild funks. During our lives, most of us will travel to different points on the continuum and, most of the time, we'll bounce back to the healthy end on our own.

But what if we don't? What if grief over a relationship breakup lingers much longer than it "should"? While we've touched on psychological treatments for specific psychological disorders, in the next two chapters, we'll explore medication and psychotherapy in detail. You'll learn what medications work for what problems, what therapy can do for you and what it can't, and how to take charge of your mental health if your own life momentarily gets off track.

The Least You Need to Know

➤ Eating disorders are not about dieting, vanity, or weight; they're complex psychological disorders in which eating is used to cope with other problems.

➤ The three eating disorders are anorexia nervosa, bulimia nervosa, and binge eating disorder.

➤ All eating disorder sufferers have a lot in common—they tend to have a distorted body image, a preoccupation with food, and low self-esteem, and they're all at risk for a number of life-threatening medical problems.

➤ Alcoholism can start out slowly or quickly, but its progression is surprisingly predictable, until the person ultimately centers his life around drinking.

➤ Kleptomania (compulsive stealing), pyromania (compulsive fire setting), and compulsive gambling are all impulse control disorders that can have serious emotional, social, and legal consequences.

Chapter 21

Better Living Through Chemistry

Two years ago, Susan had electroconvulsive "shock" therapy for her chronic depression. It was a disaster. After treatment, she had no idea how to find her house. She looked at her children and wondered when they had grown up. Snapshots of family vacations didn't bring back any memories because both bad and good memories had been erased by the electric currents that had passed through her brain. Susan has lost more than six years of her life.

Julie, on the other hand, spent most of her adult life fighting severe bouts of depression. Her numerous doctors tried antidepressants, lithium, and antipsychotics—which all caused bad side effects. Finally, at age 32 and working toward a master's degree in social work, Julie's depression was so deep that she knew it was only a matter of time before she lost her apartment and maybe her life. So Julie tried electroshock therapy.

"It's a miracle," she says. "Years ago I would have been locked up in a mental hospital. Today, my depression has lifted and I am doing better than a lot of people who never suffered from depression."

Insight

While public and private mental hospitals still exist, the number of people in them dropped from 555,000 in 1955 to 112,000 in 1988 and has continued to drop ever since.

Your mind is a sacred and essential part of who you are, so it's no wonder that psychiatric treatments have always been controversial. In this chapter, we'll take a look at medical treatments for psychological disorders—drugs, electroconvulsive therapy, and psycho-surgery. We'll look at all the ways psychiatrists try to fix the brain that is causing problems in the mind. Along the way, we'll explore the myths and realities of psychiatric medications, and look at some of the more controversial treatments from yesterday and today.

You're Not "Crazy" Just Because You See a Shrink

The biggest problem with psychiatric treatment is that too many people aren't getting it: Most people in the United States who have mental disorders never get help. In fact, surveys show that fewer than half of adults with a psychological disorder ever obtain any formal treatment and only half of those have seen a mental health professional. This means that fewer than a quarter of the people who need treatment get it.

So, who *is* traipsing to the psych doctor's office? Women (25 percent) more often than men (20 percent), college graduates (43 percent) more frequently than high school graduates, and whites more often than nonwhites. Ironically, people in higher income levels (over $35,000) are less likely to have a diagnosable mental disorder than low-income earners (poverty can make us sick), but they're more likely to visit a mental health specialist, whether or not they have a disorder. Of course, they can afford to.

Contrary to popular opinion, people who get psychiatric treatment aren't "crazy." Roughly two million of the seven million people in the United States who visit a mental health professional within any six-month period have never qualified for a *Diagnostic and Statistical Manual of Mental Health Disorders* (*DSM*) diagnosis. Instead, most of these people are seeking help with some life problem, such as marital conflict or job stress. The rest most often want help because they are anxious, depressed, abusing drugs or alcohol, or some combination of the three. Some people might say it's a lot saner to seek expert advice when life gets you down that to try and suffer through it all alone!

The Problem Is in the Hardware

"Bullet in the Brain Cures Man's Mental Problems." This dramatic headline in the *Los Angeles Times* captioned a bizarre story. A 19-year-old man suffering from severe obsessive-compulsive disorder shot a 22-caliber bullet through his head in a suicide attempt. Amazingly, he survived the injury. Even more amazingly, his pathological symptoms were cured without affecting his intellectual abilities, even though some of the underlying causes of his problems remained.

Psychobabble

Complaining about your medical treatment? Count your blessings. In the 12th century, physicians often tried to cure their patients' problems by drilling holes in their skull to let out "bad spirits."

Biomedical therapists might be awestruck by this particular story, but they wouldn't be surprised that an alteration in the physical structure of the brain would alter the mind as well. If you think of the mind as a computer, biological treatments try to fix the hardware (the brain) to heal the mind (the software). And one of the most effective ways to bring a misfiring brain back to normal is through psychiatric medication: The right dose of the right medication can dissolve hallucinations, douse depression, level out moods, and soothe anxiety. Now that's what I call better living through chemistry!

Back to Reality with Antipsychotic Drugs

In the 1950s, French psychiatrists Jean Delay and Pierre Deniker used chlorpromazine to treat the symptoms of schizophrenia and started a whole new era in the treatment of mental disorders. Today, psychiatric medications are available for just about any disorder ranging from attention deficit disorder to depression. In fact, antidepressants are so widely prescribed that we've been dubbed the "Prozac generation."

Unfortunately, early drug-based treatments were almost as bad as the problems they were intended to cure. When I was a graduate student, one side effect of one antipsychotic medication was informally called the "Thorazine shuffle," to describe the slow, robotlike movements and incredibly sedating effect of this drug. Yes, the drug would quiet the voices heard by a person with schizophrenia, but at high doses it also zombied out just about everything else.

Antipsychotic drugs have gotten a whole lot better since then. They do a great job of zapping delusions, hallucinations, and other unusual behaviors that prevent people with schizophrenia from having a life outside the hospital. Side effects still occur, however. About 40 percent of people who take antipsychotics for long periods of time eventually develop some degree of *tardive dyskinesia,* a motor disturbance that results in involuntary jerking of the tongue, face, and other muscles.

And new drugs are being discovered all the time. For example, antipsychotics developed over the past 10 years show great promise—some without the downside.

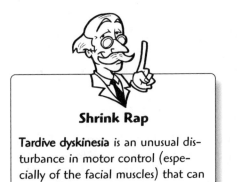

Restoril, for instance, works just as effectively as older drugs against the positive signs of schizophrenia, without the risk of tardive dyskinesia or motor problems. Amazingly, it also seems to relieve some of the disease's negative signs, such as social isolation, apathy, and reduced emotion. In short, for patients who respond to them, these new drugs don't just make life more normal, they make it happier!

Douse Depression with Antidepressants

You've probably heard as many jokes about Prozac as you have about Viagra. If you've been the one telling them, I hope you stop. At the risk of sounding like a sourpuss, clinical depression is no laughing matter. The advances we've made in treating it, though, might make you a lifelong Prozac fan.

As you saw in Chapter 18, "Mood Swingers and Scaredy Cats," depression is one of the most treatable mental illnesses—and antidepressants can play a powerful role in dousing major depression. About 70 percent of people who receive medication get better, compared to about 30 percent who are given a placebo. They work by correcting the chemical imbalance that is sometimes at the root of depression. They do so by increasing the availability of certain neurotransmitters in the brain, especially serotonin and norepinephrine—the body's "feel good" hormones.

Insight

Recent studies show that St. John's Wort, an over-the-counter herbal medication, is effective in treating mild to moderate depression with fewer side effects than antidepressant medications. However, always consult with your doctor before starting St. John's Wort.

Of course, with the good comes the bad. While the side effects of antidepressants are far less serious than the antipsychotic medications, they can still be annoying. Fatigue, dry mouth, and blurred vision are most common; a decrease in sexual libido and/or sexual performance seems to be the major bummer. Fortunately, there's a wide range of drug treatment choices, so anyone experiencing unpleasant side effects can switch fairly easily to a more comfortable medication that has the same therapeutic benefit but fewer side effects.

The Truth and Consequences of Antidepressants

Will antidepressants work for you? Only you and your doctor can answer that question. Doctors often base their clinical decisions on a patient's personal and medical history and then find the right medication through trial and error. Some people respond better to Prozac, some to Paxil, others to Zoloft. While some people are lucky enough to "hit" the first time around, others go through a couple of different medications before they find the one that works best for them.

Medication evaluation is not an exact science, and that can be frustrating. People who can benefit from antidepressants may be tempted to throw in the towel if their first few tries don't work. But the biggest barrier to giving antidepressants a fair shake is fear and confusion about what the medication will do. Here are some of the common myths about antidepressants that are still floating around:

Myth: Antidepressants make you "happy" or "high."

Reality: Alas, not true. But antidepressants can make clinically depressed people feel "normal." The dark cloud lifts, the heavy feeling in their body goes away, and they generally feel like they did before depression hit them.

Myth: Antidepressants are addictive—once you get on them, you can't get off.

Reality: Antidepressants are not physically or psychologically addictive. Some people feel anxious about getting off their antidepressants because they are afraid they will get depressed again. However, when the dosage is gradually tapered off, the fear is also reduced. And when the person stays on the medication for the recommended time, chances of relapse go down, too.

Myth: Taking antidepressants is a sign of weakness.

Reality: If you think taking insulin for diabetes or hypertensive medication for high blood pressure is a cop out, then taking antidepressants is a cop out, too. In reality, antidepressants can be as necessary as any other medical treatment.

Myth: Once you start taking antidepressants, you'll be on them for the rest of your life.

Reality: Antidepressants are typically taken for an average of six to 18 months. If a person has had at least three episodes of major depression, a doctor might suggest a maintenance dose to guard against further bouts.

Myth: Once you feel better, you can quit taking them.

Reality: Antidepressants generally kick in within two to six weeks, but it takes longer for them to do their job on the brain's neurotransmitters. Stopping antidepressants prematurely creates a risk for relapse, and,

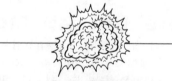

Brain Buster

Antidepressants inhibit saliva production, which can lead to more cavities and mouth infections. So, if you're taking an antidepressant, visit your dentist more often, take vitamin C, and chew sugar-free gum between meals.

according to some studies, may result in the depression becoming more difficult to treat the second time around.

Myth: Medication is all you need.

Reality: For many psychological disorders like anxiety or depression, medication is most effective in combination with psychotherapy.

Not Just for the Blues

Antidepressants, we are finding, can do more than lift your major depression. Many of the newer antidepressants (nicknamed the SSRIs, for selective serotonin re-uptake inhibitors) seem to help with lots of things, including social phobias and panic disorder. One of the SSRIs, Effexor, seems to be an effective long-term treatment for symptoms of generalized anxiety disorder. And the antidepressant Zyban, in combination with the nicotine patch, can double the odds that you kick the cigarette habit.

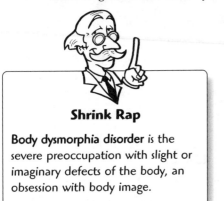

Shrink Rap

Body dysmorphia disorder *is the severe preoccupation with slight or imaginary defects of the body, an obsession with body image.*

Even people with severe body image problems may respond to antidepressants. In a recent study reported by the American Academy of Child and Adolescent Psychiatry, half of the 19 patients suffering from *body dysmorphia disorder*, a severe image obsession that is characterized by a preoccupation with imaginary or slight defects, got better after treatment with antidepressant medications. Not only did the patient stop obsessing as much over her physical appearance, she was less distressed by it. For some people, antidepressants are wonder drugs indeed!

Level Out with Mood Stabilizers

Mood stabilizers are not the same thing as antidepressants. Rather, as their name implies, they work to smooth out the extreme mood swings that characterize manic-depressive illness. The classic mood stabilizer is lithium, although some antiseizure medications such as Tegretol and Depakote are now also proving helpful in stabilizing mood.

Lithium was the first and, for a long time, the only drug that worked for bipolar illness. It is most effective at dampening manic symptoms but less helpful in dealing with the depressive side. It often decreases the frequency and severity of manic episodes, but it does not necessarily eliminate them in everyone.

Lithium is a mineral that the body produces naturally, but we don't know exactly how it works on manic depression. One theory is that lithium stabilizes the brain's sensitivity to monoamines, links in the chain of amino acids (proteins) that are necessary to life. The main problem with lithium is that at high doses it can produce serious side effects—including diarrhea, vomiting, and seizures—so anyone taking it must have his or her blood or urine tested regularly to avoid toxicity.

More recently, mood stabilizers have been used to treat other psychological disorders, but results are controversial. For example, lithium has been somewhat effective in helping clients with explosive or uncontrollable anger. And persons with other "character disorders" that involve marked mood shifts appear to receive some relief from this medication, although the jury is still out on its long-term effectiveness.

Insight

While mood stabilizers have been most effective with the manic part of manic depression, an epilepsy medication may help patients with bipolar depression. Lamictal, a drug used to prevent convulsions, seems to help relieve depression within three weeks of drug administration.

Don't Worry, Be Happy: Antianxiety Medications

Valium. Librium. Barbiturates. These minor tranquilizers, as antianxiety medications are commonly called, got a bad name in the 1960s, when they were regularly taken by more than 10 percent of adults in the United States. Unfortunately, these drugs made people feel good and were highly addictive, a dangerous combo that led to some very serious substance abuse problems. Since then, their use has declined considerably, although Valium remains the most popular tranquilizer currently in use—between 8 and 9 million Americans take it daily.

The antianxiety medications prescribed today are much safer than their predecessors. Xanax and Klonopin are perhaps the most commonly used in controlling generalized anxiety and, to some degree, panic disorder. They are best taken short term as they are still moderately addictive, and when it's time to discontinue using them, they need to be gradually tapered off to avoid unpleasant physical side effects. On the positive side, they can be lifesavers for people whose anxiety is so great that it interferes with their ability to cope with the world around them.

The most useful "tranquilizers" are those that have the largest antianxiety effect with the least sedating effect. Buspar, a new antianxiety medication, appears to be safer and less addictive than older drugs, and less sedating than the benzodiazepines (Xanax, Klonopin) which replaced the older barbiturates.

Self-medicators sometimes use over-the-counter antihistamines (Benadryl) to combat anxiety or as a sleeping pill. While it's certainly easier (and cheaper) to run to the pharmacy than to make an appointment with your doctor, self-medication for anxiety is generally not a good idea—you're better off using regular exercise or relaxation techniques to self-treat the problem. Over-the-counter drugs like Benadryl aren't all that effective in fighting anxiety, and they have more side effects than the by-prescription-only benzodiazepines.

Brain Buster

Antianxiety medication and alcohol don't mix! Antianxiety drugs multiply the effects of booze, so that the same amount of alcohol that would normally be safe can produce serious intoxication or a coma in people taking a benzodiazepine.

Sleep Now, Pay Later

Let's get one thing straight: It is rarely helpful to use sleeping pills, known as hypnotics, on a regular basis. In fact, the problems caused by sleeping pills are often worse than the problems caused by lack of sleep. The longer you take them, the less effective they become. In addition, some of them stay in your system longer than necessary, and a few, like Halcion, may cause memory problems in elderly people.

But, you say, I can't function without a good night's sleep! Ambien appears to be the most promising drug for die-hard insomniacs. This relatively new sleeping pill is reportedly highly effective, nonaddicting, and has few side effects.

Before you rush to the phone and dial your doctor, however, here's a little history lesson. Benzodiazepines were originally marketed as "nonaddicting," too—the abuse potential of many sedatives was not recognized until, well, people were addicted. And don't forget the sedative Thalidomide, used widely in the 1950s as a remedy for morning sickness. Initially believed to be safe, that drug caused horrific birth defects when taken by pregnant women.

If lack of sleep is a chronic problem for you, you're better off trying yoga, relaxation techniques, regular exercise, and psychotherapy. When it comes to sedatives, the bottom line is they should be taken with caution and used for sleep "emergencies" only.

Peeking into the Medicine Chest

Speaking of the bottom line, here's what's most likely to be prescribed, and most likely to work, for some of the most common psychological disorders.

What's Your Problem?	Your Best Medication
Obsessive-compulsive disorder	Anafranil, possibly Prozac, Zoloft, or Paxil
Generalized anxiety disorder	Klonopin, possibly Xanax (short term)
Major depression	Prozac, Paxil, Zoloft, or another antidepressant
Schizophrenia	Respiradol, Chlorazine, other antipsychotics
Bipolar disorder	Lithium, Tegretol, Depakote
Bulimia nervosa	Possibly an antidepressant
Anorexia nervosa	None (possibly an antidepressant to help prevent relapse)
Panic disorder	Klonopin, Xanax, sometimes Tofranil

Kid Stuff?

Ritalin, a drug used to treat attention deficit disorder, is the most widely prescribed psychiatric drug for children—six million prescriptions are written each year. Although few antidepressants have been tested on children, another million-plus pediatric prescriptions for these medications were written in 1998. In fact, 1.5 percent of *all* doctor visits by children in 1995 led to a prescription for a medication for the mind.

Our understanding of childhood mental illnesses is still limited, and there are gaps in what we know about the effects of psychiatric drugs on children. So far, no antidepressants have been approved by the Food and Drug Administration to treat childhood depression. But if your child was having serious psychological problems, what would you do? Would you be willing to helplessly watch your child suffer while you wait for clinical trials to be completed? Or, would you roll the dice and pray the medication that offers relief will also be safe over the long term?

The one clinical study of antidepressant use to combat major depression in children ages 8 to 18 showed promising results. The children given Prozac did significantly better than those given a placebo. There is some concern that antidepressants may cause mania in a small minority of children. Of even greater concern, however, is that many primary care physicians and pediatricians who prescribe these drugs are not adequately trained to treat childhood mental problems. Even the best treatment, in the wrong hands, can be dangerous.

Choose Your Drugs Carefully

Before we move along to other biological treatments of psychological disorders, let's nail down some basic information to help keep all these drugs straight. Medications that are used to treat psychological disorders are classified according to their clinical class, chemical class, and action:

➤ Clinical class is the drug's purpose, such as antipsychotic, antidepressant, sedative, or antianxiety. Valium is clinically classed as a sedative/hypnotic, Xanax is clinically classed as an antianxiety drug, and Prozac is clinically classed as an antidepressant.

➤ Chemical class is what the drug is made of. Xanax and Valium are chemically classed as benzodiazepines, for example. (*Benzo* means amphetamine and *diazepine* means relaxant.)

➤ Action refers to what the drug does. For example, Prozac's action is as a selective serotonin re-uptake inhibitor, rather than a direct stimulant to the nervous system, like Ritalin.

Insight

While benzodiazepines are clearly addictive, it is helpful to put this into perspective. Even some of the barbiturates with a bad reputation, such as Valium, are unquestionably less dangerous than alcohol.

There's plenty of information available about these medications, and one place to look them up quickly is the Internet. Try www.intelihealth.com and click on its drug information section. The *Physicians Desk Reference* at your local library is also a good source. And, before you take any meds, ask your doctor these questions:

1. What is the goal of this medication and how does it work?
2. For how long will I need to take it?
3. When can I expect to feel better?
4. What are the side effects?
5. Will it interact with any other prescription drug, over-the-counter remedy, food, or beverage?
6. What effect will it have on other medical conditions?
7. How will it affect my sex life?
8. How will it affect my weight?
9. How will it affect my sleep?
10. Will it interfere with any activities such as driving?

Choosing the "right" medication is as dependent on your unique body chemistry as on your psychological disorder. We now know that certain drugs, or classes of drugs, tend to be most effective with certain disorders. And, certain psychological problems don't respond to medication at all. In those cases, there are other effective treatments available—starting with, believe it or not, artificial light.

Psychobabble

Musicians and other performers have commonly used a variety of uppers and downers to maintain the long hours necessary to travel from one town to another to perform. Many, including Johnny Cash, have come close to death from addiction to amphetamines (speed) that kept them awake for days and then required the use of ever-increasing doses of barbiturates, sedatives, or antianxiety drugs to put themselves to sleep. Self-medication is a dangerous habit.

Beating Those Winter Blues

Do the gray, dreary days of winter get you down? Have you noticed a change in your mood, appetite, or sleep pattern during the winter months? Thousands of people suffer from *seasonal affective disorder (SAD)*, and it can give getting through the winter a whole new meaning.

No one really knows what causes SAD, although most of the research has focused on abnormal alterations in brain chemicals. Fortunately, we don't have to know what causes it to treat it. One of the most effective treatment options is light therapy—routine exposure to special bright lights. Under the supervision of a mental health professional, a person with SAD spends a few hours a day under the lights. Morning bright light exposure is more effective than evening exposure and, while it takes several weeks to achieve success, this treatment helps 60 percent of the time. And if it doesn't, antidepressants and therapy seem to work, too.

The ABCs of ECT

Does the thought of electric shock therapy give you the heebie-jeebies? I hate to admit it, but even with the clinical knowledge I have, it's hard for me to stomach the thought of shocking someone. But for some people who suffer major depression so profound that suicidal thoughts have begun, *electroconvulsive therapy* (ECT, commonly called shock therapy) can be a viable option.

ECT has split the psychiatric community since it was pioneered more than 50 years ago and, back then, its bad reputation was well deserved. Before modern procedures were invented, the seizure induced by the electric shock was so violent that the muscular contractions would break bones. Today ECT is painless and quite safe. Patients are given drugs to block muscle and nerve activity so that no pain or muscular contractions occur. Doctors may disagree about when, or if, ECT should be used, but all agree that the technology has steadily improved.

Some patients complain of lifelong memory lapses after ECT, but studies on the brain show no evidence of permanent memory loss, nor do brain scans show any chemical or structural changes after repeated ECT shocks. Until this discrepancy between science and personal anecdote is resolved, ECT will continue to be seen as a treatment alternative that should come only after medications and therapy have been tried and failed.

Insight

For people who don't respond to medication, ECT can be a lifesaver, even though no one knows how it works. About 70 percent of those suffering from major depression who have not responded to other treatments get better with ECT. Sometimes the depression goes away for good; other times it reoccurs after several months.

Dr. Frankenstein to the O.R.!

When I was a psychology graduate student, few things could induce more nightmares than reading about the history of lobotomies. I'll tell you the story of how they came about; maybe there's a lesson here for all of us.

It all started in 1892, when physician Gottlieb Burhardt performed operations to remove parts of the brains of six schizophrenic patients who were suffering from hallucinations and agitated behavior. A few of his patients did become calmer after the surgery, although two of them died (which should have been a clue to the grim cost-benefit ratio of this treatment). Burhardt's contemporaries were horrified at his behavior, and peer pressure kept psychosurgery to a minimum for the next 40 years.

The situation changed when several research labs in the United States began making amazing discoveries about the role of the temporal and frontal lobes in controlling emotional behavior and aggressiveness. From the late 1930s to the early 1950s, thousands of men and women were subjected to a prefrontal lobotomy, in which the front portions of their frontal lobes were surgically separated from the rest of the brain. The operation was used to treat people with severe cases of schizophrenia, bipolar disorder, depression, obsessive-compulsive disorder, and pathological violence.

Sadly, the outcome was often worse than the initial problem. While the lobotomy relieved patients of their incapacitating emotions, it left them incapacitated in new ways. Lobotomized patients showed lifelong deficits in their ability to make plans and follow through with them; they were, in fact, mere ghosts of their former selves. Sometimes, it seems, the very parts of ourselves that are the most troublesome are inseparably linked to the parts that make us uniquely human. And, from a treatment standpoint, mental health professionals should think twice before severing those links.

Psychobabble

While lobotomies are considered barbaric and ineffective today, prefrontal lobotomies were so highly regarded at one time that, in 1949, the Portuguese neurosurgeon who pioneered the technique, Antonio Egas Moniz, was awarded the Nobel Prize.

Psychosurgery Revised

While lobotomies are no longer performed, there are a rare few individuals who are helped by a new kind of psychosurgery known as *cingulotomy*. The cingulum, a small structure in the limbic system known to be involved in emotionality, is partially destroyed with radio-frequency current applied through fine wire electrodes temporarily implanted in the brain. Follow-up studies suggest that these operations most often reduce or abolish major depression and obsessive-compulsive disorder and have rarely left the patient worse off than before.

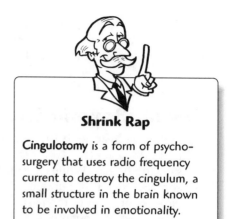

Shrink Rap

Cingulotomy is a form of psycho-surgery that uses radio frequency current to destroy the cingulum, a small structure in the brain known to be involved in emotionality.

Cingulotomy, like the earlier lobotomy, is still controversial, but to someone who has been seriously depressed for many years, and who has gotten no relief from ECT and every antidepressant medication on the market, it's something to consider. Blessedly, this degree of treatment failure rarely happens. And, no matter how you feel about it, cingulotomy does help. People who once would have spent their lives in the back ward of a mental hospital are living productive lives as a result of this procedure.

Chemistry of the Warm and Fuzzy Kind

When I think of chemistry, the organic kind isn't the first kind that springs to mind. I think of the chemistry between two actors on the movie screen, the chemistry between two people who are attracted to each other, or between two friends who just "hit it off" the first time they meet. Yep, the chemistry I think about is of the relationship sort.

It was relationship chemistry—between woman and dog—that saved Lisa Conti, a U.S. Army private. After she was raped and tortured by four men in 1987, Lisa began suffering from debilitating panic attacks and other symptoms of post-traumatic stress disorder. Between 1989 and 1995, Conti was hospitalized for psychiatric reasons more than 100 times. A few years ago, she was too fearful to walk to the end of her driveway.

Today Lisa Conti takes no medication, holds a job, and is going to college to be a park ranger. Although she still has two to three panic attacks a month, she is able to get through them without letting them interfere with her life in any way. And all because of the chemistry between herself and her dog, King. For some unknown reasons, King can sense when Lisa is about to have a panic attack and will lean against her, nuzzle her, and stand between her and a crowd. This helps her get through the attacks.

Guide dogs for the blind have been around for 80 years, but using them for "invisible disabilities" is relatively new. Dogs are now being trained to help people with agoraphobia and they may be helpful in dealing with problems like depression and bipolar disorder. And while they certainly can't correct a chemical imbalance or take the place of needed medication, for some people they may make the difference between a productive life and a life of isolation and fear. Let's have a 10-woof salute for these special dogs.

Moving Beyond the Biological

Biological treatments for psychiatric disorders have improved dramatically over the past 50 years. Medications can help conditions ranging from schizophrenia to depression to phobias. While electroconvulsive therapy (shock treatment) continues to be controversial, it has unquestionably become less physically dangerous. And the barbaric lobotomies of the past have been replaced with a less harmful form of psychosurgery, although it is still considered a treatment of last resort.

But if we learned one thing in this chapter, it's that every person is unique and problems can't be solved the same way for everyone. Medication can make some psychological disorders a whole lot better, but there are lots of challenges (marital conflict, job stress) that medication won't help at all. And, even if there's clearly an underlying biochemical problem, psychotherapy can play a critical role in learning how to prevent and/or cope with it. In the next chapter, we'll take a look at another potent weapon in the fight for mental health: psychotherapy, the talking cure.

The Least You Need to Know

➤ Psychiatric medications are often a critical part of the treatment for depression, schizophrenia, and bipolar disorder, and can also be helpful with anxiety disorders.

➤ The techniques used in electroconvulsive treatment are no longer physically harmful. However, it is still a controversial treatment and used only when medication and psychotherapy fail.

➤ Surgical lobotomies are no longer done, but a new form of psychosurgery called cingulotomy can be performed when nothing else works.

➤ Dogs are now being trained to watch for anxiety attacks in their owners.

Chapter 22

Just Keep Talkin'

In This Chapter

➤ The who, what, when, where, and why of therapy

➤ Delving deep into the psyche

➤ Breaking bad habits with the behaviorists

➤ Expanding your mind

➤ Searching for the meaning of it all

Irene was a 29-year-old woman with two children, an unemployed husband, and a severe case of depression. She turned to Dr. Aaron Beck, a pioneer in treating depression with psychotherapy, for help. She hadn't worked outside the home since she married two years ago. Her husband had been in and out of substance abuse treatment centers and Irene had become increasingly isolated. She felt that people looked down on her because of her problems and her difficulties parenting her children.

After six months with Dr. Beck, Irene was practically a new woman. She joined a tennis club, got a job as a waitress, and enrolled in a college course. She also left her husband when he refused to participate in couples' therapy and continued to treat her badly. Dr. Beck pronounced his client "depression free" and Irene proclaimed her therapy was money well spent.

In this chapter, we'll examine the who, what, when, where, and why of therapy. We'll look at the relationship between therapist and client and we'll take a peek behind the closed doors to see what actually happens in a therapeutic setting. We'll consider the

Shrink Rap

In psychotherapy, the **patient** or **client** is the person seeking professional help. Medically or biologically oriented therapists generally use the term *patient,* while those who tend to think of psychological disorders as problems in living will generally use the term *client.*

four therapeutic approaches to psychotherapy and the problems they're most effective in treating. Finally, we'll answer that question everybody asks—does therapy really work?

Half the Battle Is Getting There

Whenever I used to travel on business, the person sitting next to me on the plane or train would inevitably ask, "What do you do for a living?" and like an idiot, I always said "psychologist." Before you could blink an eye, my seatmate would be deep into a discussion of his or her latest problems. Out of desperation, I finally learned my lesson. Now I tell my travel mates that I'm a funeral director—and my travels are much more peaceful.

While travelers are often willing to unload their inner feelings to a captive audience (and a stranger) on a train, bus, or plane, people often feel shame and embarrassment about going into psychotherapy. Even if they think it's okay for someone else, they often resist the idea for themselves—as if this would be an admission of some personal flaw. And the media don't help. When we see therapist and client hopping into the sack on television, it's no wonder no one wants to see a "shrink."

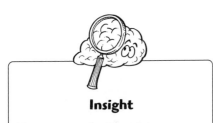

Insight

The reasons people go into psychotherapy are endlessly variable, and apparently, so are the diagnoses! Sure, you can go to therapy to cure your fear of heights (acrophobia) or snakes (ophidiophobia)—but you can also go to cure a fear of phobias, a condition known as phobophobia!

Media misrepresentations and invalid stereotypes about therapy are everywhere. But the fact is that a person's experience of therapy will depend on what brought him or her there. Just as a physician would treat cancer differently from a cold, a psychotherapist will treat schizophrenia differently from a fear of riding down escalators.

Between these extremes lies a variety of psychological problems that might drive a person to seek help. Some are short-lived but intense, such as a loss or a divorce. Some are mild but persistent and energy draining over time, like dysthymia or chronic worrying. And some problems are frustratingly repetitive, like realizing you're dating the same loser but with a different name. What all these problems have in common is that the person dealing with them feels that they exceed his or her coping skills. For whatever reason, they just can't see the light at the end of the tunnel. And, believe me, they've looked and looked for it before they come in for help.

The SCAT Team to the Rescue

Your mom is driving you batty, so you call your best friend and ask her what to do. You wouldn't dream of making a career move without talking it over with your college mentor. And, when you're feeling down, you hang around after church because talking with your minister makes you feel better. These are your informal "counselors," the ones who help you deal with most of your routine frustrations and conflicts.

No matter how good a listener your best friend is, however, there is something to be said for the skills and knowledge that formal psychological training provides. A SWAT team may rescue hostages kidnapped during a bank robbery, but when people are help captive by their problems, they turn to the SCAT team: school workers, counselors, and therapists. Here are the five kinds of mental health professionals who most often help us deal with the problems when our friends and families can't:

➤ *Counseling psychologists* specialize in the problems of daily living. They often work in community settings such as schools, clinics, and businesses, and they deal with challenges like relationship conflicts, choosing a vocation, school problems, and stress.

➤ *Clinical psychologists* are trained to treat individuals who suffer from more severe conditions, such as clinical depression, eating disorders, and anxiety.

➤ *Psychiatrists* are medical doctors who specialize in the treatment of emotional and mental disorders. These physicians generally treat more severe conditions and, in these days of managed care, are most likely to prescribe medication for psychiatric disorders.

➤ *Clinical social workers* are mental health professionals with specialized training in the social context of people's problems. Clinical social workers often work with family problems, like child abuse, and their work often involves entire families in the therapy.

➤ *Pastoral counselors* are members of a religious group or ministry trained to specialize in the treatment of psychological disorders. Pastoral counselors often combine spiritual and practical problem-solving issues.

Shrink Rap

A **psychoanalyst** specializes in applying Freudian principles to the treatment of psychological disorders. The psychoanalyst may have an M.D., M.S.W., or a Ph.D., but all complete an intensive post-graduate training program specializing in psychoanalytic theory and practice (including undergoing their own analysis).

Finding a Partner for the Dance of Therapy

What do good therapists have in common? To some extent, it depends upon the client. In a good therapeutic relationship, there's a unique and somewhat illusive chemistry that develops between therapist and client. A good therapist for you, in other words, might not be a good therapist for me. But all good therapists share certain common traits, including:

➤ They listen and you talk.

➤ They keep their problems to themselves and deal with their own issues outside of your therapy session.

➤ They don't answer the phone or nod off while you are spilling your guts.

➤ They can be completely objective about what you are saying.

➤ They apologize if they make a mistake.

➤ They protect your confidences: They wouldn't spill the beans about what the two of you talk about if you dragged them over hot coals.

A good therapist would also make a good friend, but don't make that common mistake. Your therapist is *not* your friend. Friends have needs and agendas of their own that may not always coincide with yours.

The Therapeutic Relationship

Nevertheless, you and the therapist have a relationship, and the quality of that relationship is perhaps the biggest determinant in whether or not you benefit from therapy. In fact, study after study shows the "fit" between therapist and client is far more valuable than any bag of therapeutic tricks. The ability to trust your therapist, to work as allies on the same team, and to share similar values and goals are the key ingredients to therapy that works.

Unfortunately, it isn't always easy to find a good therapist. Your first therapy session is like a blind date; you never know for sure what you're going to get. However, there are some guidelines you can use that will improve the odds that your "first date" with a therapist will turn into a trusting relationship. Let's examine what you should look for when picking a therapist and what you can expect when you get to his or her office.

Guidelines for Finding a Therapist

The best approach to finding a good therapist is the same one you'd use when seeking any professional services. Here are the basic steps to take:

➤ *Get personal referrals,* particularly from a friend or colleague who has had a problem similar to yours. If you can't find a therapist this way, check with your doctor or hospital social work department.

➤ *Interview the therapist over the phone.* Remember, you are hiring this person to be your therapist and you need to make sure she is qualified.

➤ *Ask questions.* Be sure to ask what her specialties are, how many people she's seen with the same problem as yours, and her treatment philosophy. One person may be a fabulous therapist for substance abuse problems, but have no experience with depression.

➤ *Trust your instincts.* If you don't like the person or don't feel comfortable after a few sessions, switch therapists.

What to Expect When You're Going to Therapy

Lots of what you do in therapy will depend upon the problem you're seeking help for, the therapist's style and theoretical orientation, and the nature of the relationship the two of your develop. And, no matter what problem brought you to the therapist's office, you can expect to work on the four following goals:

1. *Figuring out what's wrong.* You might think you know what's wrong; after all that's what brought you to therapy in the first place. And, most of the time, you do. However, this can be trickier than you might think. A client who comes in to deal with problems on the job may come to realize he is drinking six vodka tonics a day. So is the job his problem or is it his drinking? Good therapists will do a thorough clinical interview and ask you all kinds of questions that might seem completely irrelevant. This enables us to make a diagnosis that's helpful as a starting point.

Insight

How does your therapist rate? If you're not sure, go to www.cyber-couch.com/library/rati.tag.html and check out Dr. Thomas Grugle's "Rate Your Therapist" quiz.

2. *Figuring out what caused the problem and why you still have it.* Is your problem genetic? Does it run in your family? When did it start? What keeps it going on or coming back again?

3. *Figuring out what's likely to happen in the future.* There is no crystal ball involved in treatment. Therapists are not psychic, but they try to gauge what or who might take longer to treat and how to keep the problem from happening again. Anorexia, for example, tends to be a long-term problem and the therapist and client need to be realistic about treatment.

4. *Figuring out how to get rid of it or make it better.* What kind of therapy would work best on the client's particular problem? What does the client's social and professional environment look like? And how can the family or support system help?

The Talking Cure

While medications have helped people solve mental problems by acting on the brain, psychotherapy works on the mind. Talk therapy reprograms the thoughts, feelings, and behaviors that interfere with your ability to maximize your potential and get along in the world. No matter how much your genes may be stacked against you, the die is not cast at birth. Your environment can serve as either a powerful buffer or a risk factor.

Psychobabble

When you visualize yourself in a therapist's office, you might not picture yourself flapping your arms like a bird while your therapist accompanies your movements with drumbeats. However, shamanism, an ancient spiritual tradition that combines healing with contacting the spirit world, is becoming increasingly popular among Western therapists.

There are four major types of psychotherapy: psychodynamic, behavioral, cognitive, and existential-humanistic therapies. Each approach to talk therapy brings its own unique perspective to a client's problems.

Gaining Insight with Psychodynamic Therapy!

You should know Siggy Freud quite well by now. You've learned about his theory of personality—his beliefs that problems were caused by the tension between our primitive, unconscious impulses and the "no-no's" of society and our individual life situations. You learned that he made up a lot of cool words like *id, ego, repression,* and *resistance,* that he was partial to couches, and that he invented psychoanalysis.

When it came to setting therapeutic goals for his clients, Freud was no slacker. He wasn't interested in making a few personality tweaks or smoothing over a few glitches in his patient's behavior. He was into total makeovers, a complete personality overhaul. So, if you go to a psychoanalyst for psychotherapy, be prepared for a long trip.

Psychoanalytic therapy is a prolonged, intensive exploration of a person's unconscious motivations and conflicts. The therapist's goal is to help the patient make the unconscious conscious by discovering the relationship between present symptoms and past events. The goal is to change disturbing, self-defeating thoughts and actions by getting to the root of the problem that's causing them, which is buried in the unconscious. Psychoanalytic therapy guides the client toward insight using a number of techniques, including free association, analysis of resistance and dreams, and an exploration of the therapeutic relationship.

Free Association

One tool commonly used in psychoanalysis is free association. Daydreaming is a form of free association and so, to some extent, is brainstorming. In a psychoanalyst's office, you lay down on a couch (although some sit in a chair) and describe whatever (and I mean whatever!) thoughts or feelings come to mind, no matter how painful, personal, or seemingly trivial. The therapist's job is to help you see the underlying meaning beneath these random thoughts—a sort of verbal inkblot test—and to help you express any repressed emotions that go along with them.

Resistance

What's the most embarrassing thing you've ever done? Don't want to talk about it? Aha! You're resisting and, if I'm a psychoanalyst, I'm going to lock onto your reluctance and dig away at it like a dog after a bone. From a psychoanalytic point of view, your inability or unwillingness to discuss certain thoughts, feelings, or experiences is a clear sign of resistance, the unconscious process that prevents repressed material from surfacing and being dealt with. It's the therapist's job to help you stop resisting painful ideas, desires, and experiences so they will lose their power to control your actions.

Dream Analysis

Apparently, your superego needs a lot more rest than your id does. While your superego (your conscience) is asleep, your id (basic urges) is free to run wild, which is why psychoanalysts love to look at dreams as an important source of information about your unconscious motivations.

Psychoanalysts look at the manifest (literal) and latent (symbolic) content of dreams. If you dream about a snake chasing you, the manifest content would be the literal dream (I was walking in the grass and I saw a big, black snake that chased me into a cave). The latent content is what it really means; perhaps you were really expressing a fear of sex.

Shrink Rap

The **manifest content** of a dream is the literal story it tells. The **latent content** is the meaning that lies hidden underneath the dream's symbols, images, and actions.

Transference and Countertransference

In Chapter 16, "Psychic Self-Defense," you learned about projection and how we use it as an emotional defense mechanism. Accusing your partner of being in a bad mood when you're the real grump is projection. Well, when you do this in psychotherapy, it's called transference. A good example is jealousy: If I'm your therapist and you begin to express jealousy of my other patients, I might explore your relationships with siblings, friends, and significant others to look for the real cause. With transference, your emotional reaction to the therapist is really a carryover from past conflicts.

It works the other way around, too. I hate to tell you, but therapists don't always like every client. The good news is that, when we don't, we consider it *our* problem, not the patient's. Countertransference is what happens when the therapist has a strong emotional reaction towards a client because he is a reminder of a significant person in the therapist's life. Perhaps the client looks like the therapist's beloved first-grade teacher, or, worse, reminds the therapist of his rude and obnoxious high school coach. Psychoanalysts must be vigilant about letting their own ids spill into the therapy session, and they must recognize that any strong feelings toward a therapy client are a clue that the therapist needs to look at his or her own "stuff."

Psychobabble

South African Joseph Wolpe was the first person to recognize that the body can't be anxious and relaxed at the same time, and to apply this knowledge to the treatment of fears and phobias. He found that learning relaxation techniques can help patients deal with fear in general—whether it's the fear of heights or the prenuptial jitters.

Get with the Program: Behavior Therapy

Quit smoking in 30 days! Overcome your fear of flying and take that dream vacation to Tahiti! Get hooked on exercise by increasing your motivation and boosting your willpower. Sound appealing? You might want to give behavior therapy a try.

Behavior therapists don't care beans about your dreams. They just want you to do more of what works for you and to stop doing the things that get you into trouble. They apply the principles of conditioning and reinforcement to interfere with undesirable behaviors. They focus on the problem behavior, try to figure out how it might have been learned, and most importantly, they work with you to replace that behavior with more effective choices.

The Birth of a Phobia

Maybe you were exploring as a toddler and climbed up an unattended ladder. You got to the top and the ladder started shaking. You got so scared that you couldn't climb down and spent an agonizing 10 minutes waiting for someone to come help you. When your mom did find you, she, too, was understandably terrified. To make sure you never climbed that ladder again, she put the fear of God into you.

So now you're terrified of heights. The fear of being stuck on the ladder (which would only be a serious problem if you were a roofer) slowly mushroomed into a fear of stairs, escalators, and any building over 10 feet tall; you wouldn't be caught dead on the Ferris wheel. Even airplane rides are excruciating, especially if you accidentally get a glimpse out the window. You've managed to structure your life around your fears, but the effort is getting to be a real bummer.

Shrink Rap

Behavior modification applies principles of operant and classical conditioning to change behavior in a more adaptive direction. It generally works best with specific behavior problems: fears, addictions, impulsive behaviors, and compulsions. It's less effective at curing a personality disorder.

Conditioning Your Fears Away

No problem, a behavior therapist would say. We'll just change your conditioning with a little counterconditioning of our own. To weaken the strength of dysfunctional learned associations, your therapist might use *counterconditioning techniques* such as systematic desensitization, implosion, flooding, or aversion therapy.

Shrink Rap

In **counterconditioning**, a new response is substituted for an unwanted or ineffective one. For example, relaxation is a more effective response to a harmless situation than fear.

Systematic Desensitization

Systematic desensitization is the gradual psychological confrontation of a feared situation or event while remaining physically relaxed. If you're afraid of snakes, for example, you would list your fears about them, from mild (maybe a fear of looking at a picture of a snake) to terrifying (sleeping with one curled up next to you). After teaching your body to relax, you would imagine the feared situations, stopping whenever you got anxious and waiting for your anxiety to subside before going on to the next image.

The process is kind of like getting allergy shots. A doctor trying to overcome your allergy to ragweed begins by injecting you with gradually increasing doses of ragweed.

Over time, you build up a resistance to ragweed so your eyes and nose don't run when you are exposed. Systematic desensitization works on the same principle, and it can be so effective you might come to therapy with a snake phobia and wind up with a pet snake.

Implosion and Flooding

Implosion and flooding are the therapeutic versions of "throw 'em in the water and they'll learn to swim." Say you're a photographer with a snake phobia, but you've just been offered a dream assignment by *National Geographic* to photograph the rain forest (snake heaven) next week. You need to get over that phobia fast or forget about your career.

You could try implosion—immediate exposure (through visual imagery) to the most terrifying stimuli in order to extinguish fear associated with the entire range of fear-inducing situations. By doing this in a safe environment (the therapist's office), you can't deny, avoid, or escape from the feared situation and, by facing the fears again and again, the situation loses its power over you.

Psychobabble

Rent the 1958 Hitchcock thriller *Vertigo* to experience the fear of heights from the safety of your couch. James Stewart played a reporter with this phobia who must rescue a woman he loves from a church tower. Hitchcock loved to keep his audience off balance, and special camera techniques make the movie as unsettling as the phobia it depicts. While you're at it, rent Mel Brooks's *High Anxiety*—it spoofs psychiatry, too!

Flooding's even more drastic. This technique doesn't fool around with scary images of snakes; it takes you right to the snake house at the zoo, directly exposing you to the feared situation. If you survive the exposure, you're cured.

Why would anyone use flooding when he could use systematic desensitization? Apparently, some fears are so strong that it would either take an incredible amount of time to make any progress against it, or the person is so terrified that he is unable to make even the first move on the therapeutic hierarchy. Flooding appears to be the most effective treatment for agoraphobia, the fear of going out into public places. A ride on a New York subway at rush hour might be just what the doctor ordered!

Managing Your R&R: Habit-Forming Therapy

Think of all the risks and rewards that go into a bad habit. Take excessive shopping, for example. Just the simple act of staying out of the stores is not simple at all. Here are just a few of the reasons compulsive shoppers give for heading to the mall even when they can't afford it.

> I love the way I feel when I buy a new outfit.
>
> My sister loves to shop and she always wants me to go along
>
> Nice clothes help me feel better about my body.
>
> I'm stressed or lonely or bored.
>
> They're always having sales and I just can't resist.
>
> It's one of my few pleasures.
>
> I was poor as a kid and always wore hand-me-downs.
>
> I have to look nice for business reasons.

Maybe you could add a few of your own; I know I could! As you can see, some of these reinforcements are internal—feelings of loneliness or stress, insecurity about your body or appearance. Others come from the environment—family pressure to shop, a need to look nice for work. To control your shopping behavior, you have to think about how you might manage these risks and rewards.

Shrink Rap

Contingency management is a technique designed to change behavior by modifying the consequences.

Out with the Bad Behavior, In with the Good

An operant therapist would try to identify every single reason you overshop and systematically change them so that you quit overshopping and do something else in response to these "triggers." This is called *contingency management*, shrink jargon for a technique that aims to change behavior by modifying the consequences.

For example, if you wanted to make peace with your checkbook, you would develop a list of alternative behaviors that you could do whenever you felt the urge to shop (taking a bubble bath, going for a 10-minute walk, calling a friend) and then reward yourself every time you did this. Oprah Winfrey did this to help her with her ongoing battle with her weight. Your therapist might suggest you do the same; when you want to shop, get up and get moving—but not to the mall!

It's Positively Rewarding!

And you're not just replacing unwanted behaviors. You're rewarding yourself for a job well done. To boost your motivation in any area of your life, apply some positive reinforcement therapy—systematically reward yourself every time you engage in a desired behavior. After a trip to the gym, for example, why not sit outside and enjoy the sunshine for a few minutes or take time to read the paper? Or, take a minute to write down how much better you feel than you did before you hit the gym.

Positive reinforcement strategies can be highly effective in helping us increase the frequency of a desirable behavior. If we want to reduce our harmful behavior, though, we need to get rid of the triggers and increase the rewarding situation. For example, when a person is recovering from a substance abuse problem, she may reward herself with the love and support of AA members and stay far away from her old drinking grounds and buddies. And, if the traditional habit-forming therapy doesn't work, the therapist and client may mutually decide to bring out the "big guns": aversion therapy.

Aversion Therapy

Aversion therapy does not mean working with a therapist you hate. Instead, it's what therapists do when they are bringing out the big guns—using negative reinforcement to try to change problematic behavior. The most dramatic form of aversion therapy might be electric shock.

Psychobabble

Want to see a scary movie and a dramatic example of aversion therapy? Check out the 1971 movie *A Clockwork Orange*, based on the 1962 novel by Anthony Burgess, and directed by the late Stanley Kubrick. This movie shows aversion therapy as an extreme form of mind control. It also might give you a few sleepless nights.

Aversion therapy might fit the bill for the person who is attracted to harmful stimuli, like controlled substances, perverse sex, or uncontrollable violence. Behaviors stimulated by the desire to get high on drugs, for example, are changed by changing the consequences of the stimuli. When the patient imagines how good he'll feel from the drug, he gets an electric shock instead. Eventually, this changes his conditioning and thus, his behavior. Some alcoholics are treated with aversion therapy by being given drugs that make them nauseous when they drink alcohol.

Expanding Your Mind's Horizons

Like behavior therapy, cognitive therapy sticks with the here and now. However, cognitive therapy recognizes that before we do anything, we spend some time thinking about doing it. This therapeutic approach focuses on changing the thoughts and feelings that lead up to the problem behavior. Correct these kinks in thinking, say the cognitive therapists, and the behavior will follow. The two major ways of doing this are with cognitive behavior modification and challenging false beliefs.

Making Modifications

Cognitive behavior modification could have as its slogan, "I think, therefore I do." It combines traditional behavior modification with an examination and alteration of the unhealthy attitudes and feelings that precede the unwanted behavior. The million and one self-help books that focus on changing negative self-talk are pop versions of cognitive behavioral strategies. They're not a bad investment. Replacing negative self-statements with realistic, constructive thoughts is a powerful antidote to low self-esteem, depression, and many problem behaviors.

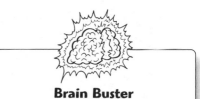

Brain Buster

Hidden expectations can zap the energy out of a relationship in no time. Avoid them by keeping track of the "strings" you attach to doing things for your partner. If, for example, you secretly expect your partner to wash the dishes whenever you cook dinner, it's best to get that secret out in the open.

Cutting to the Core Beliefs

Cognitive therapists also help people reprogram their minds to get rid of faulty beliefs. You may not be able to see these faults, but like computer bugs or viruses, they can permeate your entire view of yourself and your relationships and set you up for difficult life experiences. Some of the "bugs" are irrational or extreme attitudes such as, "I must be perfect." Some are false premises like, "If I speak up for myself, he'll leave me." And some are rigid rules that don't allow room for flexible or adaptive thinking, such as "Telling the truth hurts other people's feelings."

Oiling the Cogs in Your Mind Machine

You, too, can change beliefs that aren't helpful. Think of a situation that has given you problems in the past. Maybe you are uncomfortable at big parties and feel like a social zero as you stand in the corner and people-watch. Maybe you're frustrated that you just can't get up the nerve to ask your boss for the raise you obviously deserve. Maybe you hate what you see when you look in the mirror no matter how hard you diet and exercise. Whatever the problem is, you have the power to change it. The following five steps will get you started:

1. Write down your problem. Now, for one week, keep a diary and record every thought, feeling, and action that relates to this problem. During this stage, you are not to do anything differently, merely act as an observer. As closely as you can, write down what "triggers" thoughts and feelings about your problem and what you do to cope.

   Let's assume the problem is, "I hate my body no matter what I do to improve it." Here are some examples of ways you might think and feel about that, and how you'd record it in your journal.

Triggers	Thoughts	Feelings	Coping Strategy
Seeing an attractive woman in the elevator	I bet she never sits home on Friday night.	Angry, resentful	Stayed an extra half-hour at the gym
Trying on swimsuits	I look disgusting, maybe I'll move to Alaska until fall.	Disgusted	Bought a new outfit that didn't show skin
Getting on the scale	How can I be at the same weight? I starved all week!	Depressed, mad	Ate a piece of cake and felt a little better
Eating a meal	Ugh, my clothes are tight. I've probably gained five pounds.	Frustrated, anxious	Planned to work out harder the next day
Being tired	I'm fat and ugly and I'm tired of trying to look better.	Depressed, tired	Ate a piece of cake and felt better

2. Once you begin to understand the kind of thinking that leads to unproductive behavior, start substituting realistic statements. When you think, "I bet she never sits home on Friday night," stop yourself. Then, calmly and gently tell yourself, "This woman's physical appearance has nothing to do with me and I don't deserve to treat myself this way." Add another one: "There are lots of fish in the sea, and I will find a date who appreciates all the parts of me." The trick is that the statement must be realistic and yet not negative. Rather than, "I have no date for Friday's rock concert," substitute a positive thought: "I can order a ticket and go on my own, or I can order tickets and invite my friends to join me."

3. Develop an action plan to change some of the behaviors that get you into trouble. For instance, there's nothing wrong with an occasional shopping spree to boost your body image, but if you find your bills piling up, make a list of other ways to nurture yourself when you're feeling blue—a funny movie, aromatherapy, or reading a trashy novel on the front porch.

Psychobabble

If you find yourself obsessing over something, reframe your thoughts and you'll take away their power. For example, a parent who obsessively worried about her child's safety began calling them her "worry thoughts" and, when they popped up, she just waited for them to subside. Before she labeled them, she interpreted them as rational concerns and would spend hours either planning for her child's safety or tracking her child down to make sure nothing had happened to him or her.

These three simple steps will change your mind forever—if you do them over and over again. While they take a lot of work at first (think how long it takes to debug a computer program), over time, those thoughts that trip you up now will dissolve, and your mind will be freer to see life, and yourself, more realistically.

Find Meaning in Your Life

I have my midlife crisis all planned out. I'm going to buy a Harley-Davidson and ride it all by myself. I'm also going to learn to belly dance. I'm going to cut off my hair and still feel feminine. Yep, I'm going to knock your socks off.

Which means I probably won't need therapy. However, if I do, I'm going to look up a humanist to help me confront the question, "Is this all there is?" Humanist therapists will help you figure out where you've been and where you're going, and generally help you feel pretty good about whatever you decide. Humanistic therapies can be helpful if you're trying to make meaning out of your life and your relationships and just can't seem to do it by yourself.

At the core of the humanistic movement is the assumption that we are all growing and changing and that, despite our particular conditions of nature and nurture, we have the freedom to control our destiny by creating our own values and using them to guide our decisions. With this freedom comes a certain amount of responsibility, and part of the therapeutic work is taking responsibility for ourselves and our own happiness.

Happy Humanists

Carl Rogers and Fritz Perls were two pioneers in applying humanistic principles to therapy. Carl Rogers in particular was a major influence in shifting the focus from the

Insight

While psychology schools tend to favor one therapy orientation over another, most clinicians are eclectic. They are much more likely to match the treatment strategy to the presenting problem rather than trying to fit all of the square pegs into the round hole of their theoretical orientation.

therapist to the client. Take the time to ask a client what's wrong, Rogers believed, and he just might tell you. Furthermore, Rogers believed a client is the "expert" on his or her life and comes into therapy with a built-in desire to behave in healthy and productive ways. Provide a therapeutic place and maintain a consistent, positive regard for the client, and you can sit back and watch him grow. This therapeutic strategy evolved into what we call client-centered therapy.

Thespian Therapy

Fritz Perls, the father of Gestalt therapy, took another approach. Perls brought past conflicts directly into the therapy office and asked clients to resolve them by acting out their fantasies and dreams. If your mother died and you have unresolved feelings toward her, Perls might ask you to talk to the empty chair as if it were your mother and say all those things you either couldn't or wouldn't say to her face. He then might ask you to switch chairs and respond as your mother would—or as you wish she had. Completing this "unfinished business" would then free you to put your energy toward growth and self-actualization.

We're All in This Together

When it comes to relationship problems, it takes two (and sometimes more) to tango. When marital problems are involved, couples therapy is much more effective than individual therapy. And, in therapy, the couple is the client. The focus is on diagnosing and solving the interpersonal problems that are making the relationship sick.

Insight

While not a formal "treatment," self-help groups can be a powerful support for clients and family members struggling with addictions, mental disorders, and major life transitions. It is estimated that there are 500,000 self-help groups and 15 million people attend one each week.

Sometimes, the whole family needs help. In family therapy, the client is the whole family, and each family member is treated as part of the larger relationship system. A family therapist helps each family member see the issues or patterns that are creating problems for one or more of them. The focus is on altering the interactions as a unit, rather than focusing on any one family member. In addition, therapy focuses on situational problems rather than personality flaws or individual pathology. The family therapist might look at how one family member's eating disorder is affecting everyone's feelings and relationships, while also looking at how family interactions "feed" the eating disorder.

If you don't think families can be powerful influences on individual behavior, think about the last time you went home for the holidays. A few minutes off the plane, and we revert back to old patterns of behavior we thought (hoped) were long outgrown. We find ourselves overreacting to a sibling's ridiculous teasing or wolfing down that third piece of cake because we'd feel guilty for turning down Dad's cooking. While we never completely out-swim the quirks of old relationship patterns, family therapy can keep us from drowning in the undertow.

But Does It Work?

Of course therapy works! Why else would I be writing this book? Aside from Woody Allen, most of the people I know who have been to therapy know it works. Don't take my word for it, though; thousands of studies have been done, and here's what they have to say:

➤ *Psychotherapy works.* About 75 percent to 80 percent of people in therapy show greater improvement than the average person in a control group.

➤ *All techniques work equally well.* Each of the therapies we've discussed— psychodynamic, cognitive, behavioral, humanistic, couples and family—appear to be equally effective.

➤ *Some therapies work better for some problems.* Fear and anxiety seem to respond best to behavioral and cognitive therapies, humanistic therapies do wonders for self-esteem, and psychodynamic therapy can help underachievers.

➤ *The therapist matters.* Some therapists do much better than others, and the difference seems to be in their personalities rather than in their credentials. Therapists who are warm, understanding, and strongly motivated to help are much more effective with their clients.

Therapy can make our lives better, and depending on what we need, it offers a choice of types and techniques. In the next chapter, we'll get to the bottom line of the therapy business. You'll find out what you can change and what you can't by looking at some provocative ideas, such as the conflict between destiny and free will, outgrowing the challenges of your childhood, breaking bad habits, and getting rid of bad feelings.

The Least You Need to Know

➤ For therapy to be effective, you must have a good relationship with your therapist.

➤ There are several types of talk therapy, including psychodynamic psychotherapy, behavioral therapy, cognitive therapy, and existential-humanistic therapy.

➤ Psychoanalytic psychotherapy is a long process that seeks to remove unconscious blocks, while behavior therapy helps you change bad habits and reduce your fears.

➤ Cognitive therapy focuses on changing the false beliefs and unhealthy attitudes that lead to unhappy behavior, and the humanist therapeutic approach helps you find more meaning in your life.

➤ Couples and family therapy focuses on the dynamics of the group rather than the personality of the individual.

➤ Most therapists use a variety of types of therapy, depending upon the client and the problem to be resolved.

Chapter 23

What You Can Change, and What You Can't

In This Chapter

➤ Making the most of everyday feelings

➤ How hotheaded are you?

➤ Exploring your sexuality

➤ Getting in touch with your natural appetite

➤ Recovering from your childhood

Like millions of Americans, Suzanne is dieting. She's been dieting since she was 10 years old, when her parents, worried about the social disadvantages of being chubby, started her on a diet. But the diets have never worked. When she graduated from high school, Suzanne was five-foot-five and weighed 160 pounds. Now 28, she weighs 170. And all her life, Suzanne has counted calories, weighed portions, watched fat grams, and drunk diet shakes. She's even tried private weight-control therapists. Each time, she loses weight and it returns with a vengeance. After years of dieting, Suzanne feels like a complete failure.

Joel, on the other hand, feels great. For years, though, Joel felt different from other boys. By age 10, he realized he was gay—a realization that terrified and distressed him. Growing up in a small town, he didn't know of anyone else who was gay but he was certainly aware of the local attitude toward "queers." As a young adult, he tried hiding his feelings and dating women. He also tried psychotherapy, drugs, and alcohol. Finally, at 30 Joel came out of the closet and embraced his homosexuality. For Joel, that's when life truly began.

Over the past 30 years, we've been bombarded with self-improvement advice. The number of self-help books has mushroomed along with the belief that if you just find the right book, therapist, or technique, you can change anything about yourself and your life. But is this true? In the past 10 years, we've also identified genes that may predispose us to obesity, depression, schizophrenia—even suicide. Perhaps our nature is less changeable than we might think.

In this chapter, we'll examine the basics of self-improvement. We'll start out exploring everyday feelings, when we should listen to them, and how we can chase them away. You'll discover how much your childhood affects the rest of your life, how much of your relationship with food and sex is preset, and what you can do to promote a healthy state of mind.

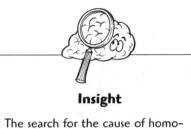

Insight

The search for the cause of homosexuality continues. While a 1993 study claimed to have found a male homosexuality "gene" on the X chromosome, a 1998 study did not support it. However, researchers have concluded from studies of twins that sexual orientation may be partially linked to genes.

Walking the Balance Beam

"God grant me the serenity to accept the things I cannot change, the courage to change the things I can, and the wisdom to know the difference." Although this "Serenity Prayer" is most often associated with the 12-step recovery movement, the advice was originally given by Friedrich Oetinger back in the eighteenth century. And it's darned good advice today.

The Advantages of Acceptance

Of course, following this advice is a lot easier once you've figured out what you can change and what you can't. Why does Suzanne feel like such a failure and Joel feel like he's finally succeeded? For one thing, Joel has come to believe his sexual orientation is not a "choice" and that the best gift he can give himself is self-acceptance and a life experience that is congruent with who he is. On the other hand, Suzanne believes that her weight is something she can control, that her problem is a lack of willpower, and if she just tried hard enough, she could do it.

Suzanne has bought into the self-improvement movement. Many psychotherapists have promoted the belief that we can improve virtually everything about ourselves if we are willing to put enough sweat into it. A glance through my community education schedule backs this up: It lists classes like "Eating to Lose Weight," "Discovering Your Psychic Pathway," and "How to Disappear and Begin a New Life." (Hey, I live in California, what can I say?)

"Can Do" or "It's All My Fault"

Living in an era of personal control has brought us many benefits. And the "can do" attitude has always been a unique part of the American character. If our society viewed drinking as an irreversible character flaw, we wouldn't have AA meetings. A society that views depression as arising from evil spirits or self-indulgence would not have pioneered research into antidepressants or invented cognitive behavioral therapy. If we don't think we can change ourselves, we may not try.

The biological movement, however, is more pessimistic about human flexibility. If mental illness is really physical illness, and emotions and mood are determined by brain chemistry, then self-help books, support groups, and psychotherapy are a complete waste of time. Medication might help correct your brain chemistry, but essentially your anatomy is destiny, and the best we can do is to help you cope with the genes you were born with. The biological movement has done a lot to take away some of the blame associated with mental illness. And, as you're about to see, it completely cured at least one.

Psychobabble

Check out Dr. Martin Seligman's groundbreaking book, *What You Can Change and What You Can't*, and find your balance between self-improvement and self-acceptance.

Curing the Insanity Plague

The worst epidemic of mental illness in recorded history began a few years after Columbus discovered the New World. It afflicted thousands of people, including Henry VIII and Randolph Churchill. The symptoms of this illness began with weakness in the arms and legs, followed by odd behavior, then delusions of grandeur, and eventually complete paralysis, and finally death. By 1884, the insane asylums of Europe were filled with men in the final stages of this disease, shrieking obscenities.

The Syphilis Scourge

The dean of German psychiatry, Wilhelm Griesinger, believed that this illness, called *paresis,* was a result of loose living, particularly inhaling bad cigars. A young physician named Richard von Kraft-Ebing was one of the few who believed it came from syphilis. It was common knowledge at the time that a person could only get syphilis once and that the trademark of this disease was a pox or lesion that developed upon

Shrink Rap

Paresis is a disease of the brain caused by a syphilis-caused infection of the central nervous system and characterized by dementia and paralysis.

Brain Buster

Are we in the middle of a depression epidemic? If you were born in the second half of the twentieth century, you're 10 times more likely to suffer from depression than people born in the first half. And, you're likely to get depressed 10 years sooner.

infection. In one of the most daring experiments in history, Kraft-Ebing injected the syphilis virus into nine men who were exhibiting symptoms of paresis. Not a single man showed signs of infection; as Richard had suspected, they already had the disease.

Supporting evidence that general paresis was caused by syphilis came pouring in and after a generation of research into finding a cure, the most common mental illness in the nineteenth century had been eradicated, as was the moral depravity explanation that had plagued it. Somehow, I don't think a great self-help book, therapy, or a support group would have had the same effect.

Balancing Between Science and Self-Help

As you can see, both sides of the self-improvement coin offer us some benefits. On the one hand, the belief that we can change whatever we don't like motivates us to problem solve. On the other hand, the biological movement keeps us from beating our heads against the wall or blaming someone for something over which we have no control. If we understand that genes do have an influence, we can also shift gears away from moral judgments and look to ways we can better cope with our gene pools.

It's Storming Inside

One of the great American myths is that we can feel good all the time. Not true. Just as we cannot avoid our genetic makeup, we cannot avoid our feelings. Yesterday, I was mad that my automotive repair guy went ahead and finished my repairs without calling me with a new estimate first. I felt sad thinking about my mom, who recently passed away. And when my son, Zachary, slept much later than he usually does, I felt a moment of pure terror at the thought that he was critically ill or something was wrong.

You Can't Feel Good All the Time

Every single day, we experience, at least for a few moments, three emotions we don't like—anger, sadness, and anxiety. These are our "bad" feelings. When we feel them temporarily, they're uncomfortable. When they get out of control, we call them "mental illness."

People often go to therapy to get rid of bad feelings and replace them with good ones. But before we take a look at what you can change about your feelings, we should also look at when you shouldn't try to.

The Language of Negative Emotions

Most of the time, your moods and feelings are status reports; they give you important information about your psychological well-being. There are times when anger, sadness, or fear carries a message and, as uncomfortable as it may be, you should listen. Often the message is that you need to change your situation instead of changing the way you feel about it. Each emotion has a specific message and is likely to urge you to take certain action:

➤ Anxiety warns you of danger. It urges you to search for ways to escape and rehearse possible coping strategies. For example, anxiety before a speech may encourage you to prepare more effectively, to mentally rehearse the words as you're waiting for your introduction, or to fantasize about calling in sick and ducking out.

➤ Sadness over the loss of something you care about urges you to crawl into your shell and lick your wounds—to deinvest in what you have lost, and ultimately save up your energy so you can learn to live without it.

➤ Anger signals that you've been trespassed against. It urges you to fight, strike out in some way, or get rid of the trespasser.

Let's take a look at when you should listen to these everyday feelings and, when they aren't helpful, what you can do to shut them up.

A Regular Case of the Nerves

The "jitters," as we often call everyday anxiety, is like the oil light on the dashboard. When these feelings start flashing, they're warning you to pay attention or else you might be heading for a breakdown. Mild, everyday anxiety is your mind's way of searching for what may be about to go wrong. Without your conscious consent, it continually scans your life for imperfections and, when it finds one, it worries about it.

Through anxiety your mind tries to prevent larger problems by making you aware of their possibility and giving you time to do a little advance planning. It may even help you avoid them. Disconnect this "warning sign" and you

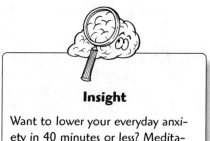

Insight

Want to lower your everyday anxiety in 40 minutes or less? Meditation and/or relaxation techniques quite reliably lower everyday anxiety levels.

may be less distracted and more comfortable for a while, but it may ultimately cost you a major overhaul. Most anxiety, however, is energy-draining and time-consuming and needs to be relieved. There are three hallmarks signaling that your anxiety has lost its usefulness as a warning and become a burden instead: intensity, irrationality, and paralysis.

Intensity

Does anxiety dominate your life? Does it prevent you from doing things you would like to do? If you're anxious more often than not, your anxiety is causing more harm than it's preventing. And if the level of your anxiety is so intense that you can't focus on anything except the worries that are causing the anxiety, it's time to do something about it.

Rational vs. Irrational

Is your anxiety out of proportion to the danger you fear? My fear of cockroaches is certainly irrational because it is much greater than any physical damage a cockroach could cause me. On the other hand, a working single mother with three children has good reason to be afraid when coworkers start getting laid off. It is hoped her anxiety will help her take steps to protect herself and her family.

Mobilizing or Paralyzing

When anxiety is too strong, it blocks effective problem solving. If your anxiety spurs you to effective action, then it may be working for you. If your fear of a life-threatening illness prevents you from getting regular medical checkups, on the other hand, it's maladaptive.

If your anxiety is moderate and not irrational or paralyzing in some way, you may be better off listening to it instead of trying to make it go away. Sometimes, it pays to channel your energy into improving your outer life, rather than your emotional life.

Digging Yourself Out of the Dumps

In Chapter 18, "Mood Swingers and Scaredy Cats," we talked a lot about the toll that the various forms of clinical depression take on those people who suffer from them. But what about everyday funks—the times when a setback hits you pretty hard or the gusto is gone? Is there any way to beat the everyday blues?

First of all, the blues, like anxiety, can be a signal that something in your life needs changing. Getting to know what triggers your blues can be a powerful way to take more control of your life. Here are three good ways to minimize the chances of the blues coloring your life, at least on a regular basis.

Psychobabble

Blues musicians know what to do when you're feeling down. "Gimme a Pig Foot and a Bottle of Beer," sang blues legend Bessie Smith. While the cholesterol or the alcohol in that remedy might prove worrisome today, listening to some lowdown gutbucket blues can actually lift the spirit.

Deal With What's Up

Handle here-and-now issues as they come up. Disputes, frustrations, and disappointments can eat away at your joie de vivre until you have the blahs and don't know why. If you and your partner have a fight, think about how it can be resolved. Does your relationship need to be renegotiated? What's up with work? Are you unhappy but afraid to talk to your boss? Learning effective communication, negotiation, and assertiveness skills can help you avoid the big mood roller coaster that you're bound to ride if you keep putting off solving life's problems.

Take Time to Grieve

You can't always change what happens to you, but you can certainly influence how you're going to recover from it. Grief is a necessary kind of "blues" and the sooner you allow yourself to mourn your loss, the sooner you'll get over it. Give yourself time to be sad about a breakup, divorce, job loss, or death and get plenty of support. Spend time alone saying goodbye and rethinking how you want your life to change now that your role is different. Unresolved grief can lead to serious depression.

Learn Optimism

People who see the glass as half full are happier than those who see it as half empty. While depression can be partly due to a neurochemical imbalance, a negative explanatory style is something you learn—and can unlearn.

Mild depression can be caused by pessimistic habits of thinking, of seeing the causes of failure as permanent, pervasive (it's going to ruin everything), and personal (it's all my fault). Learning to dispute these negative thoughts is a powerful antidote to pessimism. Not sure how to do it? Think of how you "straighten out" a friend who's in a major funk. Start telling yourself the same kind words you'd tell a friend or family member in the same situation.

Insight

Develop an optimistic outlook on life by keeping a daily gratitude journal. Write down five things you're thankful for that happened during the day. You'll be surprised how remembering those little rays of sunshine can brighten even the darkest hour.

Mad as a Hornet

Anger is one of the reasons we're at the top of the animal kingdom. To win the top-dog spot, our forebears didn't just rely on their brains to make weapons. They relied on their hot tempers to use them. Anger primed our ancestors to defend their turf and protect their offspring. And we're still doing it—sometimes just as crudely.

Anger starts with the thought that you've been trespassed against: "She's walking all over me," "He can't tell me what to do," "That's mine and no one is going to take it away." You feel angry when you believe that someone is invading your territory and stepping on your turf.

Anger also stirs up your body. Your stomach churns and your blood pressure rises. Your entire nervous system gears itself for battle, and you attack. While you don't usually think your actions through if you're really mad, the goal of the attack is a rational one: You are going to end the trespass. What you actually do with your anger, however, might be irrational; you might lash out, yell, call the person names, or slam the door and storm out of the room.

Are You a Hothead?

Did you get a few too many of the hot temper genes? Answer this quiz to see if you have your anger under control or if your anger is controlling you. As with earlier quizzes, in the space available, enter the number that best reflects your response to each of the statements in the quiz.

Anger Assessment Quiz

1 = almost never   3 = often
2 = sometimes   4 = almost always

1. When I get mad I say things I later regret. _____

2. When I get frustrated I feel like hitting someone. _____

3. I have a bad temper. _____

4. I feel annoyed when I am not given recognition for doing good work. _____

5. My quick temper has caused trouble in my relationships with the people I love. _____

6. People I know tease me about being a "hothead." _____

7. I feel really angry when I am criticized in front of other people. _____

8. I get irritated when someone isn't following what I am trying to say. _____

9. I fly off the handle. _____

10. I get angry when I am held back by the mistakes of others. _____

How'd You Score?

Total your responses and check here to see what your scoring can tell you about your temper.

15 or less: You are less angry than at least 75 percent of the people you know. Give yourself a pat on the back and spread your calm demeanor around. We need it! Have you considered teaching stress management or yoga?

16 to 20: You're in the average range, meaning people get on your nerves about as much as they do the rest of us. You aren't a hothead, however, and generally your temper doesn't cause you too much trouble.

21 to 25: You aren't a complete hothead but I wouldn't light a match around you. Seriously, you are three quarters of the way up Anger Mountain and 75 percent of your colleagues and friends are less angry than you. You might want to find better ways to keep your cool in hot situations so your energy isn't wasted on unnecessary fires.

Over 25: You're in danger of blowing a gasket! You need to chill out and find ways to handle your anger without getting yourself in trouble. Trust me, life doesn't have to be this hard.

Cooling a Hot Temper

A hot temper is a quick way to burn up any relationship. Not only do impulsive expressions of anger hurt others, they're bad for us. Chronic hostility can put us at greater risk for heart trouble than keeping our mouth shut. And children who see parents fighting constantly are more likely to get depressed and feel insecure.

On the other hand, passively standing by and letting someone walk all over you isn't healthy, either. While the suppression of anger does not appear to have the negative health effects we once thought, putting up with a bad situation over time surely does.

The most effective way to handle anger is to try to observe it from a distance, acknowledge its presence, and let it subside before you take action to remedy the situation that caused it in the first place. Here are five anger strategies that might help:

➤ Keep an anger diary. For one week, act as an observer of yourself and keep track of every time you feel irritated, annoyed, frustrated, or angry. Write down what happened to precipitate it, how it felt, what you thought, and what you did.

➤ Pay close attention to the thoughts and feelings you have when you get angry. Write down your physical warning signs that you are getting angry. Learn to rate your anger as it builds, from a 1 (mildly irritated) to a 5 (about to blow a fuse).

➤ Take a time out when you get to a 3 on your anger scale. This will allow your body's physical reaction to subside and clear your head to resolve the situation.

➤ Be open to feedback from others. Maybe you don't want to hear others say, "You're losing it," but in the heat of anger, they may be more objective than you.

➤ Examine your relationship beliefs. A hot temper often hides unrealistic and unattainable standards for oneself and others.

Psychobabble

Children who watch films of adults fighting are much less disturbed when the fight ends with a clear resolution. Most couples fight in front of their children at some point. If it happens (rarely, one hopes), go out of your way to resolve your fight in front of your children. And be sure to let your child know the fight is not his or her fault.

Can We Recover from Childhood?

Many failings of adult life are attributed to misfortunes in our childhood. Inability to love is blamed on parental neglect; commitment phobia is attributed to our parents' bitter custody fight. Indeed, much self-help is based on the premise that adulthood is a process of recovery from childhood and we can cure it by coming to grips with our early traumas.

The Contributions of Childhood Experience

How much of what happens to us really shapes our personality and determines our destiny? Many of us grow up with the belief that bad childhood experiences leave their mark. And, certainly, such experiences are painful when they happen. I can think back to a few childhood memories and, even today, feel my stomach tighten. But do they actually leave us crippled for life?

When researchers began looking at the impact of childhood on adult adjustment, they expected to find confirmation that physical and sexual abuse, parental death or divorce, and other traumas wreak lifelong havoc on the children who experience them. And they did find some evidence, but not as much as you would think. Childhood isn't destiny.

For example, losing a mother before age 11 does make you more vulnerable to depression in adulthood, but only if you are female and even then only about half the time. If your parents divorce, there is a slight disruptive effect on later childhood and adolescence, but the problems lessen with age and may not be detectable in adults. And the trauma of dealing with divorce is also mediated by the changing norms of society. Fifty years ago, a child coming from a "broken home" might have felt more deprived than today's kids who consider it no big deal to have stepparents, single parents, or some alternative family.

Insight

Adults are pretty resilient, too. While 95 percent of rape survivors experience symptoms of post-traumatic stress disorder within two weeks, about 75 percent of rape victims have recovered fully after four years. For some, it takes three months, for others, up to two years.

When Childhood Goes Horribly Wrong

While physical and sexual abuse in childhood can certainly influence adult personality, we overcome them far more often than once believed. In fact, researchers have been astonished to find that bad childhood events do not always lead to adult troubles.

Studies of adult adjustment show a relatively small relationship between what happened to us as a child and adult depression, drug abuse, sexual problems, anxiety, or anger. If there's one thing studies show of children who have experienced the most horrible trauma, it's that children are amazingly resilient. In fact, it is this resilience that may be the unexplored chapter of the human spirit.

The Genetic Component

While studies show we can triumph over a bad childhood, they also show that our genes have a definite impact on the way we turn out. Most personality studies find remarkable effects of genes. Identical twins reared apart end up being far more similar as adults than fraternal twins reared together. This shows up on a number of personality variables—depression, alcoholism, job satisfaction, intelligence, anger, and general well-being, to name just a few. If you want to blame your parents for your problems, you can blame them for the genes they gave you, but it isn't fair to blame the way they treated you as a child. And when it comes to conquering your problems, you're probably better off looking in the mirror and reciting, "The buck stops here."

What's Your Story?

Just because childhood isn't destiny doesn't mean you shouldn't take a look at it. Understanding your childhood is a valuable tool in discovering yourself. While serious psychological disorders don't necessarily follow childhood trauma, relationship habits and other patterns of behavior can continue from childhood into adulthood.

Numerous studies show the effectiveness of telling the stories of our lives when we've experienced traumatic events. This is not necessarily to find out why things are the way they are today, but to see how they were at the time and what meaning we want to give them. From a tapestry of previous mistakes you can weave a new life—and we don't have to know why the mistakes happened to change the way you represent them. Future additions to the tapestry are not determined by what was woven before. You are the weaver and although you can't always change the threads with which you work, you can change the design of what comes next.

Accepting Sexual Orientation

Let's say your life's dream is to be a grandparent. You had a great relationship with your grandmother and have always looked forward to the day when you could hold your own grandchild in your arms and pass along the family tradition of great-grandparenting. Then, one day, your 15-year-old son comes to you for a heart-to-heart talk. "Mom," he says. "I'm gay."

You love your son, but you're confused at how he can know his sexual orientation at this age. What about the prejudice and discrimination he will face in a society that touted AIDS as a moral punishment? And what about those grandchildren? Surely, he can change his mind. Maybe therapy can help.

Psychobabble

Up to 80 percent of gay and lesbian youth experience frequent verbal and sometimes physical assault because of their sexual orientation. In one study, 44 percent had been threatened with violence and 17 percent said they had been physically assaulted. Is it any wonder that homosexual adolescent males are at least three times as likely to attempt suicide as heterosexual peers?

More than one parent has sent a child to *"repar-ative"* or *"conversion"* therapy in an attempt to change his or her sexual orientation. While the jury is still out on what causes homosexuality, the verdict is definitely in on whether or not it can be changed.

On the 25th anniversary of the removal of homosexuality as a mental disorder from the DSM (*Diagnostic & Statistical Manual of Mental Disorders*), the American Psychiatric Association (APA) unanimously accepted a position state-ment rejecting "reparative" or "conversion" ther-apy. There is no scientific evidence that this type of therapy is effective in changing a person's sex-ual orientation, but there's plenty of evidence that it can be destructive. "Reparative therapy runs the risk of harming patients by causing depression, anxiety and self-destructive behavior," the APA proclaimed at the end of 1998.

Shrink Rap

Reparative or **conversion therapy** is the attempt to use psychological techniques to convince someone to change his or her sexual orientation. Studies do not support its use or its effectiveness.

What Turns You On?

Okay, we've pretty much established that our sexual orientation is here to stay. But, what about sexual preferences—the parts of the body that turn us on, the scenes we fantasize when we masturbate or imagine as we're climaxing? For boys, sexual prefer-ences have their beginnings in later childhood and are often wrapped around first encounters with sex. A "wet dream" about a girl's breasts, or a sexually arousing "play" session between two 11-year-olds, and sexual preferences can be set. Mastur-bation seals them in.

Studies show that the process is subtler if you're female. While some of us may get turned on by the sight of a V-shaped torso, as a group we're less likely to be totally captivated by a specific part of the male anatomy the way a guy can be a "breast" or a "leg" man.

Women are more likely to acquire erotic preferences for scenarios involving plot lines, intimacy, and character. Most of us get turned on by slow dancing and poetry and consider "good buns" simply the icing on the cake. No matter how we get them, though, our sexual preferences are amazingly resilient. For many of us, our adolescent preferences stick throughout our lives—although we can certainly add on!

Polishing Up on Your Gender Role

A friend of mine is an anesthesiologist determined to raise her daughter and son androgynously. Recently, her four-year-old daughter came home from nursery school.

"Mom," she said, I've decided I want to be a nurse when I grow up." "That's great," my friend said. "Yeah," her daughter continued. "I thought about being a doctor but then girls can't be them." You can only imagine my friend's frustration!

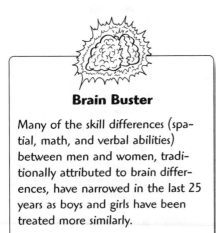

Brain Buster

Many of the skill differences (spatial, math, and verbal abilities) between men and women, traditionally attributed to brain differences, have narrowed in the last 25 years as boys and girls have been treated more similarly.

In the United States, boys and girls are firmly entrenched in gender stereotypes by the age of four. Boys are playing more with boys and girls are playing more with girls. They know the sex stereotypes for dress, toys, jobs, and games. Even children who are reared androgynously retain their stereotypes. (See Chapter 13, "Me, Myself, and I," for more on gender bending.)

However, gender roles are not deep, nor are they unchangeable. In later childhood, we still have our stereotypes about crying or kindness, but they are much weaker than the early childhood toy stereotypes. In fact, the only difference between the behavior of boys and girls as they get older is that boys are much more physically aggressive.

In later childhood and adulthood, children who are raised by androgynous parents tend to become androgynous themselves. Supporting diverse interests for boys and girls, and exposing your child to a variety of roles, works in the long run. You're just going to go through a few frustrating moments before it kicks in.

Making Peace with Your Body Size

Few things have become such a moral issue in this country as weight. Across my desk flows a constant stream of medical news articles with titles like "Obesity: An American Epidemic," "Drug Company Releases New Obesity Drug," or "Obesity Linked to Yet Another Disease." Understandably, the medical community is concerned by the fact that Americans, despite endless media attention about the connection between obesity and disease, continue to get fatter.

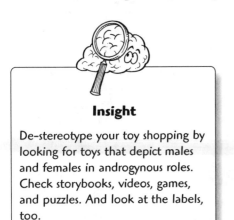

Insight

De-stereotype your toy shopping by looking for toys that depict males and females in androgynous roles. Check storybooks, videos, games, and puzzles. And look at the labels, too.

The Risks of Obesity

How much medical risk does obesity really have? We're not completely sure. If you're at least 30 percent above the normal range for your height and age, you are more likely to have health problems and be at greater risk for a premature death. If you're 10 percent to 30 percent above a "healthy" weight, the primary concern is your vulnerability to diabetes, high blood pressure, and other conditions. Being fit is probably a better health indicator than numbers on a scale and, lest we forget, if you are substantially underweight, you are also more likely to die early.

The Fallacy of Fad Dieting

The problem with all the preaching about health and weight is that the touted solution, dieting, is risky as well. As you know, yo-yo dieting may be as unhealthy as being overweight. In addition, dieting changes the way people deal with food. Dieters become more preoccupied with food, and even dream about it. The body starts hoarding energy, and normal activities use up fewer calories. It may even take fewer calories for a dieter to put on a pound than for a normal person.

A sizable number of fad dieters wind up heavier than they were in the first place. Fat cells love to hang out in those comfy places like the hips and then stand around screaming for the next fix. Fat cells, unlike other cells, demand more food. In other words, the heavier you are, the more fat cells you have, the hungrier you get. It's a truly vicious cycle.

You know it's a fad (diet) when:

➤ It recommends miracle foods that burn fat.

➤ It recommends strange quantities of only one food or one food group.

➤ It recommends rigid menus at specific times of the day.

➤ It recommends specific food combinations.

➤ It *neglects* to recommend exercise.

➤ It promises weight loss of three pounds a week or more.

Changing Your Relationship with Food

Overeating is not the same as overweight—skinny people overeat, too. Overeating is eating past the point of feeling full. There's a big difference between a weight problem and an eating problem. And, with some work, you can change your relationship with food to overcome both.

The Antidiet

Ironically enough, the way to do it is the opposite of dieting. Dieting, by its nature, teaches you not to trust your body, but to follow external rules about fat grams, calories, or some other nifty diet trick. Changing your relationship with food, on the other hand, requires you to learn to trust your body to let you know when you are hungry and when you are full.

Believe it or not, there's a healthy eater inside every one of us—if we can just find him or her. Babies are naturally healthy eaters—I've been around a lot of them and I've yet to see one go on a binge. Babies and children, if they're left alone, will eat a pretty balanced diet. Some days, four-year old Zachary eats us out of house and home and the next day he's pickier than a bird. He'll want cheese quesadillas every meal for a week and then lay off them for a month. Over time, we're coming to trust our son to set his own meal plan. We, of course, have a say in what is served and when, but he's in charge of how much.

Psychobabble

Check out some of these bogus weight-loss diets that were said to be approved by the American Heart Association: the all-you-can-eat cabbage diet, the three-day diet (lose 10 pounds in three days by eating vanilla ice cream, hot dogs, eggs, and cheddar cheese), and the grapefruit diet!

Getting Back in Touch with Your Natural Eater

While you're rediscovering the healthy eater hiding within yourself, there are some behavior changes you can make to speed the process along. For example, don't do anything else while you eat (such as read a book or watch TV) because it will distract you from your bodily signals. Also, sit down at the table when you eat. Never eat standing up at the kitchen counter or by the refrigerator.

And pace yourself. At the start of a meal, put what you consider to be a "normal" amount of food on your plate and then sit down and eat it. (If you don't know what's "normal," watch others around you.) After you've finished, wait 10 minutes and see if you're still hungry before helping yourself to another serving.

Eat a little something at least every five hours. Your body gets hungry about then and if you wait too long, you're setting yourself up for a feeding frenzy.

If you've eaten recently and get the munchies, keep a journal about your feelings before you hit the snack bar. A lot of emotional eating is the use of food to soothe or fix bad feelings. If you can begin to see what your "triggers" are, you can begin to develop other ways of handling difficult feelings. (See Chapter 22, "Just Keep Talkin'," for more about behavior triggers.)

If you need the company of others, join a support group like Overeaters Anonymous. And by all means, exercise regularly. Many people find that exercise gets them in touch with their bodies and they're much more likely to pay attention to bodily hunger and fullness cues when they're exercising regularly. Make it something you enjoy so you will look forward to doing it.

Most important of all is this final piece of advice: *Do not diet.* And, do not restrict your food choices. Nothing is "bad" in moderation.

The Wisdom's in Knowing the Difference

We can change attitudes and relationships, but not biology. The wisdom is in knowing the difference. While we can't always change our feelings, we can change how we use and interpret them. We can't change other people, but we can change how we relate to them. We can't change our natural weight range, but we can change our relationship with food. There's a message here, that perhaps we should not be so hard on ourselves. That perhaps true mental health is the right balance between being the best we can and accepting the person we are. In the next chapter, we'll take a look at some surprising research on a force that, if we aren't careful, can easily throw us off balance—the power of social influence.

The Least You Need to Know

➤ The self-improvement movement tells us we can change anything, but there are things we cannot change—we need to know the difference.

➤ Everyday moods and feelings give us status reports on our mental health. If we listen to them, we can learn whether we need to change our situation or our feelings about the situation.

➤ We cannot blame our childhood for everything we don't like about our personality; childhood has less impact on adulthood than once thought.

➤ Our sexual identity is virtually impossible to change, but we can outgrow our traditional gender roles.

➤ The best way to lose weight is to love your body and change your attitudes about food and dieting.

Part 6

Can't We All Just Get Along?

Maybe John Donne said it best: "No man [or woman, for that matter] is an island ..."
Every one of us participates in all sorts of interpersonal relationships, and the quality
of those relationships can have a real impact on the quality of our lives. From resisting
peer pressure that urges us to conform to discovering what goes into finding the great
love of our lives, it's how we handle relationships that makes all the difference. And
that's what this final section of the book is all about. When you're finished, you'll
have a firm understanding of the way that relationships shape you—and how you can
make your relationships stronger, healthier, and more fulfilling.

Chapter 24

You Can't Live with 'Em

In This Chapter

➤ Discover what a devilish situation can make you do

➤ Following the leader or setting the trend

➤ Learning the three R's of social psychology

➤ Nonconforming can be fun

➤ Find out how to get other people to come to the rescue

We'd all like to believe we would be good and heroic people, no matter what, but how can we know until we're put to the test? The best way to predict how somebody will act, in any situation, is to look at the way others actually did behave when faced with the same circumstances.

Welcome to the study of *social psychology,* which investigates how people affect one other's behavior. In this chapter, you'll take a look at how social settings influence how we think, feel, and act and you'll discover how we all use our social world to provide clues to guide our behavior.

Shrink Rap

Social psychology is the study of how people are influenced by their interactions and relationships with other people.

Of Prison Guards and Prisoners

Go to jail. Go *directly* to jail. Do not pass Go. Do not collect $200. This command may not upset you too much if you're playing Monopoly, but what if you really had to go to jail? Would being a prisoner change your behavior or could you rise above the circumstances? The answer may surprise you as much as it did the researchers in charge of the Stanford Prison Experiment.

In this study, a group of college students were asked to volunteer for a prison experiment. The participants were selected because psychological tests had shown them to be law-abiding, emotionally stable, physically healthy, and "normal." Each one was randomly assigned to play the role of a prisoner or a guard, and over the next several days they lived in a mock prison that was virtually identical to a real one.

When they played the role of prison guards, normally nice-guy students began behaving aggressively, sometimes even sadistically. The students assigned to be prisoners began to behave pathologically, passively resigning themselves to their unexpected fate of learned helplessness. The power of the pretend prison had created a new social reality—it became a real prison in the minds of jailers and captives alike.

The psychologists who designed the study were shocked by these results. In fact, because of the dramatic and unexpected effects, some prisoners began exhibiting extreme stress reactions and had to be released early. The psychologists decided to end the two-week experiment after only six days. Never underestimate the power of a bad situation.

Blame It on the Situation

Social psychologists understand that each individual's personality, core beliefs, and strong values are unique. They also know most of us believe that we're the captain of our ship, charting the course of our lives with only minor input from our shipmates. Psychologists recognize that we view situations as strong winds—sure, they may blow our sails around a little, but if we just batten down the hatches we can tough it out. Social psychologists realize that most of us think of ourselves this way—and they just don't buy it.

In fact, social psychologists believe that the *major* influence over our behavior is the social situation in which it occurs, a philosophy known as *situationism*. They argue that social situations can dominate our personalities no matter what our values or beliefs may be, and the mere presence of others can powerfully influence our behavior, even without our awareness. Let's take a look at three ways a situation wields power over us—rules, roles, and norms.

Play by the Rules

"No Shirt, No Shoes, No Service." "No Smoking." "No Gum Chewing During Aerobics Class." Think about it. We obey (or rebel against) social rules everyday, everywhere. As you proceed through your normal day, you could probably make a long list of the rules that guide you, rules so much a part of your life you hardly think about them.

Take, for example, the social rules we teach our kids. I'm currently trying to teach my four-year-old, Zachary, a few of these: "Don't take presents from strangers." "Say thank-you when someone gives you a compliment." "Answer when someone talks to you." But along with the rules I'm actively trying to teach him, I'm probably also passing along a few unintentional rules, as well, like "steer clear of mom the first 10 minutes she gets up because she growls like a bear until she's had her coffee."

We all learn rules through our transactions with others. Would you use the same language when talking to your mother as you do when talking to your friends? Would you wear the same clothes to work that you do when you go out on Friday night? Pretty quickly, we learn to size up the situation and adjust our behavior accordingly. If we don't, we learn our lesson the hard way, by having to pay the consequences for inappropriate behavior.

Shrink Rap

Situationism is the assumption that situational factors can have subtle and powerful effects on our thoughts, feelings, and actions.

Insight

Take a look at *Thelma and Louise,* the first road movie about women. Not only did this film win an Oscar for best movie in 1991, it is a powerful example of how a bad situation affects behavior.

Learn Your Roles

While we're learning about rules, we're also learning about roles—the parts we're expected to play in relation to other people in our lives. The roles available to us are determined by where and how we live and work. If you're an engineer, for example, the chances that you will be a mercenary, priest, or drug pusher are greatly reduced. But the odds you'll become a member of some technical association are higher.

Of course, most of us play many different social roles every day—wife, mother, executive, friend, and exerciser. These roles can be refreshing and energizing if they are rewarding and are comfortably reconciled to one another. But they can also become confusing and upsetting if they call for conflicting behaviors. Imagine being the top executive at a company where you have to boss people around all day. At six o'clock, however, you go home and are immediately expected to be warm and nurturing. This can cause role strain, not to mention a few extra gray hairs.

You might be wondering where we learn all the rules for our roles. Like good method actors, we have learned to gauge our roles from observation, past experience, and role models. We can't rely on simply learning a repertoire of "right" behaviors—because what's "right" in one role may be all wrong in another. A tough, no-nonsense approach to business may help the company's bottom line, but it won't earn you brownie points with family members.

That's why role models can be so powerful. They provide us with clues about how to function most effectively in various situations and in various roles. In fact, whenever you find someone who is successful in a role you cherish, latch onto them and don't let go until they promise to show you the ropes!

Psychobabble

How would you feel if you gave a friend a gift and he refused to open it in front of you no matter how much you pleaded? If your friend was from Japan, such behavior would be the polite thing to do. The Japanese place a social taboo on opening gifts in the presence of the giver for fear of unintentionally hurting your feelings by failing to show sufficient appreciation.

Conform to the Norms

Norm is not just the name of the guy at the end of the bar in *Cheers*. It's also short for *normal*. When social psychologists use it, they're talking about "normal" behavior as it's defined by a particular group. And, like rules and roles, we all have to learn how to recognize, and comply with, certain social norms.

In addition to developing expectations about appropriate role behaviors, all groups develop social guidelines for how their members should act. Individuals develop a set of norms for themselves as well: Every time you adjust your behavior to get along with someone, you're adapting to his or her norms. For example, after working for a gun-toting, card-carrying member of the NRA for a while, you'll get a sense that you might be best advised to keep your arguments for gun control to yourself, at least during your annual performance review.

Social norms can enforce certain standards of conduct. A high schooler who wants to make it with the "jock-ocracy" knows not to hang out with the school "nerds." And norms often dictate dress code and lingo, and punish members who don't conform. For example, the Amish "shun" members of their sect for breaking the "plain" dress code by wearing buttons rather than the more modest snaps on their clothes, or for dating someone outside their sect.

When you become part of any group, you soon discover the norms that regulate desired behavior in that group. Your basic training comes in two ways. First, you notice that group members act the same in certain ways—those common ways of doing things are the group's social norms. Second, you observe the negative consequences that occur when someone violates one of those norms.

If you ever switched schools growing up, you know exactly what this process is all about. The kids in each school have worked out their own norms for social membership, and it can be quite an adjustment to learn new norms each time you enter a new school. My parents switched me from a public school to a private school for a year in the seventh grade and, by the time I figured out the norms in my new peer group, I was back in my old school. For someone who became a psychologist, I was a pretty slow social learner!

Norms aren't all bad. They certainly can provide you with the comfort that comes from a clear sense of knowing what to expect from others in the group. When you know the norms, you know how you're expected to dress, what your fellow group members are likely to say and do, and what type of behavior will help you gain acceptance and approval. Norms provide us all with the first steps in identifying with a group and feeling like we belong. The question, of course, is what price do we pay for belonging?

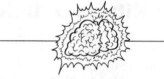

Brain Buster

Group pressure to conform can be pretty powerful. One of the best ways to avoid it is to have a strong self-concept. People who are well grounded in their identity are less influenced by even the most negative feedback from others.

The Three R's of Social School

Not all group members follow the norms all of the time. What happens when we break the behavior code of our group? How do groups rein in rebellious members, and when do they decide to cut them off? Of course, it depends on the situation— and the group. Part of a group's norms is the amount of leeway it grants it members to stray from them.

Depending on the group, your rebellion against the norms may get you some good-natured teasing, or it could get you thrown out. In any group, if you "go too far" or disagree too much with accepted beliefs or customs, you may no longer be welcome.

Even the most tolerant groups, like certain religions or churches, have their limit. And, while the degree of deviation that is tolerated varies from group to group, they all rely on the same strategies to keep group members in line. These are the three R's: ridicule, re-education, and rejection.

When I was in college, I joined a sorority that had a reputation for having all the "brainy good girls." No one ever spelled this out explicitly, but it quickly became apparent that anyone using curse words would be frowned upon. It was also clear that good grades were rewarded, and that maintaining a stellar reputation was an unspoken pledge promise we all were expected to keep.

Sure, there were a few partyers on the sorority floor, but they weren't part of the "in" clique and they certainly didn't brag about their hangovers at sorority meetings. In fact, they would be subject to catty comments, or even outright chastisement. The group made it clear that their behavior simply wasn't appropriate.

In contrast, my best friend joined a sorority that had a reputation for having fun-loving party girls in its membership. She felt equal pressure to live up to these very different expectations.

The Rituals of Belonging

You may not be a trendsetter, but you can definitely be a norm setter. Just start a new club. Charter members of any new club or group are the initial norm setters, since they're the ones who make the first rules for membership. Over time, of course, these norms will grow and change as the membership ebbs and flows—nothing stays static forever. Just as groups set the norms for our behavior, members' personalities, values, and beliefs gradually mold and shape group norms.

How does this come to pass? Each new member brings with him or her the experiences and expectations he or she has accumulated from belonging to other groups. These various expectations are spread throughout the new group as members communicate with one another. As people talk and do things together, their expectations begin to crystallize into a common perspective. We learn to understand and speak each other's "language."

But everything isn't always in constant flux. Once established in a group, norms *do* tend to perpetuate themselves. Current group members exert social pressure on new members to follow the established norms, and as these new members settle into the group, they in turn put direct or indirect pressure to conform on successive members. That's how norms are transmitted from one generation of group members to the next—and how they can continue to influence people's behavior long after the original group no longer exists.

In natural groups, like families, group rituals often serve the purpose of transmitting symbols, history, and values that are important to the group from old to new members. For example, if you were a member of my family, you'd have to get used to teasingly being called a "shockenboose" if you were acting silly. And you'd get into the habit of using the term *seeseema* at the end of a sentence to mean "very, very much." These terms are part of the Johnston-Tsakiris family vocabulary. You'd also bake cookies every Friday afternoon, celebrate Kid's Day on July 1st, and join us for our weekly pizza-and-a-movie night.

Warning: Check Your References

Cosmopolitan. Glamour. Vogue. When you read these magazines, you're applying for membership in a club—"the beautiful people club," the "sexy women club," or the "women of the millennium club." Women's magazines capitalize on both your desire to be members of these groups and your perpetual belief that you don't yet belong.

Shrink Rap

A **reference group** is a group to whom we look to get information about what attitudes and behaviors are acceptable and appropriate. It can be a formal group (church or club) or it can be informal (peers or family).

Whenever you belong or hope to belong to a group, you refer to the group's standards and customs for information, direction, and support. The group becomes your *reference group*. Parents get to see this process in action—it often comes as quite a shock when their teenager's reference group shifts from the family to peers.

Sometimes, we are most influenced by a reference group that is in fact only an imaginary set of wished-for friends and colleagues. These are called *aspirational groups:* groups we can't or don't yet belong to but in which we would like to be accepted. These can be formal groups, like the Junior League, or they might simply be social categories we find appealing. For example, in the Learning Annex catalog I get every month, there is a class on "How to Marry the Wealthy" for wannabe members of the "rich spouse club."

The more you aspire to belong to a group, the more influential it may be on your life. You may not even know the group's members, and they may not know you exist, but you'll still direct your energy toward being like the people you'd like to be accepted by.

Insight

A reference group can be a powerful force. Women entering Bennington College in the 1930s brought conservative values into a liberal political and social environment. Not only had their conservatism disappeared by their senior year, 20 years after graduating they were still liberals.

But keep in mind that if you place too much emphasis on aspirational reference groups, you can get a distorted view of what the group is *really* like. Cindy Crawford is famous for saying, "I don't wake up looking like Cindy Crawford."

This shows how unrealistic it is for anyone to think that the right clothes, makeup, skin care, or diet will give her the same sex appeal that requires 10 hours of professional attention.

Nonconformists Are Hard to Find

It's easy to understand how you might try to conform to group norms when membership in the group means a lot to you. But what about when there's no obvious reference group to concern yourself with, and no rewards or punishments for conformist behavior?

Even in such situations, people still try to find the "right" way to act. When we don't know what's expected of us, we typically turn to others in the situation for clues to help us understand what's going on. And this brings up an odd fact of human behavior: For some reason, when we don't have a clue about how to act, we automatically assume that the people around us *do*. In fact, we're so sure that they know what they're doing that sometimes we go along with them even when the facts are wrong.

Social psychologist Solomon Asch, a firm believer in the power of social influence, wondered whether the influence of the social context could actually be stronger than the "real facts." He did a study in which groups of seven to nine male college students were told they would be taking a simple visual perception test. They were shown cards with three lines of differing lengths and asked which of them was the same length as a separate, standard line. The lines were different enough so that mistakes were rare, and their relative sizes changed on each trial.

On the first three trials, everyone agreed on the right answer. Then Asch pulled a little trick. All but one member of each group were in on Asch's plan. That one member was the true subject of the study. On the fourth trial, all of Asch's confederates chose the wrong line, and the student subject had to decide whether to go along with the incorrect majority or go out on a limb and stick with the right answer. Asch found that 75 percent of the student subjects conformed to the false judgment of the group one or more times. Only a quarter of them remained completely independent.

Other studies back up Asch's findings. Between 50 percent and 80 percent of people tested conformed with the majority's false opinion at least once. A third yielded to the majority's wrong judgments on half or more of the critical trials. Asch put some variables into the mix to find out what conditions might reduce the pressure to conform. He found that people were less inclined to conform if there was someone else in the group who also bucked the status quo, if the size of the unanimous group was smaller, and if there was less discrepancy between the majority's answer and the right answer.

Psychobabble

Want to see situational power in action? Rent *Candid Camera* videos! For more than 40 years, Allen Funt demonstrated the power of situational forces to get people to do some pretty goofy things. For example, how'd you like to see pedestrians stopping at a red light when it appeared above the sidewalk on which they were walking? And what about all those highway drivers who turned back in response to the road sign "Delaware is closed"?

The power of any group depends on its unanimity. Once that is broken, the rate of conformity drops dramatically. We are also more likely to conform when a judgment task is difficult or ambiguous, when the group is cohesive, when we perceive the group's members to be competent, and when our responses are made publicly. For example, when you vote, you are more likely to go along with the majority in your group under several circumstances:

➤ if the issue is complex or confusing

➤ if most others present are friends of yours

➤ if you must vote by raising your hand instead of by secret ballot

➤ if you believe your fellow group members know what they're talking about

The Asch effect has become the classic illustration of how people conform. His studies show us just how influential the unanimous group majority can be on one person's judgment—even if the group is unanimously wrong. Unless we pay close attention to the power of the situation, and buffer ourselves from it, we may conform to group pressure without being aware that we're doing so.

The Darker Side of Human Nature

After seeing the movie *Schindler's List* three times, I read a 900-page biography of Adolph Hitler and numerous historical treatises of the events of World War II. I was under the illusion that if I read enough or understood enough, I could make sense of what happened. Surely, I wanted to believe, some character flaw made the soldiers who participated in Hitler's regime do what they did. Like many people, I wanted some reassurance that such events would never happen again and that most human beings would never behave as many did then.

I Was Only Following Orders

In the 1930s, Adolph Hitler managed to transform rational German citizens into mindless masses who were unquestioningly loyal to an evil ideology. How does one individual gain such influence over a group? How does propaganda and persuasive communication work its magic? How can people become so blindly obedient to authority?

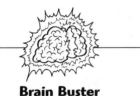

Brain Buster

During World War I, the "willingness to kill" among soldiers was only 15 percent, even though most of them were familiar with guns and hunting. To raise their willingness, today's army uses video games as training tools. The results? The kill ratio is up to 90 percent. Imagine what happens to children who spend hours at these games!

Would *you* follow a leader so blindly? We might all say "absolutely not," but a more honest answer would probably be "I hope not." A social psychologist and renegade researcher, Stanley Millgram, showed that the blind obedience of Nazis was less a product of warped personalities than it was the outcome of situational forces that could overwhelm anyone—even you and me.

Shocking News

In a controversial experiment, Millgram told volunteers that they were participating in a study of the effects of punishment on learning and memory. They were told that the experiment was designed to find ways to improve learning and memory through a proper balance of reward and punishment. Volunteers were told they'd be assigned roles as teachers or learners, but in fact the "learners" were actually actors hired by the study. The actors knew the true goal of the study: to discover just how much punishment one person was willing to inflict on another, just because he or she was told to do so.

Before the experiment began, each "teacher" was given a real shock of about 75 volts so he would know how painful it could be. The role of the learner was played by a pleasant, mild-mannered man, about 50 years old, who mentioned having a heart condition but stated that he was willing to go along with the experiment. Each time this "learner" made an error, the volunteer teacher was instructed to increase the level of shock by a fixed amount until the learning was error-free. If the teachers argued or hesitated to increase the shock level, a white-coated authority figure restated the rules and ordered the teachers to do their job.

Come on, guess. How many students do you think were willing to give serious shocks to the "learners"? Before the experiment, psychiatrists estimated that most "teachers" would not go beyond 150 volts. They predicted that less than 4 percent would go to 300 volts and less than $1/10$ of 1 percent would go all the way to 450 volts. Presumably, the 450-volters would be real "sickies"—people whose personalities were abnormal in some way.

It's nice to know that mental health professionals can be so optimistic about human nature,
but they were all wrong! A majority of the
"teachers" obeyed orders. Nearly two-thirds
delivered the maximum volts to the learner,
and the average teacher did not quit until about
300 volts. Not one of the teachers who got
within five switches of the maximum ever
refused to go all the way. To be fair, most were
very upset by what they were doing; they complained and argued with the researcher. But
they complied, nonetheless. And if you're the
one in the electric chair, that's all that matters!

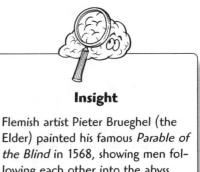

Insight

Flemish artist Pieter Brueghel (the
Elder) painted his famous *Parable of
the Blind* in 1568, showing men following each other into the abyss.
This famous picture is the source of
the expression "the blind leading
the blind."

When Authority Rules

Millgram did many similar experiments and
concluded there are several conditions under which we are most likely to obey an
authority figure:

➤ when we see a peer blindly complying with an authority figure

➤ when we can't see the target of the violence

➤ when we're being watched or supervised by an authority figure who is giving
the commands

➤ when the authority figure appears to have a higher status or more power than
we do

➤ when we can feel like we're merely assisting someone else who's doing the
actual dirty work

As you can see, all of these are situational factors, not personality characteristics. In
fact, personality tests administered to the subjects in Millgram's experiment did not
reveal that the people who obeyed fully had any different traits than the people who
ultimately refused to give more shocks, nor did they identify any mental illness or
abnormality in those who gave the maximum voltage.

How can we make sense of this disturbing news? Could it be that the subjects never
really believed that the shocks they were giving were real? Another investigator decided to find out with a similar shock test, this time making the effects of obedience
clear to the people doing the shocks. (Makes you wonder about the personalities of
some of the people who come up with these experiments!)

Once again the subjects were college students. This time, they were asked to train a
puppy by shocking it whenever it made a mistake. They could actually see the puppy
jumping around on an electric grid (in reality, the puppy only received enough of a

shock to make it squeal but not enough to hurt it). Each time the students shocked the puppy, they got upset. Some of them argued, some complained, and some even cried. But still they did it.

Then, as if this wasn't enough torture for the poor students (not to mention the puppy), an undetectable anesthesia was released, putting the puppy to sleep. The subjects, of course, thought they had killed it. The experimenter again reminded the subjects of the rules: Failure to respond was a punishable error—give more shock!

In the puppy experiment, the students had no doubt that their compliance had "harmful" consequences, so we can rule out the explanation that they rationalized their action with the belief that no harm was being done. We can also rule out callousness or meanness—the students were clearly distressed by what they were doing. So how do we explain their behavior? Let's take a look at a fascinating facet of human nature: the power of situations to "demand" certain responses.

Demanding Characteristics

In any given situation, we're constantly picking up cues about the right thing to do. We get them from watching other people, from direct instructions, or by watching the behavior or tone of a person we perceive as a leader. These cues are often called *demand characteristics,* things about the situation that "pull" us to behave in certain ways.

Shrink Rap

Demand characteristics are situational cues that influence our perceptions and our behavior. They're most powerful when social roles and situations are scripted for conformity and obedience, such as the social expectation that we should obey police officers or follow the advice of a physician.

Lots of situations have demand characteristics. When you're around a person in a position of authority, there is an underlying demand characteristic for your obedience. And this shows up in places we don't even realize. If you're a student, your role makes you hesitant to question or challenge a professor, even when you believe there is a good reason to do so. As a patient, you may leave the doctor's office only to realize that you were too intimidated to question his or her diagnosis—even if you normally think of yourself as an independent thinker. Whether you realize it or not, authority figures carry a lot of weight.

The undertow of demand characteristics can drown even the most educated professional's judgment. In a study assessing the demand characteristics of a hospital setting, 20 out of 22 nurses obeyed fake "physicians' orders" and began to administer twice the clearly labeled maximum dosage of a drug. (Of course, they were actually administering a harmless substance.) Even when there are good reasons to defy authority, it can be incredibly hard to do so.

Take Responsibility!

In psychology, as in life, the majority often rules. But not always. There's a small but not silent minority that doesn't obey blindly, that wouldn't "shock" a person or a puppy, and that will refuse to follow the doctor's orders when they are bad ones. Who are these brave individuals and what makes them different from the rest of us?

Surprisingly, the answer is rather simple. They're the people who truly feel responsible for the outcome of their actions. This isn't as preachy as it sounds; in fact, taking responsibility can simply mean that you realize that there's no one else you can blame for your actions! Our willingness to obey an authority figure increases if that authority can be blamed for any wrongdoing. On the other hand, if you feel like the buck stops with you, or if you believe that you share responsibility with the person giving the orders, you're more likely to resist any behavior that can cause someone harm.

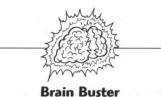

Brain Buster

Cult leader Jim Jones used an extensive amount of social psychology to keep his followers under his thumb. He created a situation in which he controlled all sources of information, social rewards, and punishments, thus maximizing the force of social norms and eliminating all points of view contrary to his own.

Becoming a Rebel with a Cause

Two reasons we're likely to obey someone blindly are the need to be right and the need to be liked. Human nature tempts us to do what others are doing in order to win acceptance and approval. And, when a situation is unclear, we are likely to rely on others for cues as to the appropriate or "right" way to do things.

When "Just Say No" Doesn't Seem to Work

Other factors can make us vulnerable to conformity, as well, such as not knowing how to disobey. For example, many salespeople count on the normal human tendency to "go with the flow." They persist in trying to make a sale even after you've told them no because they know if they keep at it, you're eventually likely to just give in and say yes. And some men refuse to believe a woman means it when she says no to his sexual advances—they just keep trying until the woman finally just goes along.

Outgrowing Childhood Rules

And, finally, we're vulnerable to conformity because we're trained that way. We all have an ingrained habit of obeying authority without question—after all, we were admonished throughout childhood to "obey our elders." While this handy rule of thumb kept us out of trouble when we were children, it can also lead us into making poor decisions if we continue to trust that someone with status or money knows better than we do!

Awareness Grants Independence

Knowledge is power. Just becoming aware of the powerful undertow that situational forces can generate is the first step in resisting social pressure and tricky situations. Also, we can analyze each situation carefully, looking for details that don't fit, the flaws in the "cover story." And we can plan ahead to deal with the forces that urge us to conform.

One of the best ways to resist unwanted influences is to build in a delay before you make a decision. Whether you're resisting the pressure to do your boss yet another uncompensated favor, or trying to avoid being strong-armed into paying more for that car than you want, delaying tactics can be your best ally. If you take a "time out" to think things over, you give yourself the space to make sure you're swimming in the right direction. Similarly, getting a second opinion from a doctor, going comparison shopping before you make a major purchase, or talking things over with a colleague or an expert before deciding on a course of action can get you out of the "total situation" and into a more balanced frame of mind.

Psychobabble

Even seminary students can fall prey to bystander apathy, especially if they're late for their Good Samaritan sermon! A study found that when a man allegedly in need of assistance was slumped in the doorway to the church, only 10 percent of the seminarians helped when they were late for their sermon. Forty-five percent stopped if they were on time, and 63 percent helped when they had no time pressure at all. Talk about needing to practice what you preach!

Give Me Some Help Here

In March 1964, 38 respectable, law-abiding citizens watched a killer stalk and stab a woman in three separate attacks. For more than an hour, the witnesses watched the killer leave, and return, only to stab her again. Not a single person telephoned the police during the assault. One person eventually did—after the woman was dead.

The newspaper account of Kitty Genovese's murder stunned millions of readers who could not understand how respectable citizens could stand by without doing anything to help. The public outrage drew national attention to the problem of bystander "apathy"—an apparent lack of concern from people who had the power to help.

Perhaps times (or people) don't change much. Three decades later, in August 1995, a young woman named Deletha Word was chased and attacked by a man whose fender she had dented. She eventually jumped from a bridge after threatening to kill herself if her attacker continued to beat her. Two young men, who actually jumped in the water in an attempt to save her, later described the other onlookers as standing around "like they were taking an interest in sports."

Why didn't someone stop to help Kitty? Why didn't more people help Deletha? First of all, because bystander apathy depends on the situation, not the person. The best predictor of whether someone will run to the rescue depends on the size of the group available to help.

Shrink Rap

Diffusion of responsibility is a weakening of each person's sense of personal responsibility and obligation to help. It happens when one person perceives that the responsibility is shared with other group members.

Oddly enough, the more people who see what's going on, the less likely any one of them will try to help. It seems that if we're in a group we tend to assume that someone else will do the dirty work. Someone else will make the phone call or stop to help the driver stranded on the side of the road. The technical term for this "pass the buck" philosophy is *diffusion of responsibility*.

That's the bad news. The good news is that, like heroic Lawrence Walker and Orlando Brown, who jumped in to help Deletha Word, people *do* help more often than not. In a staged emergency inside a New York subway train, one or more persons tried to help in 81 out of 103 cases. Certainly, the offers of assistance took a little longer when the situation was grim (if the subject was bleeding, for example), but they still came.

You Ask for It, You Got It!

Yes, there are glimmers of light in the human psyche after all! When we ask strangers to help or take responsibility for our welfare in some way, chances are they will. A series of experiments showed that when bystanders had temporarily agreed to watch someone's belongings and then a "thief" (actually a research accomplice) came along and stole them, the bystander called for help every single time. In fact, some of them even chased the thief down and tackled him.

We can convert apathy into kindness, sometimes just by asking for help. The next time you could use a helping hand, increase your chances of getting help by

➤ *Asking for it.* You might think a person would have to be in a coma to miss your need for help, but don't assume it. Let them know.

➤ *Give clear instructions.* Clearly explain the situation and tell the person what he or she could do. "My mom just fainted! Call 911 and give them this address!"

➤ *Don't let them off the hook.* "Hey, you in the red shirt, please call for a tow truck." There's nothing like being volunteered out loud to get people to take responsibility for their actions and help you.

Have I painted a grim picture of human nature? Don't be discouraged. Knowing how easily we can be adversely influenced by social situations gives us the power to recognize their pull and make a decision about whether to go along or rebel. We can guard against our conforming nature if we stop and think, delay any action, and educate ourselves objectively. And we can work with others to change the social influences that are bad for our children, such as the violence they see repeatedly in video games and movies.

Certainly, people can bring out the worst in us. However, they can also motivate us to heights that we could never attain by flying solo. In the next chapter, we'll look at one-on-one relationships and the power of love and attraction to inspire us to reach for the stars.

The Least You Need to Know

➤ Social psychologists believe that the situation we're in is a much better predictor of what we'll do than our personalities.

➤ Social situations influence our behavior through rules, roles, and norms established by the society or a group to which we belong.

➤ When we don't follow the norms of the group, we risk being ridiculed, rejected, or re-educated.

➤ Even the nicest people will follow orders to inflict pain if they believe others will do the same thing, or if they fear rebelling against authority.

➤ Nonconformists and rebels are few and far between, but if you take responsibility for what happens and take a "time out" when you feel pressured to conform, you, too, can be a rebel.

➤ If you ask strangers for help, you're likely to get it.

Chapter 25

You Can't Live Without 'Em

In This Chapter

➤ Fulfilling your prophecies

➤ Learning about how prejudice is learned

➤ Getting in touch with the spin doctor within

➤ Checking out what attracts men and women to each other

➤ Making loving last

On April 20, 1999, two students at Columbine High school in Littleton, Colorado, shot and killed 13 people, wounded 23 others, and then killed themselves. In the aftermath of this killing spree, as people asked themselves how this could happen, the causes seemed to center around the relationships among teenagers—the insiders and the outsiders—the rage at feeling excluded and the need for revenge.

While this tragedy illustrated the destructive side of human nature, the best also came through. A boy threw his body over his sister and her friend so he would be the one shot. A group of terrified teenagers comforted their dying teacher for hours, refusing to leave him even when rescuers came to their aid. Students running from bullets stopped to help wounded colleagues. A boy whose courage in holding the door open for others cost him his life.

For better or worse, we can do amazing things to and for each other. How do people stir up our most intense emotions and bring out the worst in us? Or the best? In this

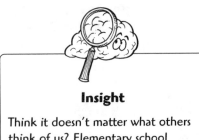

Insight

Think it doesn't matter what others think of us? Elementary school teachers were told that certain students were "intellectual bloomers" who would make great academic strides over the next year. By the end of the school year, 30 percent of these randomly assigned children had gained an average of 22 IQ points and almost all of them had gained at least 10.

Shrink Rap

Self-fulfilling prophecies are predictions about a behavior or event that actually shape its outcome in the expected direction.

chapter, we'll look at the power of our relationships, the myths and realities of attraction, the secret to long-term love, and a phenomenon that throws evolutionary psychologists for a loop: altruism.

Believing Is Seeing

If there's one lesson to be learned from the last chapter, it's the power of the situation to influence, even control, our behavior. To truly understand a situation, however, you've got to know how it's perceived and interpreted by the people in it.

Has anyone ever told you it's all in your mind, when you've described a problem? If so, you probably didn't appreciate it. Most of the time, that remark is used to dismiss or trivialize a concern.

But that's where the power of the situation is—in your mind. Certain expectations, feelings, and behaviors are set in motion when you size up a situation. This brings the situation in line with your values and attitudes. In the social world, the way you view your situation has much more influence over you than mere reality. In a very real sense, believing is seeing.

Couples have spent hours in my office trying to convince each other of what "really" happened during an argument or event, and each partner is firmly convinced he or she is in the right. And they both are—at least in their own minds. The situation is always colored by how we feel about it, believe it should be, or wish it were. Which may be why practical psychotherapists tell dueling couples "if there's no objective evidence that can prove what really happened, you're both wasting your breath."

Fields of Prophecies

What we believe and expect from each other has tremendous power in our relationships. Social psychologists use the term *self-fulfilling prophecies* to describe the circular relationship between our expectations and beliefs about some behavior or event and what actually happens. In fact, much research suggests that the very nature of some situations can be changed for better or worse by the beliefs and expectations people have about them. In essence, we often find what we are looking for.

For example, if I expect you to behave aggressively, I might consciously or unconsciously interact with you in a way that increases the odds that you'll get angry. Then, when you react aggressively, I get the satisfaction of saying, "Aha! Just as I thought!" because you've lived up to my original expectations.

Sometimes, we see the fulfillment of our expectations even if it's not there. Let's say you've just met the man of your dreams, but, on your first date, he tells you he broke up with his long-term girlfriend three months ago. If you assume any person who just ended a relationship is still reeling from this breakup, you might expect him to be upset, unavailable, or emotionally erratic. You might be reluctant to get close, and have difficulty trusting what he tells you. Even if he is one of those (rare) people who bounces back admirably, you might easily interpret his behavior as a sign that "he's not over her yet."

Of course, one of the reasons our friends warn us about "rebound" relationships is the self-fulfilling prophecies that can coincide with a broken heart. To some extent, we all bring our emotional baggage from one relationship to another. If you've been in a bad relationship, it might be easy for you to believe the worst of the next few guys you date. If you've been hurt enough, you may start to believe that the contents of every date's emotional suitcase looks the same. And you may find what you're looking for—either by picking dates with similar challenges or focusing on behaviors that confirm your dour expectations.

As you can see, relationships exist as much in our heads as they do in our interactions with the people around us. Over time, it's natural to form expectations and beliefs about how relationships do, and should, work. However, when these expectations and beliefs are negative, they can create a vicious cycle in which our attitudes and beliefs shape our interactions with others, which in turn serve to confirm our worst fears and dour predictions.

Sometimes, though, our expectations and beliefs about people arise less from our relationship histories or personal experiences, and more from family legacies and cultural myths. Let's take a look at a damaging example: prejudice.

Insight

To see just how damaging prejudice is, watch these powerful portrayals: *In the Heat of the Night* and *Mississippi Burning*. If you like older movies, watch *Gentlemen's Agreement*, a searing picture of anti-Semitism in America.

Prejudice: Social Reality Running Amok

Prejudice is an example of the vast chasm that can exist between objective reality and a distorted situation created in people's minds. A prejudiced attitude acts as a biased filter through which negative emotions and beliefs cloud the perception of members of a target group. Once formed, prejudice exerts a powerful force for selectively

Shrink Rap

Prejudice is a learned negative attitude toward a person based on his or her membership in a particular group.

attending to, organizing, and remembering pertinent information. If you think cat owners are lazy and sneaky, by gosh, you are going to find cat owners who are—and you are going to remember them far longer than any industrious, honest cat owners you might meet.

No one knows exactly why prejudice exists. At its most basic level, it divides the world into "us" and "them"—it simplifies a complicated environment by categorizing groups with shared characteristics. Blacks and whites. Christians and Muslims. Jews and Aryans. Blue-collar and white-collar. Tall and short. Jocks and nerds.

Once a category is made, individual members of it are assumed to share the same attitudes, personalities, behaviors, and/or physical characteristics. I'm sure you've heard somebody say, "They all look alike," referring to a racial group different from his own. And the impact of these beliefs affects both the person who is prejudiced and the one who is prejudiced against.

A common question about prejudice is whether there might be a grain of truth in some of the stereotypes and beliefs that support it. After all, why else would there be these negative attitudes and discriminatory actions? Let me tell you a story, and you can answer this question for yourself.

Third-grade teacher Jane Elliott was worried that her pupils from an all-white Iowa farm town were unable to understand how difficult and complex life can be for different groups. So, one day she arbitrarily stated the brown-eyed students were "superior" to the blue-eyed students. The brown-eyed students, whom she categorized as more intelligent, were given special privileges, while the inferior "blue eyes" were stuck with their lowly second-class status.

Insight

How can anyone justify paying women less than men for doing the same work? Simple: Society has the idea that women are "worth" less, intrinsically. The notion of social market value is that people are worth whatever the market will pay them. How's that for circular logic, not to mention discrimination?

By the end of the day, the schoolwork of the blue-eyed students had declined and they became depressed, pouty, and angry. The brown-eyed "geniuses" were quick to catch on to a good thing. They refused to play with their former friends and began mistreating them. They got into fights with them and even began suggesting that school officials should be notified that the blue-eyed children might steal their belongings.

When teacher Jane reversed the hierarchy on day two, the exact same thing happened in reverse. The blue-eyed children got their "revenge" and the brown-eyed children learned what it was like to be at the bottom of the totem pole. Can you imagine what happens to children who experience genuine prejudice every day?

Social Reality: Coming Soon to a Television Near You

One of the most powerful creators of social reality is the media. By the time most Americans are 18 years old, they have spent more time in front of the television than in school. And far more time than they have spent talking with their teachers, their friends, or their parents. By the time today's children reach the age of 70, they'll have spent, on average, seven years watching TV.

What's the social implication of this startling fact? Clearly, if a child spends that much time watching television, much of his or her early social reality may be created from what's on the tube!

What kind of social reality does television create? Here are a couple of statistics that illustrate how television blurs the distinction between reality and fantasy—and how it knowingly designs programming to favor the hand that rocks the remote control!

➤ On prime-time television men outnumber women at least three to one, while in the real world, there are slightly more women than men.

➤ On prime-time television there are significantly smaller proportions of young people, old people, blacks, Hispanics, and other minorities than in the U.S. population at large.

Psychobabble

Let's play a numbers game. Count up the number of prime-time television shows where guns and violence are a regular part of the action, beginning with the earliest Westerns, such as *Gunsmoke*, right up to today's cop shows. Now count the number of shows where you see people work out problems without violence. That second list's a pretty short one, isn't it?

My Bias Is My Basis

Enough about social reality. Let's talk about your reality, starting with the explanations you give yourself for the things that happen in your relationships. After all, one of the most important tasks in relationships is figuring out why people do the things they do, right?

Why did your girlfriend break up with you? Why did your parents get a divorce after years of marriage? Why is your child driving you over the edge? We all want answers to the "whys" of our lives.

Relationships, by their very nature, force us to use all of our psychological expertise to answer these questions, often on a daily basis! But the answers you come up with might not depend on what actually happened as much as you might expect. In part, your explanation for relationship events is determined by your bias.

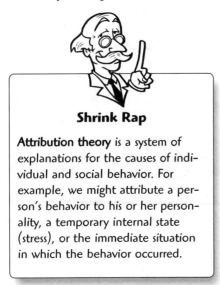

Shrink Rap

Attribution theory is a system of explanations for the causes of individual and social behavior. For example, we might attribute a person's behavior to his or her personality, a temporary internal state (stress), or the immediate situation in which the behavior occurred.

Here's an example of how it works. Suppose you're on jury duty. The person on trial for murder is a battered wife who murdered her husband in his sleep. The defense argues that this is clearly a case of self-defense. They show you impressive evidence of a long history of battering, child abuse, and unheeded calls to the police for assistance. The prosecution, on the other hand, argues that the defendant clearly knew what she was doing, that she had other options, and that personality tests show that she was a "powder keg waiting to explode." Would you vote innocent or guilty?

Your vote will be partly determined by your attribution biases. The answers you come up with for those "why did she do it?" questions are attributions. And you attribute motives and reasons to people's behavior every day. If you believe the battered wife was a harmless woman driven to a desperate act by horrible circumstances, you are likely to vote not guilty. On the other hand, if you attribute her actions to revenge or an evil character, you are likely to throw the book at her.

The FAE Club

Attribution theory is the formal study of the ways that people generate explanations for what happens, and the impact that these explanations have on their behavior. One challenge to attribution theory is that people are often biased in their efforts to explain important experiences. It seems we don't just make occasional errors in our explanations for what people do; we make them so often, they're predictable!

For example, one of our most common biases is the *fundamental attribution error* (FAE), a tendency to overestimate the influence of personality or other internal traits and to underestimate situational factors in explaining other peoples' behavior. Most of us automatically think a person's behavior is a reflection of who he or she is, especially if the behavior is negative. When your office mate bites your head off, you're much more likely to think "she's such a grump" than to wonder if she's having a bad day.

The FAE is not always wrong. There really are some people with cranky personalities or mean streaks. If your coworker is one of them, your attribution might be accurate. But your FAE is still very definitely a bias. It ignores the fact that temporary emotional states can easily get confused with personality traits (as you learned in Chapter 15, "He's

Got ... Personality"), and it doesn't take into account the power of situations to bring out the worst in people (as you learned in Chapter 24, "You Can't Live with 'Em").

In reality, the odds are at least 50-50 that a person's moodiness on any given day is due to a bad situation, but we are more likely to think it's caused by a character flaw. By reminding ourselves to check out the situation, we can at least attempt to correct for our FAE bias—and give each other a well-deserved break!

Self-Service Isn't Just for Pumping Gas

True or false: People with high self-esteem see themselves pretty clearly and like themselves anyway. (If you answered true, you're wrong. If you answered false, you realized I was asking you a trick question!)

Shrink Rap

A **self-serving bias** is a tendency to accept credit when things turn out well, and to blame the situation or other people when things go badly.

Did you know that people with high self-esteem may delude themselves more than others, and that this self-delusion might work in their favor? It's true! The conventional wisdom that says "get in touch with reality" may not always be the best advice, at least when it comes to explaining our own behavior. In fact, people with high self-esteem may have an internal self-service station—one that pumps out explanations that put them in the best possible light.

This *self-serving bias* is a tendency to give ourselves credit for good things that happen to us and to blame the situation (including other people) when we fail. You're more likely to claim you earned your promotion, but if you were passed over, you're more likely to say, "My boss is out to get me."

In the effort to protect your self-esteem, it makes sense to cast your behavior in the best possible light. Some studies show that people suffering from depression may actually have a more accurate sense of their abilities and skills than people who aren't depressed. Obviously, a self-serving bias can help you—as long as it's not extreme. After all, it does you no good to stick to a belief that the boss is out to get you when you are, in fact, slacking off on the job.

Being Your Own Spin Doctor

We are all legends in our own minds, and the bias we give to explaining ourselves and the events in our lives are stories that give us meaning and lay the foundation for our choices and plans. Not only do we want our life stories to have happy endings, we need to feel we can act them out the way we write them.

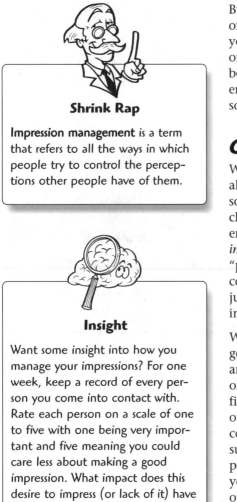

Shrink Rap

Impression management is a term that refers to all the ways in which people try to control the perceptions other people have of them.

Insight

Want some insight into how you manage your impressions? For one week, keep a record of every person you come into contact with. Rate each person on a scale of one to five with one being very important and five meaning you could care less about making a good impression. What impact does this desire to impress (or lack of it) have on how you interact with them?

But be honest. Do you act the same at the beginning of a relationship as you do six months into it? Would you eat a second piece of pie in front of your guests, or would you wait until they went home? Most of us behave differently when we are alone than when others are watching, and we act *more* differently with some people than others.

Campaigning for Acceptance

When Shakespeare wrote, "All the world's a stage, and all the men and women merely players," he was onto something. Consciously or unconsciously, we often change our behavior to influence the impressions others have of us. Social psychologists call this the art of *impression management;* your parents may have called it "putting your best foot forward." It's not that we're constantly trying to deceive the people around us, it's just that we each have a vested interest in being seen in the best possible light.

While I hesitate to quibble with Shakespeare, I'd suggest that a politician might be a better analogy than an actor. Like politicians, we tend to follow the advice of our internal "spin doctors." To secure a vote of confidence from the people around us, we campaign for ourselves and our goals quite naturally, often without consciously strategizing or manipulating others. Not surprisingly, you're most likely to "campaign" with people who have yet to cast their vote for (or against) you—new acquaintances or business associates. On the other hand, your friends and family are more likely to be treated with your "what you see is what you get" persona.

Image-Making in Intimate Relationships

Dating partners are much more concerned with their image at the beginning of a relationship. In fact, the very definition of relationship satisfaction tends to change over the course of time: Early on, couples are more likely to give high marks to a relationship when they have a good impression of each other. After they feel more intimate and secure, they want to be able to let down their guard without having to worry about being rejected. Of course, the hard part is usually the middle, right after you realize you're no longer getting flowers or gourmet meals on every date but before the true intimacy starts!

Watching Yourself on the Monitor

In Chapter 15 we talked a lot about extroversion and introversion, which together form one of the "big five" personality traits. This dimension of your personality can have a lot of influence over your attempts at impression management. Extroverts, as a general rule, try to win friends and influence people. Very shy people, on the other hand, are often more concerned about not making a bad impression than they are concerned about making a good one. They may avoid social situations, and when they can't, they may choose to fade quietly into the background.

Another personality trait that is related to how you might try to influence or control the perception others have of you is *self-monitoring*. High self-monitors are acutely aware of how they're coming across to others. They're chameleons, able to quickly shift gears and modify their behavior to please the people around them. Low self-monitors, on the other hand, show less variability in their behavior over time and across settings. They are much more likely to follow their values and beliefs, and less likely to be swayed by the spur of the moment.

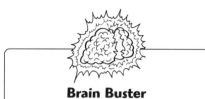

Brain Buster

Making a good impression is hard work. Research suggests that the best impression is a delicate balance between looking good, being modest, and sounding sincere.

Shrink Rap

Self-monitoring is the degree to which we vary our self-presentation to match the people we're with. Good salespeople are likely to be high self-monitors, at least in business settings.

The Highs and the Lows of It All

High and low self-monitors lead very different lives. High self-monitors have more acquaintances and casual friends, tend to choose friends who are physically attractive, and make great politicians and actors. Low self-monitors have fewer but closer friends and choose friends with values and beliefs similar to their own.

This personality trait can have practical implications if you're single. If you're looking to be wined and dined, go for the high self-monitor; if he or she finds you attractive, your date will whisk you away to France or Cancún. On the other hand, a low self-monitor is likely to wait until he or she sizes you up before bringing out the candy and flowers, but when that happens, it's more likely to lead to something long-term.

Psychobabble

Ever wonder why unpredictable, highly changeable people are called chameleons? A chameleon is a lizard with an angular head whose skin can change color rapidly so that it will blend in with its environment. And if that doesn't make it seem shifty enough, its eyes can move independently of each other, too.

Checking Your Self-Monitoring Pulse

Take this quiz to find out how your self-monitor is working. Rate yourself on the following 10 statements using the scale of 1 to 5 provided below:

Self-Monitoring Assessment Quiz

1 = never   4 = often

2 = rarely   5 = almost always

3 = sometimes

____ I have always been good at acting games like Charades or Taboo.

____ It is important to me that my friends be attractive and socially polished.

____ I would rather have a lot of variety in my social acquaintances than just a few close friends.

____ People I am with don't always know how I'm really feeling.

____ If I am not enjoying myself at a party, I usually leave when courtesy permits.

____ When I am not sure how to act in a certain situation, I look to others for clues.

____ I generally feel that people whom I date are a reflection on me.

____ I can be a chameleon with different groups of people.

____ I would change my attitudes or beliefs to please someone else.

____ I like to know what my friends think of certain books, movies, or music.

Now add up your scores. If you scored over 35, you are a high monitor. Scores of 20 or below are low monitors, and scores between 20 and 34 are middle monitors. Here's what it means:

➤ *High monitors:* Your motto might be "image is everything." You are good at schmoozing with others and if you aren't on the stage at least as a hobby, your talents are wasting away. You are a fabulous networker and get lots of invitations to parties. You know what's hot and what's not and where to go on Friday night.

➤ *Middle monitors:* Your motto might be "in everything, moderation." You are an interesting combination of rebel and politician—a lot depends on the circumstances. You are good at balancing, making a good impression, and keeping in touch with your own values.

➤ *Low monitors:* Your motto might be "do your own thing." You take pride in not always giving in to whatever's trendy. As an independent thinker, you don't get pushed around. Others often come to you for advice because they know you will tell it like it is.

Chemistry in Action

Regardless of whether you're a high, middle, or low self-monitor, if you're single, chances are pretty good you'd rate high in the "monitors other people" category. This category is also known as "checking 'em out," "eyeballing," and various other nicknames. You know what I mean—when it comes to the dance of attraction, we are constantly sizing up our potential partners.

Chemistry between two people is more than just a beauty contest, though. Physical attractiveness may give you a leg up in making a good first impression, but the power of looks fizzles out pretty quickly once the flames have been burning for a while. Second, not all men fantasize about statuesque blondes; in fact, about 15 percent of men drool over petite brunettes. And guys, if you tend to attract more flies than women, a subscription to *GQ* or a trip to Hugo Boss can do wonders for your love life. Here's a look at what men and women eyeball first:

What Men Eyeball	What Women Eyeball
Figure/build (44 percent)	Eyes (38 percent)
Face (33 percent)	How Dressed (34 percent)
How dressed (27 percent)	Figure/build (27 percent)
Eyes (21 percent)	Face (26 percent)
Legs (6 percent)	Legs (0.5 percent)

The Mystery of Attraction

Even if you like a new date's packaging, it's surprisingly hard to unwrap it and find the person inside. Most of us have a strong need to be close to others, but sometimes it's pretty hard to get there. Closeness is not automatic; it doesn't seem to "come naturally."

The irony—that close relationships are important but difficult to pull off—is painfully apparent to anyone who's gone through a divorce or relationship breakup. And since this is such a common part of the human condition, it's no wonder that social psychologists have spent a lot of time looking at what happens in the space between attraction and intimacy.

Finding the Attraction Factors

The earliest research on relationships focused on interpersonal attraction and identified key factors that determine who we like. While it might seem like a mystery to those of us in the dating arena, social psychologists have come up with some fairly predictable findings about why people go from acquaintanceship to liking or love. Here are some of the myths and realities of attraction:

➤ Absence does not make the heart grow fonder. We like people more if we see them frequently (with a few exceptions, of course).

➤ Opposites may attract, but they don't stick to each other. We generally like people who think like we do and who have similar backgrounds, values, histories, and beliefs.

➤ We like people who have qualities we value: physical attractiveness, competence, and who are generally fun to be around.

➤ We like an equal amount of give and take. If the other person gives too much, we don't respect him. If we give too much, he doesn't respect us.

From Attraction to Love

Love is a tricky concept. Definitions of love vary from person to person, but in each culture there are common themes that provide clues about what "real love" means to their members. American "clues" might be sexual arousal, attachment, and concern for the other person's welfare and, sometimes, a willingness to make a commitment.

With all those hormones and pheromones flying around, falling in love is a lot easier than staying in love. And, until recently, apparently a lot more interesting to research. It's only been over the past decade that investigators have shifted their attention from the thrill of attraction to the wonder of long-term love. Let's see what they discovered.

Gotcha! Making Love Last

What makes love last? It depends on the two people and their own ideas of what a "good" relationship means. Looking at the research on why partners stay together, four themes emerge—focused around a big question: Do you and your partner *exchange responsibility* for *communication* and *conflict* (ERCC)? Here's your ERCC checklist:

➤ *(Social) Exchange:* Long-term lovers negotiate an exchange of resources that is flexible, rewarding, and fair. For couples to stay together, they must, over time, feel they're getting about as much as they're giving—and vice versa.

➤ *Responsibility:* Cinderella and Sleeping Beauty aside, no one is going to ride up on a horse and carry us off into the sunset. And, if they did, research suggests we'd dump them eventually. Among couples who stay together, each partner takes personal responsibility for his or her own health, wealth, and well-being.

➤ *Communication:* Couples who talk about things tend to work them out. (Of course, more is not necessarily better.) Couples who can affirm the other's feelings—whether or not they agree with the content—have a leg up on the relationship ladder.

➤ *Conflict:* We all have conflicts. Meeting them head on—early and often—is what it takes to save the relationship from breaking up over them.

It's a heck of a lot easier to describe what makes love last than to do it. Research studies often can't describe the hurt feelings, stubborn beliefs, and lack of skills that so often dampen the love between two people over time. Plus, there's that age-old myth that if you have to work on a relationship, your partner must not be the "right one." In reality, if you find someone who's willing to work on your relationship as hard as you are, I'd say you've found something worth keeping.

Negotiating: Get With the Program

How do you and your partner handle conflicts? Do you find common ground or do you settle for the least common denominator? Do you take turns giving in or do you resume negotiations until both of you are happy?

Few of us would list "a good negotiator" on a dream list of the ideal mate, but maybe we should. While we often think of negotiation as a business strategy, anyone in a relationship will recognize the strength in learning to reach a compromise without compromising your relationship! Here are a few strategies for negotiation that might strengthen your partnership with the one you love.

➤ *Put first things first.* Decide what issues are most important to you and how much you are willing to give up. For example, if you're arguing over vacation plans—you want to go to Tahiti, your partner wants a trek in the mountains—you need to figure out what "qualities" Tahiti has that you might not find elsewhere. If you really just want to lie on the beach, you could give up this particular island. Or, maybe you could split the vacation and jaunt over to New Zealand for a three-day mountaineering experience.

➤ *Put yourself in your partner's shoes.* You have a close relationship with a partner you know well (hopefully). Before you negotiate, sit down and anticipate what will be important to him or her. Anticipate what your partner's objections will be and be ready to answer them. Then, listen, listen, listen.

➤ *Be creative.* The more alternatives the two of you have to consider, the less likely you are to say, "It's my way or the highway." When you fall back on ultimatums, you've left negotiation and gotten into a battle for control and a clash of wills. Come up with as many solutions as your imagination allows, and don't shy away from tossing in a few humorous ones. It's hard to argue when you're laughing together!

Psychobabble

How many lovers who lasted can you name? How about John and Abigail Adams, Winston and Clementine Churchill, Queen Victoria and Prince Albert, Gertrude Stein and Alice B. Toklas, Paul Newman and Joanne Woodward, George Burns and Gracie Allen, Paul and Linda McCartney, Harry and Bess Truman, Johnny Cash and June Carter Cash, and Hume Cronyn and Jessica Tandy.

The Truisms of Altruism

Every year, during a certain week in February, some pretty strange things happen in the good old U.S.A. In Anchorage Alaska, the police issue "kindness citations." In Fresno, California, children hand free bagels to commuters. In Columbus, Ohio, volunteers make cards for residents of nursing homes. All over the country, people commit random acts of kindness for no reason at all. In 1991, Will Glennon, writing under the pen name "Dr. Kindness," started a movement that has snowballed into a group of kindness freaks and a bunch of best-selling books.

A Kinder, Gentler Nation?

Why would a kindness movement sweep the nation? Are we looking for ego strokes? For points we can use to keep a balance in the relationship? Where's the survival-of-the-fittest competition here? Is there really such a thing as pure, unselfish concern for the welfare of others? It depends on how we define altruism.

Is It in the Genes or All in Your Head?

There are two definitions of altruism. One is biological altruism—the act of doing something for the benefit of another that increases that person's chances for survival while decreasing your own. The swimmer who jumps into the water to try to rescue a drowning person, or the person who donates a kidney to a stranger would be examples of biological altruism.

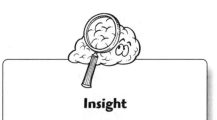

Insight

Animal altruism? At the very least, they have very good manners! For example, we know that unrelated cats will sometimes groom each other, unrelated horses will swish the flies off one another, and one hen will always step aside and wait until the senior hen in the flock has finished eating.

The second type is psychological altruism. This might be defined as doing something that rewards the other person but does not reward us, and may even be detrimental to our best interests. For example, when you face embarrassment by standing up for another person, you're exhibiting psychological altruism. The same is true when you're willing to take abuse or give up social comforts for the sake of someone else.

Some cynics argue that many people who "sacrifice" for others seem to get pleasure in the giving as well, so there is a reward for the behavior after all. According to this peculiar way of thinking, such people wouldn't be behaving altruistically.

Psychobabble

Mother Theresa is often regarded as the queen of Altruism. But there are others. Father Damien, a priest from the Netherlands, spent his life among the lepers in Hawaii. Through his work he transformed a dog-eat-dog hellhole into a place of dignity and self-respect. And he did this knowing he would ultimately catch leprosy and die.

Perhaps the best overall definition of altruism is any action that is intrinsically rewarding and that helps and rewards another person without any expectation of a return. Is it altruism, heroism, or the highest form of love that makes someone give his life for another? Whatever it is, it happens with a heartening frequency—like the high school students in Colorado who cared for each other during and after the Littleton tragedy. Social psychologists can't predict or explain why altruism exists, but they find examples of it all the time.

The Never-Ending Story

As you finish this book, you may think you've learned more about human psychology than you wanted to know—or, perhaps, you've learned just enough to make you a psychology student for life. I hope you have a better sense of understanding about yourself and others, and how to learn what you need to know to improve your life—in any situation.

We've looked at the good, the bad, and the ugly of human nature. You've learned about neurons and neurotransmitters, how children grow and how adults survive. You've seen how people can buckle under stress and rise above the toughest problems.

Maybe you'd like to relocate to Mars now that you've gotten a closer look at what makes humans tick. Or, just maybe you're convinced that the human condition is a good one after all. Because one thing that psychology teaches us is that, if we expect good from people, they usually deliver. If we let people know we care, they usually care back. And if we ask for their help, they will almost always grant it. We are still evolving, but let's hope we never lose that special and mysterious complexity that makes us all too human.

The Least You Need to Know

➤ Other people tend to behave in ways that confirm our expectations.

➤ Prejudice is a negative learned attitude.

➤ We're all self-serving in some ways—we tend to take credit for the good things that happen to us and blame others for the bad.

➤ We have built-in spin doctors for managing the way we impress others.

➤ High self-monitors match their personalities to the people they're around; low self-monitors tend to do their own thing regardless of who they are with.

➤ We're still learning what makes attraction turn into everlasting love, but we know it includes the ability to communicate and resolve conflicts.

➤ Altruism is still a mystery to social psychologists, but it happens more often than you might think.

Glossary

Affective disorders a family of illnesses in which the primary symptom is a disturbance of mood; also called "mood disorders."

Alienist a specialist who treated mental and nervous disorders before the science of psychology was developed.

Amnesia the partial or complete loss of memory; psychologically based amnesia can be triggered by a traumatic event; memory almost always returns after a few days.

Anorexia nervosa a pattern of self-starvation that occurs primarily in young girls in Western cultures from middle and upper socioeconomic classes.

Appetizer effect hunger that is stimulated by external stimuli, such as the smell or sight of food or food advertisements.

Archetype in Jungian theory, a universal symbol of human experience that is stored in the collective unconscious, the storehouse of ideas and forces shared by every human being who ever lived.

Attention a state of focused awareness coupled with a readiness to respond.

Attribution theory a system of explanations for the causes of individual and social behavior.

Behavior modification the application of principles of operant and classical conditioning to change a person's behavior in a more adaptive direction.

Binge eating disorder the official diagnosis given a person who eats a large amount of food within two hours at least two days a week for six months without purging in any way to lose or maintain her weight. This disorder is commonly called compulsive overeating.

Bipedalism   the ability to walk upright on two legs.

Bipolar disorder   (commonly called manic depression) a psychological disorder characterized by extreme mood swings of "highs" and "lows."

Blackout   a type of amnesia in which the person can still function (drive or make dinner) but later can't remember what happened.

Body dysmorphia disorder   the severe preoccupation with slight or imaginary defects of the body, an obsession with body image.

Body image   a complex array of thoughts, feelings, and behaviors that make up the subjective way a person views his or her physical appearance.

Bulimia nervosa   a disorder in which a person binges (overeats) and purges (attempts to get rid of the food).

Burnout   a unique pattern of emotional symptoms often found in professionals who have high-intensity contact with others on a daily basis; it is characterized by exhaustion, a sense of failure, and a tendency to relate to others in a depersonalized and detached manner.

Cingulotomy   a form of psychosurgery that uses radio frequency current to destroy the cingulum, a small structure in the brain known to be involved in emotionality.

Circadian rhythm   the clock that regulates your sleep/wake cycle.

Classical conditioning   when two stimuli become so closely associated that one of them can elicit the same reactive behavior as the other.

Cognitive dissonance   the inner conflict we experience when we do something that is counter to our prior values, beliefs, and feelings.

Cognitive model   a hypothetical representation of how cognitive processes work.

Cognitive processes   the mental abilities that allow you to know and understand the things around you; they include attending, thinking, remembering, and reasoning.

Collective unconscious   the storehouse of ideas and forces shared by every human being who ever lived.

Consciousness   our awareness of ourselves and all the things that we think, feel, and do.

Contingency management   a technique designed to change behavior by modifying the consequences.

Counterconditioning, a behavioral modification technique in which a new response is substituted for an unwanted or ineffective one.

Cyclothymia   a disorder in which a person experiences the symptoms of bipolar disorder, but in a milder form. The symptoms are not severe enough to disrupt normal functioning and don't include hallucinations or delusions.

Declarative memory   the portion of memory that stores information and facts.

Defense mechanism   a mental process of self-deception that reduces an individual's awareness of threatening or anxiety-producing thoughts, wishes, or memories.

Diffusion of responsibility   a weakening of each person's sense of personal responsibility and obligation to help. It happens when one person perceives that the responsibility is shared with other group members.

Dissociative disorder   a psychological disorder characterized by a disturbance in the integration of identity, memory, or consciousness.

Dissociative identity disorder   (better known as multiple personality disorder) a psychological disorder in which two or more distinct personalities coexist in the same person at different times.

Dysthymia   a psychological disorder in which the feelings of depression are less severe than those in major depression, but last for at least a two-year period.

Ego   Freud's term for the part of your personality that focuses on self-preservation and the appropriate channeling of your basic instincts.

Emotional intelligence   the ability to successfully understand, and use, emotions. It involves a group of skills, including the ability to motivate ourselves, regulate our moods, control our impulses, and to empathize with others.

Encephalization   the development of a larger brain during the course of evolution.

Event-related potential (ERP)   the measurable change in brain waves in response to a particular stimulus.

Explicit memory   the ability to retain information you've put real effort into learning.

False memory syndrome   a pattern of thoughts, feelings, and actions based on a mistaken or inaccurate memory for traumatic experiences the person claims to have previously repressed.

Freudian slip   a mistake or substitution of either spoken or written words. Freud believed that such "slips" come from subconscious wishes that pop up unexpectedly through unintentional words. By analyzing these "slips," a person might get some clues into his inner thoughts or "real" intent or wishes.

Gender dysphoria   a clinical illness characterized by a desire to be, or insistence that one is, of the opposite sex; men have this disorder two to three times more often than women.

General Adaptation Response (GAS)   a pattern of general physical responses that are triggered by any stressors, no matter what kind.

Habituation   the process whereby a person becomes so accustomed to a stimulus that he or she ignores it and attends instead to less familiar stimuli.

Hypnotizability a measure of how susceptible you are to entering a hypnotic state.

Hypothesis an answer to a question, based on theoretical assumptions, that can be tested to see if the answer can be proven wrong.

Id Freud's term for the uninhibited pleasure-seeker in your personality.

Implicit memory the ability to remember information you haven't deliberately tried to learn.

Impression management all the ways in which people try to control the perceptions other people have of them.

Judgment the process of using available information to form opinions, draw conclusions, and evaluate people and situations.

Language acquisition devices (LADs) the preprogrammed instructions for learning a language that some linguists believe all infants are born with.

Language acquisition support system (LASS) the circumstances that facilitate the efficient acquisition of language.

Latent content (of a dream) the meaning that lies hidden underneath the dream; its symbols, images, and actions.

Learning any process through which experience at one time can change our behavior at another.

Locus of control a person's perception of the usual source of control over rewards; an internal locus of control means we believe our behavior determines our fate; an external locus of control means we think our fate is controlled by external forces (destiny, luck, or the gods).

Manifest content (of a dream) the literal story it tells.

Maturation the process of growth typical of all members of a species who are reared in the usual environment of the species.

Mental retardation a condition in which a person has significantly impaired intelligence in combination with problems in living (taking care of oneself, getting along with others, and doing other age-appropriate tasks).

Mnemonics short verbal strategies that improve and expand our ability to remember new information by storing it with familiar and previously encoded information.

Morality a system of beliefs, values, and underlying judgments about the rightness of human acts.

Motivation the physical and psychological process that drives us toward a certain goal.

Natural selection the Darwinian principle that says the best-adapted traits are the ones that will be passed along from one generation to another in a species. Creatures with less well adapted traits will die out before they can reproduce, so their poorly adapted traits will eventually disappear from the population.

Nerve   a bundle of sensory or motor neurons that exist anywhere outside the central nervous system. You have 43 pairs of them—12 pairs from the brain and 31 pairs from the spinal cord.

Neuron   a nerve that specializes in information processing.

Neurotransmitter   biochemical substances that stimulate other neurons. More than 60 substances have been identified as neurotransmitters. Among these are dopamine, norepinephrine, and serotonin.

Operant conditioning   encouraging voluntary behavior that attempts to influence control over the environment. When a rat learns that pressing a lever gets more food, it has been operant conditioned to push the lever.

Panic disorder   an anxiety disorder during which the person experiences recurrent episodes of intense anxiety and physical arousal that last up to 10 minutes.

Paresis   a disease of the brain caused by a syphilis-caused infection of the central nervous system and characterized by dementia and paralysis.

Personality   the unique bundle of all the psychological qualities that consistently influence an individual's usual behavior across situations and time.

Personality disorder   a long-standing, inflexible, and maladaptive pattern of thinking, perceiving, or behaving that usually causes serious problems in the person's social or work environment.

Prejudice   a learned negative attitude toward a person based on his or her membership in a particular group.

Procedural memory   the long-term memory of how things are done.

Psychoanalysis   the field of psychology that specializes in applying Freudian principles to the treatment of psychological disorders.

Psychoanalyst   specialist in Freud's school of psychological treatment; must complete an intensive post-graduate training program specializing in psychoanalytic theory and practice (including undergoing their own analysis).

Psychodynamic personality theory   a model of personality that assumes inner forces (needs, drives, motives) shape personality and influence behavior.

Psychopathology   the clinical term for an abnormality or disorder in thought, emotion, or behavior.

Psychophysics   the study of psychological reactions to physical stimuli.

Psychosis   (also called "psychotic disorder") a general term for a severe mental disorder that prevents an accurate understanding and interaction with reality due to impaired thoughts, inappropriate emotions, and distorted perceptions.

Reasoning   a process of realistic, goal-directed thinking in which conclusions are drawn from a set of facts.

Reference group   any group a person uses to compare and evaluate him- or herself, from age-related peers to supermodels on the covers of fashion magazines.

Reinforcement   a consequence that increases the occurrence of a particular behavior over time. Reinforcement can be both positive (a hug, a raise in pay) or negative (a punishment).

REM sleep   sleep that is characterized by rapid eye movement, brain activity close to that of wakefulness, and a complete absence of muscle tone. Most dreaming takes place during REM sleep.

Repressed memory   the memory of a traumatic event retained in the unconscious mind, where it is said to affect conscious thoughts, feelings, and behaviors even though there is no conscious memory of the alleged trauma.

Retrieval cues   mental or environmental aids that help us retrieve information from long-term memory.

Savant ability   an exceptional skill in a narrow area, such as doing calculations or composing music, that is significantly higher than the person's overall level of functioning.

Schizophrenia   a severe mental disorder characterized by a breakdown in perceptual and thought processes, often including hallucinations and delusions.

Scientific method   a way of answering questions that helps remove bias from the study. First, you form your question into a statement that can be proven false, then you test it against observable facts. Other researchers who doubt your findings can duplicate your test and see if they get the same results.

Self-actualization   the constant striving to realize your full potential.

Self-concept   a person's awareness of his or her identity as a distinct and unique individual.

Self-fulfilling prophecies   predictions about a behavior or event that actually shape its outcome in the expected direction.

Self-monitoring   the degree to which we vary our self-presentation to match the people we're with.

Self-serving bias   a tendency to accept credit when things turn out well, and to blame the situation or other people when things go badly.

Shaping   a process of rewarding small steps that are in the direction of the desired behavior.

Signal detection theory   the assumption that the ability to perceive environmental stimuli is influenced by both physical and psychological factors.

Situationism the assumption that situational factors can have subtle and powerful effects on our thoughts, feelings, and actions.

Social comparison the process of comparing ourselves with others to identify our own unique abilities.

Social psychology the study of how people are influenced by their interactions and relationships with other people.

Somatization the tendency to channel emotions into physical complaints; instead of feeling angry, you might get a headache. A hypochondriac is an extreme example of somatization.

Somatoform disorder a mental disorder in which the person experiences symptoms of physical illness but has no medical disease that could cause them.

State a temporary emotional condition.

Stimulus generalization when an individual who has become conditioned to respond to one stimulus in a certain way will also respond in that same way to any similar stimuli.

Stress a general term that includes all the physical, behavioral, emotional, and cognitive responses we make to a disruptive internal or external event.

Stressors the events that trigger a stress response.

Superego Freud's term for an individual's social conscience

Tardive dyskinesia an unusual disturbance in motor control (especially of the facial muscles) that can be caused by long-term use of antipsychotic medication.

Theory a set of assumptions about a question.

Trait a stable characteristic that influences an individual's thoughts, feelings, and behavior.

Psychology Resources

Mental Health Advocacy Groups

National Mental Health Association
1021 Prince Street
Alexandria, VA 22314-2971
http://www.nmha.org.index/cfm

National Alliance for the Mentally Ill
http://www.nami.org

National Mental Health Consumer's Self-Help Clearinghouse
http://www.libertynet.org/mha/cl_house.html

General Online Psychology Resources

Minding Your Health (includes self-screening for nine psychological disorders)
http://www.mindingyourhealth.com

Self-Help and Psychology Magazine
http://www.shpm.com

Internet Mental Health
http://www.mentalhealth.com

Health Touch
http://www.healthtouch.com

KEN Consumer Information
http://www.mentalhealth.org/consumer/index.html

Psych Web
http://www.psy.www/com

PsychRef
http://maple.lemoyne.edu/~hevern/psychref.html

Mental Health Net
http://www.cmhc.com

Mental Health Infosource
http://www.mhsource.com

Sites That Have Lists of Psychology Links and Online Resources

Cyber Psych
http://www.cyber.psych.com

Encyclopedia of Psychology
http://www.psychology.org/links/resources/MetaSites/index/html

Psych Central
http://www.psychcentral.com

Resources for Specific Problems

Alcohol Resources

Alcoholics Anonymous
http://www.alcoholics-anonymous.org

Depression Resources

Depression and Related Affective Disorders Association (DRADA)
Meyer 3-181
600 N. Wolfe Street
Baltimore, MD 21287-7381
Online contact: drada@welchink.welch.jhu.edu

National Depressive and Manic Depressive Association
730 North Franklin Street, Suite 501
Chicago, IL 60610-3526
1-800-826-3632
(312) 642-7243
http://www.ndmda.org

National Organization for Seasonal Affective Disorder (NOSAD)
P.O. Box 40190
Washington, DC 20016

Depression After Delivery
P.O. Box 1282
Morrisville, PA 19067
1-800-944-4773
http://www.beharenet.com/dadinc

Postpartum Support International
927 North Kellog Avenue
Santa Barbara, CA 93111
(805) 967-7376
Online contact: THONIKMAN@compuserve.com

Wing of Madness: A Depression Guide
http://www.wingofmadness.com

Dr. Ivan's Depression Central
http://www.psycom.net/depression.central.html

Bipolar Resources

Moodswing.org
http://www.moodswing.org

Anxiety Resources

Anxiety Disorders Association of America
11900 Parklawn Drive, Suite 1200
Rockville, MD 20852
http://www.adaa.org

Anxiety Disorders Education Program
http://www.nimh.nih.gov/anxiety

Obsessive-Compulsive Foundation, Inc.
P.O. Box 70
Milford, CT 06460-0070
(203) 878-5669
Online contact: JPHS28A@prodigy.com
http://pages.prodigy.com/alwillen.ocf.html

Eating Disorders Resources

American Anorexia Bulimia Association
http://www.abainc.org

Anorexia Nervosa and Related Disorders, Inc.
http://www.anred.com

National Eating Disorders Association (NEDO)
6655 South Yale Avenue
Tulsa, OK 74136
(918) 481-4044
http://www.laureate.com/nedo/nedointro.asp

Overeater's Anonymous World Service Office
6075 Zenith Court NE
Rio Rancho, NM 87124
(505) 891-2664
http://recovery.hiway.net

The Something Fishy Website on Eating Disorders
http://www.something-fishy.org/top/html

Schizophrenia

Schizophrenia Home Page
http://www.scizophrenia.com

NAMI Consumer and Family Guide to Schizophrenia Treatment
http://www.nami.org/disorders/treatment/html

Therapy Resources

Finding a Therapist
1-800-THERAPIST

Rating a Therapist
http://www.cybercouch.com/library/rati.tag.html

Self-Assessment Resources

Minding Your Health
http://www.mindingyourhealth.com

I.Q. Sites

World's Greatest Geniuses
http://home8.swipnet.se/~we80790/Index.html

Mensa
http://www.mensa.org/workout

Personality and I.Q. Self-Assessment

Personality Psychology Links
http://www.wesleyan.edu/spn/person.html#online

Personality and I.Q. Tests
http://members.aol.com/HOON4R/personality.html

ABC's Personal Growth
http://www.helpself.com

Online I.Q., Personality, Political Tests and Novelty Games
http://universityoflife.com/serious.html

Questions About Psychiatric Medicine

Medications – Health Center's Pharmacy Page
http://www.health-center.com/english/pharmacy/meds/default/html

Index

operant conditioning, 111-113
  reinforcement, 113-116
  termination, 114-116
opiates (altered consciousness),
  101-102
optimism, 383
  personality theories, 270
oral stage (Freud), 258
organizations
  advocacy groups, 437
  alcoholism, 438
  anxiety, 439
  bipolar disorders, 439
  depression, 438-439
  eating disorders, 439-440
  schizophrenia, 440
  self-assessment, 440
  therapy, 440
organizing perceptions through
  relationships, 84-85
orientation, sexual, 149-150
  accepting, 388-390

P

pain, 79
panic disorders, 302
paranoia, 323-326
paranoid personality disorder, 252
parents
  effects on behavior, 50
    attachment styles, 50
    emotional development,
    50-52
  influences (baby research), 58
parietal lobes, 29
pathological gambling, 343
patients, 360
Paxil, 352
peer pressure (teenage self-
  concepts), 209
percent relatedness, calculating
  (nature-nurture debate), 43
perceptions
  bottom-up processing, 80
  identification and recognition,
  85-86
    context, 86
  illusions, 81-82
    directing attention, 83
  organizing through relationships, 84-85
  top-down processing, 81
peripheral nervous system
  (nerves), 31-32
  neurons, 32-34
personalities, 237-238
  defense mechanisms, 262-266

displacement, 264
projection, 263
rationalization, 263
reaction formation, 264
repression, 263
sublimation, 264
disorders, 248-249
  antisocial, 250
  avoidant, 250
  borderline, 251
  dependent, 251
  histrionic, 251
  multiple, 270-272
  narcissistic, 251
  obsessive-compulsive,
  251-252
  paranoid, 252
  schizoid, 252
  schizotypal, 250
self-actualization, 266-267
testing, 239
  Allport, Gordon,
  244-245
  Eysenck, Prof. Hans, 246
  inheritable traits, 246-248
  MMPI (Minnesota
  Multiphasic Personality
  Inventory), 240-241
  projective, 241
  Rorschach, 241-242
  stability, 242
  traits and states, 243-244
theories
  Adler, Alfred, 261
  Freud, Sigmund,
  256-260
  Horney, Karen, 261
  Jung, Carl, 260
  motives, 256-258
  optimism vs.
  pessimism, 270
  personality, 255
  self-efficacy, 269-270
  social control, 268-269
perspectives, 21-22
biological psychology, 15
  brains, 23-36
environmental (behavioral
  effects), 48
evolutionary psychology
  adapting to change, 24-25
  deterministic fallacy, 47-48
  naturalistic fallacy, 47
  species-typical behavior,
  46-47
multiple perspective disorder,
  13-14
psychoanalytic, 15-16
  experiments with rats,
  16-17

pessimism (personality theories),
  270
phallic stage (Freud), 258
phobias, 303-305
Piaget, Jean (1895-1980), 15
positive reinforcement therapy,
  370
practicing psychology, 8-9
  origins of, 8
preconscious mind, 91
predicting behavior, 5-6
prejudice, 415-416
prenatal effects (schizophrenia),
  318
preoperational stage (child development), 62
problem solving (profiling
  methods), 182-184
problem-focused coping, 197
problems, sleeping, 95-96
procedural long-term
  memory, 127
processing
  information (memory reten-
  tion), 130
  sensations
    bottom-up, 80
    illusions, 81-83
    top-down, 81
profiling, 170
  analyzing errors, 174
  behavioral observations,
  173-174
  brain scanning, 174-175
  cognitive processing, 170-171
  information, categorizing,
  175-177
  introspection, 172-173
  judgment, 184-185
  models, 171
    information-processing,
    171
  problem solving, 182-184
  reasoning, 180-181
  schemas, 178-179
  scripts, following, 179-180
  wind analysis decision-making
  strategy, 185-186
projection, 263
projective personality tests, 241
prophecies, self-fulfilling, 414-415
protecting self-esteem, 213-214
Prozac, 352
psyches (defense mechanisms),
  262-266
  displacement, 264
  projection, 263
  rationalization, 263
  reaction formation, 264

Q-R

S

X-Z

U-V

W